INTERNATIONAL AND TRANSRACIAL ADOPTIONS

International and Transracial Adoptions

A mental health perspective

CHRISTOPHER BAGLEY
with Loretta Young
Anne Scully

Avebury

Aldershot · Brookfield USA · Hong Kong · Singapore · Sydney

Published by
Avebury
Ashgate Publishing Limited
Gower House
Croft Road
Aldershot
Hants GU11 3HR
England

Ashgate Publishing Company
Old Post Road
Brookfield
Vermont 05036
USA

A CIP catalogue record for this book is available from the British Library

ISBN 1 85628 082 9

Printed and Bound in Great Britain by
Athenaeum Press Ltd, Newcastle upon Tyne.

Contents

Preface   viii

Adjustment in Adoption: A Review

1   The Institution of Adoption   1

2   Adjustment in Adoption: Follow-Up Studies   15

3   Genetic, Physical and Constitutional Factors
        Influencing Adjustment in Adoption   38

4   Adjustment, Identity and Special Needs
        Adoption: Clinical Research and Policy Change   48

5   Adjustment and Identity in Transracial and
        Inter-Country Adoption   71

**Adjustment in Adoption: Empirical Studies in
Canada and Britain**

6   A Follow-Up of Adopted Children in the
National Child Development Study   90

7   Mental Health and Adoption in a Community
Survey of Adults   114

8   Social Work Practice and the Adoption
of Special Needs Children:
A Canadian Case Study   121

**Intercountry and Transracial Adoption:
Empirical Studies and Policy Review**

9   Inter-Country Adoption: History and
Policy Formation   135

10   Further Developments in Inter-Country
Adoption   167

11   Adopted Girls from Hong Kong in Britain:
A Twenty Year Follow-Up of Adjustment
and Social Identity   195

12   Adopted from Vietnam: A Ten Year
Follow-Up of British Adoptees   207

13   Transracial Adoption of Aboriginal
Children in Canada: A Disturbing
Case Study   214

14   Transracial Adoption in Britain:
A Follow-Up With Policy Implications   240

15   Attitudes to Transracial Adoption in
Samples of Afro-Caribbeans in London,
1979 and 1989   256

Adopted Children in Residential Care: A Typology of Disrupted Adoptions

16   A Survey of Adopted Children in Two
      Residential Treatment Centres:
      Methods of Study and Initial Results   264

17   Comparison of 61 Adopted Children and
      61 Control Children in Two Centres for
      Seriously Disturbed Children   274

18   Types or Clusters of Adjustment:
      Classification of Adopted Children by
      Case Study and Statistical Methods   302

Conclusions

19   Adjustment in Adoption: Conclusions   326

References   332

Subject Index   361

Preface

Adoption is an extraordinary, exciting institution. It is a practice wrought with anxiety, grief and triumph at its outset. With the years the original anxiety can lay dormant but as the child grows, a new set anxieties may emerge as the young man or woman seeks to complete the natural identity tasks by having fuller knowledge of, and perhaps contact with, "real" parents.

If things "go wrong" for the young person the anguish of the adoptive parents who accepted this baby or child with such idealism can be intense, adding to the grief and anxiety they felt about the original adoption. Consider this case:

> Jochobed couldn't bring up the newborn child herself - the very conditions of the existence she could offer were temporary, even life-threatening. So she surrendered her little boy to the agencies of God. And his new mother was rich but childless. The boy was doted on, given a new name -Moses - and given every care and privilege which high status could give. Yet Moses struggled over his identity, over his true calling. He killed a man from the group into which he was adopted; the Bible doesn't record it, but his doting adoptive mother must have been heart broken. Moses became the ancient equivalent of a street kid - a desert kid, never to have contact with his "mother" again.

The most "natural" form of adoption, found in all world societies, is open in character. A childless couple will adopt a related child; or an individual with too many, or an unwanted child will ask a relative to take on the role of permanent care. This "custom adoption" still pertains amongst the aboriginal people of North America (Bissett-Johnson, 1984) and remains the major form of adoption in many parts of the world.

A subsidiary form of adoption relates to abandonment, in a society where lines of class, caste or religion prevent within-family adoption. Thus in India amongst Islamic people a child may be left on the steps of a mosque at dawn; a little later the child may be taken by a woman needing a child. This will be done under the benign but blind approval of the Immam, since in Islam adoption is forbidden by the word of the Prophet (whose own adopted son showed much ungratefulness to his father).

In an interesting study of "the kindness of strangers" John Boswell (1989) shows that the abandonment of children in Western Europe was a long standing practice, extending from later antiquity to the Renaissance and beyond. But Boswell's evidence also shows that the kindness of the stranger who might discover the child was often a matter of luck. Moses might just as well have been enslaved or killed as raised to the status of the Pharaoh's child. Adoption, as Ounsted (1966) has reminded us has "its dark side". Without bonding between adult and child, exploitation, servitude and abuse have been all too frequent (Bagley and King, 1990).

As the numbers of abandoned children grow small, due to the ubiquity of birth control and tolerance for termination of pregnancy, so has the institution of adoption changed. It is viewed with more critical scrutiny than in the past. No longer is it a means by which adults may easily enter the pleasurable and biologically driven role of parent. Now parents must be chosen for children, not the other way round. As Feigelman and Silverman (1983) show in their research on "chosen children", new patterns of adoptive relationship are emerging.

The traditional kinship roles implied by adoption must be reformed (Kirk, 1981); openness in adoption, and the insistent search of adoptees for knowledge about their ancestry imply important policy reforms (Haimes and Timms, 1985). Now, many other forms of child care must be considered before new, permanent parents are considered for a child.

In the present book we approach the institution of adoption as child care specialists, focusing on what appears to be the key dependent variable in adoption research: the child's mental health, both in the short and in the long run. We define mental health not just as the absence of any psychiatric symptomatology, but as the development of basic ego strength and a feeling of self-worth which enables an individual to cope with stresses later on in life, enabling also self-actualization, the development of individual gifts and talents to their fullest extent.

This research is focused on how well adolescents and young adults have fared in adoption - adopted as children following abandonment in China; as children following the death of their parents in the Vietnamese theatre of war; following adoption from single parents in Britain into advantaged, middle-class homes; adoption of black children by white parents in Britain; and adoption of Amerindian children by white, middle class parents following almost predatory inroads into the lives of aboriginal people by Canadian social workers. Some types of adoption have excellent outcomes; others do not. Our study of adolescents who have experienced adoption disruption should throw some light on why some adoptions are successful, and why others are not.

What is clear from our data is that social workers have often approached adoption practice in a cavalier fashion, ignoring the insights of sociologists such as Kirk (1964), and treating mothers who surrendered their child in a patronizing manner. Moreover, their failure to supply proper information to adoptive parents has been one of the factors which has caused great anguish and distress to adoptive parents when disruption does occur.

I would like to dedicate this book to the memory of my father, Alwyne Victor Evans Bagley, to the future of my two adopted sons, Michael Robert and Daniel Crispin, and to the future of my biological daughter, Abigail Louise Sunanda. My father was born with the surname of his adoptive parents, and I shared his anguish and excitement as he searched for his kin. I was seven years old when my mother, father and myself discovered Granny Bagley (my great grandmother) living in the village of Wing, in Rutland. She was the first biological relative my father had seen as an adult (apart from his own children). We shared his tears. Because of these early experiences, I cannot contemplate the institution of adoption without excitement or passion.

My dear wife Loretta Young, has contributed much to this book. Research assistance has been provided by my sisters, Maureen Weir and Margaret Ben Daoud. The scholarly collaboration of Anne Scully and Daria Sewchuk-Dann is also gratefully acknowledged.

Chris Bagley,
Hong Kong,
April 1992

1 The institution of adoption

Introduction

The dominant model of adoption for most Western countries in the present century has been the "exclusive" model through which a child's links to biological parents are permanently broken, and all previous kindred including, of course, the biological mother, are permanently excluded (Holman, 1973). This model has many strains and conflicts of role, as David Kirk and others have pointed out (Kirk, 1964, 1981; Sachdev, 1984).

Kadushin (1984) for example, points to the role strains and tensions between biological mothers and the placement agency; the continuing feelings of loss the biological mothers feels; the problems of meeting the psychological and social needs of the adopted child; the adopted child's rights as an adult to know about, and have contact with, a biological parent; the need to provide continuity of care for the child between placements prior to adoption; and the needs of adoptive parents to be parents in the same ways that couples are parents of biological children. Because the needs of these various parties may be in conflict with one another, adoption is potentially an institution of tension and permanent dissatisfaction.

Yet, as David Kirk says, if these potential strains are recognized and acknowledged, adoption has the potential for becoming an open and creative institution:

1

What is especially ironic is that in adoption there resides a remarkably creative potential, both for the substitute family itself, and for the members of the mainstream society. It is evidently just when differences are being candidly and lovingly acknowledged between adoptive parents and children, that there emerges between them the strongest bonds of solidarity (Kirk, 1981, p.79).

Adoption and demographic change

The changes in the character of adoption in North America and elsewhere have been well documented by Hepworth (1980), Eichler (1983), Lipman (1984), Sachdev (1984), Feigelman and Silverman (1983), Hoksberg (1986) and Simon and Altstein (1987) . These authors point to a similar trend occurring in many other countries: the number of adoption peaked in the decade from the end of the baby boom years of the late 1950s, and declined along with the decline of illegitimacy rates after 1970. For example, in Canada in 1969-70 and 1970-71 adoptions reached a peak, of 20,300 and 20,500 respectively (Hepworth, 1980). Up to 1970 out-of-wedlock babies were usually carried to term, and the stigma of illegitimacy meant that the majority of children of such mothers were placed for adoption.

Since that time - with lower birth rates, the availability of reliable birth control methods, legal abortion, and decreased stigma attached to single parenthood - the number of "normal" infants - non-handicapped and white - available for adoption has decreased dramatically. At one time, there were more "normal" babies than there were parents willing to adopt them; now the reverse is the case (Bachrach, 1986; Howe, 1987). The number of infertile couples anxious to adopt remains fairly constant, however. Increasingly, such couples are looking to the adoption of "special needs" children: children of all ages with physical or developmental handicap; older children, and children in sibling groups; ethnic minority children; and, children with emotional and behavioural disturbance (Feigelman and Silverman, 1983; Brodzinsky and Schecter, 1990).

Biological parents of adopted children

The needs of biological parents are those least addressed in the literature on adoption. Yet the mother's personal pain, both in the short run (deciding whether to give up a child) and in the long run (wondering what became of her child) are considerable (Eichler, 1983). Kirk (1981) is one of the few writers to consider the birth mother's psychological plight, although Sorosky et al. (1978) also give account of "the pain, still carried within" of the birth mother. No writers seem to have acknowledged the existence, let alone the problems of the biological fathers of adopted children. However, a humanistic literature on the psychological problems of the birth mother is now emerging (reviewed by Brodzinsky, 1990). This new literature may however reflect the fact that the balance of power has now changed in favour of the birth mother who considers "giving up" her child for adoption. Now, when healthy white babies are so scarce, and so needed by infertile couples (who continue to constitute about five per cent of all married couples) we pay attention to the needs of the birth mother, and help her come to terms with the profound loss of voluntarily separating from her child.

In the past the birth mother was often an embarrassment for placement agencies, and for adopting parents. For the adopted child, she can be a source of ambiguity, a figure of fantasy who is sought or desired with ambiguous hope and trepidation (Marcus, 1981). The model of "open adoption" (discussed in terms of its strengths and weaknesses by Baran and Pannor, 1990) in theory at least might reduce the role conflicts of various parties in the adoption role set. It is less clear whether the various forms of openness in adoption can meet the child's psychosocial needs, is there a clear recognition of the birth mother's role. Open forms of adoption (allowing some form of continuous contact of the adopted child with his or her birth mother) may actually undermine the process of successful adoption, especially when the adoptive parents have to cope with significant emotional and behavioural problems in the child (Barth and Berry, 1988). Despite some enthusiastic advocates for more open forms of adoption (Sachdev, 1990) there is no good empirical evidence that such arrangements can enhance the adoption process. Long-term research in this field is an important priority.

Adoptive parents

A distinction must be made between adopting parents who are childless, and those who either already have biological children of their own, or who prefer adoption over biological parenthood. This latter form of adoption is relatively new and is referred to by Feigelman and Silverman (1984) as "preferential adoption" - parents whose motivation to adopt varies from motives other than childlessness:

3

In as much as preferential adopting parents are not confronted with the personal crisis associated with accepting their own infertility, they are less troubled by the subtle condemnation of adoptive parents and the role stress linked with adoptive parenthood (Feigelman & Silverman, 1983 p.79).

In theory, at least, preferential adoption could mean that parents could focus on the needs of the adopted child, rather than on their own needs. They could be much more accepting of open adoption, for instance, an arrangement which traditional adopters may well find threatening.

Infertile couples have to cope with a double handicap as adopters: the personal and social stigma of being barren, as well as the stigma of taking on a child who is not theirs. Adoptive parenthood, as Kirk (1964) has shown, has a number of role handicaps for the couple - they are not like other parents, however much they wish to be so; they have to act out certain disadvantaged roles in relation to their wider kin; and they have to solve the dilemma of "ignorance versus knowledge of the child's background":

> Are they to regard themselves as just ordinary parents, no different from biological parents (which is the choice of "enchantment")? Or are they to regard themselves as different, indeed as substitute parents (the choice of "disenchantment")? Second, there is the dilemmas of how the parents are to relate themselves to the child. Are they to emphasize his difference while they are trying to become a family (the choice of differentiation simultaneous with integration) or are they to go ahead with integrative acts without the conflicting demands of revelation? The third dilemma poses the question whether the adoptive parents are to record and try to recall background information about the child. This, in a sense, is a choice between knowledge and ignorance of the child's forbearers. The fourth dilemma primarily concerns the adoptive parents whose children are born out of wedlock. Their dilemma consists of how to teach two moral imperatives, each with its claim on the parents: are they to indoctrinate the child with the necessity for premarital chastity... or are they to make less of these norms than ordinarily required, so as to protect the good reputation of the child's natural parents who bore him out of wedlock? (Kirk, 1964, pp. 50-51)

The anxiety and anguish of infertility, which often carries over to adoptive parenting, has been well described by Humphrey (1967). These acute dilemmas of adoptive parenting remain:

> ... the status of adoptive parenting continues to be deprecated in American society. This seems to be particularly clear in the case of infertile adopters who find the advent of adoptive parenthood an especially stressful period. Such stresses seem to have a specially adverse impact on the well-being of children adopted by infertile parents (Feigelman & Silverman, 1983, p.8).

The anxieties of adoptive parents are often compounded by the rigorous enquiries of adoption agencies, and the long wait between approval as an adopter and actually receiving a child. Potential adopters rejected by one agency may apply, with increasing trepidation, to other agencies and if still rejected may consider the "second best" of adopting a handicapped or minority child; or they may attempt to adopt privately or overseas.

For the determined adopters, money rather than suitability is one way of obtaining a child from some of the Latin American countries. This is particularly true of the United States, where controls on standards of professional work in intercountry adoption has been lax (Pilotti, 1984).

The ideal for the infertile couple lay in the old-fashioned adoption agency practice of providing a baby "like them" - an infant which was not only white, and healthy but who had other physical resemblances to the adopters. They regarded themselves as "ordinary parents" ignoring any differences including the child's biological background, showing moral approbation too for illegitimacy which was often the child's original status. That status would be denied, ignored or suppressed, and the fact of adoption, although usually acknowledged at some stage, would be systematically or even unconsciously ignored.

In a reprise on the theme of role dilemmas in adoption (Kirk, 1981), the survival of the exclusive model of adoption is noted: treating the adopted child as one's own, and neglecting, ignoring or suppressing differences between adoptive and ordinary parenting can lead, in Kirk's final formulation, to families with low empathy for the child's needs, poor general communication in the family, and low trust or integration in the family. Such a perpetuation of the traditional model of adoption, Kirk argues, is linked to a low degree of public understanding and sympathy with adopted children, sealed adoption records, and the obscuring of adoption as a social fact or as a credible social institution. In fact, Kirk argues that the family itself is changing, with new roles based on equality and mobility, divorce and remarriage. The new roles of the family are likely to require the same kind of changes which adoption itself requires: movement towards authenticity, empathy and communicative abilities as substitutes for those anxious to make their families more cohesive. Genuine institutional reform would free the adoptive family from the artificial props that currently try to enforce the loyalty of its children grown to adulthood.

Such reform would thus incorporate the insight that only those free to leave can freely stay. In that sense the reform of adoptive kinship has implications for the well-being of the mainstream family (Kirk, 1981, p.161).

Despite these suggestions, change is slow in coming. Research by Geissinger (1984) found, not surprisingly, that the majority of adoptive parents interviewed felt particularly anxious and threatened about proposals in the United States to allow adult adoptees access to their birth records. The adopters expressed considerable fear of loss and rejection by their adopted children if searching were allowed. Barely half would countenance the possibility of access to early records by their children, and only if both adoptive and birth parents were in agreement!

It may be postulated that the secrecy, guilt and closedness surrounding adoption which has been supported by both agencies and legal systems (Andrews, 1978) supports the weaknesses of adoption as an institution which Kirk (1981) has deplored. Increasingly, as traditional agencies opt out of the placing of "healthy, white infants," adopters are turning to private strategies including leaving vitae and "albums" with general practitioners in conservative, mostly-white areas such as Iowa, Montana and Alberta. In these areas, young women are much less likely to have terminations, and to consider adoption than women in other areas of North America.

Adopted children

Undoubtedly, the pressure to unlock adoption records, and to "open" the adoption process generally comes from adopted children, for some of whom knowledge of genealogical origin is part of identity development (Sorosky et al. 1978; Sachdev, 1984 and 1990). About a third of adopted children in a U.S. survey expressed interest in searching for birth parents (Children's Home Society, 1977). However, experience from the United Kingdom, where records have been unsealed since 1930 (in Scotland) and since 1975 (in England and Wales) have shown that a much smaller proportion of adoptees do finally seek information on birth parents. Usually the information is sought for "family tree" purposes when an adoptee has children, or gets married.

Some contact their birth parents, but almost always for positive reasons (Triseliotis, 1980; Day, 1979; Haimes & Timms, 1985). There is no evidence from the British studies that the institution of adoption has been undermined in any way. Rather, as Kirk (1981) has argued, adoption is strengthened by such easy access to birth records. Ironically, denial of such access in many parts of North America has led to a movement of adoptees which has a basis seemingly rooted in ideology rather than in psychological need (Marcus, 1981). Nevertheless, the existential anguish of some adoptees in their frequently fruitless search for birth parents, has led to an increasing number of personal accounts by adoptees engaged in a quest, which seems to assume the proportions of a search for a mythical grail whose acquisition will redeem the searcher's whole existence (Redmond & Sleightholm, 1982). The reality of open access is well but by Day (1979) in his English study:

> Primary loyalty to the adoptive parents was a marked characteristic of many applicants for their original records ... Applicants felt that more openness was needed in adoption. They thought that the legislation would help to remove the secrecy, even the stigma, with which the subject had been clouded.

The personal accounts of "voices from inside the adoption triangle" collected together by Redmond and Sleightholm (1982), are full of hope, pain, anguish and unbelievable joy, when a successful reunion with a birth parent is achieved. One of the case histories is an account by a girl who was systematically sexually abused, not by her adoptive parents, but by members of her extended, adopted kin. There is a clear sense in this account that because she was not "family," but a child of sin taken into the family from outside, normal obligations of kin did not prevail. Sexual abuse within families is now known to be much more common than previously thought (Russell, 1986), and the symbolic role handicaps of the adopted child within her wider family may put her at increased risk of such assaults. Adoptive parents can bond with their child as successfully as with a biological child, although the actual process of bonding may be rather different, especially when the child is older, or handicapped - see Smith and Sherwen (1988). This similarity to "normal" bonding provides a powerful antidote against parental abuse (physical, emotional, sexual) of the adopted child (Bagley and King, 1990). But members of the adopted child's extended family may well not have bonded to the child in this way, and are not constrained by the ordinary taboos against incestuous assault. This problem is particularly serious in the case of step-families, and Russell (1986) has shown that step-parents are at least seven times more likely to sexually assault the female children in their family, in comparison with biological fathers. Again, for all practical purposes, adoptive fathers seem to behave exactly as if they were biological fathers. This underlines once again the dilemma of adoptive parenting:

> If it is to be successful, the parents <u>must</u> bond totally to their adopted child, and she to them. But inherent in this mutual bonding is the role dilemma of the intense pressure for adoptive parents to behave as if they were biological parents <u>in every respect</u>.

Adoption by stepparents

Adoption by stepparents, when a new partner (usually male) adopts the spouse's child or children born either in a one-parent situation or in a previous marriage, is a curious variant on the institution of adoption. The adopted child has never been separated from one of the birthparents, is older, and often knows or remembers the absent birthparent, who may even have access or visiting rights. The child has adjustments which are quite different from those of "normal"adopted children, including oftentimes adjusting to relationships with biological children of the new parent.

In some provinces of Canada over half of all adoptions are adoptions by a stepparent, since remarriage is a frequent outcome of the increasing divorce rate and as the number of ordinary adoption steadily decreases (Bissett-Johnson, 1984). This author suggests that:

> Adoptions within the family, and especially stepparent adoptions, pose subtle problems of the social dynamics within the family. In many cases, the welfare of the child does not necessarily coincide with the wishes of the adult members to assert ties with him. Yet in intrafamily adoptions if social inquiry or home-study reports are made at all, they may lack the depth of studies made for placement in adoption of a child by strangers (Bissett-Johnson, 1984, p.217).

The stability of a second marriage is, in statistical terms, not clear but it may be that the adopted child in such families is more at risk for disruption of family life, and subsequent maladjustment than adopted children placed by social service agencies with strangers. Stepparent adoptions could, in fact, distort the figures on adoption disruption or breakdown, and it is important to know what proportion of clinically disturbed adopted children were, in fact, adopted by a stepparent.

In Britain, the various problems of the stepparent adoption were recognized in the 1975 Children Act. Following this Act, stepparents were not allowed to adopt children they acquired through marriage. They could, however, take out guardianship orders which gave them day-to-day care and custody; but guardianship did not eclipse the child's surname nor the rights of the other biological parent to have access. Foster parents, too, were given the right under this British Act to apply for guardianship if a child had been with them continuously for three years. Guardianship gave the foster parents legal protection against arbitrary removal of the child by social workers and others.

The adoption of children with special needs

Adoptions of older children, ethnic minority children, those with physical and mental handicaps, and those with emotional and behavioural problems has increased dramatically since 1970 (Hardy, 1984; Cole and Donley, 1990). Before that time such children were considered unadoptable (Churchill, 1979). Now, a cheerful philosophy that "no child is unadoptable" seem capable of fulfilment. Adoption work with special-needs children concentrates on matching a particular child with a particular parent or parents, rather than approving parents in advance, with the automatic guarantee of child after an appropriate wait.

Another trend is for foster parents to adopt children who have been with them for months or year (Ward, 1984; Shapiro, 1984). A variation on this practice is known as "legal risk adoption, in which potential adopters accept a child, knowing that the legal issues surrounding permanent guardianship are not yet settled." (Lee & Hull, 1986). This is part of the welcome trend towards "permanency planning" which aims to prevent the drift of children between foster homes (Maluccio and Fein, 1983). Subsidies are often available for such adoptions, since foster parents often would have adopted the child but for the fact they would have lost a fostering allowance. Feigelman and Silverman (1983) indicate:

> Our results clearly show that the rapidly expanding interest in finding adoptive homes for special-needs children that has occurred since the 1960s is linked to larger changes in family and

9

social structure. The data indicate that as the trend toward sharing work and child care roles and other modern family patterns enjoy widening social support, the numbers of families amenable to adopting special-needs children is likely to increase ..... We have found that there is substantial acceptance for adopting blacks and other minorities, among the upper classes and the political left. The less affluent and members of adoptive parent groups seem to be more positively disposed to adopting the retarded and the handicapped (pp. 54-55).

Feigelman and Silverman (1983) also argue that in special needs adoption there is a much greater potential for Kirk's principal of "acceptance of difference" by the adoptive parents, in ways which can reduce the role handicaps and dilemmas of traditional adoption, a point reinforced by David Kirk in his foreword to Feigelman and Silverman's (1983) book.

Social structure and social work practice in adoption

The most radical critique of conventional social work practice in foster care and adoption is that by Mandell (1973), whose Marxist analysis still echoes uncomfortably in schools of social work. It is easier to ignore than refute her thesis that:

The litany of foster care and adoption is the litany of poverty: unemployment, underemployment, inadequate public assistance grants, poor health and medical care mothers carrying the burden of child care alone (p. 16).

Day (1979), in an equally penetrating attack, shows that the reason that so many black children were retained in institutions and in a later period were offered to whites, is that social service agencies operated with racist assumptions, and while they were adept at removing black, Native and poor white children from their families, they hardly considered supporting these same families by economic measures, so that the families or communities involved could retain their own children.

Social workers have traditionally maintained an excessively narrow model of adoption practice. Traditionally, they have selected as potential adopters white, middle-class couples of conventional behaviour and values and good material standards. Black and Native communities particularly have failed to meet such criteria. Adoption is indeed as Benet (1976) has argued, a political institution, by means of which the children of the poorer classes and of immoral youth could be controlled by removal, with the additional benefit of meeting the needs of childless, middle-class couples. Holman (1973), another radical critic of adoption, called the practice "trading in children". At its worst, adoption is unpleasantly reminiscent of the practice of slavery itself. Indeed, the lifelong pain of the mother who is forced to give up her child for adoption is strikingly similar to the accounts of slaves whose children were removed for sale to other plantations (Eichler, 1983).

The dilemma for policy makers in this area is identified by Silverman and Feigelman (1990) in their review of the outcomes (largely positive) of transracial adoption:

> Perhaps the most disturbing part of our review of the transracial adoption literature is the extent to which it is ignored in formulating adoption policy. We are not recommending transracial placements as a panacea for the problems of family disintegration among nonwhites in the United States. But their success suggests they may at least be a useful resource. The effort to expand intraracial placement for minority children, however, does not require the cessation of transracial placements. At a time when few black leaders are sanguine about the deplorably low income and employment levels found among minority underclasses, as the rates of adolescent out-of-wedlock pregnancies continue to mount, transracial placement is a resource that cannot easily be ignored. (Silverman and Feigelman, 1990, p. 200).

Changing social work practice and the new character of adoption

The traditional rigidity of adoption caseworkers is changing (Hoksberg, 1986; Sachdev, 1990). Yet in some jurisdictions such as the conservative mid-west regions of Canada and the U.S.A., change is slow in coming. Adoptive placement of special-needs children in Ohio and Alberta for example, has lagged behind the practice in other areas. The norm in Ohio and Alberta was until 1989 for white infants "surrendered" (at the gunpoint of moral pressure) by unmarried mothers, to be placed with childless couples. Although the number of such babies available for adoption in Alberta is declining, the placement of any "normal" infant at all is in marked contrast to European countries such as Sweden and the Netherlands where such placement has virtually ended (Hoksberg, 1986).

The following vignette, an account of the annual meeting of the

Calgary Chapter of the Alberta Adoptive Parents Association in January 1985, illustrates the more conservative, or traditional practice of adoption. The speaker, at this meeting, was the supervisor of adoptions for Edmonton and Northern Alberta. A matronly, much concerned lady, she exuded warmth, and had clearly caused great satisfaction to the thousands of adopters she had served. Her audience consisted almost entirely of the young couples, mostly in their thirties, who had been accepted as adopters and were waiting, with articulate impatience, for "their" child.

The audience was told that 1,600 adopters had been approved; lists were now closed, and couples would have to wait up to three years for their white infant. None seemed interested in a special-needs child, and responded warmly to the social worker's account of how she went about matching adopt their child. She required a photograph of the approved couples, and noting hair and eye colour and height of the adopters, compared such characteristics with those of the birth mother and child. She was adamant that child and adopters had to look like one another, and come from parents of the same build and stature as the adopters. "We don't want the child to stick out like a sore thumb, do we?" she asked her audience rhetorically. She matched too on "educational potential," trying to place a child of a well-educated mother with well-educated adopters! Moreover, pains were taken to place the child well away from the community in which the mother lived. Clearly, like the adoptive parents she served, this social worker was locked in an "exclusive" model of adoption, with all attendant role strains which Kirk (1981) has identified.

By 1990, the social worker referred to above had retired, and a new Child Welfare Act now favoured forms of open adoption in most cases. But this practice brings new anxieties for the adoptive couples - not only must they cope with the role handicaps outlined above; they have to negotiate with the birth mother, and with some type of continued contact with her.

A new adoption literature is beginning to appear. James Gritter's Adoption Without Fear (1989) carries on the dust jacket, a picture of a birth mother handing over her child to adoptive parents. Below is the message, "Seventeen couples tell their emotion-filled experiences with open adoption." One potential problem with open adoption is that by allowing regular contact of the biological parent(s) with the adopted child (and thus reducing adoption to a form of long-term, albeit legally secured, foster care) is that this will increase the anxieties, insecurity and role-ambiguity of the adoptive parents, and will in the long-term fail to serve the needs of the adopted child. This possibility is illustrated by the research of Raynor (1980) and Bohman and Sigvardsson (1990) - these two sets of research, in Britain and Sweden, both found that children in long-term foster care had significantly poorer outcomes than adopted children, even when the adopted and the foster children were placed at a similar age.

Philip Hepworth (1980) in his book <u>Foster Care and Adoption in Canada</u> reaches an important conclusion on policy issues in adoption:

> Adoption statistics reveal that striking changes in the character of adoption have taken place during the last 20 years. These changes are almost all direct consequence of changes in Canadian society. Adoption as such is increasingly a simple term for a complex social institution. The number of adoptions is not simply a reflection of the number of illegitimate births. Most adoptions now involve a natural parent of the child being adopted. It is the combined number of divorces and of unmarried mothers who have originally kept their babies that is the main explanation for this development. We must ask, though, if adoption occurring in widely differing circumstances is the same process, involves the same type of emotional relationships and is likely to have the same degree of success. The answer to these questions is likely to be no, but we have no evidence on the long-term outcomes of different types of adoption. (Hepworth, 1980, p.177).

Conclusions

Adoption is an ancient institution, but in its development in Western Societies adoption rigidified into a closed institution which created many role ambiguities for both adoptive parents, and adopted children, and also excluded and indeed stigmatized birth mothers. Adoption has developed as an institution which has primarily served the needs of childless, middle-class groups. Social workers, as servants of the existing moral order, have actively assisted this process in practising an "exclusive" model of adoption, which has incidentally done severe disservice to the needs of disadvantaged ethnic minority communities, whose potential for community support of traditional types of custom and kinship adoption have been ignored (Morrow, 1984).

Two parallel, linked developments are changing the institution of adoption, however. First of all, the traditional supply of normal, white children available for adoption is drying up; secondly, many children previously considered unadoptable are being placed with new parents.

13

Sometimes these adopters are the traditional childless couples, but increasingly new types of people are adopting children with special needs. Yet another type of adoption is becoming increasingly common: this is adoption by stepparents of the biological children of their new husband or wife. Some of these are women, who in earlier times, would have surrendered an out-of-wedlock child for adoption.

The face of adoption is becoming increasingly varied, and systematic follow-up studies of the various forms of adoption are necessary if we are to understand why these various forms of adoption are necessary, if we are to understand why these various forms of adoption work or fail to work, and the kinds of support they need. Some progress in this area has been made (Hartman and Laird, 1990; Schaffer and Lindstrom, 1990; Cole and Donley, 1990), but much more policy development and practice research needs to be done on the important social institution of adoption.

2 Adjustment in adoption: Follow-up studies

Introduction

An obvious, but fairly difficult way of establishing the problems which adopted children and their adoptive families may have, is to follow-up from placement a group of adoptees and their families. Ideally such a study should include a non-adopted control group, and a reasonably large and representative sample so that generalizations can be made. Follow-up at more than one stage of the child's life is also necessary to have the fullest picture of adjustment, since problems at any point in time may reflect a temporary difficulty in relationships during adolescence (Bohman and Sigvardsson, 1990). For reasons of expense and logistics (including the funding and the stamina required to undertake longitudinal studies), good follow-up studies are both difficult to undertake, and few in number. However, the three major studies in this area from Britain (Bagley, 1977 and the chapter in this volume, further analysing the National Child Development Study data); from the United States (Hoopes and Stein, 1985); and from Sweden (Bohman and Sigvardsson, 1990) have provided some of the richest data on adjustment in adoption which is available.

Triseliotis (1980) reviewed earlier British and American studies of adoption follow-up, and was unable to find many reliable studies, leading him to conclude that: "One neglected area of child welfare research is how people who have grown up in public care are functioning in adult life". However, his conclusion (based on a review of the studies of a number of earlier researchers) was that adoption and long-term foster care had, in the large majority of cases favourable outcomes in terms of adjustment in young adulthood. Adoption appeared to be especially helpful for "special needs children, such as older children or those with some form of handicap, in terms of comparison with outcomes for children with similar problems who were not so placed."

Earlier American studies

Jaffee and Fanshel's (1970), <u>How They Fared in Adoption</u> is the most cited of the earlier American follow-up studies. These authors studied the "life adjustment" of one hundred adults who were adopted before the age of three years. The respondents were divided for purposes of statistical analysis into three groups of 33 with "few problems", 34 in the "middle range"; and 33 in a "high problem" group. It is difficult to infer from these categories whether the third of adopted children with "many problems" were disturbed at a level requiring clinical intervention or support. The authors do make clear however (p. 307) that many of the "problems" reported, such as conflict with parents, had disappeared by the time the adoptees were young adults.

Significant correlates of being in the problem category were: age at placement; sex - boys were more often seen as problematic in their adjustment; family structure - adjustment was somewhat better in families where there were existing children; social status - children in higher status families "tended to encounter more personality problems over their years than did their counterparts reared in lower status families." The final conclusion of this report is interesting.

> It is our view that agencies ought to go beyond their present primary role of acting as "brokers" i.e. bringing couples and babies together. Rather, we believe they should become experts on adoptive family life.... (Jaffee & Fanshel, 1970, p.315).

It is salutary to note that thirty years after this was written many adoption agencies in North America still seem to have a narrow focus, and have little expertise in, or understanding of the general dynamics and potential problems of life in adoptive families after placement (Cole and Donley, 1990). In a general conclusion on the Jaffee and Fanshel Study, we should note that despite the numerous citations of the study, it is based on a relatively small, geographically limited sample; lacks a control group; has a rather unclear definition of research methods; lacks standardized assessment methods; and lacks statistical sophistication in data analysis. However, an appropriate control or comparison group is difficult to obtain in adoption research.

Ideally one needs two comparison groups - children who were not adopted (but who are similar to the adopted group) and who remain in institutional care, temporary foster care, or in an unstable one-parent family; and children growing up in "normal" family situations. An example of a study which has achieved such a research model is that of Tizard (1977), which we review below.

Besides Jaffee and Fanshel (1970), another earlier American study which is frequently cited is Kadushin's (1970) study of the progress of 91 Wisconsin children who were specifically placed for adoption between 5 and 11 years. All were "white, healthy and had normal intelligence." Extensive pre-placement work, including consulting the child's own preference preceded these adoptions. At the time of follow-up 58 percent of the children were aged between 12 and 17. The principal criterion to ascertain the "success" of the placements was the level of satisfaction in the experience expressed by parents. The proportion of adoptions judged to be fully successful was 78 percent, with 15 percent judged to be marked by chronic problem behaviours in the child; but in only 2 of the 91 adoptions had the child been removed for residential treatment. However, Kadushin did not directly interview or test the adopted children, so we have no clear indication of their own views of the adoption process. A control group was not used.

Despite the limitations of Kadushin's study, we should note that it has influenced much adoption practice by agencies in North America, stimulating the trend towards the adoption of older and special-needs children which resulted in the view that "no child is unadoptable" (Churchill, 1979). Kadushin argues that his findings point to the possibility that a stable, supportive environment can overcome the effects of many early traumas which would otherwise have disposed the children to maladaption and delinquency. While the evidence he presents does not directly prove this point, it is certainly consistent with Clarke and Clarke's (1976) review of the evidence on the long-term outcomes of early deprivation.

Kadushin includes in his monograph a review of 14 follow-up studies of adoption in Europe and the United States, using various but presumably compatible methods of assessing success and failure in outcome. These 14 studies involved a total of 2,236 placements: on average, 74 percent were rated as successful, 11 percent equivocal, and 15 percent unsuccessful. Kadushin's comments on agency practice, and the process of adoption are worth quoting:

By far the most important thing the social agency does for the child is to provide him with an adoptive home. All else is commentary. All the case work efforts in easing transition, all the case work in follow-up during the post-placement year, is frosting on the cake of potential for change provided by the environment .... Adoption is not psychotherapy. But its psychotherapeutic potential is like that of a good marriage, a true friendship, a new satisfying job, or an enjoyable vacation. It can help to repair old hurts. (Kadushin, 1970, p.267)

Longitudinal studies

The most comprehensive and methodologically sophisticated studies of adopted children are represented by the Swedish work of Bohman and his colleagues (Bohman, 1970, 1980, and 1982; Bohman and Sigvardsson, 1990; Von Knorring et al., 1982). Bohman obtained his first sample through a Stockholm social service agency which dealt with cases of "unwanted pregnancies" - children born to women who, for various reasons had been unable to obtain an abortion. Of the 624 children identified, 168 were adopted as infants; 208 were placed in foster homes (although some of these children were later adopted, and others returned to biological parents for temporary periods); and the remainder stayed permanently with their biological parent or parents. For each of these three groups, an age and sex matched "normal" control group was studied. Bohman and his colleagues followed up the children in each of the three groups when they were aged 11, and adjustment was estimated by teachers rather than by parents. A "problem child" was defined as one with behaviour disturbances or nervous symptoms of a severity that would merit treatment in a mental health clinic.

Small but statistically significant differences did emerge between the three agency groups and the controls: 18 percent of agency children compared with 10 percent of controls were behaviourally disturbed, falling in the "problem child" category.

However, within the three agency groups those adopted in infancy were better adjusted, and across all three groups girls had significantly fewer behavioural problems than boys. In sum, the results at age 11 indicated that adopted children were doing better than similar children who were not adopted at birth; but not so well as controls. However, less than one percent of children in any group were so disturbed or maladjusted that they needed to be removed to a therapeutic institution. (Bohman, 1973, p.22)

At age 15, adjustment (again, teacher assessed) was rated in seven categories ranging from: score 7, (pupils with obvious bad adjustment, truancy, abuse of alcohol or drugs, criminality) to score 1 (pupils functioning well according to their age, in different social roles, goal-directed, and achieving well). Only one of the adopted boys had a score of 7 (severely maladjusted), and none of the adopted girls. Likewise, only three adopted boys and one adopted girl were in the next most severely maladjusted category (score 6). In fact, there were slightly more severely maladjusted children who were control subjects. A significant excess of adopted children occurred however, in the middle range of adjustment, with a slight dearth of adopted children in the very well adjusted categories. In contrast, "unwanted children" who stayed in biological or foster homes and who were not adopted displayed a significant excess of seriously disturbed behaviours. Bohman made a special study of aggressive traits in all groups, and found that the adopted children (unlike the non-adopted agency children) were no more aggressive than the control subjects.

> The results suggest that overall, adopted children show an excess of mild emotional and behavioural problems, but no excess of marked disturbance. The results support the conclusion ......that this investigation clearly shows the importance of an early and well-prepared placement of children born after unwanted pregnancies and that such placements may protect the children from future social maladjustment. (Bohman, 1973, p.25)

Bohman and his colleagues have also published a number of papers on the possibility of genetic transmission of behaviour problems in adoptees. While this research will be referred to in the subsequent chapter on health and constitutional factors in the adjustment of adoptees, it is appropriate to discuss this work here since the model which Bohman (1980) develops provides an important link between the two types of work - the follow-up studies (conducted mainly by social workers and agency psychologists), and the studies in behavioural genetics (conducted by psychologists and behavioural geneticists who are interested only in adoption as a "natural experiment" rather than as a helping process).

The work of Michael Bohman and his colleagues integrates these two traditions in a humane way which can be of considerable value in social work practice. The Swedish group has tried to identify factors which could assist in making adoption placement, and which can give an indication of support needed during adoption. Thus, Cloniger et al. (1982) and Bohman et al. (1982) found in linked studies of 822 men adopted at an early age by non-relatives that lower social class, criminality and alcoholism in an adoptive parent were linked in complex and indirect ways to the development of "petty criminality" in the adoptees when they were adults. Later adoptive placement associated with several unstable placements prior to adoption (particularly likely in disorganized "problem" families) interacted with genetic dispositions, to increase the risks of alcoholism and minor crime in later life. It appeared however that the quality of the adoptive home could overcome many of the early problems, and there was no direct or deterministic link between criminality or personality disorder in a birth parent, and the development of such conditions in an adopted-away child.

Bohman (1980) in reviewing these studies, suggests that although this work does support other adoption studies on genetic transmission of schizophrenia, affective disorder, personality disorders, and alcoholism, the adoption work cannot show what the mode of transmission is (recessive, or direct), nor whether single genes or collections of genes are involved. On balance, however, the Swedish evidence seems to shows that: (a) genetic factors explain a small but statistically significant part of the variance in maladjustment in adoptees; (b) genetic vulnerability interacts with environmental stresses in leading to higher vulnerability and the emergence of certain abnormal behaviours; (c) adoptive parents can, with appropriate support, diminish these risks, even in children who seem initially to be markedly vulnerable; (d) when behavioural problems do emerge in adopted children, or in the adulthood of adoptees, they are much less serious in nature than those recorded in the birth parents. There are two possible reasons for this: either some of the genes involved are "recessive" in nature, skipping generations; or quality parenting gives the adoptees greater strength to deal with problems when they do arise.

The largest study undertaken by the Swedish group is of the link between early stressful experience and adult adjustment in 2,215 adoptees born 1930-1949 (Von Knorring et al., 1982). The study was based on data linkage from centralized child welfare records to the government central registry on people with psychiatric illness. It was found that 136 of the 2,215 adoptees (6.1%) had received treatment for a psychiatric illness by the time they were, on average, 40 years old. This period prevalence rate was slightly but not significantly greater than that expected in an unselected sample of the general population. The authors identified early stresses from birth up to the time of the adoption to check for any link with later psychiatric disorder. Only one statistically significant link was found. Other potentially important factors such as number of placements prior to adoption, and history of abuse, were <u>not</u> related to later adjustment.

The one significant link was that between being placed for adoption at between 6 to 18 months (with the greatest risk between 6 and 12 months) and the later occurrence in adulthood of "reactive neurotic depression," such as acute depression with features of anxiety following the loss or departure of a partner. While Von Knorring et al. do not advance any theory to account for this finding, it is certainly compatible with psychoanalytic theories of separation (see Bowlby, 1979) which suggest that between the age of 6 and 18 months the child has an embryonic sense of self which is deeply threatened by prolonged separation experiences. Interestingly Belsky (1985) reports that children placed in day-care between 6 and 18 months (but not children placed before 6 months) have the most disturbed reaction to this temporary separation from a parent.

Further integration of findings on the follow-up of the "unwanted" children who were later adopted, with the work of the Swedish behavioural geneticists who have studied adoptees, is presented by Bohman and Sigvardsson (1980 and 1990). These papers report the follow-through till their 18th year of the adopted and nonadopted cohorts of "unwanted" children, and controls, born in 1957, with a further check on the central register on criminality and alcoholism when the adoptees and other children were aged 23.

By age 15, any psychiatric disturbances in the adoptees had largely disappeared; but the "unwanted" children who went to foster homes, and back and forth to biological parents had become appreciably worse. The data for the follow-up at 18 confirmed the picture at age 15. The adoptees had similar levels of adjustment and achievement in comparison with the nonadopted, normal controls. In contrast, the nonadopted controls who grew up in unstable homes were much more maladjusted than their normal controls. At age 23, adopted children had an 18.0 percent incidence of crime (major and minor) and alcohol related crimes, and drinking problems - compared with 15.5 percent of controls, a nonsignificant difference.

However, in the 96 children who grew up in unstable circumstance (including foster homes), 29.2 percent had recorded events of crime and alcoholism. Bohman and Sigvardsson attribute the poor outcome in the fostered group to poor placement practices, changes in foster homes, and uncertainty about their role by foster parents. On the question of genetic factors causing a higher a higher prevalence of crime and alcoholism in adoptees, the authors conclude that these findings provided only partial support for such a hypothesis. While genetic factors could account for the slight increase of the deviant conditions in the adoptees, the results also indicate that adoption has had many positive effects. In a further review of the data on the 23-year follow-up of the three groups of originally "unwanted" children, Bohman and Sigvardsson (1990) conclude:

> The results of our longitudinal studies indicate that the long-term prognosis for adopted children is in no way worse than for children in the general population, providing the adoptive home is psychologically well prepared for the task of rearing a nonbiological child. The study at 11 years admittedly indicated an increased frequency of nervous disturbances and maladjustment. This was, however, largely overcome in the subsequent follow-up studies. With regard to the very high frequency of criminality and alcohol abuse among the biological parents, the conclusion is warranted that adoption largely reduced the risk of social incompetence and maladjustment. The conclusion is supported by the comparison with the children who were taken back by their biological mothers or who had grown up in foster homes... Finally, our studies have demonstrated the advantages of a longitudinal, prospective design. If, for instance, the investigation had been restricted to the first, cross-sectional follow-up at age 11, then conclusions concerning adoption would have been quite different from those we have now reached. (Bohman and Sigvardsson, 1990, pp 104 and 106)

A further important longitudinal study has been reported by a Danish group (Eldred et al., (1976) who followed up a cohort of adoptees placed between 1924 and 1947. All 5,500 placements in Denmark were identified, and 216 were sampled through a stratified random procedure for intensive study. Since the researchers were primarily interested in genetic aspects of psychiatric illness, the sample was selected in the following way: group 1, 79 adoptees with a biological parent with a diagnosed schizophrenic or manic-depressive illness; group III, 99 adoptees whose birth parents had no history of mental illness; and group II, 38 individuals in whom birth parents had no psychiatric history, but one of whose adopting parents developed schizophrenia or manic-depression.

This research throws interesting light on the adoption experience as well as an adjustment in adoption. Adoptees learned about their adoption at an average age of 11 years, with a range of 4 to 17 years; but 13 percent of the subjects had never learned of their adoption. A fifth of those learning of adoption during or after adolescence reported very negative reactions to this news. Such revelation contributed to the development of neurotic patterns, but not to serious mental illness. Age at placement was also unrelated to later mental illness, though children who were adopted when older were more likely to know about their adoptive status from the outset. Another interesting finding was that children placed by agencies had no better outcome than children place privately by third parties. About one-fifth of adoptees, especially those placed later, had some contact with a biological parent after adoption. Such contact was associated with better satisfaction with the adoption process, as reported by the adult adoptees.

None of the environmental factors (including multiple placements prior to adoption, age at placement, and mental illness in an adopting parent) predicted the development of psychotic illness in adoptees. The best predictor of serious mental illness was psychosis in a biological parent with whom the child had no contact after adoption. While this finding points to the influence of genetic factors, these data also suggest that a child who is genetically at risk (because of the illness in biological parent) and who is brought up by adoptive parents without mental illness, has a 50 percent reduction in the expected incidence of serious mental illness.

In general, this Danish research suggests then that good adoptive care reduces the possibility of schizophrenia happening in biologically vulnerable individuals by at least half (Wender et al., 1974). It should be noted, however, that two independent analyses of the Danish data using different criteria have suggested somewhat different proportions (Kendler et al., 1982; Lowing et al., 1983). The general principle - that a good adoptive home can reduce the risk of psychosis in vulnerable individuals - remains, however.

The British National Child Development Study

The comprehensive Scandinavian work is paralleled by the long-term follow-up study of adopted children and control subjects in the British National Child Development Study. This study followed up from birth to age 16 (and beyond) all 16,000 children born in one week in England and Wales in 1958 (Davie et al., 1972). The cohort was followed up through the school system, and even if parents did not co-operate, data were obtained from teachers and school doctors on children at ages 7, 11 and 16 if they had been born in the crucial week in 1958.

Data were obtained at birth from parents, doctors and public health nurses. Of the children in the study, 640 were born out-of-wedlock, to single mothers. By the time they were seven, 182 of the 640 surviving illegitimate children were adopted. It was thus possible to compare adopted children, with non-adopted children from a similar social background, as well as the remaining "normal" children in the cohort (Crellin et al., 1972).

The follow-up to age seven of the adopted children showed that they had many advantages in the largely middle-class homes into which they had been adopted, in comparison with the children in one-parent families whose deprivation was reflected in poor levels of achievement and higher than average levels of maladjustment, measured by the Bristol Social Adjustment Guides, completed by teachers: on this measure 24 percent of the non-adopted children, who remained in one-parent families were maladjusted, 16 percent of the adopted children, and 13 percent of the remaining children in the study. Since the adopted children had lower birthweights, more neglectful parental care, and more congenital physical problems than the children born in "legitimate" circumstances, the level of adjustment in the adopted children was surprisingly good (Bagley, 1977). The follow-up of the children to age seven indicated, then, the powerful advantages of adoption over a one-parent situation. Stable, middle-class circumstances had largely overcome the marked disadvantages evident at birth.

The importance of longitudinal work in adoption is demonstrated by the report of the study of adopted and other children at age 11 (Lambert & Streather, 1980). This book was titled <u>Children in Changing Families,</u> a reflection of the remarkable change in the fortunes of the children in one-parent families, which was reflected in the adjustment of those originally classified as illegitimate. By the time they were 11, only 20 percent of the original illegitimate, nonadopted children were with a single mother - most mothers had married and stabilized their family situation. Even the lone mothers had reasonable security in public housing and income support. These changes were reflected in the improvements in behaviour and scholastic achievement in the "illegitimate" children at age 11.

The situation of the adopted children had, by contrast deteriorated somewhat at age 11, compared with adjustment at age 7. Put in perspective: "The attainment scores showed that adopted children, as a group, were doing very well indeed at 11. They were reading significantly better than legitimate (main cohort) children, they were doing just as well at maths, their social adjustment was no worse, and although not significantly so, they were slightly taller" (Lambert & Streather, 1980, pp. 132-133).

A further report of the follow-up when the adopted children were 16 (reported in detail in a later chapter in this book) shows that their adjustment and achievement had in fact improved, although it still lagged slightly below that which their class position would predict, based on comparison with 12,000 nonadopted children. The two comparison groups in this phase of the study are the "normal" children; and the 143 children who were separated from their biological mother after birth but who were not adopted, going instead into foster care, care of relatives or their father, or into institutions of various kinds. The behaviour, adjustment and achievement of these children was dramatically worse than that of the adopted children.

The British data which we analyzed shows too how disadvantaged the children were at birth: their birth mothers, usually single teenaged girls, often smoked late into pregnancy, had significantly more obstetric abnormalities both before and during birth, had lower levels of hemoglobin, more often worked past the 33rd week of pregnancy, and came late to antenatal clinics. Forty percent of the adopted children had low birthweight (below the first quartile for the whole cohort). They had more congenital problems of hearing and sight, and at age 16 significantly more (21%) than the main cohort (16%) were wearing glasses.

Educationally, the adopted children have better achievement levels than the general cohort at age 16 in English language and reading skills. The verbal advantages of the adopted children almost certainly reflect their social class advantages - 43 percent had a father in the highest social class groups, compared with 25 percent of the general cohort children. Social class advantages were also reflected in the height of the adopted children - by age 16, 29 percent were above the 3rd quartile for the whole cohort, compared with 25 percent in the general cohort children and 12 percent in the maternally-separated controls. Behaviourally the adopted children were slightly disadvantaged: 11 percent had received psychological help for a behavioural or emotional problem, compared with 8 percent of the general cohort children up to age 16; but 22 percent of the maternally-separated children had received professional help for problem behaviours.

A report by the child on relationships with parents, indicated that adopted children had significantly <u>fewer</u> conflicts with parents, in comparison with children in the main cohort. Parents were described as often anxious for the adopted child's welfare however, and there was some evidence from the data that the anxiety of the parents had transmitted itself to the adopted children. Overall, however, this British study shows that the adopted children have by age 16 adjusted very well, with only minor differences in adjustment and achievement from the average child in a stable, two-parent family. This British longitudinal study provides powerful support in favour of adoption as an institution which can meet the needs of children deprived early in life.

Other British studies

Barbara Tizard's (1977) book <u>Adoption: A Second Chance</u> reports a study that is well-controlled, but followed-up relatively small samples until they were eight years old. Her total sample of 65 (plus "normal" controls) are divided into three groups. All children were initially admitted in their first year of life to child care institutions. A third were adopted, a third returned to a biological parent (usually a single mother), and the remainder stayed in the institution. Half of the children returning to a biological parent either returned to the institution or went to foster homes. The children in institutions had various movements and instabilities.

By the age of eight the adjustment and achievement of the adopted children was largely similar to those of the "normal," community sample. "... the only problems described more frequently by adoptive parents were over-friendliness and attention-seeking.... A small minority of the adopted children displayed difficult or unusual behaviour which was not reported in any of the home-reared children - extreme disobedience, frequent and violent tantrums, overactivity, rocking, impulsiveness - and excessive "goodness". Five of the twenty children were described as showing one or more of these unusual behaviours". (Tizard, 1977, p. 120)

Children remaining in the child care institutions had relatively good outcomes as well, but children restored to biological families were much more maladjusted at age eight than the normal control group: two-thirds of the restored children compared to 15 percent of the adopted children, had been referred to a doctor or a psychiatrist because of problem behaviour.

Tizard's final conclusion is important, and worth quoting:

Long-term fostering only exists as a form of child-care because the natural parent is permitted or even encouraged to abandon care of the child, and to prevent the child from receiving stable permanent care in another family. In the case of the foster children described in this chapter it is clear not only that they are unlikely ever to return to their natural mothers but that right from their birth, or at least from early childhood, this was never a realistic possibility. Objectively, there seems little justification for the almost limitless irresponsibility which is permitted to natural parents in their relationships with children . (Tizard, 1977, p. 211)

A further report on the children in the above study who spent at least their first two years in residential care has been made by Hodges and Tizard (1989), when the three contrasted groups (adopted, restored to biological mother, or remaining in residential care) were aged 16. A new control or comparison group of children growing up in conventional two-parent homes, without any maternal deprivation or disruption of early life was also studied.

The results showed, first of all the advantages of the stable environment provided by the adoptive homes was apparent in the areas of IQ, social and family relations, and general behaviour. The adopted children had a mean IQ of 110; those returning to a biological parent a mean IQ of 97; and those remaining in care, a mean of 96. The social and behavioural profiles of the adopted children (who came from very deprived and disrupted early environments) improved over time, and was markedly better than the behaviour of the other two groups. Nevertheless, in comparison with the "normal" control subjects, the adopted children were significantly more worried, fearful and overparticular, and had more nervous tics and mannerisms (all signs of anxiety neurosis). However, the adopted children showed very few signs of externalising, aggressive or delinquent behaviour disorders, in marked contrast to the children restored to a biological parent. These important results demonstrate, once again that although adoption cannot totally make up for early deprivation, neurological damage, or negative heredity the outcomes for adopted children are much more favourable than in similar children who remain with a biological parent. This study once again reinforces many other studies in showing that many adopted children tend to develop signs of anxiety and nervousness - presumably a reflection of styles of adoptive parenting, rather than of early trauma or heredity.

Another British study of note is that by Raynor (1977) who attempted to trace in adulthood 288 individuals placed for adoption by two agencies between 1948 and 1951. Raynor was able to locate 160 families (55.5% of those adopting). She could find no reason from an examination of the placement records to suppose that those not traced were any different from those in the survey. Raynor was able to interview 105 of the adopted children from the 160 adoptive families. She comments that, "It was surprising ... how many parents were not prepared to leave this decision to respond to the researchers to their grown up sons or daughters, now 22 to 27 years old, but instead refused the invitation for them without consulting them." (Raynor, 1977, p. 39). Some reasons for this emerged from the interviews with both parents and adopted children: many adopted parents appeared to be anxious about the security of their role as adoptive parents. They seemed overprotective, were often unwilling to discuss the adoption with the adopted child, gave less information about birth parents than they actually had available, and seemed reluctant to let go of their children following adolescence. Many adopted children responded by being extremely dutiful, pondering to parental whims and wishes long into their own adulthood. Many adult adoptees, while generally well-adjusted, had a "truncated identity" which prevented them from being fully independent.

Overall, 73 percent of the adult adoptees interviewed had good or excellent life adjustment according to parental reports, while six percent of the adoptees had very poor adjustment (had criminal histories or were mentally ill). However, although no control group was used, it is unlikely that this proportion would differ much from an unselected group in the general population. Age at adoption did not contribute to any particular outcome, except that foster parents who had later adopted were more open and accepting of the child's original family, and were able to tell them more about the original parents of the child. Too often the parents who had adopted children as infants revealed the adoption too late in the child's life, and treated it after revelation as a topic that was not to be discussed. Embarrassment about not being the biological parents of a child whom they loved so dearly, and sometimes so desperately, was the main reason why some parents would not allow their adopted children, now adults, to be interviewed. In four cases, the adopters had never told the child that he or she was adopted.

Raynor's study has a number of interesting implications for the understanding of mental health in adoption. In terms of Kirk's (1964) model, most of Raynor's adoptive parents were operating at the "denial of difference" level which, in theory at least, prevented the adoptees from full actualization of their potential, and might actually impair their mental health in subtle or indirect ways. A case example from Raynor's study illustrates this: an adopted boy aged 11 was caught taking coins from his mother's purse. He didn't know that he was adopted. Mother told him, on discovery of the theft, "I'm not your Mummy, Daddy is not your daddy, Mary is not your sister. We picked you out from a lot of babies and now you let us down." Raynor comments, "When the children were told before five years of age, more than a third reacted with pride or pleasure and most of the others with indifference, but when they were told between five and eleven the proportion 'really pleased or proud' dropped sharply and the reaction of several children was shock or bitterness ... our experience in this study tends to support the advice given to adoptive parents by social workers over the years - to tell the child early before someone else does." (Raynor, 1977, p. 42).

Overall, Raynor gives a picture of adoptive parents who often have a lot guilt about being infertile, and not having biological children. These feelings of guilt are subtly transmitted to the adopted children, who have to cling tight emotionally because they are not "real" children. Yet despite this, adoptive parents and adoptive children often love one another deeply; and sometimes obsessively.

It is interesting to contrast Raynor's insights with those of the more formal epidemiological studies of Bohman (1980) and the National Child Development Study. While these studies indicated no excess of severe maladjustment or delinquency in the adoptees, they have shown that adoptees have an excess of minor types of maladjustment.

These epidemiological studies have not examined the subtle processes of adoption, and the interaction of parents and children around the issue of adoption. Raynor's study reaches the same conclusion as the epidemiological studies (an apparent excess of sub-clinical adjustment problems in adopted children with few major problems of adjustment) but produces evidence that these sub-clinical problems may be related to interactions related to adoption (and the avoidance of the issue of adoption) itself. Her insights are rather different from the identity theories ("genealogical bewilderment") advanced by writers such as Sorosky et al., (1978) in The Adoption Triangle. Raynor's theories seem more akin, in fact, to the ideas put forward by the Canadian researcher David Kirk (1964). Kirk's extensive studies (of more than 2,000 families with adopted children) in America and Canada deal with the "shared fate" of role handicap of both parent and adopted child. Kirk's "theory of adoption and mental health" based on this work is that an acceptance of the genealogical difference between parent and child is likely to best cope with the role dilemmas of adoption, and foster the best mental health outcomes for children.

Kirk's examination of role relationships in adopted families has led to important and testable hypotheses. It is curious that social psychologists working in this field have rarely tested Kirk's hypotheses with regard to adjustment in adoption, and Kirk (1981) himself, in a revision and reflection upon his theory, reports no empirical studies which have tested his theory of mental health in adoption. However, putting together Kirk's anecdotal and case history evidence with the clinical insights of Raynor and others with the epidemiological work of Bohman and others; and with the work of some identity theorists such as Sorosky, Hoopes and Stein and others, there is enough evidence for a general proposition:

> The problems and peculiarities of adoptive parenting produce a particular type of personality in many adoptive children, marked by a sub-clinical neurosis characterized by forms of guilt, anxiety, and over-attachment to over-protective parents.

Further U.S. studies which are reviewed in the following section do not contradict, and sometimes support this proposition. The studies on transracial and transcultural adoption which are reviewed later complicate this proposition however, in that the seemingly acute role difficulties in adopting a child who is racially different from his or her adoptive parents have led to a different style of adoptive parenting, with rather successful outcomes.

Later U.S. studies of adjustment in adoption

The first study worthy of mention is that reported by Hoopes and Sherman (1969). In following up 100 children placed for adoption by the Pennsylvania Children's Aid Society, the researchers set out to investigate the hypothesis that adopted children would have poorer mental health than "normal" controls because "they suffer deep trauma in early life because of forced separation from the natural mother, and later on they are liable to have acute identity crises because of loyalty to both the natural and adoptive parents." The research did not confirm these hypotheses however.

The adopted children and the controls were studied in their mid-teens using various clinical and educational measures.   No statistically significant differences in adjustment or achievement were found between the adopted adolescents and controls, when mean scores on the various measures were compared.   The authors explain this finding by the fact that the children were "unexceptional," white infants, placed with middle- and upper-class parents, after careful selection procedures. This study then, like many others, found no excess of gross pathology and maladjustment in adopted children in their teenaged years.

The further work of Stein and Hoopes (Hoopes, 1982; Stein and Hoopes, 1985) is important in that it represents a well-controlled, longitudinal study of children placed in infancy, followed up to late adolescence. All of the adoptees in this additional study were white, and were adopted in white, middle class families. The initial sample was of 260 adoptees and controls, studied when they were between eight and twelve years old. On the Bristol Social Adjustment Guide (a measure of emotional and behaviour disorders) the adoptive children had significantly higher scores than the comparison group of non-adopted children in the same school classes. However, the adoptees were judged by teachers to have problematic behaviour in only 15 of the 150 areas in the scale used (compared with 8 of 150 in the controls), leading the authors to conclude: "There is ... a degree of additional risk for the adopted child, with a greater incidence of problem behaviour reported for the group of nonadopted children than for their nonadopted classmates. It should be noted that the percentage of adopted children who develop serious problems is very small and represents expected variations within the normal range of behaviour." (Stein, 1982, pp 98-99).

Stein (1982) also attempted to predict adjustment within the adoptees, from information gathered about parents. She found that parents who were less secure and more controlling of their adopted children, had children who were more insecure and anxious on the Cattell personality measure. Moreover, parents' own self-concept was a good predictor of child adjustment. These findings indicate that some adoptive parents are anxious in their roles as adoptive parents, have poorer self-conception of themselves as parents and in turn are controlling, dominating and overprotecting of their children, who in turn manifest rather anxious behaviours. Nevertheless, this anxiety when it occurs, is not grossly pathological or "clinical" in nature. These results strongly support the proposition about overprotectiveness in many adoptive parents, advanced above.

Another interesting finding from the Delaware study was that on a sociometric test of how popular the children were in the classroom setting, the adoptees had just as many friends and were just as well adjusted in a social sense, as their non-adopted peers. Overall, the self-concept of the adopted children (as measured by the Osgood semantic differential scale) did not differ from that of the non-adopted controls, except on one important dimension. Adoptees' ratings of "myself with my father" were significantly higher than those of controls. Hoopes speculates that since the adoptive fathers described themselves as particularly assertive, uninhibited, secure and relaxed (on the Osgood measure, in comparison with control parents), their adopted children may draw particular identity strengths from their fathers.

Fifty of these adoptees (and 41 controls) were studied again when they were in senior high school, aged between 16 and 18 years. The measures selected by Stein and Hoopes (1985) reflected their theoretical view of child development, which was strongly based on the descriptions of identity stage development of Erikson (1968). The adoptees were found to be doing surprisingly well, and the slight elevation on measures of behaviour disturbance observed in their elementary school years was no longer evident in late adolescence. On the Offer Self-Image measure (Offer, et. al. 1981) there was no significant difference between adoptees and controls; while on the Tan Ego Identity measure (Tan et al., 1977) the adoptees actually had significantly better levels of ego integration than controls.

On a complex measure of sociometric functioning derived from the work of Moreno (1953) the adoptees had as wide a circle of friends and respected social figures (including parents) as the controls. Moreover, identity integration and development was associated with a wide range of social acquaintances who were respected and liked. A comparison within the adopted sample of adolescents with and without a sibling who was the biological child of the adopting parents found no significant differences in adjustment, contrary to earlier findings (e.g. Ternay et al., 1980).

While these findings overall, present a very optimistic view of adoption outcome, Stein and Hoopes (1985) remind us that their results are derived from white infants placed in advantaged, white homes. It is not clear whether these findings could be generalized to other types of adoption such as those of older children, or of children racially different from their parents. Nevertheless, the hypothesis from the Delaware study is that problems of adoption are relatively few (although some parents are overprotective and overanxious, traits which they pass to their children to some degree), and the strengths of adoption as an institution can also apply to various "special need" categories of adoptive children.

In a later review of these findings, and of subsequent work on identity formation in adoptees Hoopes (1990) argues that in comparison with "ordinary" children, adoptees have some special identity tasks - for example, integrating knowledge and affect concerning biological parents, personal ethnicity in relation to parents and peers, and the role demands of being adopted. There is no evidence however that these additional tasks in identity resolution (in the Eriksonian paradigm) have in general impaired the self-concept of adoptees. True, adoptive parents have special tasks, as Brodzinzky (1990) make clear. But there is little evidence that adoptive parents (who are usually carefully selected by social work agencies on grounds of emotional maturity) are unable, as a group, to meet these challenges. This is clearly brought out in Janet Hoopes' (1982) research: adoptive parents are specially selected, have special motivations in parenting, and usually have special strengths in this task. The one weakness in adoptive parenting may be over-involvement, over-possessiveness, and over-commitment. But it is better, in our judgment, for parents to err on the side of love. It is coldness, rejection or inconsistent loving which causes the most profound damage (Bowlby, 1979).

Clinical researchers (e.g. Brinich, 1990) argue from individual case histories that the additional identity tasks faced by both adoptive parents and adopted children may interact with other stressors in producing particular kinds of outcomes. Nevertheless, the weight of the evidence from random or unselected samples of infant adoptees, without overt physical or mental disability, and belonging to the same ethnic group as their parents is that manifest identity problems are few, and psychological outcomes in terms of good adjustment and mental health are unlikely to differ from those in the general population.

Lindholm and Tavliatos (1980) used a rather different methodology in an essentially epidemiological study of school children of all ages (from kindergarten to 12th grade) in Fort Worth, Texas, which identified 3032 children, 41 of whom had been adopted. Teachers completed Quay's Behaviour Problems Checklist for each child. Overall, adopted children (particularly boys) were reported to have significantly more conduct problems, personality problems, and problems of "socialized delinquency". The differences between adopted and nonadopted children peaked at age 14, and then declined as children grew older. The authors stress, as many other researchers have done, that the amount of serious maladjustment in adopted children was small, limited to just two of the 41 cases.

Another study dealing with 'ordinary' adoption is that by Brodzinsky et. al., (1984), which employed a factorial design sampling 130 adopted children placed by several New Jersey agencies, stratified by sex (half were male) and current age (equally distributed between 6 and 11 years). Controls obtained from the New Jersey school system were matched for age, sex, socioeconomic status and current family intactness. Mothers of the adopted children and the controls completed two standardized measures of child adjustment, while teachers rated children separately on profiles of achievement and behaviour. Analysis of variance of measures indicated that:

Overall, adopted children were rated by their mothers as lower in social competence and as manifesting more behaviour problems than nonadopted children .... Mothers of nonadopted girls rated their daughters as more frequently and more effectively involved with others and/or more successful in school than did mothers of adopted girls .... there was a significant difference between adopted and nonadopted girls for depression, social withdrawal, hyperactivity, delinquency, and cruelty. In each of these categories adopted girls were rated higher than nonadopted girls by their mothers (Brodzinsky, et. al., 1984, p.585).

Somewhat fewer differences emerged in the comparison of parental rating of adopted and nonadopted boys, and there was a trend on some variables for perceived problems (particularly those related to externalized aggression) to diminish with age. Teacher ratings added to the complexity of the picture: adopted boys were better adjusted than girls at age 6-7, but by age 10-11 this pattern was reversed. These authors draw the general conclusion that:

Adopted children are typically not manifesting severe pathology, but only display slightly more extreme forms of behaviour than are found among nonadopted children .... the adopted children actually are doing very well considering the SES background of the typical birth parents, and the fact that adopted children are more likely to experience increased stress and poorer prenatal care during gestation... Adoptive parents, and mental health professionals, need to be informed and educated about the potential problems associated with this form of family life, but they also need to reassured that in the majority of cases the adopted children adapt quite successfully both in psychological and academic areas (Brodzinsky et. al., p. 588-589).

It should be noted that this well-designed study looked only at children who were not transracially adopted or placed later in life. Brodzinsky (1984) makes some interesting observations on adoption revelation, based on his work with a total sample of 300 adoptees aged 4 to 13. While following the advice of modern practice, all adoptive parents had told their children of their adoptive status before their fifth birthday, Brodzinsky found that the majority of the younger children had little clear idea of what adoption meant, at any level of understanding. This was not surprising when the difficult idea of adoption is considered in the light of Piaget's theory of concept formation in young children:

The four-year-old may well say that he is adopted, but just what does this mean to him? Probably no more than it does when the young child volunteers the fact that he is Catholic or Jewish, American or English. To the child these are just words.... However, an early disclosure of adoption information also occurs in the context of a warm, loving and protective family environment, thereby minimizing the chances of children finding about their status from an outside and often unfriendly source. (Brodzinsky, 1984, p.31)

Most importantly, early revelation provides a basis on which adoptive status can be elaborated, cognitively and emotionally, as the child grows older. But the 'simple facts' alone, at an early age, are just not enough. Brodzinsky advocated that parents and children need continued support in elaborating the meaning of adoption for themselves and their children. They need to be 'open' about adoption in more ways than one. Brodzinsky's theory of mental health in this respect bears many resemblances to Kirk's earlier theory of "acceptance of difference" (Kirk, 1964).

Several further studies of self-esteem in adoptees and controls should be noted. These studies accessed the adopted children and controls through the school system. Culley (1970) in a study of 58 adopted adolescents found that adoptees and controls, "did not differ in regard to self-concept, self-acceptance, and concept of ideal life. However, the nonadopted perceived their peer group as having a better self-concept than did the adopted.... The nonadopted viewed themselves as being a more cheerful person, whereas the adopted viewed themselves as being a more thoughtful person". (Culley, 1970, 5659). In a later study with a similar design, Norvell and Guy (1977) could again, find no overall difference in the self-concepts of adopted adolescents in comparison with control subjects.

These results are in accord with the later work of Stein and Hoopes (1985), summarized above, and with Simon and Altstein's (1987) work on transracial, adolescent adoptees which again found that they had similar levels of self-esteem, compared with their non-adopted peers.

Conclusion

This review of follow-up studies of adoption reinforces the idea that adoptive parenting differs in some important respects from ordinary parenting. Some of the problems and difficulties which may emerge in adoption seem attributable, in part, to the tendency of adoptive parents to treat their children 'as if' they were their own, without accepting the nature of the child's origins or the inherent differences which adoptive parenting has in comparison with ordinary parenting.

While few parents today conceal the fact of their child being adopted, few seem to follow-though adequately the fact of early revelation in ways which would be most helpful to the child's psychological development. Agencies have largely failed in follow-up and support of adoptive parents with the difficulties and challenges of adoptive parenting.

The follow-up studies show a small excess of marked psychopathology in adopted children: this could be due to genetic factors, a risk which the environment of a good adoptive home may well diminish. Adopted children often demonstrate a sub-clinical neurosis or personality style, marked by anxiety, worry and over-attachment to their adoptive homes - a personality style which may reflect the anxiety and overprotection of the adoptive parents themselves.

A number of common trends emerge in many of the follow-up studies: in the early years boys seem to do somewhat more poorly than girls. However, the longer the period of follow-up, the more do early problems of adjustment diminish, so that in the long run adopted children's adjustment shows few differences from that of children who grow up in stable homes with both biological parents. The longitudinal studies reviewed indicate that at least three-quarters of adopted children will grow up to be normal adults; but 10 percent of adoptions will have failed to meet the children's development needs, and five percent of adopted children will, as adults, have very poor psychological adjustment. These are precisely the same proportions which have emerged in the control or contrast groups in these longitudinal studies. What is not at all clear from these studies however is whether the adjustment problems in the contrasted groups (adopted and nonadopted) have different aetiologies, or indeed are clinically similar.

Scholastically, adopted children tend to do well, but with achievement somewhat less than that which the social class levels of their adoptive parents would have predicted in ordinary circumstances, but significantly higher than that predicted by the social status of the surrendering birth parent. In studies where nonadopted controls, born in similar disadvantaged circumstances to the adopted children were followed up, it is clear that the educational and behavioural adjustment of adopted children is rather successful. Where children have been separated from their birth mother early in life, but have not been subsequently adopted, outcomes are often unfavourable.

In general terms then, adoption is an institution which meets the needs of children who would otherwise not enjoy stable family life.

3 Genetic, physical and constitutional factors influencing adjustment in adoption

Introduction

Of all my literature files, that on biological, or genetic influences on the behaviour and adjustment of adopted children is the most bulky. There are well over a hundred studies in this area, published mostly in journals of psychiatry and behavioural genetics. Ironically, this literature pays little attention to problems of adoptive parenting and how adopters may help children overcome inherited or early acquired physical or temperamental factors which may be potentially handicapping. Instead, most of the studies treat the adopted child with a cold and clinical detachment, seeing the child simply as a means to an end - demonstrating the degree to which behavioural, intellectual or other problems in the adopted child reflect genetic factors, and the degree to which the family environment created by the adopting parents modifies the child's behavioural and emotional adjustment.

Despite their clinical detachment and the disinterest which many of these studies show for the adoption process, these studies have to be taken account of since their very scientific detachment does provide data which alert us to potential difficulties in the institution of adoption, difficulties which social work support for adoption may be able to overcome. Before going on to review these studies briefly, I will consider studies on other aspects of biological influence on the adjustment of adopted children: biological impairment acquired early in life through perinatal circumstances or deficiencies in early nutrition; the influence of gender on adjustment; and the effects of early child abuse prior to adoption on the later adjustment of the child.

Early circumstances and early trauma

The British National Child Development Study (Crellin et al., 1971) has produced the fullest evidence that the prenatal and birth circumstances of adopted children are likely to be extremely disadvantaged. In a study of some 180 adopted children in a national cohort of all children born in Britain in one week in 1958, it was shown that mothers who gave up infants for adoption were particularly likely to be disadvantaged teenaged mothers who smoked during pregnancy, attended prenatal clinics irregularly, had more complications of pregnancy, had children with lower birth weight, and with more minor physical complications of hearing and sight. These differences were dramatic when the early circumstance of the adopted children were compared with those of a control group. What is most remarkable about this data set is the outcome of these physically disadvantaged adopted children by the time they were 16. By then, these adopted children taller, brighter and heavier than children in disadvantaged working class homes (see the subsequent chapter in this book). This was entirely a reflection of the advantages which being placed in middle class homes had bestowed. In other words, this study provided powerful evidence of the beneficial effects of an enriched environment on the growth and development of adopted children.

Bohman's (1970) Swedish work of an adoption cohort followed through to adulthood provides somewhat similar evidence (Bohman and Sigvardsson, 1990). Adopted children had lower birthweight, and their mothers had many more complications of pregnancy and birth. Up to the age 11, a significant link was found between complications of birth and pregnancy, and problems in reading and writing. Low birthweight was also related to problems of maladjustment at age 11. But these links were barely significant and had disappeared by the time the adoptees were in their teenage years.

American research has confirmed that mothers who relinquish children for adoption are more likely to be unsupported teenage mothers with unplanned pregnancies, and receive less prenatal care (Yogman et al., 1983). However, the widespread availability of abortion in the United States has meant that in recent years many unmarried teenagers who were hostile to their pregnancy can have an abortion, rather than having to bring an "unwanted" child to term (Kirman, 1983). This fact it reflected too in the greatly decreased supply of babies available for adoption. At the present time the majority of unmarried teenagers giving up babies for adoption are Roman Catholic (Yogman et al., 1983), a reflection of strictures within the Catholic church against abortion.

Another possibility that has to be considered is that young, single girls who get pregnant are also marginal individuals, not only in terms of psychological characteristics, but in also terms of physical health. There is more evidence too, from the work of Cadoret et al. (1976) and Cadoret (1990) that such health problems may be transmitted genetically to the adopted child, so that adopted children may have an excess of both medical and behavioural problems in adolescence.

Sex and adjustment in adopted children

Boys are more often given up for adoption; and boys are in general more likely to appear in deviant populations. When these two factors are controlled for, it emerged in Cadoret and Cain's (1980) American study, that adopted boys did have significantly more behavioural problems in adolescence. Nevertheless, the relationship was not a straightforward one: adopted boys had no excess of behaviour disorders in stable adoptive homes. But when the home was stressed by divorce or psychiatric illness in an adopting parent, boys were much more likely to become disturbed, in comparison with girls. Moreover, the vulnerability of the boys to stress appeared to be inherited, when data on biological parents was taken into account.

Bohman's (1970) follow-up study of a Swedish cohort also showed that adopted boys were more likely than controls to be disturbed in early adolescence, while girls showed fewer differences when compared with their control group. However, these differences disappeared as the adopted boys grew older (Bohman and Sigvardsson, 1990).

Schechter and Bertocci (1990), speculating about "the meaning of the search" for birth parents by adoptees discuss the different kinds of identify development in males and females which may impel the adoptee to search. Women appear to search more than men, but for reasons of identity linked to sex-role development, rather than because of greater maladjustment or unhappiness in adoption.

In their report on breakdown and disruption in older child adoptions, Barth and Berry (1988) indicate that chronic acting out behaviour (more likely in males) is a factor associated with adoption breakdown. However, it is clear that aggressive and delinquent behaviour is more common in boys, while girls react to loss and stress by more internalizing behaviours. It is also possible that biological families, faced with the chronic stressors of poverty, adult male aggression and desertion etc., will release into care aggressive male children, but will retain girls. Thus the statistics showing a high proportion of acting-out boys in the special-needs adoption categories may be biased by much earlier child care decisions. We provide some supportive evidence for this idea from an empirical study of fifty cases in which a judge of the Alberta Family Court dispensed with all rights of biological parents in cases of child abandonment, neglect and abuse (Bagley, 1988).

The inheritance of I.Q. in adopted children

While the I.Q. of adopted children is not directly related to adjustment, the research in this area provides an important model in both adoption and I.Q. research. If adopted children are removed from disadvantaged and generally lower I.Q. parents at birth, and placed with advantaged, and generally higher I.Q. adoptive parents, how will the children turn out intellectually? The answer to this question could have important implications for the debate about the degree to which intellectual characteristics are inherited. Studies in this field reviewed by Munsinger (1975) indicated that both heredity and environmental factors were at work in influencing the adopted child's intellectual development. Later studies of black children adopted by white parents indicated too that black children have above average I.Qs. when adopted by middle class, white parents (Scarr and Weinberg, 1976 and 1976 and 1977; Tizard, 1977). Scarr and Weinberg (1977) also show that the beneficial environmental effects for the black children were most marked in children adopted in the first year of life. Two American longitudinal studies both show that the environment provided by the adoptive family is an important and significant influence on the adopted child's basic I.Q., although some genetic influence remains (De Fries et al., 1981; Horn, 1983). Horn suggests from his data on 300 adopted children in Texas that the influence of genetic factors on I.Q. declines as the children grow older, and the powerful environmental effects of adoption assert themselves. Maughan and Pickle's (1990) British research provides additional data showing that children of disadvantaged parents adopted into middle class homes have, by their early adult years, acquired cognitive and intellectual styles close to those of non-adopted, middle class children. It should also be noted that children adopted past infancy, who have experienced either severe malnutrition, physical abuse, or both, tend to have poorer intellectual and behavioural outcomes.

This could reflect the fact that such abuse and neglect causes CNS trauma to such children (Martin and Beezley, 1977; Bagley, 1991e).

In an important study of 321 adopted children by 101 Massachusetts families Berbaum and Moreland (1985) found support for the "confluence model" - that is the I.Q. of a child adopted in infancy was best predicted by the combination of the birth parents' I.Q. levels, and the intellectual level of the adoptive parents. Both environmental and genetic factors, probably in about equal portions, contribute to intellectual development in adopted children. Labuda et al. (1986) suggest that the relative influences of these two factors remain stable throughout early childhood. There are obvious procedural and methodological difficulties in these kinds of studies however - adoption agencies may try and place children with adopters with similar educational achievements as a birth parent, and this has to be controlled for; and both birth and adoptive parents, as well as the adopted child, have to be subjected to carefully administered, individual I.Q. tests. Furthermore, even when the most careful controls and test procedures are employed, about half of the variance in I.Q. test scores of adoptees remains unexplained (Labuda, et al., 1986; Rice, 1986).

The best prediction for genetic factors seems to be with regard to verbal I.Q. and reading ability, according to data from ·the large-scale Colorado Adoption Project (Cardon et al., 1990). The findings from adoption work by behaviour geneticists generally support those models of the influence of heredity on intelligence produced from twin studies (Bouchard et al., 1990). Indeed, adoption research has now replaced the evidence from twin studies as the most important source of data on genetic influence on intelligence (Locurto, 1990).

However, it should be emphasized that the largest source of data in this field, the Danish study of more than 4,000 adoptees followed-up into early adulthood showed that the combination of intelligence levels of biological and adoptive parent, and social class of adopting parent predict less than two thirds of the variance in the intellectual achievements of the adoptees (Teasdale and Owen, 1986). While predictions of this accuracy are quite rare in psychological research, nevertheless these findings imply that anyone trying to predict exact intellectual outcomes on the basis of rather comprehensive information will be wrong about one third of the time. However, the implications of these findings for those involved in adoption placement are that there is a reasonable probability that well-educated adoptive parents will raise adopted children whose educational achievements will be average, or above average. Indeed, there is important evidence that adoption can significantly raise the I.Q. of children whose original potential was thought to be very depressed, because of mental retardation in parents, or because of adverse experiences in the child's early life. This is well brought out in the classic American work of Skeels (1966), and in the Swedish studies reviewed by Bohman and Sigvardsson (1990).

The temperament of adopted children

Important research from the New York Longitudinal Study of children with and without CNS problems at birth or acquired early in life, has shown that all children have an individual temperamental style which is probably genetic in origin, although insults to the central nervous system can modify temperamental style in negative ways (Thomas and Chess, 1977). Three main types of temperament have been identified: 'easy' (about half of all children), characterized by persistent good mood, adaptability, and ease of comfort in the face of stress; 'slow- to-warm-up' (about 25 percent of all children), characterized by shyness, social withdrawal and lack of responsiveness to stimuli; and 'difficult' children (about 12 percent) who are irregular in biological function, have intense, negative reactions to stimuli, find it difficult to adapt to new situations, withdraw prematurely or are aggressive in interaction, as infants cry a great deal, and are difficult to comfort. Children with a 'difficult' temperament are particularly likely to develop behaviour problems in childhood and adolescence if there is a 'lack of fit' between parental rearing style and the child's temperamental characteristics (Thomas and Chess, 1977).

Is it possible that adopted children are more likely than those in the general population to have a difficult temperament (because of either genetic factors or poor prenatal care or difficult birth circumstances)? Evidence on this question is mixed. Carey et al. (1974) confirmed that between 12 and 14 percent of both adopted children and control infants had a 'difficult' temperament. However, only 38 percent of the adopted infants, compared with 51 percent of the controls had an "easy" temperament. The differences were accounted for by the fact that significantly more of the adopted children had either 'slow' temperament, or temperamental styles which were difficult to classify. Maurer et al. (1980) studied 162 adoptees followed through to mid-adolescence, and found that in both sexes, difficult temperament in infancy was a significant predictor of behavioural problems of various kinds. The difficult temperament in infancy was particularly important in predicting hyperactivity and associated maladjustments in both males and females. Overall, 19 percent of 'easy' temperament infants had signs of maladjustment in adolescence; 31 percent of the 'slow-to-warm-up' infants; and no less than 68 percent of the 'difficult' adopted infants were maladjusted in adolescence. The 'difficult' infants were most likely to display antisocial conduct disorders, sometimes associated with hyperactivity; while the 'slow' children were most likely to be withdrawn, anxious or depressed. These are very interesting findings, which imply that different approaches to child-rearing, responsive to the child's particular emotional and behavioural needs, might well have prevented adolescent maladjustment.

Cadoret et al. (1976) compared two groups of adoptees, one with difficult temperament in infancy, and later hyperactivity and associated conduct disorder; and a contrast group with easy temperament in infancy, and normal behavioural development in later childhood. Adopted boys were much more likely to fall into the original group of disturbed adoptees, and this was controlled for in selecting the contrast group. An examination of the background histories of the <u>biological</u> parents of the two groups showed that the disturbed group of adoptees (all placed during infancy) were much more likely to have had a biological parent who had antisocial personality disorder, or other psychiatric condition. There is clear evidence from this and a related study (Cunningham et al., 1975) that hyperactivity is a personality trait which arises from 'difficult' infant temperament, a temperamental style which is genetic in origin, and which is related to behavioural deviance in a biological parent. Childhood hyperactivity has the potential to develop into antisocial personality.

Adopted children are likely then, because of genetic factors to have a higher risk of difficult temperament in infancy. Such a conclusion has important implications for adoptive parenting. The adopted child is not an ordinary child, similar to a biological child of the adopting parents: an adopted child is one who may have special needs for a particular type of parenting in relation to temperamental style. As Thomas and Chess (1977) have shown, it is by no means inevitable that an infant with a difficult or hyperactive temperament will develop behaviour problems. The crucial variables are likely to be parental attitudes, interactions and handling of a child with special needs (Cadoret, 1990).

The possible inheritance of alcoholism, criminal behaviour and antisocial behaviour and personality disorder in adoptees

Both the American follow-up study of adoptees by Cadoret and Gath

(1978) and the Danish study by Goodwin et al. (1977) have indicated that children adopted in infancy who had an alcoholic birth mother were slightly more likely than a similar group of adoptees but with no history of alcoholism in a birth mother to become 'early drinkers.' Such behaviour was also environmentally stimulated however, in that marital discord in the adopting parents seemed likely to precipitate the emergence of drinking behaviour in adoptees.

A similar model of interaction of genetic vulnerability and environmental stress emerged in the Swedish follow-up studies of adoptees (Bohman et al., 1982) with regard to 'petty criminality': stress in the child's life increased the risk of such behaviour only when a biological parent had a criminal history. Similar findings emerged too in the Danish adoption study (Mednick et al., 1984).

What is most interesting about all of these studies is that the prevalence of crime and alcoholism was substantially less in the adoptees than that expected if the children had grown up with a biological parent. In other words, growing up in a stable adoptive home was a powerful protective factor for the large majority of adopted children who were at-risk genetically.

Possible inheritance of schizophrenia, psychosis and affective disorder in adoptees

There is a considerable technical literature in this area, published by behavioural geneticists interested in identifying the degree to which major types of mental illness could be inherited. I will not review this literature in detail here: suffice to conclude that a number of American and European studies (e.g., Kendler et al., 1982; Wender et al., 1974; Lowing et al., 1983; Gottesman and Shields, 1982; Baker, 1986; Cadoret, 1990; Roy, 1990) show that biological parents of adopted children appear to have an excess of psychiatric morbidity of various kinds which is in some cases transmitted to their adopted children. Parental instability due to mental illness appears to be an important reason both for conceiving an unwanted pregnancy, and also for being unable to care for the child.

Again, the incidence of psychiatric disorder in the adopted children in these studies was much lower than in children reared by a biological, mentally ill parent. The degree of risk of developing schizophrenia in an adopted child with a schizophrenic parent is illustrated in the study by Lowing et al. (1983). The expected incidence of schizophrenia in the general population is about one percent; in an adopted child of a schizophrenic parent it is about three percent; but in a child of a schizophrenic reared by a biological parent it is ten percent. In other words, adoption greatly diminishes the risk of developing schizophrenia in an individual with some genetic proneness for the disease. The same conclusion can be drawn for affective disorders such as manic depression (Parker, 1982).

Cadoret (1990) concludes her review of the genetic influences on conduct disorders which emerge by the time of adolescence in adopted children:

> In how many cases of adoptees who come to clinics are biologic parents antisocial, depressed, and so on? Perhaps a large part of the variance in adolescent conduct disorder can be ascribed to biological background. Furthermore, the actual findings with adoptive families suggest that environmental variables, such as behavioural or psychiatric problems in other adoptive family members, play an important role. This role may be very different from many of the psychodynamic models put forth in the past. (p.40)

Conclusions

Certain biological factors - genes for some types of psychiatric and personality disorder, certain types of inherited temperament, and psychobiological problems linked to poor prenatal care and birth conditions of natural mothers - are likely to put adopted children at greater risk for the development of psychiatric or behavioural problems in childhood, adolescence or young adulthood. However, given the potential risks for a minority of adopted children (perhaps ten percent of all adopted children) it is remarkable that the institution of adoption has protected them so well against stresses or dysfunctonal interactions which could precipitate mental disorder. Nevertheless, given the powerful potential for adoption to prevent the emergence of such disorders, we conclude too that adopting parents should receive much more support for their role than has hithertofore been the case. This is clearly brought out in the work of the Swedish psychiatrist Michael Bohman (Bohman, 1981; Bohman and Sigvardsson 1980 and 1990). Bohman concludes that:

> Looking at the very negative social heritage for the whole cohort of these unwanted children, the conclusion is warranted that the

intervention and decisions made by social welfare authorities and the adoption agency at the time of the child's birth have had a very decisive influence on later life opportunities and careers, in both positive and negative directions (Bohman and Sigvardsson, 1980, p.31).

In Bohman's analysis, the decision to remove and place for adoption the child of a mentally ill parent has profound positive consequence for the later development and mental health of child. An extremely useful synthesis of the literature on genetic problems of adoptees, and the general identity and self-concept development of adopted children is presented by Black (1983).   Black is concerned to dispel notions of "bad blood" which have plagued adoption in the past, and caused needless worry to both adopters and adoptees. She argues that the movement toward openness in adoption should mean that adopting parents should get the fullest information about psychological or physical problems of the biological parents, and be counselled by an expert in   genetics about the implications of that background for the special parenting inputs needed. As Black points out, it is incumbent in this process for social workers to obtain a very   detailed social and biological history about the child and his or her birth parents <u>before</u> adoption is planned.

Finally, we turn once more to the evidence provided by the crucially important longitudinal study from infancy to adulthood of the large cohort of adoptees and control subject studied by Bohman and Sigvardsson. In their most recent report of data from this cohort they comment:

> In regard to the very high frequency of .... criminality and alcohol abuse among the biological parents, the conclusion is warranted that adoption largely reduced the risk of social incompetence and maladjustment. This conclusion is supported by the comparison with the children who were taken back by their biological mothers or who had grown up in foster homes. Among those children, maladjustment and school failure were common and persistent features over the years. (Bohman and Sigvardsson, 1990, pp 104-105).

4 Adjustment, identity and special needs adoption: Clinical research and policy change

Introduction

Follow-up studies of cohorts of adopted children, and systematic surveys of children placed by an adoption agency have provided the clearest picture of adjustment in adoption. These studies, reviewed in Chapter 2, have shown that in general adopted children have good adjustments, although there may be characteristic types of adoptive parenting which led to a higher incidence of sub-clinical neuroses.

The studies reviewed in the present chapter are based on non-random samples usually obtained from a clinic or counselling agency, or from personal contacts or networks of the particular researcher. Such studies could give a biased picture of adoption. While a number of such studies have suggested that adopted children are likely to be overrepresented in say, child guidance clinic populations, it should be borne in mind that referrals to clinics, and clinic selection of cases may be selective. The British National Child Development Study of adopted children (Seglow et al., 1972) found for instance that adopted children were more likely than others to have had tonsils removed or (for male children), to have been circumcised. There was no medical need for these procedures, and they could best be described as prophylactic, or the referrals of parents anxious for their child to have the best of services.

Likewise, the British study found that adoptive parents were particularly likely to enter their children for private schooling, and to refer them for educational testing and other psychological procedures, including counselling. But there was no evidence from this large scale epidemiological study that the adopted children were disturbed to such an excessive degree that they actually needed, in most cases, such referrals. Many very disturbed children who were not adopted were never referred to or assessed by any helping agency. Ironically, the British work indicates the possibility that referral may actually give the child a self-perception of himself as a difficult child with problems. Put another way, the referral may be part of the process by which parental neuroses are transmitted to the child.

Studies of adopted children in clinic settings, and studies of non-random groups of adoptees are nevertheless interesting and potentially important in identifying sub-types of mal-adaption in adoption, or in focusing on problems which may beset at least a few adoptees. Such studies could have important implications for social work practice in post-adoption support.

Clinical studies

Jackson's (1968) study of "unsuccessful adoptions" is fairly typical of the earlier clinical studies of adoption. Jackson, a psychiatric social worker at an English child guidance clinic became interested in adopted children because of what seemed to be the excessive number of such children referred to her clinic. Jackson collected data on 40 such referrals, and concluded that neither the age of the child at adoption, nor the age or manner in which the adoption was revealed to the child, were causally related to the child's maladjustment. Rather, Jackson points to chronic neurosis (in 30 of the 40 mothers) in an adoptive parent as an important causal factor in the children's problems. The mothers were variously described as, "perfectionist, over-anxious, over-moral...hysterical, unstable, deeply depressed, overpowering, immature, mentally cruel...rigid, paranoid, overprotective." Further, a quarter of the adopted children had parents with unstable or disrupted marriages. All of the children had been adopted by older, childless couples. It should be noted in this connection that Humphrey (1967) and Humphrey and Kirkwood (1982) found, in English work, that childless couples waiting to adopt often had neuroses surrounding their inability to conceive. Indeed, inability to conceive in some couples could itself be psychologically grounded.

Ounsted (1970), an English psychiatrist, writes about "the dark side of adoption" based on the fact that "...it became apparent to my colleagues and myself at the Park Hospital for Children in Oxford, that

we were seeing an unexpectedly large number of adoptive children...many of the children owed their disabilities either to some innate handicap, or to defects in the structure of their families" (p. 25). Ounsted found that three percent of his child psychiatric patients were adopted, at least twice the number expected from general population figures. In these estimates, step-parent adoptions were excluded. He notes too that 8 percent of children in residential centres for disturbed
children had been adopted.

Ounsted compared 80 children adopted by non-relatives with a similar number of controls. He concluded that in a significant number of adoption placements, children were placed with couples with pre-existing psychological problems which prevented them from parenting "difficult" children. These parental factors included non-consummation of marriage, and a chronic dislike of children which prevented the adoptive parents being able to bond to the child. Ounsted found too that the clinic adoptees were particularly likely to have been placed after the first six months of life, so that there was often an interaction between traumatic experiences of the child and parental incapacity and neurosis. Ounsted concludes that adoption placement practices have to improve:

Adoption is in every case a matter that can only be permitted through a properly organized and approved adoption society. Such societies ought to build into their organization follow-up and research units that act as regulating systems, continually correcting practice as errors are identified. We have too, to press forward with scientific study of that bonding precess which links the developing infant to the adults who care for it (Ounsted, 1970, p. 35).

Still, in 1990 most adoption agencies have no systematic follow-up or monitoring of adoption placements. Tizard's studies (1977 and 1987) are amongst the few British examples of such monitoring.

Turning to American work in this area, a few studies have systematically surveyed child guidance clinic or residential centre populations with the purposes of identifying adopted children in such populations. Menlove (1965) surveyed 1,314 children attending an out-patient psychiatric clinic and found that 59 (5 percent of the total) had been adopted. The adopted children were then compared with a control group of clinic attenders matched for age, sex and race, and socioeconomic status. Menlove notes that in general adoptive parents tended to have much higher social status than did parents of non-adopted children attending the clinic: exact socioeconomic matches were difficult to obtain. The major symptom difference between adopted children and controls was a much higher incidence of hyperactivity and associated aggression in the adopted children. The adopted children were also more likely to have displayed firesetting, impulsiveness and sexual acting out. Adoption after six months was particularly likely to be associated with symptoms of hyperactivity and aggression.

Brinich and Brinich (1982) surveyed 5,135 adult psychiatric patients and found 113 who had been adopted as children. This proportion (2.2%) was similar to the proportion of adoptees in the general population. The patients who had been adopted as children did not generally differ from patients as a whole, and no factors in the adoption history predicted adult psychiatric status. This study is particularly interesting in the light of studies of psychiatric genetics which seem to suggest that adopted children <u>do</u> have somewhat increased risk for mental illness in adulthood, because of genetic vulnerability inherited from biological parents.

Brodzinsky and his colleagues (1984) in reviewing previous research on adjustment in adoption concluded:

> At present it is difficult, if not impossible to interpret this confusing empirical picture. The degree to which the results of studies using clinic populations can be applied to adopted children in the general population is limited by the sample selection biases inherent in this approach and by frequent failure of those studies to use appropriated control groups. In addition, these studies, as well as studies using nonclinical samples, also have been plagued by other methodological problems. These problems include poorly matched controls (when controls have been included), small sample size, narrow age range of subjects, narrow range of outcome measures, and questionable reliability and validity of measurement instruments and procedures. (p. 583)

Brodzinsky and his team tried to overcome the shortcomings of previous work by obtaining carefully matched controls for the group of adopted children aged 6 to 11, from elementary schools. Both teachers and mothers completed measures of adjustment and learning which had known reliability and validity. Nevertheless, this study had a notable weakness: adoptive children were obtained through public advertisement from adoptive parents, adoption support groups, personal referrals, schools, and social work agencies. These recruitment methods produced a sample of 130 matched controls obtained from elementary schools in

51

the New York area.

Results of this controlled study indicated that the adopted children were described by their parents as being slightly more disturbed (particularly in the areas of hyperactivity and associated aggressive activity), and had more problems of learning. Nevertheless, there were some promising trends in the comparisons - the adjustment of the older adopted children was better than the adjustment of younger children. "Moreover... adopted children are typically not manifesting severe pathology, but are only displaying slightly more extreme forms of behavior than are found among non-adopted children. This finding is important to keep in mind when evaluating the risk associated with adoption. It is all too easy, given the kinds of results found in the present study to lose sight of the fact that adopted children are doing very well considering the SES background of the typical birth parents, and the fact that adopted children are more likely to experience increased stress and prenatal care during gestation." (Brodzinsky et al, 1984).

Brodzinsky argues further that although adopted children may be particularly vulnerable to stress, good adoptive parenting can help protect these children from such stress, or help them overcome it. Furthermore, he argues, adoptive parents need continued support from social welfare agencies in this important task.

Further evidence in support of the idea that adopted children may be subject to prophylactic referrals, or referrals which meet the needs of overanxious parents comes from the American study of Andrea Weiss (1985) who compared 47 adopted children assessed in a privately-funded adolescent inpatient unit for adolescents. The comparison group of 93 adolescents were admitted to the unit in the same period; no attempt was made to find exactly matched controls. When the two groups were compared, no significant differences with regard to race, sex or social class emerged. However, the adoptees were significantly younger than the comparison subjects on first referral to the hospital. They exhibited milder symptomatology (more neurosis, less psychosis) than the comparison group, and stayed in the hospital a shorter time.

Rogeness and his colleagues (1988) also compared adopted children referred to a children's psychiatric hospital (in Texas) with non-adopted children in the same clinic. Of 763 consecutive admission, 66 (8.7%) were adopted. The adopted children tended to display significantly more problems of hyperactivity, learning problems, and personality disorder, conditions for which there is often a genetic history, a history of CNS perinatal trauma, or both. The non-adopted children overall had more serious psychiatric disorders, including schizophrenic-like illnesses. Blitz and Glenwick (1989) confirmed a finding from previous American research, in showing that previously adopted adolescents, now in residential care, were significantly more likely than non-adopted children in residential treatment to have attention deficit disorder.

Some clinical writers, sensing rather than measuring family interactions in systematic ways have claimed that some adoptive parents have latent or unconscious hostility towards their adopted children (e.g. Schneider and Rimmer, 1984). Whatever their motivation, it is unfortunately true from clinical evidence that some adoptive parents (hopefully a small minority) do abuse and maltreat their children (Sack and Dale, 1982).

Brodzinsky and Brodzinsky (1992) in a study whose methodology is more substantial than that of psychoanalytical writers who claim to have special insights into hidden family pathology found that family structure and composition bore no relationship to the adopted child's adjustment. In this study of 130 adopted children aged 6 to 12 living in various family constellations, the presence or absence of siblings (biological or adopted), the sex of siblings, and the child's age in relation to siblings bore very little relation to psychological outcomes. "Family structure, while complicating the dynamics of adoptive family life, plays a minor role in adoption adjustment," the authors report.

We can locate only two recent British studies of previously adopted children in residential care. Packman (1986) in a survey of 361 children assessed for child care placements found that two of 361 children assessed for child care placement found that two percent were adopted - a proportion probably not greater than the proportion of adopted children in the general population. Howe (1987) located only 20 previously adopted children in care in three English counties, a rate of 0.95 percent. Two thirds of these children had been adopted during infancy, and most were admitted to care in their early teens because of acute behavioural problems, often involving hyperactivity and aggression within the home. Unlike other children in care, the adopted children's families usually remained intact, and there was little evidence of neglect or abuse by the adoptive parents.

Concepts of identity

Identity is a complex topic, and definitions of and understanding of the term may vary between different disciplines (e.g. social psychology, learning theory, symbolic interactionism, psychoanalysis). For many years mainstream psychology ignored the possibility that measuring self-concept and identity could be an important method of understanding and predicting human behaviour. Nevertheless, relatively recent research with the framework of social learning hypotheses have shown that self-esteem, self-concept and identity are powerful mechanisms through which individuals understand and interpret the world around them, how they might react to these stimuli, and how they organize their lives in relation to others (Coopersmith, 1981; Rosenberg and Kaplan, 1982).

The manner in which individuals evaluate aspects of their lives which they feel to be important (which is of course a socially constructed reality) is incorporated into a person's self-esteem. Self-concept represents the combination of those aspects of self the individual considers to be important with the various dimensions of evaluation (e.g. good-bad, strong-weak, capable-incapable, wise-foolish etc.) which the individual has adopted from various interactions and cultural symbols. How significant others interact with oneself, and give information, messages, rewards and punishments is crucially important in the formation of global self-concept, which becomes increasingly complex as the individual grows older. By adolescence global self-concept is synonymous with an individual's identity. For a minority group adolescent, such an identity is grounded in important ways in the ethnic self-consciousness a youth has. How the wider society perceives and evaluates the young person's ethnicity (e.g. skin colour and features), how the ethnic group as a collective entity views such ethnicity, and the degrees of consensus amongst minority group members on how to present one's ethnicity to the world in relation to the social and interpersonal tasks which are necessary all mean that identity is both a crucial aspect of healthy personal functioning, will vary quite markedly from group to group, and from individual to individual (for a schematic and theoretical overview of these concepts see Bagley et al., 1979 and Young and Bagley, 1982).

An adopted child whose ethnicity is both different from that of his or her parents, and is also to some degree stigmatized by the prejudice and oppression of the wider society has a set of identity tasks which are both unique for transracially adopted children, and are also rather complex. Both the fact of being adopted and the fact of being ethnically different from most people make the identity tasks facing the adopted adolescent, in theory at least, substantially more difficult. Indeed, the positive outcomes in most transracial adoptions (reviewed by Silverman and Feigelman, 1990) come as a pleasant surprise to those who work in this field. In fact, having an ethnically different child could make the role of the adoptive parent in "accepting difference" as Kirk (1965) termed it, easier rather than more difficult.

Research on the foundations of self-esteem has consistently shown that there are two, independent contributors to the formation of self-esteem in the years up to adolescence. Not surprisingly, these aspects of self-esteem are derived from the quality of parenting the child receives. The first dimension of parenting which contributes to self-esteem is the basic love and warmth which parents give. This flows naturally from the mutual bonding which usual occurs spontaneously between parent and adopted child. Even in cases of older child adoption, bonding will occur in course of time, and there is much that a well-prepared adoptive parent can do to facilitate this bond's development (Smith and Sherwen, 1988). Mothers who adopt an ethnically different child bond to that child just as speedily as those with a same-race child (Singer et al., 1985).

The second major factor underlying the development of a health self-concept and a strong framework of identity and self functioning is usually independent of the first dimension (love and warmth), but is equally important.

The second major correlate of self-esteem is not as intuitively obvious as parental love and warmth. It involves, the mixture of authoritative parenting (parents who have some wisdom and knowledge, and can earn the respect of their children); consistency of norms and rules governing behaviour; a clear framework of expected punishments and rewards for breaking rules; consistent reactions by adults to such rule-breaking; consistent knowledge transmitted to the child about his status in both his family and the wider world; a coherent and ego-enhancing account of a child's ethnic identity (wherever that is relevant); and consistency and continuity of key figures in the socialization process (families broken by death and divorce will lack such continuity, at least for a time). Put another way, unpredictable adults, and unpredictable sanctions for rule-breaking, and reactions by adults that veer between indulgence and rage are likely to give a child both fragmented identity or self-concept, and a globally poor self-esteem.

Once a global self-concept or identity has developed in adolescence it will usually guide may aspects of behaviour throughout life. Self-concept measured in the early years of secondary schooling can with some accuracy predict school failure, school drop-out, drug and alcohol use, suicidal ideas and behaviour, and teenage pregnancy (Rosenberg and Kaplan, 1982).

Conversely, the child with an integrated, well-functioning identity framework has what ego psychologists (e.g. Erikson, 1968) term ego-strength. Such ego strength contributes to degrees of invulnerability to later stress factors in the interpersonal environment (Anthony, 1987).

Kirk (1965) uses Lewin's theory of identity and ego in describing the kinds of parenting which can provide the most ego-enhancing conditions for the development of the adopted child. The parent of the adopted child must be open and honest about origins, respecting their child's uniqueness and difference from a biological child.

The idea of identity foreclosure in the work of Hauser (1971) describes the ego status of the oppressed, minority group adolescent, but Hauser's description of "negative identity" is also relevant in considering the roles of adopted parent and adopted child:

> Negative identity is the adolescent derivative of a failure to resolve the set of issues belonging to the developmental stage of conscience formation. It is the phase of ego development in which the conflicts between guilt and initiative become most prominent. (Hauser, 1971, p.44).

The dilemma of resolving the struggle between guilt and initiative is derived from Erikson's ego psychology (1968). In this schema of self psychology, the individual at each stage of development (in infancy through adulthood) is presented with a series of dilemmas which have to be adequately resolved before that individual can move to the next stage of life (in psychological terms) and tackle a new set of identity tasks. A child from parents who have offered neither consistent love nor a consistent framework of rules and family structure in which interactions are predictable, and additionally belongs to a stigmatized ethnic minority group, and as well has been adopted away from traditional cultural supports is at grave risk indeed. Such an adolescent may have a fragmented identity structure, a poorly integrated self-concept, and minimal self-esteem. Fortunately, we meet very few such individuals in clinical work, although in the research in residential treatment centres for adolescents (described in subsequent chapters) a number of such adolescents with devastated identity have been encountered. Psychological treatment of such individuals presents many difficult challenges.

Identity conflicts in adoptees

American work in this area has used a different methodology from the epidemiological or controlled studies outlined in previous chapters. These American studies have been psychoanalytic in nature, and claim that the adoption process is fraught with psychological hazard. The evidence for these propositions comes from the psychoanalysis of children and adults who recall childhood events related to their adoption. Thus Weider (1977 a and b) makes generalizations for the whole institution of adoption, based on the psychoanalysis of three patients, aged 9, 17, and 27 who had been adopted in the first few weeks of life. Weider claims that the experience of loss and problems in rebounding in these first few weeks of life is deeply traumatic at an unconscious level. This trauma is exacerbated, according to Weider, when the child is told of adoption before he or she can incorporate such information logically or emotionally. A possible outcome are fantasies of 'family romance', in which the adopted child develops fantasies of being descended from some famous person. In adolescence however, these fantasies develop into rage against the supposedly famous parent who has abandoned them. Weider suggests that suppressed rage is a frequently experienced trait in adolescent and adult adoptees, a theme extended in the work in Goodwin et al. (1980). Certainly adoptees have changing concepts of themselves and the imagined qualities of birth-parents change as he or she enters adolescent (Rosenberg and Horner, 1991).

The work of Sorosky and his colleagues (Sorosky et al., 1975, 1976 and 1984) including their well-known book The Adoption Triangle extends this theme, again drawing in a highly selective way from small, non-random samples of adoptees, adopters, and birth parents. Sorosky argued that the identity conflicts which adoptees experience are linked to unresolved attachment to the birth parent:

> Many adoptees are preoccupied with existential concerns and a feeling of isolation and alienation due to the break in the continuity of life-through-the-generations that their adoption represents. For some, the existing block to the past may create a feeling that there is a block to the future as well. The adoptee's identity formation must be viewed within the context of the life cycle, in which birth and death are closely linked unconsciously. (Sorosky et al., 1975, p. 25).

In order to heal the "broken identity," or the unconscious conflicts of the adopted child, Sorosky et al. (1978) advocate the practice of open adoption, or at least the unsealing of adoption records so as to allow adolescent adoptees knowledge about, and ultimately access to their birth parents. Open adoption is a radical process which involves a consultation between birth parent and potential adopter about what is in the child's best interests. After adoption, the child's birth parents (usually the mother) would become an 'aunt' who might have periodic contact with the child. However, whether such arrangements are absolutely in the child's best interests is difficult to say, and no evaluations are available at the present time of the practice of fully open adoption.

In social policy terms we can say however that placement of the child within an extended family, giving guardianship rights rather than adoptive status to the new parents may have certain advantages. Such 'adoptions' would be much closer to traditional types of adoption in which children were cared for by kin rather than by strangers. These types of adoption could be used much more often by social welfare agencies.

One interesting aspect of the proposals of Sorosky and colleagues are their practical similarity on many points to those of Kirk (1981). While Kirk does not discuss open adoption per se his proposals for the reform of adoptive kinship are certainly compatible with Sorosky's proposals. Kirk advocates the acknowledgement by adoptive parents of the differences between their own parenthood, and that of parents and children who are 'biologically' related. Kirk argues that in such openness adoptive parents:

1. Put themselves empathically into the special place in which the adopted child finds her/himself. Such empathy is conducive to:

2. Readiness to listen to the child's questions about his/her background even though such questions may be troublesome for the adoptive parent.

3. Such readiness to listen and answer questions, however uncomfortable, enhances the child's trust in the parent and therefore the bonds between adopted child and adoptive parents. (Kirk, 1981, pp. 147-158).

Kirk does not advocate any particular pattern of reform with regard to the unsealing of adoption records; rather he poses the question of reform in the institution of adoption as a possible "compass for the mainstream family." He argues that the arbitrary closeness of adoptive kinship bonds - imposed by legal and administrative fiat -may be dysfunctional for parent-child relationships, and may indeed be out of step with those relationships which have developed in other kinds of families.

Problems in the adoption of older children

With the decline in the number of 'ordinary' infants available for adoption, agencies have increasingly placed older children for adoption. While such developments could have many positive developments for the children involved, they also pose challenges to the institution of adoption.

A number of case studies of 'failure' in older child adoption have been reported by writers seeking to improve placement practices and post-adoption support in this area. Most older adoptees have the conscious experience and memory of loss; they may have bonded to one or more figures (natural parent, foster parent, residential child care worker, etc.) before being placed with adoptive parents. Bowlby (1979) argues that such loss initially involves two stages: a numbing, yearning searching for the lost person; and then disorganization and despair. Only after this stage of "true sorrow" can any kind of resolution take place. Anger and aggression are common following such loss, and may be directed at the newly adopting parents, even after a careful and gradual introduction. If such initial anger is not well-handled, permanent harm can be done to the adoptive relationship. Sometimes the older adopted child will be very controlled in his adoptive home, and only later will be aggressive and disruptive. Holmes (1979) reports such a case which was successfully handled by the adoptive parents; and another case in which the adoptive parents ultimately rejected a boy whose aggression they could not understand or cope with.

A complicating factor in older child adoptions is the fact that such children may have been the subject of abuse and neglect in their early years. Sack and Dale (1982) report twelve such older child adoptions. All had been physically abused or neglected in the first two years of life, and all manifested following adoption, "A behavioural pattern that was intermittently provocative and punishment seeking, with an ability to elicit a sense of bewilderment and betrayal in the adoptive parents." All the adoptive parents were considered highly competent by the agencies concerned at the commencement. All (like many adopters of older children) had successfully raised biological children. Sack and Dale present these dismal case histories of adoption failure, "...as a way of drawing attention to much needed research, both in better understanding the early attachment process in older child adoptions, and in better understanding the relative impact of abuse in influencing the child's subsequent attachment capacities." Such research is still urgently needed to assist the growing practice of placing older, previously traumatized or abused children for adoption, and we need more studies of the kind reported by Barth and Berry (1988).

There is evidence from the American Humane Society Survey of the treatment of sexually abused children in American that such children are frequently placed in foster homes, and that foster parents are given little help and advice in handling the effect of past traumas (AHS, 1984). The same conclusion applies to adoptive placement - sexually abused children may act out sexually, and may assault younger children; or, since they have been trained to act seductively towards adults, they may encourage further sexual abuse by a foster or adoptive parent. Evidence of this comes from case studies (Powers, 1984; Bowman et al., 1985) in which adoptive parents were completely unprepared for sexual acting out in their newly adopted daughters. Powers (1984) argues that placement practices relating to most older children (whether or not they have been previously abused) by adoption agencies are often "hurried," paying insufficient attention to preparing the child and the parents for the adoption experience. This is especially true in the case of the previously abused child. In such adoptions "love is not enough" (Braden, 1981). Braden argues from U.S. evidence that over half of children over two who are available for adoption have experienced abuse of some kind, be it emotional, physical or sexual. A first key to successful adoption of such children, Braden argues, is the fullest sharing of information with the new parents about the child's background. A second step is networking the adoptive parents with support groups, including other adoptive parents as well as relevant professionals. This approach is rather similar to Hartman's (1984) ecological model for working with adoptive families beyond placement.

Because of the risks inherent in the relationships of the older adopted child and his or her new parents, a number of practitioners have written accounts of family dynamics in the adoptive family, and ways of dealing with problems as they occur. These reports include a general guide for new parents of older adopted children; literature addressed to social workers engaged in post-placement support (Pannor et al., 1977; Bass, 1975; Kraus, 1978; Katz, 1980; Frances, 1982; Shapiro, 1984; Hartman, 1984); and literature addressed to clinical social workers striving to heal families in which the child-parent relationship is under strain (Blotcky et al., 1982; Cohen, 1981). Blotcky and his colleagues suggest, for example:

> Due to current trends making it increasingly possible for adolescents to locate their biologic parents, therapists must respond by at least considering the involvement of the biologic parent in the treatment. In certain carefully selected cases of severely disturbed and very resistant youngsters, it may be the participation of the biologic mother which is crucial to the adolescent's working through a common, core intrapsychic psychopathologic configuration involving idealization of the lost

biologic mother and splitting of object relations (Blotcky et al., 1982, p. 281).

The approach of these workers draws heavily on the psychoanalytical approach of Sorosky et al. (1978) on 'open adoption' mentioned above. This approach has profound theoretical differences, but some practical similarities with the 'systems' or 'ecological' approaches advocated by Cohen (1981) and Hartman (1984).

A further area of literature is available for practitioners, - on possible courses after an adoption has broken down, or is disrupted beyond repair (McEwan, 1973; Fitzgerald, 1979). McEwan advocates the 'readoption' of the child as soon as possible, with close negotiation on the transfer of the child between the old and the new adoptive parents.

In the past five years the literature on adopting older children (including those with a variety of special needs) has expanded rapidly, paralleling the welcome increase in such placements by social work agencies. The push towards permanency planning for children in care has meant that adoption (including adoption by foster parents with continuation of subsidy) of many children previously considered to be unadoptable, can now be successful. (Weitzel, 1984; Coyne and Brown 1985 and 1986).

The pioneering work of Skodak and Skeels (1949 and 1965) has demonstrated that mentally handicapped children adopted at an early age can benefit greatly from the security and social stimulation that an adoptive family can provide, with significant increases in measured IQ over time. In Australia Hockey (1980) also showed (in a study of 137 mentally handicapped children adopted over a 30 year period) that in three quarters of the sample the outcomes were good or excellent. Hockey argues from her data that adoption disruption could probably be avoided in the majority of cases if those children had been placed earlier in life: congenital abnormalities of movement, perceptual and cognitive ability should not be seen as barriers to infant adoption.

In the years since Hockey's report the practice of placing handicapped infants for adoption has increased around the world. Follow-up studies of such adoptions (Hardy, 1984; Coyne and Brown, 1985; Rosenthal, Groze and Aguilar, 1991) indicate long-term success rates of about 80 percent of placements. Katherine Nelson (1985) in a study of 200 Chicago area families who adopted 256 children (56 percent of whom were mentally handicapped) suggests that disruptions could be minimized if the placing agencies remained in touch with the adoptive families as a continuing resource for co-ordinating special education services, and medical care when this was needed.

A rather greater challenge now seems to be the successful placement of older children who have suffered neglect or abuse (physical, emotional and sexual) in previous settings (Kagan and Reid, 1986). Most research on the adoption of older children (including adolescents previously in residential care) comes from the United States. Reid and his colleagues indicate from a study of 26 New York cases that ".... the difficulty in maintaining youths in adoptive homes was directly related to the intensity of loss, anxiety and rage that youths carry with them from previous family experienced, as the ability of adoptive parents to tolerate the manifestations of grief." (Reid et al., 1987). Reid suggests that adoptions of older children with prior histories of neglect and abuse should be seen as part of a continuing care progress, with adoptive parents working co-operatively with other members of the youth care team. Occasional spells of the adolescent in residential treatment care should not be viewed as a failure of adoption, but as part of the continuation process of care, therapy and healing. In such adoptions there has to be, in Trudy Festinger's (1986) term "a necessary risk". While adoptive parents of older, special needs children must be able to care affectionately for such children, "love is not enough" (Sandmaier, 1986).

In the field of research on adoption the work of Richard Barth and his colleagues (1986 and 1988) stands out in terms of careful methodological analysis and substantive importance. Barth and his team show that as more older children with special needs are placed for adoption, so the number of adoption breakdowns or "disruptions" (temporary breakdowns) increases: about 10 percent of such adoptions will disrupt within a year of placement. "In the face of the possibilities of failure or difficulty, social workers should strive to offer a more professional service, with improved practice based in good research since older child adoption has become arguably than the most essential component of successful child welfare services." (Barth and Berry, 1988, p.3)

In the California sample of 120 families studied by Richard Barth nearly a half had some kind of disruption in the five years following placement (mean age at placement was 8.2 years). The research team sought to identify factors which could predict disruption (temporary separation of the child from the adoptive family). Many factors which in theory could be associated with disruption failed to reach statistical significance. Transracial adoption (in 13 percent of cases) had as good an outcome as within-race adoptions, for example. A major factor underlying disruption was lack of preparation of adopters by social workers, inadequate information given about the adopted child, and poor follow-up and support by social service teams. The profile of the most successful adoptions was as follows: a female child, for whom this was a first-time adoption; no history of sexual or emotional abuse of the child; only moderate behavioural or emotional problems in the child before placement; a high degree of prior preparation for the prospective adopters; realistic expectations of the child's behaviour and emotional responses by the new parents; and extensive follow through and support from the placing agency. Barth and his colleagues stress that many adoptions would not have disrupted if the parents had been better prepared, been given more information about the child, and had been offered better post-adoption support. Children who have suffered prior sexual abuse need special kinds or support when they are later adopted (Bowman et al., 1985; Bagley and King, 1990).

Group counselling for adolescents recently placed in adoptive families is a useful strategy in ongoing programs of support for new, blended families (Cordell et al., 1985). Special programs of support for the adoptive parents of older children have also proved their worth (Katz, 1986, Ward and Lewko, 1987), and can minimize the possibilities of adoption disruption (Partridge et al., 1986).

Another important principle which research studies have underlined is that sibling groups should never be broken up simply in order to make placements easier. Siblings will have likely bonded strongly to one another, and the oldest sibling will have a special role in being a "parent" to his or her siblings. Approaching these particular dynamics requires that the new parents be given appropriate information and support in this special role (Le Pere et al, 1986; Ward, 1987).

Another welcome development in adoption practice is support for foster parents in adopting long-stay foster children (Mica and Vosler, 1990). Sometimes the placement is at the outset, one of fostering in a "legal risk" situation in which no-one is sure whether the child is legally available for adoption (Drotar and Stege, 1988; Mica and Vosler, 1990). At other times social workers will put the idea of adoption to the foster parents of long-stay children when it is clear that they are legally available for adoption. Obviously, providing legal support for permanence in a fostering situation has many advantages. When permanence is assured, dynamics in the family will likely change in a more relaxed and committed direction. When the adopted child is 18 he or she will still have a permanent family for support and contact through the various adult milestones - something which foster children rarely have as young adults.

Most child welfare legislation in North America and Britain allows social work departments to offer continued financial support for foster parents who adopt children with special needs; subsidized adoption is now quite widely used to support parents who would not otherwise be able to consider adoption, because of the additional costs in caring for a special needs child (Byrne and Bellucci, 1983). Such subsidies can be highly cost effective, since they are likely to prevent or minimize the need for expensive residential care for the child (Powers, 1983).

A parallel but equally welcome development has been the pioneering English scheme in which professional foster parents are recruited and trained as full members of the social work team. This program (the Kent family placement service) places disturbed or difficult children and adolescents with individual families rather in residential care. A ten-year evaluation (Hazel, 1986) has shown that this program is highly cost effective even though it involves paying a full professional salary to one or both foster parents; and, most important, it serves the psychological needs of troubled children far more effectively than expensive alternatives, such as residential care.

The adoption of stepchildren

Stepchild adoption, although common, has received little attention in the social work literature. Partly this is because the prospective adopter usually approaches the court for an adoption order independently of adoption or social service agencies. Usually too Courts have approved such adoptions without much scrutiny (Bissett-Johnson, 1984). In the main this is because the child has never been separated from and will remain with, his or her biological mother. But it is now clear that relationships between the new parent and his adopted child are often fraught with conflict, to the extent that the 'adoption' is at risk of breakdown (Sager et al., 1983).

After presenting a number of case histories of such breakdowns, Sager and his colleagues (1983) advocate that the child's perception of the situation, and wishes with regard to relationship with both the departed biological parent, and the new stepfather should be carefully considered by the Courts, who should make an order other than complete adoption, in most cases:

> Contact with the biological parent can prevent the 'hidden parent syndrome'. In this syndrome the child's ambivalent feelings and questions about the absent, secret, or not discussed bioparent have no outlet and therefore remain submerged and presumably have a deleterious effect on personality development. The most

flagrant example is when the child embraces the hidden parent's alleged destructive behaviour (negative identification). (Sager et al., 1983, p. 318).

Adoptees seeking reunion with birth parents: A problem of identity?

The evidence on the extent to which adoptees have a need to seek out birth parents is somewhat contradictory, and in part reflects different methodologies as well as differing cultural contexts in which the research has been carried out.

Sorosky et al., (1978) are among the most vocal advocates of opening adoption records so that adoptees can have knowledge of, and ultimate access to, birth parents. His argument coincides with the position taken by lawyers and social policy analysts who use quite different types of evidence and reasoning (Small, 1979; Campbell, 1979). Small argues, on the basis of legal and policy analysis:

> An estimated one-half million adopted children in the U.S. will attain full adult status but will be deprived of the right of direct access to information concerning their parentage. The societally sanctioned sealing of birth and adoption records, begun in the 1920s and made to apply retroactively, was designed to keep the circumstances of an adopted child's origins confidential. The laws were enacted to remove the stigma of illegitimacy from the public record. Yet, the very fact of sealing records perpetuates enduring and widespread hostile, negative and punitive attitudes toward adopted people. Arguments that deny an adult citizen direct access to his or her original birth records became rationalizations in defence of discrimination. (Small, 1979, p. 38).

Personal accounts, such as Florence Fisher's dramatic and anguished search for her 'real' mother illustrate the identity crisis which being adopted may bring, and the permanent neurosis into which this can develop (Fisher, 1973).

The more systematic, but non-random collection of case material does seem to suggest that a significant number of adult adoptees have a deep-seated but frustrated need to have knowledge of or access to a birth parent (Wishard and Wishard, 1979; Pavoa, 1982). Pavoa argues from her American case material that the search for a birth parent is a symbolic search for identity. All human beings, she argues, have this existential need; but in adoptees it takes a special form. For most adoptees the 'search', whether psychological or actual seeking, is resolved in a fantasy manner. The sought for or imagined-about birth parent is rarely known intimately, even when that parent is actually located. It is interesting to note that Scottish evidence seems to support this proposition. Triseliotis (1973) in a study of adoptees who sought information on a birth parent (in a country where open access to birth records has been available since 1925) showed that the large majority of children adopted in infancy did not avail themselves of this opportunity. Those that did were predominantly children placed after infancy, who both had some memory of a biological parent and who had experienced psychological trauma prior to adoption.

In England and Wales open access to birth records was granted by the 1975 Children Act. Five years later, only two percent of individuals aged 18 and over who were legally eligible to seek these birth records had done so (ABAFA, 1981). Moreover, a study of the first people who sought this birth records from the General Register Office in London found that only 28 percent actually had the intention of seeking out a birth parent. For the remainder, the information was for 'family tree' purposes only. The motivation for seeking such information was usually some type of kinship transition, such as getting married or the birth of a child. Of those seeking information, less than five percent were judged to be doing this in relation to a neurosis or chronic identity problem affecting mental health.

The British evidence, then, suggests that most adoptees do not have a deep-seated need for knowledge of a birth parent. In America and Canada it is likely that those who seek a birth parent with such desperate anguish, in the face of seemingly overwhelming difficulty (Marcus, 1981) are seeking because of a psychological motivation arising from maladaption perhaps caused by failures on the part of adoptive parents, but perhaps caused too by traumatic factors unconnected with adoption. What we can conclude (with Day, 1979) is that the opening of the original birth records of adoptees would strengthen rather than undermine the institution of adoption.

In recent years a policy of "open" adoption has been advocated as a counter to the secrecy about origins which was maintained by the placing agencies, a policy which colluded actively or passively with the tendency of adoptive parents to act as if they were the child's biological parents, denying the many important differences which distinguish an adopted child's identity tasks as he or she passes through the various stages of life, up to adolescence and beyond. Kirk (1981) advocated a more open approach to adoption policy and adoptive kinship and it appears that a variety of approaches to adoption reform can fulfil the reforms which Kirk and others have advocated. As Haimes and Timms

(1984 and 1985) have noted, movement in adoption policy and practice towards meeting the best interests of the child (rather then the needs and wishes of childless couples) has opened up possibilities for a much greater degree of information sharing between biological parents, adoptive parents, and adoptive chid. A form of open adoption within the Napoleonic legal code has been practised in France since the last century (Verdier, 1988) - but the possibility of lifting the veil of secrecy surrounding adoption has caused consternation for many North American practitioners, despite progressive changes in British practice (e.g. Triseliotis, 1985) which have largely escaped the notice of North American practitioners.

Although there has been an earnest debate in the professional literature on the pros and cons of forms of openness in adoption (e.g. Sorich and Siebert, 1982; Borgman, 1982; Pannor and Baron, 1984; Dukette, 1984; Wells and Reshotoko, 1986; Groth et al., 1987), the shortage of adoptable infants has meant that profound changes in adoption practice have become inevitable. Many of these changes have meant that private adoptions, with the birth mother as the major decision maker, have become common while agency adoptions of infants have greatly declined in number (Butler, 1986).

British policy (described by Haimes and Timms, 1984) has avoided the anguished demand for information abut birth parents, which has marked the "search process" of some North American adoptees (e.g. Marcus, 1979; Sobol and Cardiff, 1983), and the anxious pleas of some adoptive parents for keeping the adoption records sealed (Geissinger, 1984). Canadian and American policy is now moving towards the openness which has pertained in Britain and other European countries (Berry, 1991). On both sides of the Atlantic there seems to be much agreement in arguing for a moderate amount of openness in adoption placements (Reid et al, 1987; Triseliotis and Russell, 1984). Evolving practice often allows the birth mother (and father where he can be contacted) to exercize choice after meeting the adoptive parents. Nevertheless, once the decision to release the child for adoption has been made, the birth mother will have no knowledge of the actual whereabouts of the adoptive parents. Photographs of the child may be sent to the birth mother who will have no knowledge of the actual identity or whereabouts of the adoptive parents. Photographs of the child may be sent to the birth mother at regular intervals, and when the adopted child reaches the age of 18 he or she may choose to make contact with the birth parent(s), following support and counselling in this process by a specialist worker.

We can conclude with Sachdev (1991) that much greater openness, including the opening birth records of adoptees to both biological parents and adopted children would strengthen rather than undermine the institution of adoption.

Conclusions

The various clinical and non-random studies of adoptees provide many interesting insights into the institution of adoption. The cause of some adoption failures or disruptions, as well as possibilities for strengthening or supporting adoption can be derived from this work.

Identity problems or maladjustment in adoptees are far from universal. However proposals for the 'opening' of birth records for all adoptees can be readily accepted on the basis of various studies. Opening such records might not ease the pain of adoptees searching for birth parents; but such a move would strengthen the credibility and stability of the institution of adoption, and should encourage openness in the adoptive relationship itself, as Kirk (1981) advocates.

Although the number of adoptees with psychiatric disturbance extending into adulthood is probably not very much greater than in members of the general population, it does seem clear from studies of clinic and hospital populations that adoptees are somewhat overrepresented. However, many of these referrals are prophylactic in nature, while other referrals reflect an ongoing process of treatment for problems which originated in abuse or neglect before the adoption.

However, there is evidence from some clinical studies that adoptees may develop a particular type of personality orientation. Some evidence for this supposition comes from a survey of the 7,000 members of 'Yesterday's Children,' an American adoption reform group. This is a self-selected group, and it is not clear to what degree it is representative of adoptees as a whole. Nevertheless, Cullom-Long's (1984) survey of these 7,000 adoptees provides interesting information on a least a segment of adopted families:

> This study shows that people who discover their adoption by accident carry a strong sense of betrayal into other relationships and that almost all adoptees sometime in their lives suffer from low self-esteem and a fear of abandonment stemming from their adoption ..... fear of abandonment makes many adoptees hang on to unsuitable friendships and romantic relationships. Adoptees have a strong feeling of being different usually starting at age 6 or 7, when they realize they are adopted. In the past, adoptees often

felt stigmatized, but children adopted today may feel that they are 'chosen children'...At some point (usually adolescence) almost all adoptees have a sense of detachment from their adopted family and a feeling of rootlessness...A disproportionate number of adoptees in this survey had entered the helping professions - psychology, teaching, social work... Adoptees feel a strong desire to marry and have children. Many female adoptees said that pregnancy was a special event because it was their first chance to be biologically connected to another person (Cullom-Long, 1984, pp. 1-10).

Cullom-Long argues that the adoptees she surveyed are generally representative of adoptees as a whole in America. While this has yet to be established, her study provides many important insights into ways in which adoptive parenting can be strengthened, and her work dovetails with many of the other clinical studies of adoption cited earlier in this chapter. Kirk's (1981) characterization of "adoptive kinship" as "a modern institution in need of reform" is certainly supported by the studies cited in this chapter.

Indeed, the institution of adoption is already changing, in part because of the decreasing availability of 'ordinary' infants who can be adopted. Thus Feigelman and Silverman (1983) title their book on adoption, "Chosen Children: New Patterns of Adoptive Relationships." The traditional adopters - childless couples - now find it increasingly difficult to adopt, and preference is now given by agencies to the degree to which potential adopters can meet the needs of a special child. 'Preferential adoption' in which the adoptive parents choose to adopt for reasons other than infertility creates new patterns of relationship in the adoptive family which are potentially supportive of the adopted child's needs in ways which traditional adoption has not been. This is particularly important, argue Feigelman and Silverman (1983) because the kinds of children which these couples tend to adopt are likely to have past traumas or problems which make their present adjustments difficult:

Since these parents are more likely to adopt children with serious mental or physical problems, the services of child care professionals may be most relevant to helping these families deal with their children's problems. The shared experiences of other adoptive parents may also provide aid and comfort to families facing difficulties...Traditional infertile adopting couples appear to require different social services. Their problems - the recognition and acceptance of infertility, then deciding to find and adopt a child - may point to a need for adequate preplacement and onset family counselling services. Our results, indicating that parental crisis and trauma are recurrent phenomena, suggest that the need for these kinds of services is unsatisfied. Our data also suggest that the anxiety and uncertainty generated by the crisis of infertility are communicated in many cases to the adopted children and adversely affect their adjustment. (Feigelman and Silverman, 1983, p.80).

These authors, like many others point to both the strengths and weaknesses of adoption in meeting the needs of children who would otherwise grow up without the benefit of stable family life. Virtually all of this work draws attention to the lack of support services for families and children once the adoption has taken place. With these recommendations we strongly concur. The experience of children in residential child care centres, presented in subsequent chapters, supports the view that much stronger post-adoption support services could in many cases prevent the need for some adopted children to be admitted to therapeutic child care centres.

5 Adjustment and identity in transracial and inter-country adoption

This chapter is about the ways in which white adoptive families have served, and can serve the psychosocial and cultural needs of black and mixed-race children, and those adopted across cultural and national boundaries. We are principally concerned with adoptions of children of Afro-Caribbean heritage born in the United Kingdom or in the United States of America, and adopted by white parents of European heritage. However, some of the literature and findings on inter-country adoption (which is also often transracial) and on adoptions of Amerindian children in Canada and the U.S.A. are of interest, and will be referred to in this chapter - these types of adoption are dealt with more fully in separate chapters in this book.

In a society in which physical differences in appearance are not a factor of social differentiation or discrimination, "transracial" adoption would be unnoticed and unremarkable, just as the adoption of a child with say, red hair by a couple with brown hair would be an event of unremarked except for the fact of adoption itself. What is so important in differences in hair texture and skin shade? The answer must be that some physical differences between human beings are allied with cultural and value differences. As sociologists of "race" have averred (e.g. Rex, 1972), race is a crude biological concept, and is sociologically meaningless; what is relevant is the concept of ethnicity, which implies a coherent and enduring set of cultural ideals, values and customs maintained by a particular group of people (an ethnos, or folk). Crucial to the maintenance of ethnic identity is endogamy - the degree to which members of ethnic group marry and have children by members of that same ethnic group. Marriage outside the ethnic group ("mixed-race" marriage - see Bagley, 1979 and Bagley and Young, 1984) may threaten the continued existence of some minority ethnic groups, and may be considered deviant for this reason. Similarly, adoption of black children by white parents (and of white children by black parents) is politically controversial, and may be classed as a form of deviance. Does such deviance (wanting to transcend traditional "racial" barriers in non-prejudiced and creative ways) when added to the other problems of adoptive parenting (including the role strains identified by Kirk, 1964 and 1981) make transracial or transethnic adoptive parenting an impossible proposition?

The evidence we review and present in this book offers a firm "No" in answer to this rhetorical question. Just as racial and ethnically mixed marriages are a growing reality in today's society, with successful developmental outcomes for children of such marriages (who are neither black nor white, but both), so too are the large majority of black adoptees in white homes emerging in the 1980s and 1990s as bright, emotionally stable young men and women, with secure identities and friendships which transcend traditional racial and ethnic divisions.

One of the paradoxes, indeed the tragedies in this progressive development has been the conservative, even the reactionary policy of many modern adoption agencies in refusing to consider the placement of black and mixed-race children with white couples, or with mixed-marriage couples.

Simon and Altstein (1987) comment on the situation in the United States:

> Trans-racial adoption was not halted because data indicated that it was a failure, that adoptees and/or adoptive families suffered any damaging social or psychological effects. It was not stopped because transracial adoptees were experiencing racial confusion or negative self-images. It did not end because there were no longer any non-white children in foster care or in institutions requiring permanent placements. It was not eradicated because the supply of families willing and able to adopt a child of another race was exhausted. Transracial adoption died because child welfare agencies no longer saw it as politically expedient, even though none of the 50 states recognizes race as a sufficient factor in

denying an adoption. (Simon and Altstein, 1987, p 143).

Silverman and Feigelman (1990) conclude in their overview of studies of transracial adoption (TRA): [The European research] ... presents little challenge to the picture presented above of transracial adoption as a generally successful enterprise from the perspective of the adopting parents, adoptees, and the investigators completing this study." (Silverman and Feigelman, 1990, p. 199)

Follow-Up studies of adoption of black children by white parents

Identity is important for all children, and crucial for ethnic minority children who face many disparagements to self-esteem from the external world (Young, and Bagley, 1982). The family of the black child - including the adoptive family - has a special task in giving that child secure feelings of identity and positive self-worth. It is significant that Kirk's (1964) theory of the need for a special and separate identify for the adopted (but not necessarily transracially adopted) child draws on Kurt Lewin's account of the need for "exaggerated identity" in the child from a persecuted minority group (in Lewin's writing, the Jewish child).

The adopted child, like the young adult in Triseliotis' (1973) study of the search by adopted people for their origins demands that, "I want someone that's like me, that's part of me." Adoptive parents can never fully occupy that role, and face the difficult task of giving the child an identity which incorporates a set of absent natural parents, and in the case of the transracially adopted child, a particular ethnic group. The earlier research literature (up to 1984) indicated that transracially adopting parents had been only partially successful in this task. While Rita Simon (1975) in Illinois has shown that white parents do in many cases transmit to black children a positive sense of ethnic identity, Diana Robertson (1974) in Los Angeles found that the majority of the white parents in her sample did not have black friends, or black playmates of the child; nor were they particularly concerned with informing the child about black culture, or the positive elements of being black. In the national American study of Grow and Shapiro (1974) a relatively important factor in lack of successful adjustment in the pre-adolescent children studied was lack of recognition by parents of the children's blackness. Overall however, at least three-quarters of the 125 adoptees had adjusted successfully by the age of nine.

In a comparative review of the American literature on transracial adoption, Joyce Ladner (1977) gives numerous examples of white parents who failed to give their black children any adequate sense of black identity, but instead isolated them from black people and black culture. As Ladner stresses, the silence or ignorance of parents on this issue is important and disturbing for children who inevitably know they are black. But Ladner also gives encouraging examples of how transracial adoption can work: a home which provides love, warmth and security and gives the child a positive sense of racial identity in the context of black and white playmates and a racially mixed circle of friends, is likely to provide the basis for successful adjustment in adolescence and adulthood. Costin and Wattenberg (1979) and Morin (1977) also point to positive successes in American transracial adoption.

In a follow-up of the adjustment of 30 mixed-race, adopted children in Britain (Bagley and Young, 1979) we found that perhaps a fifth of the parents interviewed not only had little contact with the black community, but also held some stereotyped views of black people in Britain and were not concerned to transmit to their child any positive feelings of black identity. One should stress however, that overall the adjustment of these adopted children was excellent. However, the oldest child in this research was only eight, so none had reached the age when Sorosky and his colleagues (1975) suggest that adopted children are particularly likely to suffer conflicts of identity. Sorosky puts this time in late adolescence and early adulthood; but Berlin (1978) writing about the transracial adoption of Native American children suggested that such "estrangement from self" often occurs in early adolescence.

Barbara Tizard (1977) concludes her follow-up study of a British sample of adopted children, some of them mixed-race, with a spirited defence of adoption as "a second chance". Her argument for a greater acceptance of adoption in child welfare policy is based on her impressive and carefully controlled study which shows that adoption has many advantages over both restoration to natural parents, and growing up in foster or group homes.

Tizard forthrightly exposes however, those adoptive parents who in her sample were failing to meet the child's needs for an adequate ethnic self-concept. She cites four families with black children who had not yet told the child about his or her ethnic background:

Mother: I don't quite know the best time to tell him he's partly West Indian. I think we should make a point of letting him know. When we are on holiday a boy was obviously African, and our child was teasing him - calling him "Blackie" and the boy was obviously upset. We spoke very severely to our son about teasing people for being crippled, or coloured. And we wondered if that would have been a good time to tell him - but we didn't - and the time passed.

The adoptive parents of this child were passing him as white. Similarly, the adoptive mother of a child with a West Indian father had concealed the fact that he was 'coloured' from the child, and told the interviewer: "There are certain traits in his character which are definitely the traits of a coloured person. There's his lack of concentration. Also, he'll suddenly switch off if he thinks you're going to tell him off - you can tell by his eye - he'll just go into his own little world. This is a thing that the coloured races do - one notices these little things" (Tizard, 1977, p. 181). Another child was told about his ethnic origin, but in such negative terms that Tizard attributed the child's present anxiety and aggressiveness to the adoptive mother's attitude:

> Mother: We told him that his Mummy didn't want him and that as soon as his Daddy knew he was on the way he left her. And he said, "didn't I have a Grandma" - and we said yes, but she didn't want you either. And we told him they didn't want him because of his colour. It's hard, but its best they know from the start (Tizard, 1977, p. 181).

The message from Tizard's account (like that in many other studies) is that adoption works, other things being equal; it is often in the child's best welfare interest, and should be contemplated more readily than it has been in the past; nevertheless, adoptive parents need to be chosen with care, and naive social workers have like some adoptive parents, have ignored the child's need for ethnic identity.

The dilemmas of white parents adopting black children have been brought out in Barbara Jackson's (1979) study of family experiences in inter-racial adoption. The need for a child to discover 'who she is' is brought out in the following quotation from an adoptive mother:

> My daughter Patricia came home from school one day quite perturbed. She said, "I'm not an immigrant, am I? I do eat meat don't I?"

These dilemmas and problems are graphically described in Joyce Ladner's penetrating study Mixed Families, (Ladner, 1977), an account of 136 transracial adopters in America, together with an analysis of the "politics of child welfare" which institutionalization, foster care, and adoption involves. Ladner makes it clear that the majority of the families she interviewed were transmitting to the black child a proper sense of ethnic identity, in the context of a loving and caring family. But it is clear too from Ladner's study that 'love is not enough' or, at least naive caring which ignores the child's social roles in the wider community, and his or her needs for a secure and stable identity in a society in which racism still thrives:

> Many parents feel that if they love their adopted child and provide for his or her emotional needs, there should be no serious problems ahead. The notion that love is sufficient is indeed naive. That most of the parents who adopt these children love them is probably indisputable. But whether they understand what their differential needs are and will be as they grow to maturity is a more important question. Are they willing to transform their white suburban middle-class lifestyles to accommodate their child's needs, which, ultimately, are their own needs? Many parents have not been willing to do so, even though they love their child and provide for all of his or her physical needs. That they have been insensitive to certain psychological and emotional needs he or she will have - needs that are related to identity - is most important. White parents who adopt black youngsters must also be willing and able to identify not only with their black children but also with blacks generally. They cannot be permitted to isolate their child and view him or her as 'different' from other blacks, but rather they must perceive their child to be an extension of other blacks. (Ladner, 1977, p. 140).

It is quite clear from these earlier British and American studies that a minority (but a crucially important minority) of white adopters had failed in this task, due to their own naivete or racial biases, explicit or implicit, and the biases of the agencies and the social worker who placed black children with them.

Further research in Britain does nothing to allay these fears (Gill and Jackson, 1983). These workers followed up 36 black or mixed race children, described when they were younger in a previous study (Jackson, 1979). At the time of this follow-up the children were adolescents aged 12 to 16. The majority of the white parents lived in predominantly white areas. Sixty percent of the children had no black friends; likewise, their parents only atypically had contact with black people. The adolescents themselves generally had good self-esteem, and the majority gave no sign of behavioural maladjustment. Nevertheless, a sixth of the children (predominantly boys) did have problems of peer relationships and self-esteem, but it is not clear whether these problems were limited to conflicts over ethnic identity.

Simon and Altstein (1981) expressed some reservations about the success of a minority of adoptions in their follow-up to adolescence of 204 black children placed with white, American parents. One in five families was found to have:

> A level of stress and tension which is profound and which the parents believe are directly a result of the adoption. The most common problem cited by the parents is the adopted child's tendency to steal from other members of the family. Typically, the accused child is a boy. Another serious problem is the parents' discovery' that their adopted child has disabilities that are either genetic or a consequence of the child's foster home experiences. A third theme to emerge in the follow-up study is parental guilt. A few parents believed that adopting a child of another race had caused problems with their biological children, some of whom felt estranged and left out. (p. 200)

Nevertheless, as Simon and Altstein stress, over half of these adoptions were highly successful - the majority of the children in successful transracial adoptions were leading emotionally and socially successful lives in racially integrated schools and neighbourhoods. The studies of Simon and Altstein (1981) and Gill and Jackson (1982) did not employ control groups, a methodological deficiency made good in Feigelman and Silverman's (1983) American study of 372 adoptees in a national sample of adoption agencies and associations of adoptive parents. All adopters were white, and seventeen percent adopted white children; 13 percent adopted black children; 43 percent adopted Korean children; 4 percent adopted children from Colombia; and 22 percent adopted children of other ethnic and cultural origin. The children had been previously studied in 1975 (Silverman and Feigelman, 1981). The differential levels of adjustment indicated by the follow-up five years later when the children were adolescent (in 1981) were largely similar to those found in 1975.

Results from the second follow-up indicated that Korean and Colombian children (adopted from overseas) were the best adjusted and the most highly achieving, with white children in an intermediate position, with black children more poorly adjusted. Over half of the black children were described on the basis of a variety of indicators, to be maladjusted in adolescence, compared with about a third of the white children, and a quarter of the Korean and Colombian children.

Regression analyses by Silverman and Feigelman (1981) indicated two reasons for these differences. First of all, later age at placement (more common for black children) was related to degree of maladjustment: placement before age five (including most of the inter-country adoptees) was generally related to good adjustment. A second factor predicting maladjustment was the opposition of family and friends of the white adopters to the adoption - particularly likely to be the case in the adoption of a black child.

Paradoxically, adopting an overseas child is more acceptable to the families and friends of the white adopters. However, this factor did not explain fully the very high levels of achievement and adjustment of the Korean adolescents in comparison with white adolescents born in America. The authors cannot explain these findings: but they do point to the paradox outlined earlier, that adopting an in-country minority child carries stigma for white parents, whilst adopting an overseas child (who is not usually 'black') does not.

We should note also McRoy and Zurcher's (1983) American study, comparing the adjustment in adolescencee of 60 black children adopted by white, and by black parents. These authors use a symbolic interactionist framework to explain the somewhat poorer adjustment of the black children adopted by white parents. Simply put, black parents with a supportive network in the black community give the black adopted child a more grounded identity and adjustment. The black child adopted by whites has to cope with both the usual adjustments which adopted children (and especially older adopted children) have to make, as well as the fact of having a stigmatized identity in a largely white world.

McRoy and Zurcher's concluding recommendation is a familiar one, which modern adoption researchers have emphasized again and again. This recommendation has to be reiterated because it identifies an important weakness in social work practice of adoption agencies:

Adoption agencies should recognize that their role does not end when the adoption is legally finalized. Postplacement support services should be an integral part of the agencies' continued service to transracial adoptive families, in order to help parents facilitate the development of a positive and unambiguous racial identity in the child. Support groups for parents and children are recommended in order to provide a vehicle in which their concerns and problems can be discussed together with black and white adoption staff and other families who have transracially adopted (McRoy and Zurcher, 1983. p. 145).

Identity issues in transracial adoption

Identity problems, and in consequence problems of adjustment, should in theory be much greater in black or Amerindian children adopted by white parents. However, the studies reviewed an above suggest that most (but not all) white parents can meet the identity and adjustment needs of the adopted black child (Ladner, 1977, Simon and Altstein, 1981). When parents are poorly selected or fail to support the black child's identity needs, outcomes can be catastrophic for the black child or adolescent, as the case studies presented by Tizard (1977) make clear. Rosenthal's (1982) study suggests that the black child of divorcing white parents is in 'triple jeopardy' - in addition to the usual problems of adapting to the role of a black child in a white family, these children had to endure considerable pre-divorce stress in an increasingly dysfunctional family; and finally had to endure the loss of the adoptive parent to whom they had bonded, usually the father. Rosenthal concludes that:

> The five families in our sample who adopted racially or ethnically different children all later proved to have negative racial attitudes which did not surface during the agencies' two pre-adoption interviews. All five families also proved to have more severe emotional difficulties than were initially apparent. Our experience in this study points to the need, therefore, for more careful screening of families who seek to make these sensitive transracial adoptions (Rosenthal, 1982, p. 43).

Rosenthal's proposals are based on a study of only five cases. More optimistic evidence comes from a rather larger study of the adjustment of transracial adoptees by McRoy and Zurcher (1983), who compared the adaptation in adolescence of 60 black children 30 adopted by white parents, and 30 by black parents, in Texas. Overall, there was no difference in the adjustment of the two groups on standardized mental health scales. Black children in white families positively identified themselves as 'black' significantly more often than those in black families, who more often expressed "no preference to race"; and those adopted by whites were also much more likely to use the term 'adopted' as a self-description. These are interesting findings, and point to the fact that carefully selected white parents of black children not only "accept the difference" in Kirk's terms; they also are successful in fostering both the mental health and the identity development of adopted, black children.

Kirk (1984) himself avers, in a foreword to Feigelman and Silverman's (1984) <u>Chosen Children: New Patterns of Adoptive</u>

Relationships, that recent work shows, "...that transracially adopted black children do not develop the serious adjustment and identity problems that some have predicted and that living in close proximity to Afro-Americans is not essential for being well adjusted. Many adoptive parents questioned say that they are prepared to accept the unsealing of adoption records. All of these findings are contrary to widely held beliefs in the field of child care and social work." (p. xiii, Foreword to Feigelman and Silverman, 1984).

Problems which can occur in transracial adoption, and potential solutions are well illustrated by McRoy al.'s (1988) further study of clinical problems encountered in a sample of 100 adoptees in Texas. One mother reported that:

> in kindergarten, when Paul passed the milk out, boys wouldn't take it from because he was black. One white kid told him each day that whites hated blacks. He was afraid to come home and tell us what was happening because we were white, and the kid got him convinced that whites didn't like blacks and he couldn't figure it out. He used to have real bad asthma attacks when he was upset. Fortunately, his Godparents were black and they used to talk to him about race. After a while his asthma cleared up. (McRoy et al., 1988, p.35)

The final conclusions of McRoy et al. (1988) are important: although adoption placements of older children who have some earlier experience of neglect or abuse followed by a period of residential are more likely than infant adoptees to develop clinical problems, the fact of being adopted is not in itself a major cause of the emergence or persistence of clinical problems. Furthermore, transracial adoptions are no more likely than inracial adoptions of older children to be associated with later emotional disturbance. Similar conclusions were reached by Barth and Berry (1988) from their Californian data on adoption and disruption: ethnic difference between parent and child is not in itself a factor in the development of adolescent problems.

In 1987 Rita Simon and Howard Altstein reported the third phase of a longitudinal study of 96 parents and 218 children. The children were about equally divided between those who were transracially adopted, and those who remained with their birth parents. A small sample (16) of white, inracial adoptees was also studied. The adolescent adoptees and controls completed a number of measures of self-esteem and ethnic identity.

The follow-up study found that about a fifth of the transracially adopted had significant psychological problems. These difficulties were profound enough to precipitate disruption of the adoption in seven percent of cases. In the group of successful transracial adoptees, cross-ethnic dating and friendships were common in contrast to the experiences of children who had never been adopted, and who remained with the parents, white or black. Measurement of self-esteem indicated that there were no significant variance in self-esteem levels across the various groups of adoptees and controls. The finding that transracial adoptees have self-esteem levels similar to those of most other children replicated the findings of another American study (McRoy and Zurcher, 1983).

In another longitudinal study of transracial adoption Johnson at al. (1987) reported on their Chicago sample when the children were aged eight years. This study showed that the black children in transracial adoptions had similar profiles on measures of identifying self with black people, in comparison with children in ordinary black families. However, only a third of the transracially adopting families maintained regular contacts with black friends. In the elementary school years at least, this type of contact did not appear to be crucial for the development of identity in transracial adoptees.

Further work in the field of transracial adopted in the United States is well summarized by Silverman and Feigelman (1990). this research indicates that children who are ethnically different from their parents usually identify with both the ethnicity of their parents, and that of people who are physically like them. In this respect the identity tasks of the transracially adopted child are rather similar to those of the non-adopted, mixed race child who has parents from different racial or ethnic backgrounds. Some further studies of transracial adoption, including policy implications of this research are offered in Chapters 14 and 15, below.

Inter-country adoption: Studies of adjustment

Adoptions across racial and cultural lines began in the post-war years with the adoption by North Americans of children from Korea following the involvement of the U.S. military in that country. Since then children have been adopted overseas from other Asian countries and from Central and Latin America, in large numbers by U.S. and European families (Weil, 1984). Korean children remain the largest single group of children adopted from overseas by American parents.

Such adoptions pose an interesting methodological problem in adoption research. In theory, since such children have to make cultural adaptations and may suffer ethnic stigma as well as making the usual adjustments of an adopted child, their adjustment might be rather poor. 'Adjustment' for such children has to be seen in relative terms however, and the obvious control group - children in similar circumstances who were not adopted, such as residents of orphanages in the sending country - has rarely been studied.

The follow-up studies of children adopted across cultural boundaries are worthy of note, since they seem to disconfirm the pessimistic critics of such adoptions: rather, they show that the adjustment of transculturally and transracially adopted children is in general no worse than that of 'ordinary' adopted children. This could be because parents who adopt an ethnically different child approach the inherent role handicaps of adoption in a more open and accepting fashion; it could also be that many parents who can accept an ethnically different child have a qualitatively different approach to parenting which supports the identity development of their adopted children (Simon, 1975). Studies from Europe (Bagley and Young, 1981; Gardell 1979), have been in agreement in their findings: Asian children adopted by European families have adjustment and achievement levels which are similar or above those of their non-adopted, European peers. These findings are particularly surprising in view of the fact that many of the placements look place after the child's first birthday, because of inevitable delays in formalizing the adoptions and overcoming the many legal and procedural hurdles. Many of the children had experienced abandonment, malnutrition, had minor physical handicaps, and experienced early life in orphanages varying in quality.

The American work by Wood (1972), Winick et. al. (1975) and Kim (1977 and 1978) reveals a similarly optimistic picture. Wood (1972) studied the adjustment of 133 Korean children in adolescence or adulthood, who had been adopted by American families at least five years before. The most salient problems of adjustment were seen in children placed after age four, and in children placed where (after their first year) there was a younger sibling. Problems were encountered most frequently in the early grade school years, and by adolescence such problems had largely disappeared. Little evidence was reported by the parents or the children themselves to indicate that community reaction to being oriental in a white or black family had any negative salience. Wood concluded that her findings provided clear grounds for continuing such adoptions, and she saw no difference in adjustment in comparison with same-race placements. No formal control group was used however.

The methodologically sophisticated study by Winick et. al. (1975) published in Science examined the influence of early malnutrition on later intellectual development, through the study of 138 children born in Korea and placed with American adoptive parents at an average age of 18 months, between 1958 and 1967. Since the placement agency used was similar to that in Wood's study there is probably an overlap in subjects with Winick's study. All subjects were female, full-term, and without handicap or chronic illness. Standardized I.Q. scores were obtained when the children were aged between 6 and 12 years. The sample had been selected to include three groups: clearly malnourished in the first year of life (N = 41); moderately nourished (N = 50); and well nourished (N = 47). The mean I.Q. of the well-nourished group was 112; of the moderately-nourished 106; and of the malnourished 102. Thus even malnourished children achieved 'normal' intelligence levels after placement in middle-class, American homes. Neither schools nor the adoptive parents themselves had knowledge of previous nutrition history. It is interesting to note that the malnourished children had mean heights similar to children in Korea; but children from the other two groups were significantly taller than norms from Korea had predicted. While these findings do not relate to emotional adjustment, there seem good grounds for supposing that good nutrition and emotional support might go hand in hand in these adoptive families.

Kim (1977) studied the self-concept of 406 Korean children adopted by American couples up to the age of 10, with follow-up when the children were aged 12 to 17. The children were sampled from a much larger population of Korean adoptees to include (1) children placed in the first year of life, and (2) children placed after 6 years. Results indicated normal grade achievement for those placed before age one, but retardation of about one and half grades for those placed after six. However, a quarter of the later-placed children were physically handicapped (usually following polio) or had been diagnosed as mental retarded before placement. Surprisingly, scores of this latter group on a standardized self-concept measure did not differ from normative levels for the Tennessee Self-concept Scale. Early placed children, not surprisingly, had average or above average levels of self-reported adjustment. In all subjects reported difficulties in adjustment were said to diminish over time, even in the physically and mentally handicapped groups. Noting Kirk's argument that adoptive parents should "accept the totality of the child's back-ground", Kim sought to find whether adoptive parents were supporting a positive ethnic identity in these Korean children. Kim found in fact that only a minority of parents emphasized the child's ethnic identity. The presence or absence of such emphasis was not related to self-concept in adolescence. However, consistency and warmth of family environment was related to adolescent self-concept, a finding which reflects general findings pointing to the family warmth and structure as the primary source of self-esteem for the developing child (Coopersmith, 1981; Thomas et al., 1977).

Kim's finding in this respect is similar to our own conclusions from a follow-up of 98 Chinese adolescents adopted as infants by British parents: self-esteem levels (measured by the Coopersmith Scale) were, on average, significantly higher than in non-adopted, white controls (Bagley and Young, 1981). This high self-esteem reflected parental warmth, and the concern (including the "overconcern" of some parents) for their adopted children's well-being. Emphasis on ethnicity either actively or passively, was not related to self-esteem. It is important to note however that in our study none of the parents devalued the ethnicity of the child. Those who live in inter-ethnic situations will know that somatic aspects of identity such as hair colour, features and skin colour rapidly become the least relevant factors in interaction. Interaction is based on the personality of the individuals, on their human characteristics. This process has been described in America by the anthropologist Ashley Montagu (1977), and seems in many cases the inevitable outcome of ethnic interaction in which the parties have no preconceived stereotypes. However, when parents retain latent or active ethnic stereotypes which they use as factors guiding interaction, symbolic interaction theory advises us that distorted patterns of interaction may emerge, and the weaker party in the interaction may internalize these negative view of self.

The hypothetical model in the accompanying table sets out some theoretical possibilities. It is assumed that structural values concerning the status of ethnic minorities affect the consciousness of children (including adopted children) from such minorities, and also that families can support the identity of such children through the fostering of a "global self-esteem" which can foster ethnic pride which is sufficient in degree to defend the young person's ego in the face of ethnic devaluation offered by the larger community. In clinical work in Canada I have encountered a number of Native children whose adoptive parents have been unable or unwilling to extend the love of their adopted Native child to that child's ethnicity, and the wider community of Native children to which that child is inevitably, in structural terms, linked. Ironically, it seems easier to be an adoptive parent of a child adopted from Korea than the white adoptive parent of a Native or Metis adopted child who was born in Canada.

To return to Kim's (1977) study of children from Korea adopted in the U.S.A.: Kim's general conclusion is as follows:

In spite of drastic changes of their life environment, including personal and ethnic status, language and culture, they have made an impressively healthy normal developmental adjustment and most likely they will continue to do so in the future ... in the process of this development, the attitudinal interactional environment of the adoptive family appears to have played the most important role, whereas other factors such as the child's age at the time of placement, the length of placement, racial background, ethnic cultural pattern etc., are found to be not as important. (Kim, 1977, pp. 12-13).

We should note one more study of 21 Korean children adopted by American couples in the New York area (Kim et. al., 1979). This research reported some early problems in the behavioural adjustment of younger children, which appeared to be diminishing with age.

A Hypothetical Model of Relationship of Ethnic Difference in Adoption and its Relationship to Adolescent Self-Esteem, Assuming Other Family Factors Held Constant

Values of Social Structure	Parental Action Concerning Ethnicity	Adopted Child's Outcome
Accepts ethnicity of group (oriental)	Accentuate ethnicity	Self-esteem + +
	Accept ethnicity	Self-esteem + +
	Deny/Ignore ethnicity	Self-esteem
	Devalue ethnicity	Self-esteem -
Ambiguous about ethnicity of group (black)	Accentuate ethnicity	Self-esteem +
	Accept ethnicity	Self-esteem
	Deny/Ignore ethnicity	Self-esteem -
	Devalue ethnicity	Self-esteem --
Stigmatizes ethnicity (East Indian, Native)	Accentuate ethnicity	Self-esteem
	Accept ethnicity	Self-esteem -
	Deny/Ignore ethnicity	Self-esteem --
	Devalue ethnicity	Self-esteem ---

Note: Assumptions about status of ethnic groups in Canada derived from Henry and Ginzberg (1985) and from personal observations.

Follow-up studies of adoption of native children by white families

Adoption of indigenous black and aboriginal children in North America presents somewhat different problems for adoptive parents. The need for black and Native children to be adopted outside their own ethnic communities is itself an indicator of the profound structural inequalities which affect the lives of individuals in those communities. How do Native children, 'far from the Reservation' fare with white adopters? Although such adoptions are quite common in Canada (Hepworth, 1980) there is little good evidence from follow-up studies on the adjustment of such transracially adopted children.

A review of what studies exist in this area, including American outcomes of transracial fostering and adoption of Native children has been undertaken by Green (1983). Green's conclusions are that such transracial placements have, in many cases, a very poor outcome. Whether this is due to problems which existed before placement, to maladjustment in the adoption itself, or to a combination of factors is not clear from any study. Methodologically, the most sophisticated study in this is that of Fanshel (1972) who followed up 97 Native children placed in white adoptive homes in the United States, up to five years after placement. Only the parents were interviewed, and the reports by the majority of these parents that the children were well settled, were not corroborated by any interviews or testing with children. Fanshel remarked that, "It is to be expected that, as our Indian adoptees get older, the prevalence of problems will increase" - as Berlin (1978) has found in another study of Native children.

Unfortunately, such follow-up was not undertaken by Fanshel. With the passing of the Indian Child Welfare Act in the U.S.A. giving autonomy in child welfare services in Indian Bands, such adoptions have largely ceased (Sink, 1983). Ironically, such adoptions have continued in Canada, and a significant number of Indian and Metis children were up to 1983, being sent to the United States for adoption by white parents (Kimelman, 1983). The fate of these children is largely unknown.

Further studies of intercountry adoptions

Andresen (1992) indicates that in 1989 some 7,000 children were adopted in Norway from overseas. (If Britain adopted children overseas on this scale then over 80,000 intercountry adoptees would come to Britain each year, rather than fewer than 500 a year arriving at the present time). Andresen studied a random sample of 160 adolescent adoptees born overseas, using the national register of all adopted children as a sampling frame. The sample was stratified so as to represent children adopted at different ages, and from different countries - 72 percent of all international adoptees in Norway came from Korea in the 1970s. Teachers and parents of the sample completed a number of measures of behaviour and achievement when the adoptees were in mid-adolescence. Control subjects were non-adopted, Norwegian children attending the same school classes.

Results indicated that the adopted children were more often described by teachers as "restless", "fidgety" and with "poor concentration". Overall 16 percent of adoptees and 10 percent of controls had scores on the Rutter scale indicating maladjustment of clinical proportions. In addition, nearly twice as many adoptees as controls had problems in arithmetic achievement (which is known to correlate with overactive behaviour in children with some CNS impairments - see Bagley, 1986b). This combination of overactivity, poor attention span and some impairment of spatial and numerical abilities occurred more often in boys, in children who were more than three years old on arrival in Norway, who came from countries other than Korea (implying the possibility of early malnutrition and CNS impairment in these children). However, "Most of the adopted children in this study were found to be quite well adjusted... As many adopted children may have lived in quite unsatisfactory conditions in early life, it is gratifying that such a high proportion of them seem to be well adjusted at 12-13 years of age. Although adoptive children have somewhat more problems than their non-adopted classmates, the problems are seldom of a magnitude that would classify the child as maladjusted." (Andresen, 1992, p.436)

Two edited volumes containing a number of research reports on adoption have added much to our knowledge of adjustment so transracially and interculturally adopted children. Brodzinsky and Schecter (1990) have gathered together a valuable set of papers on the psychology of adoption including a review by Silverman and Feigelman (1990) of twenty years of research on transracially and internationally adopted children. This chapter includes an overview and update on their own follow-up of 713 white American families who had adopted American black, American white, Korean, Vietnamese, and Colombian children: "..... findings are congruent with the research already presented ... black adoptees adapt reasonably well to their white homes ... most of their emotional and developmental experiences can be traced to their preadoptive experiences. This also seems true of Asian and Latin American transracial adoptees." (p. 198)

The second volume of note is Altstein and Simon's (1991)

compendium of seven chapters reporting the adjustment of internationally adoptees in various countries in North America and Europe. Included is a report from the present writer on adoptions of Amerindian children in Canada (Bagley, 1991) which formed an earlier version of Chapter 13, below. Apart from our own pessimistic conclusions about Canada, the various chapters in Altstein and Simon's book are rather optimistic about the outcomes for children adopted from Latin America and Asia by European and American parents. The editors conclude however:

> The major findings that emerge from these cases studies [of America, Canada, Germany, Netherlands, Israel, Norway and Denmark] are the variations that exist across societies. One should not generalize from the experiences of any one society. Although the age of a child may be important in each society, how that variable interacts with the motivation of adoptive families, the homogeneity or heterogeneity of the adoptive society produces scenarios sufficiently different to make it difficult to predict how successful ICAs are likely to be as overall strategy for helping homeless, parentless children in Third-World countries. (Altstein and Simon, 1991, p. 191)

Similar conclusions reflecting "optimistic ambivalence" about the future of intercountry adoption are drawn by a number of researchers whose work is reviewed by Tizard (1991). While everyone who writes about ICA expresses the hope that countries from which the children come will soon be able to provide within-country solutions, nevertheless for many intercountry adopted children outcomes can be rather successful, despite cultural and ethnic differences, early problems of nutrition and other health problems (reviewed in Chapter 10).

Conclusions

The first thing do be said about transracial and intercountry adoptions is that in a more ideal world, principles of social justice would ensure that families would not be oppressed by poverty to the extent that children have to be abandoned or given up to orphanages and welfare agencies. Extended families can almost always cope with children whom relatives are unable to care for, particularly when their basic housing needs are met and they receive a small fostering allowance which allows them to meet the child's basic material need (1). While conservative administrations often resist allocating such subsidies for support of family life, all of the alternatives are much more expensive n both human and financial terms.

Nevertheless there are countries such as India and China whose stage of development and huge population mean that there are literally millions of children growing up in orphanages. Many of these children could be adopted in other countries provided that the United Nations guidelines are followed (see Chapters 9 and 10). Research studies have indicated generally favourable outcomes for both transracial and intercountry adoptions, despite the gloomy predictions of some ethnocentric writers. As international boundaries become less rigid, as world communications increase, as populations migrate in larger numbers, as traditionally separate ethnic groups now work together on terms of dignity and equality, meet and marry so is the adoption of children across traditional racial and cultural barriers becomes boundaries more viable than it ever was. The evidence reported in the following chapters supports that idea.

However, the removal of children from families for arbitrary and often reactionary reason has also occurred in countries such as Canada (in the case of aboriginal children), Argentina (adoptions of children whose parents were executed by the military), and many former Communist regimes in Eastern Europe where children were compulsorily removed from dissident or imprisoned parents, and placed for adoption.

End note

(1)   The use of the extended family for child care is widely used in many parts of Asia, Africa and North America. For example, my Jamaican father-in-law (following African tradition) has 25 children by four wives. All of these wives are known as Mrs Young, and all of his children take their father's surname. Children of different wives often spend long periods in the homes of their half-siblings - the movement is usually determined by the preference of an adult for a child of a particular age or sex to fit in with the particular family's current needs.

One of my wife's cousins, descended from an East Indian father and with skin fairer and hair straighter than is usual in our family, was a teenaged single parent. At the infant health clinic in rural Jamaica she was introduced in 1984 to an American woman who offered her $500 if she would give up the child for adoption. This event is retold in our family with both amusement and outrage. Loretta Young and I have undertaken a number of studies comparing the cognitive styles, identity and psychological orientation of members of our large, extended family (many hundreds of people) resident in rural Jamaica and following migration in Toronto, Edmonton, Calgary and New York (Bagley and Young, 1983 and 1988).

6 A follow-up of adopted children in the National Child Development Study

Introduction

Adoption is frequently a favoured solution for the long-term welfare of children who have been separated from their natural mother, or whose natural parents are unable (in society's convention at least) to care for the child. Barbara Tizard (1977) on the basis of her systematic research, writes enthusiastically about the benefits which adoption can bestow on children whose early life has been disrupted in various ways. In her comparison of various outcomes for children who had been in care early in their lives, adoption seemed to have the best emotional, behavioural and educational outcomes by follow-up age eight.

Similar conclusions were drawn from the first follow-up study of adopted children in the National Child Development study, conducted by the National Children's Bureau in London (Seglow et al., 1972). This survey of all children born in England, Wales and Scotland in one week in March, 1958 followed up some 14,500 children to age 7, and was able to compare these findings with detailed socio-medical data gathered at the time of the child's birth. Further follow-ups of the cohort have been undertaken at ages 11, 16 and 23. Detailed secondary analysis of the enquiry at 16 years is now possible, since data from the follow-up surveys have been deposited with the SSRC Survey Archive at the University of Essex.

Six hundred and forty children in the 1958 survey were born to single mothers; by the time they were seven, 182 of these children had been adopted by people other than their own mothers. It was possible to trace 180 of the adopted children: four had emigrated and one had died, while thirty parents declined to be interviewed. This left 145 families who were interviewed in a special study of adoption.

It was found that despite early social and biological stress, outcomes for the adopted children in social, psychological and educational terms were excellent, leading the authors of the report to conclude: "We can have considerable confidence in adoption; a good environment can overcome birth vulnerabilities and adverse experiences; adoption should be more readily considered for older children and those with handicaps..." (Seglow et al., 1972, p.161). These conclusions were based in part on the contrast between the adopted children and those born in similar disadvantaged circumstances, who remained with their natural, unmarried mothers. This latter group were still suffering serious socio-economic disadvantage, and this was reflected in the behavioral and educational circumstances of their children.

In the follow-up comparison at age 11 of the adopted children and those originally in one parent situations, 115 adopted and 294 one-parent children were available for study (Lambert & Streather, 1980). The most remarkable finding in this further follow-up was the positive progress made by the children of single parents over the four year period. Some of the mothers had married; others had stabilized their social situation, taking full advantage of housing and income support of various kinds. By the age of 11 the educational and behavioural profiles of these children in one-parent families were generally similar to those of their peers.

In contrast, the early promise of the adopted children was not reflected in a wholly favourable outcome at age 11. After comparing adopted children with non-adopted children in homes of similar social class background," .... the finding of most importance and concern is that when such factors were taken into account, adopted children's social adjustment was poorer than that of legitimate children, and showed signs of having deteriorated relative to that of other children since the age of 7... Many of them (the adopted children) would have been starting to adjust to the knowledge that their adoptive parents were not their natural parents and coming to terms with their own identity." (Lambert Streather, 1980, p.133).

An independent analysis is the NCDS data for the adopted children at age 11, concluded more optimistically after comparing the adopted children with the main sample that, "The only difference reported to the disadvantage of adopted children was in ease of setting for a few moments. We have a picture of the adopted children as cheerful, co-operative, rather bubbly, and not particularly disturbed in any area. On the Bristol Social Adjustment Guide for Children, completed by teachers, adopted children showed some excess of behaviour disorders, but this difference did not reach an acceptable level of significance." (Bagley, 1977, p.47).

Other longitudinal research on adoption, particularly the Swedish work of Michael Bohman (Bohman, 1981) suggests that the longer one follows up adopted children, the more they resemble members of the general population - a finding which might apply to all groups with early adverse circumstances of development. There is, however, some suggestion in the work of Bohman and others that adopted children may carry more genes than members of the general population for certain types of personality disorder (Bohman, 1981; Cadoret, 1978). The implications of this genetic research using adopted subjects however are that the influence of environment is much stronger than the influence of genes: but this is not to say that genes have no effect on development at all, and much may depend on the kinds of stresses placed upon a child with some genetic vulnerability. Since there is no specific linage between behavioural problems in a biological parent and any problems in the adopted child, we can conclude too that environment plays an important part in determining the type of reaction that vulnerable individuals will display. In general, any behavioural reaction in an adopted child will be milder than that in a biological parent (Von Knorring et al., 1983).

Adopted children in the NCDS study at age 16

In further follow-up study of the adopted children in the NCDS cohort, we have compared the adopted children not with children born to single mothers and never or rarely separated from them, but with children permanently separated from their mothers (because of maternal death, chronic hospitalization, separation, divorce, or surrender to foster or institutional care) by the age seven. Our basic hypothesis is that maternal separation in the first seven years of life followed by adoption will have a much more favourable outcome than maternal separation in this period not followed by permanent transfer to an adoptive family. There is both ethological evidence (e.g., Bowlby, 1979) and socio-behavioural evidence from empirical work with children(e.g., Rutter, 1987) to support such a proposition. However, there are also studies (reviewed by Brodzinsky and Schechter, 1990) which show that adopted children face identity problems, role handicaps, negative genetic heritage, and anxiety in adoptive parents, factors which might mean that adopted children are more at risk for stress factors than "normal" children.

Comparison of adopted children with non-adopted groups

An important question yet to be answered is whether the adjustment and performance of the adopted children is at a level which the social class of their adoptive parents might predict. It is important to bear in mind that in the entire group of children in the British National Child Development Survey (NCDS), parental socioeconomic status has been shown to be an important predictor of scholastic performance and behavioural problems (Wedge & Essen, 1982).

Control subjects for the 127 available adopted children at age 16, were randomly selected so as to obtain a population with a similar proportion of children in each of five social class groups, similar mean sibship sizes, and similar sex ratios. Given the large pool of non-separated control subjects to draw from, it was possible to undertake individual matching for sex and sibsize and blue-collar/white-collar parental background, ensuring that overall, proportions in each of the five social class groups were similar. Missing data for a number of subjects meant that comparisons are often based on variable numbers. A comparison of adopted children available for interview at ages 7 or 11, but not at age 16 with those who remained in the cohort on a range of social and psychological variables, could find no significant differences. This suggests that families who declined participation or who could not be traced when their child was 16, did not represent any kind of special sub-group of adoptive families.

The results in Tables 1 and 2 show, first of all, the very disadvantaged circumstances of the adopted children at birth. Their biological mothers had lower haemoglobin levels, worker longer into pregnancy, visited antenatal clinics much later, and had proportionately more children than controls who fell into the low birth weight quartile. Yet by age 16 the group of adopted children actually had somewhat more members who were <u>above</u> the fourth quartile in height, in comparison with controls. This difference was not however statistically significant, and the picture in comparing the adopted children and their matched, non-separated controls on this and other indictors is one of similarity rather than difference. The adopted children seem to have been doing somewhat poorer scholastically than the controls, but the differences were not marked.

On the behavioural indicators the adopted children at age 16 show very similar profiles to the matched, non-separated controls, with very few children falling into extreme categories of behavioural and emotional disturbances. The one exception concerns the item "Can't settle to anything for more than a few moments": 20 per cent of the adopted children fell into this category, compered with ten per cent of controls. Adopted children seem more likely to lie to others, and to be unpopular with other children; and relationships with mother seem slightly poorer than for the controls. But these are the only significant differences amongst a long list of comparisons, and might well have occurred by chance.

The adopted children began life in very disadvantaged circumstances, most often as children of teenaged, single parents who obtained very poor perinatal care, which was clearly reflected in the children's early physical status. Some disadvantaged mothers did not surrender their child for adoption, and the kinds of outcome experienced by these children who suffered subsequent maternal separation without adoption by age seven can be seen in Table 1. These maternally separated children were much more likely to have been referred for psychiatric consultation for a variety or reasons, and by age 16 were also significantly shorter than the remainder of the NCDS cohort, while the adopted children who suffered subsequent taller. This presumably reflects both social stability, and the advantages of good nutrition bestowed in a middle class home. The maternally separated children who had not been adopted were by age 16 under-performing scholastically to a significant degree, and had many more teacher-rated symptoms of behaviour disorder. In contrast, the comparison between the adopted children and the non-separated main cohort indicates a picture of similarity rather than of difference.

Discussion and conclusion

In contrast to the view of adoption which emerges from the clinical work reviewed by Brodzinsky and Schechter (1990), and our own study of previously adopted children in residential treatment centres reported in this volume, this British study has produced an optimistic picture of outcome in adoption. Since it is based on a national survey and includes some 70 per cent of all children born in one week in 1958 who were subsequently adopted, and followed up to age 16, the results have particular importance and can be generalized to the institution of adoption. Various estimates indicate that between two and four per cent of the population had been adopted, and it is likely that the "disrupted" adoptions described by clinical workers represent only a small proportion adoption as a whole.

One of the interesting features of adoption is the anxiety of the new parents in wanting to do the best for their long awaited children. In the NCDS cohort the adopted children were much more likely to have two types of elective surgery, circumcision and tonsillectomy. This kind of surgery is essentially prophylactic, and many of the referrals -to tutors, psychologists and specialists of various kinds - made by adoptive parents were made by parents anxious to avoid the onset of any major problem. This chronic anxiety is a frequent feature of adoptive parenting and seems to be reflected in high levels of sub-clinical anxiety in the adopted children themselves, who often cling to the parental home for longer periods than non-adopted children.

We have gathered together the theoretical advantages and disadvantages of adoption, based on this and other studies, in Table 3. Adopted children start life with many disadvantages, both physical and social, and many also carry a greater genetic potential for the development of problem behaviours. Adoptive parents themselves have faced the stigma of infertility, and the role handicaps inherent in adoptive parenting (Kirk, 1964).

On the credit side however, adopted parents are usually carefully chosen by social work agencies on grounds of marital stability and good mental health, and they tend to be materially advantaged as well. Adopted children are usually only children, and their new families tend to be stable, loving and devoted to the child. Yet the parenting style of the adopters may be one marked by excessive anxiety, and over-indulgent care. Whatever these problems, the outcomes for the adopted children by age 16 are remarkably good. Although not doing as well scholastically as their non-adopted, middle class peers, nevertheless the adopted children are doing quite as well as the average child, and much better than children who were separated from their natural parent but who were never adopted.

Indeed, the real comparison group for adopted children's outcome must be those children who might have been adopted, but who were not given stable, alternative care for whatever reason and who remained in the care of relatives, foster homes, or institutions, often going back and forth to maternal care within the context of disadvantaged and often neglectful parenting situations. Given this kind of comparison, adoption as an institution appears to be dramatically successful in terms of developmental outcomes by mid-adolescence. The evidence from this survey indicates that permanent family care through adoption must be considered to be an important and viable option in social work with maternally-separated young children.

An interesting verification of our results (albeit using a different control group) comes from the preliminary analysis of data from the NCDS cohort of adoptees at the age of 23 (Maughan and Pickles, 1990). This study compared the 155 available adopted children with a sample of legitimate children who had never been adopted, and the original comparison group of out-of-wedlock children described by Lambert and Streather (1980). Interesting sex differences emerged in adjustment, with the adopted women at 23 doing just as well as those from the main cohort on indicators of adjustment, employment and social participation. The adopted men were slightly disadvantaged on these various indicators compared with the sample from the main cohort. However, both adopted men and women had markedly better adjustment on all indicators in comparison with the out-of-wedlock children who were never adopted. For example, 31 percent of these disadvantaged, non-adopted children became teenaged mothers compared with 11 percent of the adopted women, and 9 percent of the main cohort sample. The women born out-of-wedlock but never adopted had particularly poor outcomes (seeming in many cases to continue a cycle of deprivation). This finding underlines once again the potentially powerful effects of adoption in offering a fair future for many otherwise disadvantaged children.

Table 1
Outcomes at age 16 for children who by age 7 were adopted, maternally separated, or remained with both natural parents

	Proportion in		
Variable	Adopted children N = 81 to 127	Separated children N = 96 to 143	Non-separated children N = 9,196 to 10,760
Perinatal Variables	%	%	%
1st visit of birth mother to antenatal clinic after 24th week of pregnancy	47.4	32.6	14.8
1st visit after 28th week of pregnancy	32.7	14.6	6.9
1st visit after 36th week of pregnancy	8.6	2.4	1.9
Mother's haemoglobin level below 70% during pregnancy	13.0	9.5	8.0*
Fetal distress at birth	10.6	23.3	8.9
Mother worked full-time after 33rd week of pregnancy	24.5	6.8	5.5
Birthweight below 1st quartile for whole group	39.5	25.0	24.9*
Medical Report When Child aged 16			
Referred to psychologist/ psychiatrist	10.9	22.4	7.5
Referred because of: School problems	6.4	4.8	3.3
Disturbed relations with parents	0.9	3.2	0.2

Table 1 (continued)

Variable	Proportion in:		
	Adopted children N = 81 to 127	Separated children N = 96 to 143	All other children N = 9,196 to 10,760
	%	%	%
Aggressive behaviour and/or delinquency	1.8	4.0	0.9
Below 1st quartile in height for whole group	11.9	28.9	24.1
Above 3rd quartile in height for whole group	29.3	11.6	24.9
Child attends, or recommended for special schooling	4.4	9.0	3.1
Ethnic appearance: European/Caucasian	98.2	92.7	98.1
Black/Afro-Caribbean	0.0	1.6	0.7
"Mixed-race"	1.8	7.3	0.9
Physical or mental handicap of child	3.5	0.0	1.3*
Significant sight problem	21.0	11.6	15.8*
Significant hearing problem	3.6	9.3	3.7
School Report When Child Aged 16			
Attends private or independent school	14.2	1.4	5.4
Special help for behavioural problems	12.3	21.6	7.1
Recent contact with welfare agency	11.4	46.3	12.2

Table 1 (continued)

Variable	Adopted children N = 81 to 127	Separated children N = 96 to 143	All other children N = 9,196 to 10,760
	%	%	%
Well below average in mathematics	31.5	55.5	34.1
Exceptional ability in mathematics	5.6	2.2	11.6
Well below average in English	19.2	40.4	23.8
Exceptional ability in English	12.0	3.7	16.3
Exceptional ability in foreign language	10.5	2.1	11.2
Exceptional ability in science	8.0	3.2	11.6
Exceptional ability in social studies	12.5	2.3	13.9
Child's handicap needs special schooling	3.2	7.7	2.4
Child most suited for:			
Degree level education	8.9	2.7	11.4
Diploma level	11.7	5.4	12.7
No tertiary programme recommended	29.7	33.8	27.5
School suggests child leave school at 16	37.9	63.4	43.9
Child delinquent	10.3	22.3	8.3
Often apathetic	31.2	62.0	29.2
Resentful or angry when corrected	21.6	40.7	21.3
Bullies others	10.6	20.6	7.5

Table 1 (continued)

Variable	Proportion in:		
	Adopted children N = 81 to 127	Separated children N = 96 to 143	All other children N = 9,196 to 10,760

Teacher rated behaviour (Rutter Scale Items) at 16

	%	%	%
Very restless	22.5	40.7	19.5
Truants from school	18.7	29.5	20.0
Squirmy, fidgety	20.9	29.5	16.3
Often destructive	5.6	18.7	6.4
Frequently fights	11.3	20.1	9.2
Unpopular in class	23.5	23.0	15.6
Often worries	36.3	47.1	36.5
Quick-tempered	23.3	36.2	19.8
Often miserable	21.6	23.3	14.0
Often absent from school	16.1	31.1	24.2*
Often disobedient	21.6	30.7	17.4
Often can't settle	21.0	36.7	20.3
Often fearful	22.6	31.2	22.5*
Often fussy or overparticular	7.5	14.9	9.5*
Often tells lies	19.2	29.8	15.3
Has stolen in school in past year	4.1	11.6	4.7

Educational Test Results at Age 16

Reading:> 3rd quartile for whole group	27.8	8.3	24.6
Mathematics:> 3rd quartile	27.0	6.8	25.8

Table 1 (continued)

Variable	Adopted children N = 81 to 127	Proportion in:	
		Separated children N = 96 to 143	All other children N = 9,916 to 10,760

Teacher's Global Ratings of Behaviour

	%	%	%
Extremely impulsive	5.7	9.3	3.4
Extremely moody	3.2	15.1	5.3
Extremely aggressive	7.4	7.2	2.9
Extremely withdrawn	1.6	4.3	1.8*
Extremely lazy	10.6	12.2	8.8

Family Situation at Age 16 (Parental Report)

Child has no older siblings	82.7	46.8	59.1
Child has no younger siblings	83.1	35.1	57.2
Current mother-figure not biological or adoptive mother	2.9	63.0	2.8
Child has no regular mother figure	4.8	7.6	1.2
Currently in foster care	0.0	8.4	0.1
Currently in residential care	1.0	9.2	0.1
Natural or adoptive mother has died	2.5	13.2	0.9
Current father figure not adoptive or biological parent	8.6	49.6	11.1

101

Table 1 (continued)

Variable	Adopted children N = 81 to 127	Separated children N = 96 to 143	All other children N = 9,196 to 10,760
	Proportion in:		
	%	%	%
No regular father figure	4.5	16.0	7.1
Father figure is foster parent	0.0	5.9	0.1
Natural or adoptive father has died	6.7	5.9	3.8
Separation from parent(s) due to their divorce	1.0	16.5	5.3
Father (when present) in higher white collar occupation (I or II)	43.3	19.8	25.3*
Father (when present) in lowest blue collar occupation (IVb or V)	17.5	25.0	18.4*
Mother has paid employment	64.6	53.6	66.9
If mother employed, in unskilled work (IVb or V)	11.0	38.0	25.4
Father: education beyond age 16	38.8	14.0	20.8
Mother: education beyond age 16	36.3	17.0	21.3
Parent(s) wish child to have full-time education beyond 18	44.2	13.7	32.5

Table 1 (continued)

Variable	Adopted children N = 81 to 127	Separated children N = 96 to 143	Proportion in: All other children N = 9,196 to 10,760
	%	%	%
Child has appeared in court because of criminal offence	3.1	6.2	4.8*
Child receives free school meals (poverty index)	3.9	22.6	9.6
Family had serious financial problem in previous year	4.8	17.1	9.8
Family live in rented apartment	5.9	15.6	8.7
Family live in council (public) housing	24.0	50.0	41.3
Family live in owner-occupied house	67.3	33.8	49.7
Accomodation has 3 rooms or less	6.8	12.8	7.8
Child has own bedroom	88.5	60.3	61.1*
Child has lived in present dwelling 10 years or more	41.4	33.0	48.2*

Parent Descriptions of Child's Behaviour at 16

Variable	Adopted	Separated	All other
In past year: Suffered stomach pains or vomiting at least weekly	0.0	3.4	1.3*
Wet pants or bed at least weekly	1.0	3.4	0.8*

Table 1 (continued)

Variable	Proportion in:		
	Adopted children N = 81 to 127	Separated children N = 96 to 143	All other children N = 9,196 to 10,760
	%	%	%
Severe temper outburst at least weekly	2.9	11.3	5.6*
Occasionally or frequently stole things	6.7	6.8	3.2
Very restless	19.2	29.1	15.7*
Squirmy, fidgety	18.2	15.4	13.3**
Often destroys things	2.0	7.7	2.5
Frequently fights	9.7	17.1	12.3*
Not much liked by other children	3.9	14.5	3.5
Often worried	45.2	40.2	39.4*
Often irritable	42.3	38.5	40.1**
Often miserable or unhappy	20.1	18.8	15.7*
Frequently bites nails or fingers	23.1	35.0	29.0
Often disobedient	21.1	28.2	19.6
Can't settle for more than a few moments	20.2	20.5	12.1
Fearful of new situations	25.0	27.3	22.0**
Often tells lies	21.2	21.1	12.6
Bullies others	3.9	12.0	5.6

Table 1 (continued)

Variable	Proportion in:		
	Adopted children N = 81 to 127	Separated children N = 96 to 143	All other children N = 9,196 to 10,760
	%	%	%
Fit/convulsion after 1st birthday	5.8	2.6	2.7**
Saw specialist for behavioural problem in past year	7.8	17.1	4.2
Adolescent's Own Report at Age 16			
Wishes to stay in school/college after age 18	24.4	6.8	22.9*
"Above average" in mathematics	13.2	5.5	16.1*
"Above average" in English	20.3	15.6	24.2*
Parents "very anxious" for me to do well in school	31.7	13.7	23.3
"I get on very well with my mother"	76.6	71.0	87.3
"I get on very well with my father"	78.3	69.6	80.2

Note: Statistical significance of differences between proportions calculated by the Chi-squared test. All comparisons are significant at the 0.1% level or beyond, except where indicated: * indicates statistical significance less than 5%, but greater than 0.1%. ** indicates that the differences are not statistically significant. Because of missing data, numbers of subjects in each cell varied.

Table 2

Comparison of behavioural and educational outcomes in adopted children and non-separated controls (matched for sex, social class and number of sibs when index child aged 16)

| Variable | Proportion in: | | Significance of Chi-squared |
	Adopted children N = 81 to 127	Non-adopted controls N = 144 to 207	
	%	%	
Perinatal History			
Birth mother's 1st visit to antenatal clinic after 24th week of pregnancy	47.4	10.1	.001
1st visit after 36th week of pregnancy	8.6	1.1	
Mother's haemoglobin level below 70% during pregnancy	13.0	7.4	.052
Bleeding in pregnancy before term	5.7	5.1	.175
Other obstetric and/or pregnancy abnormality	26.0	17.3	
Foetal distress at birth	10.6	6.2	.09
Mother worked full-time after 33rd week of pregnancy	24.5	2.4	.001
Birthweight below 1st quartile for all children	39.5	21.2	.001
Medical Report on Child at Age 16			
Referred to psychologist/ psychiatrist	10.9	4.9	.272

Table 2 (continued)

| Variable | Proportion in: | | Significance of Chi-squared |
	Adopted children N = 81 to 127	Non-adopted controls N = 144 to 207	
	%	%	
Below 1st quartile in height (average for all children)	11.9	14.5	.642
Above 3rd quartile in height	29.3	27.5	
School Report when Child 16			
Attends private or independent school	14.2	10.5	.226
Well below average in mathematics	31.5	25.9	.059
Exceptional ability in mathematics	5.6	15.1	
Well below average in English	19.2	15.5	.082
Exceptional ability in English	12.0	20.8	
Child's handicap needs special schooling	3.2	1.1	.638
Child most suited for: Degree level education	8.9	17.6	.043
Diploma level	11.7	15.2	
No tertiary programme recommended	29.7	20.8	
School suggests child leave school at 16	37.9	31.5	.081
Resentful or angry when corrected	21.6	20.0	.845
Bullies others	10.6	6.2	.504

Table 2 (continued)

| Variable | Proportion in: | | Significance of Chi-squared |
	Adopted children N = 81 to 127	Non-adopted controls N = 144 to 207	
	%	%	
Teacher's Global Ratings of Behaviour (Rutter Scale Items) at 16			
Extremely impulsive	5.7	3.1	.321
Extremely moody	3.2	3.6	.943
Extremely aggressive	7.4	3.0	.137
Extremely withdrawn	1.6	1.0	.831
Extremely lazy	10.6	7.6	.749
Parent Descriptions of Child's Behaviour at 16			
Very restless	19.2	13.2	.129·
Squirmy, fidgety	19.2	11.6	.195
Often destroys things	2.0	1.0	.825
Frequently fights	9.7	9.5	.962
Not much liked by other children	3.9	1.6	.513
Often worried	45.2	39.5	.071
Often disobedient	21.1	15.8	.063
Can't settle for more than a few moments	20.2	20.3	.047
Fearful of new situations	25.0	23.0	.297
Often tells lies	21.2	10.4	.021
Bullies others	3.9	4.1	.866

Table 2 (continued)

Variable	Adopted children N = 81 to 127	Non-adopted controls N = 144 to 207	Significance of Chi-squared
	Proportion in:		
	%	%	
Saw specialist for behavioural problem in past year	7.8	3.1	.167
Delinquent acts recorded	10.3	6.5	.395
Truants from school	18.7	16.4	.731
Squirmy, fidgety	20.9	14.5	.141
Very quarrelsome	11.3	7.0	.268
Not much liked by others	23.5	14.7	.041
Worries about many things	36.3	33.0	.653
Rather solitary	27.2	26.2	.693
Irritable, touchy	23.3	17.0	.170
Twitches or mannerisms of face or body	3.2	2.5	.827
Frequently bites nails or fingers	11.7	11.5	.856
Often absent from school for trivial reasons	16.1	16.3	.925
Often disobedient	21.6	15.0	.111
Can't settle for more than a few moments	21.0	19.0	.663
Tends to be fearful in new situations	22.6	22.0	.947

Table 2 (continued)

| Variable | Proportion in: | | Significance of Chi-squared |
	Adopted children N = 81 to 127	Non-adopted controls N = 144 to 207	
	%	%	
Fussy or overparticular	7.5	9.5	.802
Often tells lies	19.2	12.7	.167
Has stolen things in past year	4.1	4.1	.989
Unresponsive, inert, apathetic	31.2	27.0	.560
Often complains of aches or pains	4.9	5.1	.805
Adolescent's Own Report at Age 16			
Wishes to attend college or university after leaving school	32.5	31.6	.905
Parents "very anxious" for me to do well in school	31.7	24.3	.053
"I get on very well with my mother"	76.6	88.1	.033
"I get on very well with my father"	78.3	79.7	.931
Very poor relationship with one or both parents	7.1	8.5	.631

Table 2 (continued)

Variable	Proportion in: Adopted children N = 81 to 127	Separated children N = 96 to 143	Significance of Chi-squared

Test Results at Age 16

Variable	%	%	
Reading comprehension:			
Below 1st quartile for whole group	13.1	15.4	.629
Above 3rd quartile for whole group	27.8	29.0	
Mathematics:			
Below 1st quartile for whole group	18.0	17.6	.515
Above 3rd quartile for whole group	27.0	31.6	

Note: Chi-squared calculations based on tables of various sizes, categorized according to the original parameters of data from the National Child Development survey, collected by the National Children's Bureau of London. The original data can be accessed by independent researchers, on application to the Survey Data Archive, University of Essex, Wivenhoe, Essex, U.K..

Table 3
Outcomes for adopted children at age 16: A model of positive and negative factors potentially influential on adjustment in the NCDS cohort, from conception through childhood to adolescence

---

Early Disadvantages

Poor prenatal care.　　Lower birthweight.

Higher incidence of physical and sensory disability, because of various perinatal hazards.

Initial bonding failure?

Early separation from biological mother.

Separation from foster mother for those adopted past infancy.

Problems of bonding to new mother figure.

Later Disadvantages

Genetic potential for behaviour problems?

Role handicaps of adoptive parents?

Adoptive parents overanxious, with overly high expectations?

Adoptive parents older, so higher proportion of parental deaths.

Adopted child's special identity problems in adolescence and young adulthood, with desire to seek out biological parents?

Long Term Advantages of Adoptive Parenting

Well-educated parents.

Parents usually economically stable.

Adopted child is an only child, or in a small family.

Private schooling for adopted child quite frequent.

Good housing conditions.　　Adoptive parents' low divorce rate.

Adoptive parents screened for good mental health and marital stability through home studies by social workers.

Adoptive parents more likely than other parents to seek help, treatment and guidance for their child.

Table 3 (continued)

Typical Outcomes for the NCDS Cohort of Adopted Child by Age 16

Mental health generally good; slight excess of anxiety and related disorders, and of overactive behaviour.

Mental health and behavioural outcomes dramatically better than children who were maternally separated early in life, but who were not adopted.

Little manifest evidence of serious identity crises.

Relationships with father good; some problems of relationship with mother?

Academic motivation high.

Achievement, generally as predicted by the advantaged socio-economic situation of the adopted children.

---

7 Mental health and adoption in a community survey of adults

While adoption is often the preferred child welfare solution for meeting the needs of a child who might otherwise grow up in an unstable or less than optimum environment, and while the traditional type of infant adoption can often meet the needs of couples who would otherwise be childless, the evidence reviewed and presented by Brodzinsky & Schecter (1990) makes it clear that being an adoptive parent is by means easy, and that adoptive parents may need strengths which are quite different from those involved in ordinary parenting.

Brodzinsky (1990) argues that:

> Even research with nonclinical, community-based samples suggests somewhat greater psychological vulnerability for adopted children as compared to non-adopted children..... Moreover, the increased vulnerability of adopted children generally does not emerge until the elementary school year. (p.3)

Brodzinsky argues further that sometimes adoptive parents may have difficulties facing the stress imposed by the problems of raising adopted children (which may reflect both early physical and psychological trauma of the child, and a negative heredity) problems which interact with the lingering psychological problems of childlessness and infertility of the parents, and the role problems which may be inherent in adoptive parenting, and being an adopted child.

Social work practice can assist the important institution of adoption by the careful selection of adoptive parents, and by continued support for adoptive families once the child has been placed. Such long-term support is likely to be highly cost-effective if it prevents the emergence of serious behaviour problems in the child, and the possibilities of disruption (Hoopes and Stein, 1982; McRoy, Grotevant and Zurcher, 1988).

The present study: Methods

The present study appears to be unique in that it identifies, through random sampling of an adult population (in the city of Calgary, Western Canada) two groups not hitherto sampled in this way - adoptive parents, with adopted children ranging in age from infancy to adulthood; and adults aged between 18 to 67 who were themselves adopted. The survey of 679 adults which yielded the two populations (23 adult adoptees, and 24 adoptive parents) was designed as a community mental health survey to estimate the prevalence of suicidal ideas and actions, and as part of long-term study of the mental health of women (Bagley & Ramsay, 1985 & 1986; Ramsay & Bagley, 1985).

The expectations or hypotheses for this study are:

(a)   adoptive parents, because of the fact that they have been carefully screened for good mental health, marital stability, and stability of economic circumstances, will have significantly better mental heath and marital stability than other members of the general population; and

(b)   adult adoptees, in contrast, will have somewhat poorer mental health and social adjustment than members of the general population.

The validity and reliability of the measures mental health and stress have been described in detail in previous publications (Ramsay & Bagley, 1986; Bagley & Ramsay, 1985 & 1986; Bagley & Young, 1990; Bagley, 1991). Beck's Hopelessness Scale is a well-established clinical measure (Beck et al. 1974). The Middlesex Hospital Questionnaire, developed in England (Crown & Crisp, 1981) has been factorially shortened for use in community mental health survey (Bagley, 1980) and

115

includes a number of diagnostic sub-scales. The suicide prediction scale of Cull & Gill (1982) is now well-established, and is the best psychometric predictor of suicidal ideas and behaviour in our community survey (Ramsay & Bagley, 1986). The self-esteem measure has been factorially derived from the Coopersmith SEI (Coopersmith, 1967), and the general factor of self-evaluation was developed as an adult self-esteem scale (Bagley, 1989). Poor self-esteem is conceptually important, since we have shown the individuals with a negative self-image are particularly vulnerable to stress, and the likelihood of developing a major depression (Ingham et al, 1986; Bagley & Young, 1990).

Results

A comparison of adopters and adoptees with the remaining respondents subjects (Table 1) indicates that their age and occupational levels are somewhat different from the remainder of the sample. The adopters are more likely to be middle-aged, middle class, and in stable marriages; the adoptees, while younger than the main sample, are more likely to be in professional roles or to be full-time students. These are advantages presumably bestowed both by the way in which adoptive parents are selected by social work systems, and the inputs which adoptive parents make in child rearing, and should in theory provide a basis for the development and maintenance of good mental health in both adopters and adoptees.

We decided however to see if the adoption process is associated with differential levels of mental health when relevant demographic factors are controlled for. This was achieved by selecting from the main sample two controls for each adopter and adoptee, exactly matched for sex, age (birth in the same or an adjacent year), and occupational level. Where more than two controls were available, a random selection process was used.

Table 2 and 3 present a comparison of the two groups, adoptees and adopters, with the control subjects. The proportions of the contrasted groups with scores on three categories for each variable ("low" scores in the lowest quartile for the whole sample of 679 subjects; "medium" scores in the range of the middle 50 percent of scores for the whole series; and "high" scores in the highest quartile for the whole group) are presented.

The most striking of the results in Table 2 is the non-linear relationship between mental health scores in the comparisons of the adoptees and their controls. Chi-squared analysis does establish some

116

significant variations of being adopted across the mental health categories. But the excess of cases amongst the adoptees occurs by and large in the <u>middle</u> range of scores, and not in the highest range indicating poorer adjustment. Thus the adoptees have fewer individuals with very good mental health than the controls; but they also have somewhat fewer individuals with very poor mental health.

In contrast, the adopters (Table 3) - who are not of course, the parents of the adopted children in Table 2 - show significantly better mental health than controls on a number of the measures.

Conclusions

This research indicates that adopters, as we would expect, have rather better adjustment than individuals in the community of similar age, sex and social class. This is almost certainly a reflection of the manner in which adoptive parents are selected by social work agencies. The adoptees do <u>not</u> show an excess of individuals with poor mental health, despite some gloomy accounts of difficulties in adoption which have emerged from some clinical researchers (e.g. Brinich, 1990). The adoptees in this random sample do however show an excess of individuals with mild mental health problems, a finding which may be compatible with some of the clinical studies reviewed by Brodzinsky and Schecter (1990). All of the adoptees in this survey are white, were adopted by white parents before their second birthday, and had no physical or mental disability as children. While we can make no generalizations from these data for children with special needs, transracial adoptions, or adoptions of older children, we can conclude that for the large majority of the adoptees in the present survey, adoption as an institution seems to have worked well in laying the foundations of life-long adaptation.

Table 1
Comparison of 23 adoptive parents, 24 adults adoptees and 632 remaining adults in a community mental health sample

Variable		Adopters	Adoptees	Remaining community sample	Chi-squared
Age:	18-29	8.7%	33.3%	23.1%	1166.3 (8,679)
	30-39	43.5%	29.2%	33.9%	p < .001
	40-49	21.7%	20.8%	16.6%	
	50-59	17.4%	16.7%	15.0%	
	60 +	8.7%	0.0%	11.4%	
Marital Status					
Single		0.0%	37.5%	12.5%	1043.2 (8,679)
Separated/div.		4.3%	8.3%	7.1%	p < .001
Widowed		8.7%	0.0%	5.1%	
Married		87.0%	45.8%	70.2%	
Single with partner		0.0%	8.3%	5.1%	
Sex					
Male		43.5%	41.7%	40.8%	2.9 (1,679)
Female		56.5%	58.3%	59.2%	n.s.
Occupation					
Unskilled		0.0%	0.0%	1.1%	675.2 (6,679)
Semi-skilled/skilled		30.4%	37.5%	54.4%	p < .001
Professional		60.9%	33.3%	30.8%	
Homemaker/student		8.7%	29.2%	13.6%	

Table 2
Mental health in 23 adult adoptees and 46 non-adoptees in a community mental health sample

Variable	Low Category		Medium Category		High Category		Eta	Significance of Chi-squared
	Adopted	Non-Adopted	Adopted	Non-Adopted	Adopted	Non-Adopted		
Beck's Hopelessness Scale (prediction of suicide potential)	8.7%	17.4%	73.3%	64.8%	18.0%	17.8%	.13	.207
General psycho-neurosis (Total MHQ Score)	4.3%	9.6%	91.4%	77.4%	4.3%	13.0%	.08	.437
Depression (MHQ)	8.7%	22.6%	74.0%	51.8%	17.3%	25.6%	.15	.035
Phobia (MHQ)	26.1%	17.7%	48.0%	57.0%	25.9%	25.3%	.13	.252
Somatic anxiety (MHQ)	26.1%	16.8%	69.6%	63.0%	4.3%	20.2%	.14	.043
Free-floating anxiety (MHQ)	21.7%	16.9%	65.3%	63.7%	13.0%	19.4%	.17	.054
Obsessionality (MHQ)	13.0%	22.6%	69.7%	51.4%	17.3%	26.0%	.17	.021
Complaining, anxious and aggressive personality (Cull and Gill's Suicide Prediction Scale)	13.0%	21.8%	74.0%	52.6%	13.0%	25.6%	.30	.013
Self-Concept (Coopersmith Adult Scale)	26.1%	29.1%	60.9%	45.7%	13.0%	25.2%	.09	.217
Suicidal Ideas and Actions	39.1%	50.0%	34.9%	24.9%	26.0%	25.1%	.06	.475

Note: "Low" and "High" categories based on division of scores into lowest and highest quartiles for normative groups as closely as possible. Eta is a measure of non-linear association across nominal categories, and is based on analysis of variance. When relations are perfectly linear, values of Eta and Pearson's r coincide. For explanations of these statistical techniques see Nie et al's (1975) explanation of the SPSS programs, which were the basis for all of the above calculations.

119

Table 3
Mental health in 24 adult adopters and 48 non-adopters in a community mental health sample

Variable	Low Category		Medium Category		High Category		Eta	Significance of Chi-squared
	Adopted	Non-Adopted	Adopted	Non-Adopted	Adopted	Non-Adopted		
Beck's Hopelessness Scale (prediction of suicide potential)	12.5%	17.3%	75.0%	64.8%	12.5%	17.8%	.15	.056
General psychoneurosis (Total MHQ Score)	37.5%	9.2%	62.5%	77.0%	0.0%	13.8%	.07	.302
Depression (MHQ)	50.0%	22.6%	41.7%	52.1%	8.3%	25.3%	.12	.218
Phobia (MHQ)	37.5%	17.7%	54.2%	57.0%	8.3%	25.3%	.09	.503
Somatic anxiety (MHQ)	37.5%	16.8%	62.5%	63.0%	0.0%	20.2%	.15	.041
Free-floating anxiety (MHQ)	48.0%	28.6%	52.0%	52.0%	0.0%	19.4%	.14	.049
Obessionality (MHQ)	50.0%	22.6%	50.0%	51.4%	0.0%	26.0%	.13	.053
Complaining, anxious and aggressive personality (Cull and Gill's Prediction Scale)	25.0%	21.8%	62.5%	52.6%	12.5%	25.6%	.11	.372
Self-Concept (Coopersmith Adult Scale)	50.0%	29.1%	25.0%	45.7%	25.0%	25.2%	.04	.495
Suicidal Ideas and Actions	62.5%	50.0%	16.7%	24.9%	20.8%	25.1%	.07	.353

Note: "Low" and "High" categories based on divisions of scores into lowest and highest quartiles for normative groups as closely as possible. Eta is a measure of non-linear association across nominal categories, and is based on analysis of variance. When relations are perfectly linear, values of Eta and Pearson's r coincide. For explanations of these statistical techniques see Nie et al's (1975) explanation of the SPSS programs, which were the basis for all of the above calculations.

8   Social work practice and the adoption of special needs children: A Canadian case study

Introduction

The horizons of adoption practice are changing. The practice of placing infants who are biologically similar to their adoptive parents is rapidly disappearing in North America and Europe, since very few infants are now "surrendered" for adoption. Parallel to this trend, the practice of adoption of special needs children has expanded.

In Alberta, Western Canada, the program of special needs adoption has been termed the "Wednesday's Child" program. Wednesday's child may be full of woe, but the program is so named because it is associated with television advertisements broadcast each Wednesday by CKUA, a commercial station broadcasting in Calgary and Edmonton. The presenter in Calgary is the host of well-known women's health series, and she is featured with special needs children in a park or in the zoo.

A special needs child in this social work definition is one who if an infant, has some special medical need (e.g. arising from congenital malformation, a chronic medical condition, a disability, or a condition such as fetal alcohol syndrome). Past infancy, the special needs child will have little or no contact with a biological parent, and will be in a sibling group, or have specific behavioural or medical needs, will perhaps belong to a minority ethnic group, or will simply be older (of school age) with some family disruption in his or her background, but no overt behavioural or emotional problems.

Research undertaken by Alberta Family and Social Services has shown that the successful adoption of one special needs child by age 7 can, at 1990 costs, save the public purse around $150,000, assuming that the child stays with the adoptive parents until age 18, and makes no special demands on social service agencies. Clearly, adoptive parents represent the ultimate in volunteerism, saving the welfare state over a million dollars for every ten special needs children successfully placed.

In Alberta the special needs adoption program began in 1981. In that year 76 children in the special needs category were placed; in the same year, 620 ordinary or traditional infant adoptions were finalized. In 1985 240 special needs adoptions were completed, and 264 ordinary adoptions. In 1990 the number of special need adoptions had risen to 674, and the number of ordinary adoptions had fallen to 53.

By 1991 the adoption department of Alberta Family and Social Services had ceased to make any placements in the traditional, infant category, leaving this role instead to a number of newly licensed private adoption agencies. These agencies usually practice a form of "open" adoption, allowing the biological parent to meet the prospective adopters, with freedom to choose which adopters she would like to parent her child, and request some form of limited contact (usually an annual photograph, and a report of the child's progress). The Child Welfare Act has been amended to facilitate this process, and the institution of adoption has changed radically in Alberta as a result. It will be much easier for both child and biological parent to make contact later on, if either of them should wish this to happen.

A study of special needs adoption

In this chapter we report a survey of 342 special needs children placed with adoptive parents in Alberta by 1985. All adoptive parents with whom a "special needs" child was placed between 1981 and 1984 were sent a postal questionnaire, and over two thirds of those who could be located, returned the questionnaire. Table 1 indicates that less than a half of these children were of full European origin. A quarter were Metis (a traditional mixed group, descendants of unions of early French settlers and Amerindian people), while another quarter were of traditional aboriginal or "Indian" descent. "Non-status" with reference to someone described as an "Indian" means that the child's family did not have status under the Indian Act, and came from a group which had never signed a land treaty with the British colonial government. The Alberta Child

Welfare Act makes special provision for respecting the cultural rights and identities of "Treaty Indians", but not for other groups. It is an unanswered question as to why so many children with ethnic minority status had lost contact with their biological families, and seemed to be suitable for adoption placement, usually with white families with no knowledge of or interest in the child's aboriginal heritage.

Table 2 lists the characteristics of the adopted children. Only five of them were in fact infants with special medical needs, while 105 were aged less than five. One hundred and twenty five of the children (36.5%) were aged between seven and nine years at the time of their placement.

Table 1
Ethnic background of special needs children placed for adoption

Ethnic Background	Number	Percent
Caucasian	152	44 %
Metis (Mixed)	86	25 %
Indian (Status)	64	19 %
Indian (Non-Status)	16	5 %
Black	1	0.2%
Oriental	2	0.6%
Other	21	6 %

Table 2
Characteristics of 342 special needs children placed for adoption

Special Need	Number
Age 2 to 8	176
Sibling group	85
Developmentally Delayed	74

Table 2 (Cont'd)

Premature/Small for Dates/Difficult Delivery	67
Medical Problems (heart, lungs, kidneys)	64
Multiple Foster Home Placements	57
Behavioural Problems	55
Age 9 and over	55
Speech Problems	51
Emotional Problems	48
Learning Disabilities	35
Fetal Alcohol Syndrome	33
Physical Abuse	28
Born to parents with problematic backgrounds (psychiatric problem, mental disabilities, drugs, alcohol)	25
Sexual Abuse	17
Physical Abnormalities (eg club foot, cleft palate)	17
Blind/Visually impaired	15
Deaf/Hearing Impaired	10
Cerebral Palsy	9
Down's Syndrome	6
Mentally Handicapped	5
Muscular Dystrophy	1

Note: Many Children fall into more than one category.

Table 3
Characteristics of adoptive mothers

Ethnic Background	Number	Per cent	Total Number* of Responses
Caucasian	294	95.1%	309
Metis (Mixed)	6	1.9%	
Indian (Status)	4	1.3%	
Oriental	2	0.6%	
Black	1	0.3%	
Other	2	0.6%	

Table 3 (Cont'd)

Educational Background	Number	Per cent	Total Number* of Responses
Less than grade 8	2	0.7%	294
9 to 12	105	36 %	
University	101	34 %	
Other Post Secondary	86	29 %	

Occupation	Number	Per cent	Total Number* of Responses
Homemaker	187	67%	280
Semi-Skilled	4	1%	
Skilled	4	1%	
Technical	6	2%	
Managerial	9	3%	
Professional	70	25%	

Age	Number	Per cent	Total Number* of Responses
20 to 29	70	24%	295
30 to 39	186	63%	
41 to 49	39	13%	

* Number of mothers is less than the number of children in the survey because a number of sibling groups were placed.
Variable Ns also reflect variations in response to some questions.

Table 4
Information given to adoptive parents about child's background

	Yes	per cent	No	Per cent	Number of Responses
Birth History	229	72%	87	27%	316
Record of Immunizations	185	62%	114	38%	299
Illness to Which Child is Susceptible	38	45%	166	55%	304
Developmental Milestones	116	40%	177	60%	293
Intelligence Assessments	97	33%	201	67%	298
Developmental Assessments	107	36%	188	64%	295
Speech Assessments	59	21%	220	79%	279
Account of Special Needs	148	51%	142	49%	290
Reason for Apprehension	269	85%	46	15%	315
Length of Stay in Foster Care	246	82%	54	18%	300*
Adjustment to Foster Care	202	70%	86	30%	288
Reasons for Changing Foster Homes	135	57%	101	43%	236

* The total number of responses varies as respondents did not answer every question.

Lack of information on early history

A surprising outcome of this survey was the sometimes haphazard nature of information given to the adopting parents. In theory it is essential to give the new parents the maximum amount of information about the child's medical, social and psychological background, but it is clear from the responses of the adoptive parents to the questionnaire that there were huge gaps in the information given. Sixty per cent of parents received no information on child's developmental milestones, and 49 per cent received no clear assessment of what the child's special needs actually were! In fact, there was no standard protocol for informing parents about the child's background and needs, and apparently no professional standard of social work practice for doing so.

The following comments from adoptive parents illustrate the frustrations which this lack of information caused the adoptive parents.

a)   "Child's birth history, record of immunizations, illness to which child was susceptible, record of developmental milestone? - none were available even though she was a ward of the crown from birth!!! I would have loved to have them. None were kept and we are sorry no one cared enough to do their best for her!" (The adopted child was a 5 year old caucasian girl with severe behavioural and emotional problems and a history of multiple foster home placements).

b)   "We should be given all health records on the child in case of emergency. We are only given facts they thought were necessary. Too much history on special needs children is kept confidential. We need more for the child's sake. We have learned so much more about our child since we have signed the final papers and now we have a better understanding about his problems and can help him more." (The adopted child was a one year old caucasian boy. The boy's biological mother had German Measles during pregnancy and the boy was born deaf, blind and mentally retarded).

c)   "We were led to believe that our daughter had a strictly physical handicap. We were shocked to learn after the placement was completed that she also had emotional and behavioural problems and would always require special education classes." (The adopted child was an 8 year old Metis girl with a kidney condition. She also had emotional and behavioural problems and was

127

developmentally delayed).

d)　　"We still feel badly that we received as little information as we did. When the child grows and starts to question his background prior to adoption we can't tell him anything - not even his ethnic origin. This is a great void in his life. Put yourself in his position." (The adopted child was an 8 year old boy whose ethnic background is unknown. He had learning disabilities).

e)　　"Our children are particularly disappointed to have no baby pictures or any records of the years before their adoption. With the emphasis on finding your "roots" at school recently, this becomes even more difficult for adoptive children." (The adopted children were a brother age 6 and a sister age 7 of Metis background. The were developmentally delayed, physically abused and had multiple foster home placements).

f)　　"We came to feel that there was a cover-up on the part of the agency so that this child would be taken off public assistance! Not to say that we wouldn't have taken him, but it would have made life easier if we had the information which we required. e.g. In the first two months after placement, he had 12 falls when he walked across a bare floor! After the adoption was finalized and we were in the children's hospital and the doctor gave us reams of information that your agency had not made available to us." (The adopted child was a 5 year old boy with Treaty Indian Status. He had Fetal Alcohol Syndrome, behavioural, speech, and learning difficulties, and was hearing impaired. As well, he had been born prematurely and was diagnosed as "failure to thrive").

g)　　"Much of the information was not in the child's file. Much of the information in the files is either incomplete or inaccurate." (The adopted child was a 13 year old girl of Metis background. She had behavioural problems and difficulties with speech. She had been "institutionalized" and had been physically and possibly sexually abused).

Lack of permanency planning

Many of the adoptive parents were rather scathing about what they correctly perceived as the inconsistencies, lack of standards and professional practice in social work, which had delayed decisions about permanency planning and had in some cases allowed children to drift through a series of foster homes. Such drift of course, makes the successful adoption of special needs children more difficult and can be a cruel denial of child's need for emotional stability in a permanent family. Fifty five per cent of the adoptive parents surveyed were critical of social work practice which had resulted in unnecessary delay in the permanent placement of their child.

The following comments were made by adoptive parents on the basis of their understanding of the child's needs, and his or her previous experiences:

a) "Don't keep these children bouncing around the system so long. Each day is very important, and very harmful to the child. As soon as they are made permanent wards they should be out to their new home - not 6 months to 2 years later." (The adopted children were two brothers, age 7 and 8 of Metis background. They had behavioural problems, speech difficulties, learning disabilities, were developmentally delayed and had multiple foster home placements).

b) "I think more effort is needed in searching adoptive homes for these kids. They are too easily lost in the present system. There are children placed in foster homes and no real effort is being made to find an adoptive home where they would feel the love and permanence that comes with being part of the family; really not just sort of. We know some foster kids that are not even sure what their name is! These kids are available for adoption, but there is no effort being made." (The adopted children were a boy age 1 and girl age 4. They were not siblings but both had Treaty Indian status. One child was visually impaired and had a club foot. The other one was developmentally delayed).

c) "If there are lots of special needs children 'out there' just waiting for placement - let the adoptive "waiting parents" know. Pictures and information on the children could be circulated to social services offices. We were under the impression that there were just are no children available!" (The adopted children were two brothers age 5 and 6 of Indian (non-status) background. The were developmentally delayed and had behavioural problems and speech difficulties).

d) "One thing we feel very strongly about is how long the children are kept in foster homes before they are finally adopted. I am sure that in most cases the social workers know right from the start if the parents are going to change their ways or if the child is eventually going to have to be taken away. In our case, our boy was in a foster home for 2 years not more than 8 miles from us. We sure would have enjoyed having him sooner and he would not have had such a hard time separating from the foster family." (The adopted child was an 8 year old boy of Metis background. He had learning disabilities and had been physically abused).

e) "More advertising is needed so more people will adopt these wonderful children." (The adopted children were two brothers age 5 to 6 of Treaty Indian status. They had behavioural problem and learning disabilities).

f) "When mother is deceased when child is 3 months of age, it shouldn't take 2 years to become available for adoption." (The adopted child was a 2 year old boy with Treaty Indian status. He was developmentally delayed).

g) "As in all government organizations too much time was spent. We wanted the child so let us get on with the job. Child suffered many stomach aches because he was worried whether or not he would be adopted." (The adopted child was a 6 year old boy of Metis background. He was developmentally delayed).

h) "I felt our child was not placed soon enough. We saw him on television and it took six months before he was place with us. This is too long. Precious months were lost for him and for us. These months cannot be regained." (The adopted child was a 1 year old boy of caucasian background. He was deaf, developmentally delayed, and had many allergies).

Placement practice

The adoptive parents made a number of perceptive criticisms of the social work practice involved in placing the child with them. One puzzling feature of practice was the great variation in the number of pre-placement visits made by social worker: a quarter of potential adopters had only one visit from a social worker, who often seemed anxious to finalize the adoption process without either preparing the adopters adequately, or informing them about the child's backgrounds. Only 26 per cent of the adopters had what seemed to be adequate preparation and information, including five or more visits from a social worker who was able to do full assessment of both the strengths of the potential parents, and the needs of the child being placed for adoption.

Among the many comments made by the adoptive parents on this haphazard selection and placement practice were the following:

a)   "We felt very unprepared when we went on the visits. We were just told to go. Our worker gave us no tips, advice, etc. The child's worker was of no help at all. As a result we got to know the foster parents quite well. After the visit we were told that this was not a good idea. A bit of planning ahead would have avoided this." (The adopted child was a two year old Inuit girl. She was deaf).

b)   "In our case they flew a social worker down from Edmonton twice. The child had social workers coming out of his ears. Social worker from Edmonton, one from Calgary and our social worker. This made him quite nervous. I wanted one social worker at a time." (The adopted child was a 13 year old boy of Metis background. He had behavioural problems, learning disabilities and was visually impaired).

c)   "The quality of a worker is so important. Our first worker was excellent. After worker changed we had virtually no contact with our new worker and it's very frustrating when you are unsure what's going on." (The adopted child was a 9 year old boy with Treaty Indian status. He had behavioural problems).

d)   "We never knew which worker to call - ours or the child's." (The adopted child was a 6 year old girl of Metis background. She had Fetal Alcohol Syndrome, development delays and learning disabilities).

e)   "We had to deal with three different social workers which only added to the confusion. One did the homestudy, another the placement and another, the post placement services." (The adopted child was a 4 year old girl of Metis background. She had developmental delays and speech difficulties).

f)   "When the social worker called she told us that the cleft lip was in her words, "gross". In fact our daughter was not gross! Education of social workers on the type of defect the child has should be mandatory and they should never tell the prospective parents that the child looks "gross" or any other negative comments. Let the prospective parents decide for themselves. Also the social worker should be versed in what can be done for the child in terms of therapy, surgery, etc. and advise parents immediately before the child is seen." (The adopted child was a two month old girl of Caucasian background. She had a cleft lip and cleft palate).

g)   "Our worker was not familiar at all with the child or his past. I feel that workers should be familiar with each charge (as much as possible)." (The adopted child was a 7 year old boy of Metis background. He was deaf and had developmental delays).

h)   "More visits were possible for us but were made difficult. Someone thought the child did not understand enough to come to our home for visit. Visits were arranged and cancelled for foster family and social worker's reasons and conveniences. We wanted the children to visit each weekend for one month, but his couldn't be arranged." (The adopted child was a 4 year old boy with Treaty Indian status, and a developmental handicap).

Satisfaction with the adoption experience

Although a number of parents expressed significant concerns about the adoption process, the majority of them (83%) were satisfied with their adoption experience as is indicated below.

Table 5 Parental satisfaction with adoption

Level of Satisfaction	Number	Per cent	Number of Responses
Very Satisfied	191	63%	304
Somewhat Satisfied	60	20%	
Unsatisfied	28	9%	
Very Unsatisfied	25	8%	

Sixty three percent of parents said that they would be willing adopt another child with special needs. A third of parents did not wish to adopt again and 4% were not sure.

One satisfied adopter wrote:

"We are doing great. He is the best thing that has happened to us. He makes us laugh and he is very smart. We may be a little prejudiced but we feel he is the best little boy ever and we keep getting reminded by our families how lucky we were to get him. No word can say or show how much we love him. Our sincere thanks for him. For making our dream come true." (The adopted child was 2 year old boy of Caucasian background. He was born prematurely, suffered from asphyxia at birth, had visual problems and was developmentally delayed).

What is striking about this survey is the good will, maturity, integrity and commitment of the adoptive parents in the face of the often awkward, inept and sometimes incompetent practice by social workers. The parents were critical of social work practice, but in perceptive and constructive ways and the large majority were clearly enjoying the challenge of caring for their special child.

Conclusion

If the adoption of a special needs child is successful, it will make a remarkable contribution to the lives of a young person who might otherwise grow up in unstable and relatively uncaring circumstances, with many negative outcomes possible. A stable, loving home can overcome the potential for negative development in the lives of such children.

Two dilemmas of this adoptive parenting are yet unresolved. The first relates to the child's ethnic identity. It has been traditional practice in Alberta to move aboriginal children from their extended kin for trivial and often imperialistic reasons (a practice which seems to be ending now, with new understanding of the importance of biological family and cultural integrity in continuity of child care). Nevertheless, the physically and developmentally delayed children from ethnic minority groups (children whose condition often resulted from maternal alcoholism during pregnancy) are in our experience the most marginal in terms of acceptability to stressed minority groups, who will fight to retain, or regain, non-handicapped children. But social and community development in aboriginal communities has not reached a level at which these developmentally and physically disabled children can be coped with. The adoptive parents are willing to care for these children: but what emphasis should they place on the child's ethnic identity and roots? This is a dilemma for which professional counselling can offer no definitive answer.

We do no know however from our survey of adopted adolescents of aboriginal background (reported in another chapter of this book) that many of these young men and women do have acute identity problems. But the children in that survey were not disabled in any way, and could well have been placed with their kindred - and in the changing social work practice of today, would be unlikely to fall into the special needs category.

The second dilemma for parents of special needs children is the degree to which they should seek, and accept, continued specialist help in meeting the child's development needs. There is a great temptation in adoptive parenting to revert to the "exclusive" role, treating the child as if he or she were one's own biological child (Kirk, 1964). Yet there are problems in this withdrawal from contact with social services, for if things go wrong, if significant problems occur in say, adolescence, the parents may be isolated, blame themselves or the child, and be unwilling or unable to seek professional help.

For their part, social workers who are subject to many pressures of work load, are often glad to close a file and forget about the adoptive parent with whom they have placed the child. Yet, if special needs adoption is to be both successful and cost effective, regular and systematic follow-up and support for the adoptive parents is crucial. At the present time special follow-up and support services are organized on a haphazard basis, this role being given to voluntary agencies in the large cities.

There is clearly a need for systematic research here. We need more long-term follow-up surveys to find out just how successful these adoptions have been, what stresses they face, and what support services are necessary. Given the profound needs of many of these special needs children, even if only half of the placements were fully successful we would still conclude that the program had some remarkable successes, and it would certainly have been cost effective in dollar terms. The question of dollars is a crucial one, for it seems likely that dollars spent on counselling and support services for special needs adoption could be highly cost-effective in the long-term. Unfortunately, social services bureaucracies do not traditionally account in the long-term; nor do they usually account in terms of successful outcomes for human beings.

9 Inter-country adoption: History and policy formation

Introduction

Since 1945 at least half a million children have been adopted across cultural boundaries, into families of profoundly different cultures, and often of different ethnic or racial characteristics. But adoption across national and cultural boundaries is certainly older than the disruption of peoples and families which followed the second world war; it is as old as adoption itself, which is a very ancient institution.[1] There is perhaps an analogue of modern inter-country adoption, in which children from the poorer countries of the Third World are adopted by families in the more prosperous Western countries, in the traditional practice in East Africa in which "taboo children" (born of too-close relatives, or one child of triplets) were abandoned by the Luo close to Nandi settlements. The Nandi people were known to be especially generous in taking in abandoned children.[2]

The Second World War undoubtedly increased some forms of international co-operation, and ultimately produced a much greater degree of inter-cultural relationships, and perhaps understanding, than had existed before. But this war also resulted in large numbers of children being orphaned or irrevocably separated from their parents. In addition too the victorious troops of America created many illegitimate children in the countries which they occupied. From 1945 separated, orphaned or abandoned children from Greece, the Middle East, Italy, France, Germany, Korea, Philippines, Hong Kong and Thailand were adopted in North America. Since 1960 growing numbers of children from various countries in the Far East, the Middle East, North Africa, and Central and Southern America have been adopted by parents in North America and Western Europe.

Such adoptions are controversial. They may create profound problems in international law;[3] they may run the risk of creating problems of adjustment in children who have to adapt to a new culture and a new language;[4] they may create problems of identity in adolescent children who are of a different ethnic group from their adoptive parents;[5] it has been claimed that the continued practice of inter-country adoption retards the growth of child welfare services in the sending countries;[6] and even encourages parents to abandon their children in the expectation that they will be adopted in the West.[7]

The most bitter critics of inter-country adoption allege that wealthy adopters from the West come to the poor countries of the Third World in the wake of war, earthquake or famine, and take many healthy children, leaving behind older or handicapped children to remain in institutional care.[8]

These claims are vigorously contested by advocates and practitioners of inter-country adoption, who point out that such adoption is often a by-product of in-country child welfare programmes, and is confined to children (many of whom are in fact handicapped) who would die of malnutrition or lack of medical care, or who would suffer severe deprivation in orphanages in Third World countries.[9]

In an earlier argument on the problems currounding inter-country adoption [10], we asked: "Are the deprivations experienced by children in institutional care in the Third World of so profound a nature that inter-country is justified - or does the concept of deprivation formulated by observers from developed countries involve some ethnocentric assumptions? To what extent do children moved from one country to another for the purpose of adoption experience certain trauma, reversible or otherwise, as a result?

"To what extent do children from developing countries, adopted by parents in developed countries, experience psychological or social difficulties because of their particular ethnic and cultural heritage? To what extent do the adoptive parents unwittingly alienate the children of inter-country adoptions from their cultural heritage? How successful, in overall terms, are these inter-country adoptions, in comparison with other kinds of adoption, including within-country transracial adoptions?"

The further problems which we will discuss in this chapter concern the legal, social and administrative practices which are necessary to safeguard the interests of the various parties - natural parents, the child, and the adoptive parents; and finally, we will address the difficult and important policy question: what should British and Canadian policy be, at both the national level (in terms of appropriate social and legal measures for admission of inter-country adopted children) and at the level of local authority social work practice?

In Britain the various policy dilemmas over inter-country adoption have meant that many organisations who might be involved in this practice prefer to remain " on the fence". International Social Service of Britain, once actively involved in inter-country adoption, is now only involved in cases after they have provided difficulties for other agencies; and as late as the 1980s the British Association of Social Workers had not been able to issue clear guidance to its members on appropriate practice, despite much interest and concern about the practice voiced in various professional meetings.

The Association of British Adoption and Fostering Agencies has been more explicit in its opposition to inter-country adoption, while a number of voluntary associations in Britain, such as Parent-to-Parent Information on Adoption Service, the Homeless Children's Aid and Adoption Society, have expressed vocal and practical support for inter-country adoption.

There are two types of inter-country adoption (abbreviated as ICA). One involves the adoption by migrants to a country of a child, usually a relative, from their home country; the other involves the adoption of a child in a Third World country by parents from the West, who are unrelated to that child. It is this second type of ICA which is the source of controversy, and leads to reservations by some British agencies. It should be stressed that this British reluctance stands in contrast to practice in America, Canada, and in many European countries.

We have approached the policy problems surrounding inter-country adoption in three ways. First, we have examined a great deal of documentation including published studies, unpublished material held by various international organizations, and unpublished thesis material, mainly from the United States. Secondly, we have also interviewed officials concerned with policy and practice in statutory and voluntary agencies concerned with inter-country adoption, in Britain, India, Hong Kong, Canada, U.S.A., Switzerland, and the Netherlands. Finally, we are engaged in a continuing study which involves interviewing families in Britain with adopted children from Vietnam and Hong Kong. Such empirical data on the adjustment of inter-country adopted children in adolescence and beyond, is crucial in deciding whether such adoption is in general terms, in the best interests of the children involved.

Fundamental principles in inter-country adoption: The Leysin seminar of 1960

In 1960 some 80 experts on child welfare from sixteen European countries, the United Nations, International Social Service, and the International Union for Child Welfare held a meeting at Leysin in Switzerland, convened and financed by the U.N., to consider the problems posed by the growing number of inter-country adoptions, and the possible legal, social and economic solutions. For reasons which are not clear, no representatives from Third World countries (from whom most inter-country adopted children come) were invited to, or attended the conference.

The Leysin conference is important, because its lengthy report[11] is frequently referred to as an authoritative statement on practice in inter-country adoption. The U.N. document is, without doubt a lucid and magisterial statement of the problem. It also seems true that the excellent principles which emerged from the Leysin conference have been widely ignored in practice. For these and other reasons we are summarizing this conference report in the following pages.

The conference took as its starting point a number of principles for ICA set forth by International Social Service in 1956. The principles grew out of the day-to-day service of International Social Service (ISS) in casework with children and families involved in ICA. A group of experts met in 1957 under U.N. auspices, and confirmed the essential validity of these principles. The twelve principles were discussed and slightly modified by the Leysin seminar, and were commended as guides to practice. These principles are:

Principle 1: "That adoption is the best substitute for care by the child's own parents or close relatives, provided that adoption is based fundamentally on the welfare of the child".

The principles that the overriding consideration in decisions about adoption and child custody should be the child's welfare, or the child's best interest, is a feature of many European legal systems, including that of Britain.[12] Members of the seminar cited numerous cases known to them in which inter-country adoptions had not been based fundamentally on the welfare of the child. For example, couples are sometimes allowed to adopt Third World children to fulfil their own needs - to bolster a failing marriage, or to try and improve the emotional state or morale of an adult. Indeed the lack of general control, or indeed the policy of some agencies, may allow children from the Third World to be adopted in the

West on less stringent criteria than would be applied to in-country adoptions. Another type of case cited concerned children in materially poor circumstances but part of a stable family group, being given to adoptive parents from the West in order to have various kinds of material advantages.

The seminar suggested that more stringent procedures should be applied in the countries of the potential adopters, to make sure that unsuitable couples do not adopt.

Principle 2 "That sufficient consideration should be given to possible alternative plans for the child within his own country before inter-country adoption is decided upon, since there are various hazards inherent in transplanting a child from one culture to another."

What is implied here is that each child should be considered on a case-by-case basis, and a plan formulated which is in the child's best interest. Only exceptionally should older children, children who are part of an economically deprived family group, and children who have been institutionalized for long periods be adopted overseas, since it was felt that such children might have considerable problems of adjustment in a new culture.

Principle 3: "That increased efforts should be made in each country to examine at as early a stage as possible whether certain children should be adopted within the country, rather than remaining indefinitely in institutions because of rather slight family ties; that careful examination should be made of the values to the child of any ties which act as an obstacle to adoption".

It was observed that, "In almost every country, even those where the number of persons seeking to adopt far exceeds the number of children available for adoption, it is a common phenomenon to see institutions filled with children".

Principle 4: "That efforts should be made in each country to find adoptive homes, within the country, for children with certain mental or physical defects, and for children whose family background presents an obstacle to adoption".

The Seminar makes it clear however that many children from such backgrounds have also been successfully adopted overseas. Indeed in developing countries where resources are often diverted to healthy children who can benefit the country economically, Western countries may have a particularly valuable role to play in providing adoptive homes for handicapped children who would not otherwise be adopted, but would have to spend their lives in institutions. The Seminar also stressed that positive action should be taken to place children with adoptive families (preferably in their own country, but overseas if this is not possible) when lack of contact with a natural parent has left them "in limbo". Similar policy proposals have been made for children in institutional care in Britain and in the United States[13].

Principle 5: "That extremely careful consideration should be given to all possible alternatives before a child is removed from his own relatives for adoption; that a parent, regardless of social and legal status, should have the opportunity for full consideration of what is involved, including legal and psychological consequences, before a decision is made that adoption is the best plan for the child; that concepts of modern child and family welfare should prevail over economic and social factors".

The Seminar noted frequent violation of this principle in inter-country adoption, as in the following case: a child was allowed to go to another country without his parents understanding that giving consent to the adoption, which they assumed would ensure the child's education and material welfare, meant a permanent break with their child. But they still wanted to keep in touch with the child, and made efforts through several channels to do this. the adoptive parents were deeply troubled by these continued efforts, and the child was torn in his sense of belonging between two sets of parents.

The above principle, like Principle 2 concerning alternative plans within the child's own country is frequently violated to some extent, but especially so in periods of great stress and times of emergency, when the importance of individuals is apt to be lost sight of. The Seminar recommended that special care should be taken in times of national disasters to prevent hasty placement of children outside their countries. Too often external agencies, or foreign adopters themselves, seize on the fact of poverty in developing countries and the desire of parents to ensure the material and educational well-being of their children. The recent situation in Romania is a case in point. Natural parents may be pressured in such circumstances to signing documents which they do not understand, not realising that they may be relinquishing contact with their child for ever. In such circumstances foreign agencies should provide material assistance for the families, rather than removing a child to adopters in another country. It was pointed out too that in many countries the term "adoption" does not imply the irrevocable cutting of ties with one's original family. In many cultures, adoption of male children is common by couples who themselves have no male heirs; this ensures that property is passed through a patrilineal inheritance.[14] The adopted child usually comes from the same clan as the adopter, and the natural parents still keep contact with the child, and benefit materially from the arrangement. Clearly, natural parents were thinking of this cultural form of adoption in giving consent in the case cited above.

Principle 6: "That those who have ties, legal or emotional, to the child should be helped to understand thoroughly the meaning of adoption in the culture of the new country; that the child, if old enough, should also be prepared for the implications of adoption and life in the new country; that unless this can be done and the consequences accepted by all concerned, the child should not be considered for inter-country adoption".

This principle, like Principle 5, is aimed at preventing too hasty a placement for adoption and emphasizes the importance of the factor of consent in its fullest meaning.

In relation to this important matter of consent, the need for case-work service in each case in which adoption is envisaged is evident. In recommending that provision should exist for dispensing with the consent of the natural parents, or for the transfer of parental rights under certain circumstances, the Seminar agreed that it can be extremely difficult to determine when this step is in the child's best interests, for example, the point at which the child can be considered to be abandoned by his or her mother who had placed him in an institution and presumably showed no further interest. It was agreed that determining the best interests of the child must always be arrived at on the most careful individual basis, with the most skilled service available. In order to carry out this principle there needs to be a skilled intermediary agency which operates between local services in both the countries involved, and which ensures that proper standards are maintained. This intermediate agency should carry out a number of tasks which are safeguards of inter-country adoption. These safeguards are incorporated in Principles 7 to 12.

Principle 7: "That an adequate home study of the prospective adopters should be completed before a child is suggested to, or placed with a couple with a view to inter-country adoption, as well as an adequate study of the child's background, physical condition, and personality development; that it is recognized that a home study of the adoptive parents may have a limited value when the parents are living in a temporary setting, so that there are often valid reasons for not considering such couples as prospective adoptive parents unless they live in one setting for a sufficient length of time where they can be studied by a social worker who is sufficiently familiar with their culture, and an appraisal of them in their own community can be obtained, before a child is suggested or placed with them".

The Seminar felt strongly that an adequate home study should be made be a reputable child welfare agency. Cases were cited in which a child had been placed with potential adopters before a preliminary home study in the country of normal residence had been made. It was felt that couples travelling or living temporarily abroad who received children "on the spot" should be strongly discouraged from this practice. Among the cases cited was the following: a couple made a weekend visit to another country and in the course of their visit a five-year-old child was entrusted to them by his guardian who had the impression that they were a stable and well-to-do couple. Two years later, not having had any news of whether the child had been adopted, the guardian asked the specialized international agency to arrange for a "home study" and to secure a recommendation as to whether the adoption should be completed. The social study made by a local child welfare agency revealed that the adoptive parents were on the point of divorce; they were not at all well-to-do but in very precarious financial circumstances; the adoptive mother seemed mentally disturbed; the couple were too old to adopt under the adoption law of their country; the child had not been registered with the proper authorities, and was in the country illegally. However, the child had been living with the couple for two years and had established emotional ties with them.

The Seminar noted, too, with much disapproval, the practice of some couples of obtaining a "home study" in their own country prior to their departure abroad, in search of a child. It was stressed that home studies are only realistic when the social worker concerned has a clear idea of the child who may be placed, and the nature of that child's needs. Only then can a relevant home study be made, and a placement which will serve the child's welfare interests be made. It is essential too that social work agencies investigating the child's background should be fully conversant with the language and cultural customs of his natural parents.

Principle 8: "That the process of matching together child and adoptive parents in inter-country adoption should be a shared responsibility between the child welfare agency which makes the home study of the prospective adopters and the child welfare agency responsible for the child, with the participation of the specialized international social agency acting as intermediary between the two. All relevant factors which are accepted as valid in matching child and adoptive parents in local adoptions shall be taken into consideration, with special attention to the factor of religion".

Too often in the past, the Seminar reported, "matching" in inter-country adoption had been a haphazard and unplanned step. The following case, among others, was cited: a serviceman on duty in a foreign country was touched by the plight of a child in a poorly run institution. He befriended the child, became attached to him and persuaded his wife to allow him to being the child home for adoption. When the child arrived, his wife literally "couldn't bear the sight of him", and a local child welfare agency had to be called in at the point at which the wife's neglect of the child becomes so obvious that the neighbours complained.

Principle 9: "That before the legal adoption is completed, there must be a trial period of not less than six months under the supervision of a social worker attached to a qualified agency, able to understand the cultural patterns of the prospective adopters and of the child; in the case of older children, this period should be longer. That there is opposition to proxy adoptions except under certain exceptional circumstances where prospective adopters and child have lived together for a reasonable time and established a satisfactory parent-child relationship".

Experience had demonstrated that proxy adoptions (when a third party adopts the child on behalf of the prospective adoptive parents, and travels to the country of the prospective adopters, there transferring the adoptive status) are a fertile field for unqualified and unscrupulous intermediaries who use this method to circumvent basic safeguards. A case was cited, among others, of a couple who had been repeatedly turned down by adoption agencies in their own country because of the wife's mental illness, who adopted a child by proxy through the intermediary of lawyers. Another child adopted by proxy was found to be mentally retarded, and was rejected by the adopters; in another case, a child adopted by proxy was so seriously maltreated by the adoptive parents that criminal prosecution had to be taken. Many cases are seen, too, in which children have left their countries for adoption abroad, through the proxy system, before consents valid in both countries have been prepared.

Principle 10: "That care must be given, before the adoption plan is finalized, that pertinent documents necessary to complete the adoption are available, particularly that all necessary consents are in a form which is legally valid in both countries; that it must be definitely established that the child will be able to immigrate into the country of the prospective adopters and can subsequently obtain their nationality".

What can happen is that a child may be adopted abroad; the adoptive parents return to their own country, only to find that they are not entitled to bring the child into their country, since the adoption is not legally valid in their country. In practice, many immigration authorities give way in the face of a _fait accompli_, and they are allowed to keep the child. The dilemma of what to do is then placed with local welfare agencies, who may have to take the child into care if the potential adopters are totally unsuitable. What often happens is that a _de facto_ adoption emerges because the local authority is reluctant to take on the expense and problem of taking a young, foreign child into care.

Principle 11: "That care must be given to assuring adequate protection of the child in his new country, and that, in view of the difficulty of exercising guardianship functions across national boundaries, the value of the former legal guardianship needs to be examined; that legal responsibility for the child in the new country should be established promptly".

The need for this principle was emphasised by a case, typical of others, in which a couple travelling abroad adopted a child by the law of his country. Soon after the couple returned to their country the child welfare authority asked for a report on the child. It was learned that the adoptive parents had decided not to keep the child, and without consulting the child welfare authority had "given" the child to relatives for adoption. No person or social agency in the country of the adoptive parents had any legal authority to act on behalf of the child.

Principle 12: "That steps should be taken to assure that the adoption is legally valid in both countries".

But, the Seminar noted, conflicts in laws are so great that the attainment of an adoption which is valid in both countries concerned may be impossible in many cases. That was true in 1960, and is probably still true. A later a survey of conflict of laws in inter-country adoption by Ingrid Delupis[15] pointed to many confusions and conflicts in international law surrounding ICA.

The Seminar, after having considered the six general principles and the six principles pertaining to safeguards, came to the conclusion that all of the principles would be better observed in practice if there were some form of centralization of adoption services. In the years that have passed since that recommendation, only the Netherlands has to our knowledge, centralized the administration of inter-country adoption. In other European countries matters have improved to the extent that large organizations, particularly Terres des Hommes based in Switzerland, dominate the field and because of their size are open to government influence in adopting good practice. In the Third World although International Social Service periodically inspects local agencies through its regional offices, there is no organization specifically concerned in any region with co-ordinating inter-country adoption. There is much variation in practices, standards, and legal requirements for inter-country adoption between countries with which we are familiar, such as Hong Kong, Thailand, Korea, India, Bangladesh and Sri Lanka.

The Leysin Seminar also considered in detail the application of case-work in inter-country adoption, since there was concern that each individual inter-country adoption should be carried out so that it would be in the best interest of the child, the natural parents or guardian, and the adoptive parents. It is clear however that deciding a child's best interest is very difficult, and must involve casework of high quality at all levels and careful social enquiries with all parties, in both countries concerned. All too often agencies involved in inter-country adoption do not have the resources, expertise or willingness to carry out such work. This is particularly true at the present time, in our opinion, of many adoptions from the Third World by Americans and Canadians. With the plethora of American agencies or lawyers specialising in adoption work, and the differences in American State laws, it seems that many adoptions are made which do not meet adequate professional standards. Many of the case histories showing difficulties and dangers of ICA are drawn from American experience. The rich, determined and childless American couples, with powerful lawyers at their disposal in both their home country and the country in which they wish to adopt a child are often a match for under-financed and under-staffed regional offices of international bodies concerned with child welfare. The growing trend in North America is for adoptions from Central and South America, and much of this practice, according to our information, is organized through specialist (and highly paid) lawyers in Florida and California.

The report of the Leysin seminar observed that "Adoption in general involves the deepest human emotions - the longing of couples for children which awakens compassion in the hearts of most of us because it seems so human, so natural". (p.36). This powerful motivation of couples to acquire a child, and the naive motivation of others to rescue children from apparently substandard material circumstances, means that very often careful adoption practice which ensures the welfare of all parties is ignored, swept aside, or even criticized. It is urged by some that an overly legalistic approach to inter-country adoption makes the process very drawn out, and even blocks it altogether. But the children in institutions grow older, and even months are vital. Experience indicates that although children can adapt to a new language, such as English, when they have already acquired another, the process can also have its traumas. The adoption of children before they have acquired speech, and indeed while they are still infants, appears to have theoretical advantages.

The two overriding principles of the Leysin seminar were that: (a) adoption is the best substitute in the absence of care from the natural or extended family; and (b) the welfare of the child must be the principal objective at all times. The twelve principles were established in order to ensure those welfare interest. Yet it is clear, writing three decades after the Leysin seminar, that in a large number of cases of the ICA those twelve principles are not been applied. In many other inter-country adoptions only some of the principles pertain, and only in a minority can good practice be said to be the rule.[16]

International organisations in the field of inter-country adoption

There are many organisations concerned with inter-country adoption which work within particular countries, or between two particular countries; but only three specialist organizations work between many countries, and are large and influential enough to effect international policy. These organizations are International Social Service, Terres des Hommes, and the International Union for Child Welfare. It is important to understand the history and current policies of these organisation before a proper appraisal can be made of the pros and cons of inter-country adoption, and the problems of implementing appropriate practice in this field, including a more universal adoption of the twelve principles of Leysin.

International social service

International Social Service (ISS) grew out of international responses to the manifest problems of refugees and homeless children scattered across many countries as a result of the First World War. The basis of International Social Service, which has its headquarters in Geneva, is to offer skilled social work service (using the highest standards of casework) to families and individuals whose problems cross international boundaries. ISS is non-denominational and non-political, and is still a voluntary organization existing on a small and fluctuating budget. Its income comes from various charitable and fund-raising activities, and grants which are made by a number of the countries that it serves.

From its foundation ISS was particularly concerned with the problems of refugees and migrants, and set up offices in countries where such individuals would be most likely to find themselves. Services were offered to all, regardless of race, religion, nationality or political affiliation, a condition which led to clashes between the Nazi government and the ISS branch office in Germany, which was eventually closed down. Much work was done in America assisting newly-arrived immigrants who had difficulty in understanding or overcoming American entry regulations, and bringing families to join them. Another area which concerned ISS was the conflict of law between countries which affected migrants. Most frequently these problems concerned marriage, divorce, and maintenance of dependents.

The Second World War and the refugee problems it caused gave additional impetus to the activities of ISS, and it is in this period that ISS became involved in advising on, and monitoring, international adoptions. Ruth Learned in her history of ISS tells us that, "Another war situation in which all the ISS Branches were plunged, grew out of the many hasty marriages and extra-marital relations between members of the armed services and nationals of other countries. These often resulted in divorce, desertion, bigamy, and, above all, illegitimately fathered children who, however counted, numbered many thousands, and appeared wherever armies were stationed. They were not only the embodiment of tragedy, but also their support was an almost intolerable burden on war-weakened governments. The result was bitterness, both personal and official amounting to much serious ill-will, that governments were aroused. Cases concerning these children were referred to ISS not only by social agencies, but frequently by embassies and ministries of foreign affairs". (p.54)[17]

There were often legal obstacles to be removed if the best solution for the many children separated from their parent or parents was to be found. In Britain, where there were many such children, the Family Welfare Association (a unit of which was to become the British branch of ISS in 1953) was designated by the Home Office as the centralizing agency for these cases.

Another major task for ISS was the problem of the many hundred children of forced workers in Germany, now separated from the parents and in institutions in Germany and Austria. Some were eventually reunited with their parents by ISS. Others were adopted by German families; and many were adopted in America, Sweden, and other countries. On these varying post-war experiences, Ruth Learned comments, "Through all its handling by casework methods of special war-created problems - from the paternity cases to the uprooted children - the role of the ISS was becoming clear. For it had demonstrated the value of the case approach, through analysis and counselling, to supplement mass refugee planning. As the official bodies became more and more aware of the need for such individualized service, as opposed to mass solutions, there followed inevitably an increasing recognition of the kind of role ISS could play in helping to find solutions for those who did not readily fit into mass schemes". (p.58)[17]

As various governments recognized the valuable role which ISS could play, appreciating the professional approach of its workers, and their freedom from ideological biases, more financial support was forthcoming and new branches were opened - in Brazil in 1952, in the Netherlands in 1951, in Australia in 1954, and in addition branches in France, Italy, United States, Germany, Greece, Britain and Uruguay, and in various parts of Asia.

In the decade following the Second World War, ISS did not confine itself to inter-country service for displaced persons and refugees. The most important new development was the increase in inter-country adoption of children, beginning in the immediate post-war period. ISS became aware that many adoptions took place across national boundaries which were not subject to the usual safeguards and social enquiries which were conventional for in-country adoptions. The wide divergence of national laws, attitudes and placement practices, and the scant international co-ordination in protective measures convinced ISS that in inter-country adoption, above all else, urgent international consultation was needed.

Several ISS branches concerned with this problem had for some time been furthering working relationships with child welfare agencies in their respective countries which had become increasingly aware of the difference in local and national conditions and practices. With this experience, ISS was not unprepared when special United Stated legislation permitted, even invited, inter-country adoption on a large scale. The U.S. Displaced Persons Act of 1948, amended in 1950, provided for admission of 10,000 "orphans" of specified nationalities.

Only 4,182 of that number came to America before the programme ended in June, 1952. The Refugee Relief Act passed in 1953 provided for the admission of 4,000 more children before December 31, 1956.

A variety of factors led to these Acts - military personnel stationed in foreign countries found adoptable children more available than at home and tended to adopt on the spot (and as a consequence put pressure on their Congressman when difficulties were encountered in bringing the child to the United States). The U.S. Congress also expressed a general concern for war orphans, and illegitimate children of U.S. servicemen, in Austria, Germany, Greece, Italy and Japan.

The special Acts stimulated the efforts of couples in the United States to seek foreign children for adoption, with the result that there were far more homes offered than there were adoptable children to meet the demand. Up to the time of its identification with this programme for adoption of "foreign orphans", ISS had confined itself to a service in which a foreign child was already known or recommended to a family offering a home in another country. In expanding its services to accept referrals of children for adoption in a foreign land by parents quite unknown to them, the ISS branches agreed on the principle that a child should be selected only if adoption within its own country was not, for one reason or another, feasible; further, that emphasis should be placed primarily on the need of the child for adoption and only secondarily on the wish of the would-be adoptive parents to find a foreign child.

ISS did not conceive its function to be one of finding children for prospective adoptive parents but rather that of making a careful choice of parents most suitable for a particular child. There was need of "matching" with utmost care and sensitivity. Detailed information on the child was obtained, and similarly detailed investigations of the potential adopters in America were commissioned. ISS was subsidised in this activity by a voluntary organization based in Los Angeles, the World Adoption International Fund (WAIF) and by assistance by the U.S. State Department branches in the sending countries of Austria, Greece, Italy and Japan. Altogether ISS branches and co-operating agencies in 14 countries combined to make the North American inter-country adoption programme possible.

The valuable experience which ISS gained in this programme, and the policy documents circulated by ISS to other organizations led to the establishment of the Leysin Conference in 1960. The principles emerging are the chief guides for practice today, and are largely based on the experience and expertise of ISS.

The practice of inter-country adoption (ICA) is, of course, controversial, and an internal debate on the practice has been continuing within ISS about future policy for some years. ISS branches in various regions are autonomous both in fund-raising and in the development of regional policy, and clearly some branches are more in favour of ICA as a solution to the problems of certain orphaned or abandoned children in the Third World than are others. It is fair to say that the American branch, for example, is much more in favour of ICA than is, say, the Hong Kong branch. those in the sending countries seem to be more sanguine about the inter-country adoption than those in the "receiving" countries, where the wealthy, the child-hungry, and the naive "do-gooders" put considerable pressure on ISS to assist them in obtaining a Third World or refugee child. But the early experience of ISS, for example in Greece after the civil war, indicated that in the wake of civil turmoil many premature and indeed disastrous decisions could be made to adopt a child overseas when later events showed that the biological parents turned up wanting their child, or had changed their minds, or had not understood what "adoption" meant.

As the International Council meeting of ISS in November, 1967 concern was expressed about the wide variations in standards in ICA and the difficulties experienced, particularly in certain areas of the world, in working in accordance with the basic principles formulated at the U.N. Seminar at Leysin in 1960. ISS was being increasingly asked to supervise inter-country adoptions in countries where it had no branches; sometimes such work had to be done by ISS "correspondents" - social agencies of apparent integrity but with varying professional standards, acting on behalf of ISS. [18] Correspondents were, in theory, regularly visited by ISS branch officials, but lack of funds often meant such consultation might take place every other year. Another important problem noted at the 1967 meeting was the increasing number of international adoptions which were by-passing the supervision of ISS. In addition, the Leysin principles were re-examined in detail. While they were generally reaffirmed, Principle 1 "That adoption is the best substitute for care by the child's own parents or close relatives, provided that adoption is based fundamentally on the welfare of the child" was subjected to particular scrutiny. Delegates pointed to the fact that thinking on adoption policy had changed since 1960; more emphasis was now placed in all countries on vigorous efforts to enable a natural mother to look after her child, and adoption was seen as a solution only after these efforts had clearly failed. The ISS meeting suggested that this principle should be clearly applied, too, in the countries of the third World from which children in inter-country adoptions tended to come.

The meeting stressed once again that in-country adoption should be considered first, when adoption was the best solution; that the highest standards of casework, with careful enquiries and counselling of all parties should be adhered to in inter-country adoption; and every effort should be made to ensure that natural parents or relatives understood the final nature of adoption.

The debate on ICA policy has continued within ISS. The British director has reported to the head office in Geneva of "the feelings of frustration" of local authority social workers who were faced with unsuitable placements from abroad which they were unable to disturb without damage to the child concerned and at which, therefore, they were forced to connive. Adoption workers in Britain, both in statutory and voluntary agencies, face tremendous pressure from thwarted adopters, unable to adopt locally because of the "baby shortage". The media itself occasionally presses for inter-country adoption without realising the difficulties involved. The net effect of this pressure from parents and publicity in certain newspapers was to increase the number of unsupervised inter-country adoptions.

In America the office of ISS has also frequently approached by couples wanting to adopt internationally, in the years since 1960. ISS policy in America on inter-country adoption had changed over the years, largely in response to the change in international needs. In the years following World War II, activity was concentrated on orphaned or abandoned children in Germany, Austria, Greece and Italy. The U.S. State Department gave much assistance, both Legal and financial, to the adoption of these children in America.

The American branch of ISS then had to respond to the emergency situation created by the Korean war, where many orphaned and racially mixed children needed homes which existing Korean society could not at that time provide. The same situation had existed immediately after World War II in Japan. In Hong Kong the massive population increase which followed the 1949 revolution in China resulted in a rather large number of abandoned and orphaned children, many of whom were subsequently placed in the United States (a number were placed in Britain in the early 1960s; we have conducted a personal follow-up of the adjustment of these children, now young adults - see below). With an increase in prosperity in Hong Kong in the late 1960s, and the development of indigenous welfare services the need for international adoption from Hong Kong subsequently diminished.

In a memorandum to the Adoptions and Foster Care Bureau of the American State Department dated November 1970, ISS in America suggested that: "It would be naive for us to deny that there are children in many countries of the world who are living in institutions or who are orphaned and homeless and who could benefit from adoptive placement.

Whether inter-country adoption planning is the most feasible way of meeting the needs of such children is another question. We already made reference to the highly specialized services that we believe are absolutely essential for inter-country adoption planning. In most developing countries - where one finds children who are victims of poverty - social services are not wide-spread and those welfare sources that do exist or are being developed, must focus on basic health and welfare needs of the entire population".

The ISS memorandum noted too that there were many countries which did not favour the idea of "exporting" their children; and other countries where wealthy foreigners could bypass existing social agencies set up to safeguard the rights of children and the interests of natural parents involved in ICA. Cases were cited from Thailand where the role of wealthy foreigners in combination with unscrupulous lawyers and weak government officials had acted to export children for adoption in America in a manner which flouted many of the Leysin principles. The situation in Vietnam was also chaotic, but here the US State Department, together with various voluntary agencies, was able to offer a better casework service which could serve the long-term interests of children.

The debate within ISS has continued, with various branches, in Canada, Australia, Hong Kong, Britain and America exchanging carefully reasoned memoranda putting different points of view on inter-country adoption. The various points raised in these memoranda illustrate the complexity of the problem of ICA. It was noted that in some European countries there was something of a vogue to adopt internationally; wealthy and well-meaning adopters often put pressure on countries such as Vietnam, Peru and Nigeria which had experienced civil war or natural disaster, to give up children for adoption; often these pressures had to be resisted, for the children could frequently be reunited with kin, or adopted within their own country.

An ISS voice from Sweden pointed to a "double standard" in that country. The development of social welfare programmes in Sweden had made it possible for single mothers to keep their babies without stigma or hardship; but the success of this programme had meant that childless couples were unable to adopt because of the small number of mothers giving up their children. So the demand was satisfied in poor countries of the Third World: "The Swedes are now turning to Asia, particularly Korea, for children, and hundreds of Asian children are now adopted in Sweden yearly. The placement of these children in Sweden has become somewhat a political issue in Sweden: ... The argument of opponents of ICA (very much a minority voice) has been that the Swedish ministry operates a double standard, in failing to attempt to implement welfare standards in Third World countries in which it is interested, which would prevent the need for children to become adopted."

Another apparent double standard is operated by some agencies carrying out home studies of prospective adoptive parents wishing to adopt a foreign child. Frequently out of misguided kindness (according to an ISS observer) they approve homes which they would not approve for placement of native children, because of their sympathy for what they consider to be the needs of foreign children. But, the ISS representative argues, families who adopt a child from another country or from another race and culture, have _more_ adjustments to make, and probably face more problems in bringing up a child who may face certain problems in relating to peers and the wider environment. These parents really need to be very special people, and their suitability needs to be _more_ not less carefully scrutinised.

The ISS representative in Hong Kong wrote with dismay that: "I recently had the occasion to meet with the Director of a large adoption agency in California, and it was obvious that he was in Asia shopping for children. He told me that while American children are becoming less available for adoption because of legalised abortions, the pill, etc., he has many white families wanting children but he had fewer children to place. He came to visit to find out if we could place Hong Kong children and was obviously disappointed we did not have any for him. Later when I saw him again in the Philippines, he told me triumphantly that he had found an orphanage there that would supply him with children ... From where I sit in Asia, I feel strongly that there is over-emphasis in some of ISS's programmes on inter-country adoptions; in this field we are beginning to collect more enemies than friends. There are those who think we are monopolistic - still others who think we are not doing enough. I have a strong fear that unless we can control this problem within us, it will destroy us. I feel we should really sit down and think through very thoroughly what part our organization should play in inter-country adoptions". This senior official of ISS is clearly reacting to the pressure placed on ISS to assist other agencies wanting to import children from Third World countries, and to relax, or even abandon, the high standards evolved from the Leysin conference. Because of its long experience in ICA and its general prestige, ISS has come under more rather than less pressure in the intervening years to assist inter-country adoption. The alternative is a diminution of its international authority and the rise of alternative organisations such as Terres des Hommes which are vigorous and unequivocal in their advocacy and practice of ICA.

Even if we can dispel fears of the later problems of adjustment of children adopted across cultures, we still have to face the basic policy issues raised by ISS workers. The ultimate paradox in adoption work, both nationally and internationally, is that the child's general welfare interests (which is the cardinal principle in adoption) can probably be served by adoption, in that the outcome is on average, at least as good as that in "normal" families; but the very success of these placements may mean that the development of services which would prevent family break-up, or allow mothers to keep their children, is neglected. In Britain, Robert Holman[19] for example, has been critical of the over-enthusiastic use of adoption; while Barbara Tizard[20] has advocated its greater use. Barbara Tizard's views are based on her research showing the remarkably successful outcome in adoption placements, research paralleling that carried out by the National Children's Bureau on successful adoption[21] in comparison with unsuccessful outcomes of one-parent families.[22]

It is at this point that the policy dilemma begins. Should we, because of the manifest success of adoption placements advocate the continuation or the increase of such placements; or should we turn instead to preventing the need for adoption placements? This is both a national dilemma, and an international one. What kind of balance should be struck between continued international adoptions for children who would otherwise grow up in emotionally-handicapping institutions, perhaps malnourished, and indeed in some case dying of starvation? What efforts should be made in parallel to adoption to prevent the need for adoption, by increased international aid and the strengthening of the child welfare agencies in the countries concerned? To what extent, indeed, do the richer countries have a vested interest in keeping child welfare facilities in poorer countries underdeveloped, so as to ensure a continued supply of babies for the childless rich, or for those motivated only by the need to be fashionable, or the motive of patronising pity?

As child welfare services grew and developed in countries such as Korea and Hong Kong, and as the practice of adoption became more acceptable in these societies, international organizations, including ISS, began to concentrate on the needs of "hard to place" children - often older, and handicapped - who could not be placed locally for adoption. Added to this category were children from minority racial groups or of mixed racial background. The ISS office in Hong Kong had, in the 1970s to supervise the transit of babies from Indochina to Europe, America and Australia, and as a result of their involvement, "the office became inundated and disrupted with calls from people wanting an Indochinese baby". Yet very few babies were actually now available in Hong Kong for adoption, and ISS reported: "It is not an uncommon practice for members of our foreign community to go elsewhere in Asia to look for children to adopt or for Chinese families to do the same in Taiwan. Because of the problem of black market in children in some of these countries, the activities of these families have become of concern to the police, the immigration department, and ourselves ... ". It seems that in this search for children, it was the needs of parents that were being fulfilled, not the needs of children, and that many of the Leysin principles were being ignored.

In further policy documents, International Social Service directors have outlined several alternative policies on ICA. The first alternative proposes that in view of the many international agencies now working in field of ICA, ISS should withdraw from this field, and concentrate on its other roles and functions, such as the social advocacy role for migrants, which had been neglected so far.

The second alternative proposal is that ISS should revert to its original position, that inter-country adoption cases should only be handled between units, when other agencies requested ISS to help them with cross-boundary casework problems.

ISS has emerged from this debate with a continued resolve to be involved in inter-country adoption, both advising and supervising wherever possible, so far as limited resources will permit. The director of the British branch of ISS has summarised the possible direction of the policy role of ISS, in a cautious policy of both assisting where necessary, but discouraging ill-advised action, in international adoption. A country's children (she writes) represents its future and very few governments would consent to sending large numbers out of the country unless they were under pressure of various kinds. Many countries in Africa and the Far East are putting up barriers to prevent children leaving and the desire of people in the United States and Western Europe to obtain children is seen as a new kind of rather patronising colonialism.

Adoption on the Western pattern was unknown in the East until comparatively recently and is still, according to ISS experience, not properly understood. The signing of consent forms and other procedures is often meaningless and parents do not understand that they are handing over their children for good and will hear nothing more of them. They seek news later, often with heartbreaking results, and ISS is no longer able to assist after the adoption has been finalised. Underdeveloped countries which do allow children to leave in large numbers may have no incentive to develop their own child care services; adoption may be a simple solution, for the problems are simply exported. This could have generally a negative influence on general child welfare services, and ultimately more children would suffer than benefit from the continuation of ICA. Worse still as has been alleged in Korea, foreign agencies may persuade mothers to give up, or at least abandon children in the sure knowledge that they will be adopted overseas.

ICA can also be cheap option for a country with problem children, and those children may even be turned into a source of income. The alternative forms of child care developed within the country require funds and expertise which might not be developed because of ICA.

Some affluent countries may have the option of an ICA programme as an alternative to assisting in developing a total child care programme in that country. In these circumstances, ISS would certainly advocate the development of indigenous services, but would not set its face in any dogmatic fashion against international adoption for individual cases. The worst situation of all, which ISS would very much like to remedy, is that in a country of widespread poverty a woman may be tempted or obliged to sell some children for purposes of adoption in order to support the rest of the family. A second, most undesirable situation is where women are encouraged to have children to supply an ICA market. The Australian branch of ISS commenting on this practice in the Far East, sees it as a form of prostitution. ICA should be considered, the Australian workers suggest, only if there exist no better alternatives for that child within its own country. "This proposition suggests that, all things considered, a child is best placed within its own country if a satisfactory placement of any kind is available. And countries do vary greatly in this regard. At present there are far fewer local alternatives for children in Bangladesh than there are in the Philippines ..." On this view, it is only in countries like Bangladesh where death from starvation is a very real alternative to ICA, that the practice can be advocated on any scale.

It can be said, writing in 1990, that International Social Service will continue its involvement and its quiet, careful advocacy and practice in inter-country adoption, supervising certain cases, discouraging many potential adopters, and trying to encourage high standards and the development of indigenous services wherever possible. One is continually impressed by the high professional standards maintained by ISS, despite an extremely limited budget; it will continue to have a major voice in the development of practice and policy in this area. Its most potent influence is in the receiving countries, where it can advise governments on ways of controlling the practice of ICA so as to ensure that only properly selected and motivated adoptive parents are involved, and that visas are not given for the entry of a child unless the fullest safeguards and enquiries have been applied in the country of origin. British practice, as it has evolved, probably ensures maximum safeguards and enquiries have been applied in the country of origin. At the present time, ISS workers in Geneva attempt to influence world opinion in areas where it is relevant to do so: they have pointed to a recent addition to the Geneva Convention which says that children should not be removed from a country in times of crisis. Yet in the civil war in Lebanon, many children have been taken overseas for adoption. The situation is Romania is analogous. Concern has been expressed by ISS about the current situation in Colombia, from where up to fifty children a day are being sent to Europe and America for adoption. The pressure from ISS for proper procedures had meant that some infants had been returned from Switzerland to Colombia, because proper consents had not been obtained in the country of origin. Here again we see the dilemma of work in this field. What do authorities do in the receiving country when faced with this fait accompli? Here is a child, having endured considerable upset and disruption in being brought from Colombia to Europe. Which now is the lesser of two evils, allowing the child to stay even when consent was not properly obtained for adoption, and the present adopters are perhaps unsuitable; or sending the child back, further disrupting the infant's life, to be housed once again in a large and underfinanced orphanage?

In India the ISS workers informed us, the debate which exercised Western consciences - whether to accept ICA, however imperfect, or whether to be rigorous about the condition, and prevent many potential adoptions - was viewed with some astonishment. The choice as the Indian workers saw it was "death now or an identity crisis in Europe 14 years later"; yet often the choice is not that simple. A European couple travelled to India in order to adopt; ISS thought they were manifestly unsuitable, and opposed the adoption in the Indian courts (there is no adoption law as such in India, but a couple may apply to the courts for permission to take a child abroad for purposes of adoption); but the couple, well-financed, won their case. ISS, with limited funds, cannot really afford such legal expenses.

Everywhere, ISS needs more and better "correspondents" in the countries in which it does not have branches. Some branches, such as the British, will not co-operate in ICAs from countries where ISS has no correspondent. The American branch of ISS is less stringent on this score, and generally seems the most sympathetic of the ISS branches to ICA. Yet a liberal policy can lead to cases like the one quoted to us by ISS in Geneva. An American woman, divorced, was travelling in India. She took a liking to a child she met, and the parents agreed that she could "adopt" the girl, whom she thought was 12. Adult and child duly left for the States, where it was found that the child was 15, not 12, and was too old to be given an immigrant visa as an adoptive child (the upper age limit for such a visa is 14). The outcome of this case is not known.

Terres des Hommes

It is difficult to imagine an organisation dealing with children more different from ISS. Terres des Hommes (TdH) is pioneering, passionate, sometimes overly emotional, and accepts inter-country adoption as part of its general brief for the welfare of children in a world-wide setting. "Terres des Hommes is the wolf howling over its dead or dying cub - so that the world may at last fathom the suffering of the world and be appalled by it - and at the same time it is the relief given to children in particularly profound misery," declares the publicity material of TdH, amply illustrated with photographs of children burned by the fires of war, limbs shot away by shrapnel, and wasted and dying with starvation.[24]

With headquarters in Lausanne, Switzerland and branches in many European countries, TdH has active programmes in some forty countries of the Third World. TdH's first work in ICA was in Algeria, with children abandoned or separated from parents in the civil war. From the start, adoption was seen as a reasonable, and often the most desirable solution to the problems of starving, handicapped or abandoned children in the countries in which it operated. While often working over-enthusiastically and unprofessionally in its earlier years, TdH took active steps to place both older and handicapped children, and to ensure optimum support for families after placement of an ICA child. It certainly could not be said that TdH was taking "the healthiest and the most beautiful children" from these Third World countries.

By the 1980s TdH was placing children for adoption from Bangladesh, Cambodia, Camaroon, Colombia, India, Palestine refugee camps, Korea, Peru, Togo, Vietnam, and a number of other countries. The children have been placed in France, Belgium, Germany and Denmark and Switzerland where TdH has branches (the Dutch branch does not place children, since this activity is centralised in a government agency). The European branches are autonomous, and we were unable to find a central record of how many children, in total, had been placed for adoption. The Swiss headquarters estimated however that at least 300 children were placed with adoptive parents in Switzerland alone every year since 1970, most of them from Korea.

Terres des Hommes have stressed to us that international adoptions are becoming a smaller proportion of their work, and their current activities include much in-country aid, and general advocacy of the welfare of children which is neglected in many official development programmes. The kind of work being done is illustrated by a typical issue of the TdH newspaper, which records current activities, with numerous appeals for financial and other support. One issue for example, gives up two of the broadsheet's four pages to Lebanon. "Papa est mort, maman est morte", a caption declares, next to a photograph of three unhappy-looking children; a photograph of 9-year-old Andre shows that his right eye has been shot away by a bullet; Janine, aged thirteen, has had both her legs blown off - the scarred stumps point at us accusingly from the page, and we are exhorted to support TdH work in strife-torn Lebanon. Less conventional is the article about two brothers, aged ten and six, imprisoned by the government of Salvador for alleged subversive activities. The letter which TdH has addressed to the President of the Republic of Salvador is reproduced - outrage is expressed at the senseless and bizarre act of imprisoning children for alleged political crimes. This action by TdH illustrates its general role as an advocate for the world's children, a secular missionary organization fighting humanistic battles in all quarters of the globe. Inter-country adoption is a relatively small part of its work, and is only used when it seems absolutely necessary - for example, when older or handicapped children cannot be adopted in their country of birth.

In Germany, where TdH in independent, at least eight thousand children have been adopted from Third world countries in the past 26 years. According to information given to us by International Social Service, TdH did not at the outset operate full professional standards in adoption placement. However, because of pressure from ISS via the official Youth Department, TdH in Germany now makes good home studies, and co-operates fully with ISS in all aspects of adoption. At the present time between four or five hundred children are placed each year for adoption in Germany by TdH. These children come mainly from Latin America, India and Bangladesh, and Korea. A considerable number of Vietnamese children were placed before the ending of the civil war in that country. TdH in Germany is also involved to some extent with the placement of children of immigrant workers. In both Germany and Switzerland there is pressure for women to release their children for adoption in this way, since the child may well be declared an "illegal immigrant", liable to deportation! The only way the mother can keep her job is by giving up the child.

Each European branch of TdH has different emphases, and a somewhat different policy over inter-country adoption. We were told by officials in other child welfare agencies in Geneva that in some Third World countries TdH operates carefully, making sure that all safeguards and alternatives for the child are considered before adoption; but in other countries certain TdH branches may operate with less care and may offend some of the Leysin principles.

In Switzerland a division over various aspects of child care policy at one time split TdH to the extent that there are now two branches, one in Lausanne, and the other in Basel. One major cause of the division seems to have been over the policy of bringing children to Switzerland for medical treatment, and returning them to the original country. It was felt by many that it was unwise to return them; and perhaps unwise to have brought them to Switzerland in the first place. The alternative policy of providing in-country aid has been strongly advocated. The Lausanne branch of TdH puts more emphasis on adoption as a solution to the problems of certain children; but nevertheless, in-country solutions are actively sought. It is to the credit of TdH that its involvement in Nigeria after the civil war was aimed at reuniting children with family and kin groups, rather than adopting them overseas as some individuals in Europe had advocated.

Terres des Hommes is an important organization, not least because it has been involved in the inter-country adoption of thousands of children, and will continue to be so. When questioned about this policy, officials of TdH point to the sheer enormity of the problem - the millions of children in the world malnourished, starving, suffering premature death, subject to disease, and the ravages of civil war. Inter-country adoption has involved a few thousand children, a tiny fraction of the suffering children of the world. It has not, TdH argues, detracted from their vigorous programme of offering aid and assistance in any country where it is needed and accepted; ICA has been a small, but integral part of their programme, and is operated with great care, and increasing skill. We found it somewhat difficult to obtain information on the full extend of TdH activities and policies - the autonomous branches did not see a great need to maintain central documentation and statistics, and those involved in the child care programmes tended to see the writer as an outside researcher, offering nothing to starving children, and asking nonsensical questions about adoption policy. But we could not but be impressed by the vigour, the determination, the secular moral purpose, the efficiency, and indeed the success of Terres des Hommes.

International Union of Child Welfare

Unlike ISS or Terres des Hommes, the Geneva-based organization International Union for Child Welfare (IUCW) does not deal with actual cases, and is never involved directly in adoptions. Indeed, the policy of this influential organization is clearly against international adoptions. The IUCW is concerned in its policy reviews, to ensure that proper adoption practices are followed within countries; but adoption between countries it sees as by and large unnecessary. The scope of the IUCW's concern can by judged by the authoritative and sometimes polemical articles which are published in its quarterly, the International Child Welfare Review.

Perhaps the most extreme voice to be heard in the International Child Welfare Review was that of Professor Thomas Melone, writing from the Cameroon in 1976.[25] He argued, first of all, that homeless and orphaned children in Bangladesh, Vietnam and Cambodia had been brought to this condition by the imperialist apportionment of resources to the rich, developed countries; or indeed by wars in these countries fostered by the imperialist powers. Melone viewed with considerable distaste the adoption agencies which proceed in the wake of war and famine, picking out, as he saw it, the healthiest and the brightest children for adoption in the West. The supposed altruism of the couples involved he saw merely as an expression of the guilt which the rich people of the West feel for the poverty and degradation of many Eastern countries:

> It is clear that the circumstances of the Vietnamese/Cambodian crisis, and above all the unforgettable spectacle of the mass exportation of Vietnamese or Cambodian children who were brought to light in differing terms the so-called 'orphan problem'. The photograph of President Ford with a weeping Vietnamese baby in his arms incontestably makes use of the situation and as such acts as an alibi ... The American charter planes which evacuated the supposed orphans were in fact chartered by so-called charitable American organizations which sold children at exorbitant prices to cover the budget for their other domestic activities. In addition to these rescue missions, there was a wave of intensive propaganda which created a fashion ... Is political publicity, which acted as a cover for this new form of slavery, an isolated phenomenon, or will these new traders in human lives, in no way put off by world-wide criticism, spread their influence and render traditional adoption in the West so totally different that its primary objectives will be radically changed? (Melone, 1976, pp.22-23).

Despite this polemical view, there is ambiguity in the writing. Melone argues that, "... In the traditional African milieu for example, there are no orphans as such". Yet the powerful devastations of famine and war also can destroy traditional social organization, and to insist that no child shall be adopted may be to condemn children to live in the fearful conditions of the orphanages which have existed in Vietnam, and elsewhere. Indeed, Melone makes the error of generalising from kinship organization in Africa (where exchange of children between kin, and indeed within clans, is common and accepted practice) to Asia (where adoption across caste lines is impossible, or where only boys are adopted within kinship networks, and where family adoptions are forbidden by the Koranic principles of Islam).

Melone asks, rhetorically, "... will the young emigrant, while making a significant contribution to economic life, never be more than an additional member of the marginal community which, in so many Western cities, to make up of all those confined to ghettoes of people from the same origin because of an imposed or desired difference? In other words, will these newcomers become English or Bengalis, Biafrans, and Vietnamese of the United Kingdom? ... What will be the adoptee's country? If, in answering this question, we are bound to say the country of origin, then there can be no hesitation in stating that the mass exodus of young people exported for good amidst loud proclamations, purportedly for humanitarian reasons, is a new form of war aimed at deriving the traditional enemy of his human resources". (pp.24-25).

Yet these words ring hollow and do not accord with experience. In our follow-up studies in Britain we have not encountered marginal adolescents, victims of racism; rather, we have encountered cheerful, Anglicized teenagers, full of self-confidence, dating freely with their English peers. They are materially privileged and well-educated, and some plan to work in their country of birth when they have acquired relevant skills. Britain today is a multiracial community, and a significant sector of the community, including the transracially adopted, move freely within a network of multiracial and increasingly intermarried acquaintances. The emerging theme is one of harmony, rather than oppression.[26] The position of extreme critics of ICA, is an ideological one; we have the impression that same of these critics would rather let a child die for principle, than let it be adopted from a Third World country by a foreigner.

The formal position of IUCW is not as extreme as Melone's but it is significant that his voice is given a hearing by this organization. The official position of IUCW can perhaps best be summarized by the statement of Pierre Zumbach, the Secretary General, at the time of the Vietnam crisis, when a massive airlift of children in orphanages was being considered. Basing its arguments on the experience gained in Nigeria, Bangladesh and the Southern Sudan, IUCW offered a number of arguments for great caution in the practice of inter-country adoption. It is wrong for Westerners, Zumbach argues, to impose their own cultural standards of welfare on a people whose standards are quite different.

162

The experience of Nigeria is instructive. At the end of the so-called "Biafra war" in Nigeria more than 10,000 children, immediately labelled as orphans, were destined either to be put in orphanages or indeed to be evacuated by Western relief organizations. One Western group even chartered a plane to try and "rescue" some of these "orphans". Yet in truth no child in Nigeria is ever an orphan. If his or her parents cannot look after him, then relatives or indeed anyone in the same town or village will accept the responsibility. In Africa, children are prized, and the duties of caring and socialization fall not just on the immediate parents, but on the whole community.

After the Nigerian civil war, IUCW financed a number of local social workers who after several months of careful searching, placed all but 42 severely handicapped children with local families, with whom their good up-bringing seemed to be assured. The Nigerian experience is a powerful argument in favour of caution in the field of inter-country adoption. It was possible to carry through such a policy in the relative stability and calm which followed the ending of the civil war. Probably such calm did not exist following the end of the Vietnamese civil war in 1975, and the dilemma of various child welfare organizations working in that country was extreme. Should children in institutions be evacuated? Or should the organizations stay and try and co-operate with the Communist authorities in an uncertain military and political situation?

The situation in Romania, in which children abandoned in large orphanages were discovered following the fall of the Communist regime has presented a severe challenge to groups such as IUCW. Clearly in the scramble by westerners to find adoptable children, the U.N. guidelines were frequently violated and some children were literally bought and sold. At the present time (May, 1992) the Romanian government has forbidden most out-of-country adoptions, because of numerous abuses.

Conclusions

The practice of inter-country adoption is well-established, and is likely to grow rather than diminish as links between developed and developing countries continue. At some point in the future when developing countries have adequate child welfare services, and have developed satisfactory adoption and fostering services on an inter-country basis, inter-country adoption may become unnecessary. Our work in India has made it clear however that in-country adoption can, for many years to come, provide a reasonable family life for some children who would otherwise grow up in institutions.[27]

International organizations in this field have gathered considerable experience of the difficulties involved in inter-country adoption in recent years, and the procedural rules which have emerged from the experience of these countries in inter-country adoption have been accepted by many countries. Abuses in inter-country adoption have indeed occurred, but it is clear too that the adoption of the Leysin principles and their subsequent modification in the past two decades has prevented many abuses - such as payments being given to a parent to induce the giving up of a child; adoption by unsuitable people; and disregard for the principle of the child's welfare, and the legal rights and needs of the natural parents. Certainly in India, in our fieldwork in Bombay and New Delhi there was no evidence we could find of abuse or neglect of the child's welfare needs in inter-country adoption.

In our view Britain has an important role to play in increasing the number of inter-country adoptions which take place. The procedures initiated by the government for ensuring that all legal and professional safe-guards are followed both in Britain and in the sending country are stringent, and were praised for example by the Indian adoption workers we interviewed. A major difficulty however is that the activities of the British government in assessing children and adopters have not been co-ordinated with the activities of the Home Office in issuing visas for entry of children adopted overseas, or admitted for the purposes of adoption. In contrast to the help given to us by the Department of Health and Social Security, the Home Office did not reply to our letters on this topic, and telephone calls could not reach any responsible person. We have retained the distinct impression that the Home Office treats the issue of visas for inter-country adoption in the same manner as it treats the issues of visas for Commonwealth immigrants and refugees. This, in our view is fundamentally wrong and mistaken for it causes hardship to the adopted children (who may have to wait for long periods in foster homes or institutions before joining their new parents), as well as deterring potential inter-country adopters. Some change in the policy of the Home Office is clearly necessary. Additional difficulties are created by the uneven and sometimes hostile policies of some local authorities in Britain.[28]

A further need is for a British adoption agency, either statutory or voluntary, to specialise in or centralise the work of assessing potential adopters and liasing with countries from which children are adopted.

We have drawn an unfavourable contrast between Dutch and British policy in another context[29] and it is clear too that the Dutch with a tolerant and internationally-minded outlook are leaders in the field of inter-country adoption, with policies which Britain might emulate. Since

164

1975 all inter-country adoptions have had to be centralised, in the state-supported Netherlands Intercountry Child Welfare Organisation (NICWO). For this reason organisations such as Terres des Hommes do not operate as adoption agencies in the Netherlands. The population of the Netherlands is only a quarter of that in Britain, and if Britain were involved in inter-country adoption on the scale of the Netherlands, some 2,800 children a year would be placed, instead of the present figure of less than 300. The children placed with Dutch families come mainly from India, Korea, Haiti, Indonesia, Colombia, Bangladesh, Lebanon, Brazil, and Sri Lanka.[30] It is clear that Britain has much to learn, and indeed to emulate in Dutch policy in this respect. It is perhaps significant that the director of the NICWO, on reading our report of difficulties which British adoption agencies were experiencing in finding homes for black children, asked us to negotiate with British agencies to see if any of these children could be placed with Dutch adopters.

With regard to the adjustment of inter-country adopted children, our research with a group of Chinese children placed with British adopters has confirmed the optimistic conclusions drawn from research with inter-country adopted children in Europe and America.[31] By the time they are adolescents, the large majority of inter country adopted children appear to be well adjusted, without overt identity problems. They reflect the material advantage, love and family stability which adoptive homes so often provide. We have little doubt that the best welfare interests of the Chinese children we studied have been served by inter-country adoption. If British families were to adopt children from Indian institutions on the scale of, say, the Dutch there is again little doubt that the needs of such children would be well served.

End notes

(1)   Goody (1969).
(2)   Jones (1974).
(3)   Delupius (1976).
(4)   Alstein and Simon (1991).
(5)   Bagley and Young (1982).
(6)   Byma (1974); and Rorbech (1991).
(7)   Mangold, T., British Broadcasting Company, London - personal communication.
(8)   Melone (1976).
(9)   Alstein and Simon (1991).
(10)   Bagley (1977).
(11)   United Nations (1960).
(12)   Bagley (1977).
(13)   de Hartog (1969).

(14)   Freedman (1970); and Brady (1976).
(15)   Delupius (1976).
(16)   von Overbeck (1977).
(17)   Learned (1960).
(18)   This account is based on documents on inter-country adoption made available by the ISS head office in Geneva.
(19)   Holman (1975).
(20)   Tizard (1976); and Tizard and Phoneix (1987).
(21)   See Chapter 6 in this volume; and Maugham and Pickles (1990).
(22)   Ferri (1976).
(23)   Simon and Alstein (1987).
(24)   The information in this section is based on documentation and materials supplied to us by Mme. Suzanne Bettens of Terres des Homes, Lausanne. We are grateful to Ms Suzanne Hines for translating materials from the French.
(25)   Melone (1976).
(26)   Verma and Bagley (1984).
(27)   Bagley (1979).
(28)   Bennett and Mostyn (1991).
(29)   Bagley (1973 and 1983).
(30)   Hoksbergen (1991).
(31)   Altstein and Simon (1991).

10 Further developments in inter-country adoption

A major trend in inter-country adoption (ICA) in the past decade has been the refinement of the standards which should in theory govern the practice of ICA have been refined, and the acceptance of these principles by a number of a growing number of countries; but abuses of the formal procedure are still possible, and do frequently occur. Emergency situations, such as the recent civil upheavals in Romania and Yugoslavia test well-established procedures and show how easy it is for the guiding principles which emerged from the Leysin conference in 1960 to be usurped or by-passed.

Legal developments and the movement towards international accord

Documents based on the Leysin principles and their amendments were tabled in a debate at the United Nations General Assembly in 1980, reflecting the work of an expert group convened by the UN Economic and Social Council in 1978. Revised proposals were tabled at the end of 1985, indicating slow but steady progress in reformulating the original draft agreement in ways which seemed to be acceptable to many countries (UN, 1979 and 1985). The 1985 draft document (entitled "Declaration on Social and Legal Principles Relating to the Protection and Welfare of Children, with Special Reference to Foster Placement and Adoption, Nationally and Internationally") was finally adopted by the U.N. General Assembly in 1986.

According to the International Children's Rights Monitor (ICRM, 1987) the slow progress in reaching any kind of agreed document reflected some apparently fundamental disagreements on the nature of adoption as one of the solutions for children without parents; and the low priority given by the United Nations to the general issue of adoption. One persistent problem has been the refusal of certain Islamic countries to accept a universal draft on principles and practices of child adoption, since in Islam The Prophet has specifically forbidden the faithful to adopt children. Mohammed himself had an adopted son, who turned against his father. On these grounds Mohammed, in obeisance to the word of God, farbad the faithful from adopting non-biological children.

In the United Nations sub-committees concerned with the drafting the Convention on the Rights of the Child there was "fierce opposition of practising Muslim States to agreement on a declaration mentioning adoption, a practice which is not recognized by the Quran." (Luecker-Babel, 1986). The preamble in the Declaration on the Rights of the Child declaring that: "The principles set forth hereunder do not impose on States such legal institutions as foster placement or adoption" could not allay the fears or objections of these Muslim states.

In a statement made before the Sixth Committee of the U.N. General Assembly in 1984, Libya summarized this Islamic stand as follows: "Adoption is forbidden by the Quran and this prohibition cannot be open to any interpretation whatsoever. This is because, on the one hand, the biological family of the child is repudiated by adoption and its right to pass on its name and to have a line of descendants would, henceforth be no longer guaranteed. On the other hand, adoption could also obscure the line of descendants and the child who has lost his/her biological family could unwittingly marry a near relative." (UN, 1984).

We have described the large number of orphanages in India containing, over the whole country more than a million children who cannot be adopted,because of their Islamic religious origins (Bagley, 1979). In 1991 the situation in India remained unchanged, except that the numbers of children growing up in institutions has increased significantly (see Table 1). Proponents of Islam claim that children's needs for family life are met through absorption into the religious life created by these communities of children. Yet from our own observations, and those of others (e.g. Khan, 1991) these huge orphanages provide only minimal care, and cannot be an adequate substitute for ordinary family life.

The U.N. principles concerning adoption practice are embodied within a longer document pertaining to the rights of the child. Luecker-Babel (1987) comments that: "The general principles established in the first part tend to ensure the protection of the child and various of his/her rights (right at all times to a name, nationality and legal representation; right of the child to know his/her family origins). Strangely enough, no explicit mention is made of the right of the child to live and grow up in his/her biological family." The apparent reason for this omission is the view pressed by some Islamic countries that the needs and rights of religious institutions in caring for children transcend the priorities of both foster and biological families in caring for children.

The six U.N. resolutions on adoption could not be passed until the formal acceptance by the United Nations of ten Principles on the universal rights of the child. These ten principles, paraphrased and summarized are:

1. Children shall enjoy the rights set out in the U.N. Declaration without discrimination or exclusion based on race, colour, sex, language, national or social origin or other particular grounds.

2. Children shall be specially protected so as to enhance and maximise physical, emotional intellectual, spiritual and moral development in an atmosphere of freedom and dignity. In the enactment of laws to this end, the child's best interests shall be of paramount consideration.

3. The child shall be entitled from birth to a name and nationality.

4. The child shall enjoy the benefits of social security, including the adequate income and means of subsistence for his or her parents.

5. The child who is physically, mentally or socially handicapped shall be given special treatment, education and care required by his or her particular condition.

6. Children shall be given love, understanding and security by those who care for them, whether in their family of origin or in some other institution.

7. The child shall have the right to education, play and recreation, based on principles of equal opportunity, and with specific recognition of the child's individual needs and talents.

8. The child shall in all circumstances be among the first to receive protection and relief.

9. The child shall be protected against all forms of neglect, cruelty and exploitation.

10. The child shall be protected from practices which may foster racial, religious and any other kind of discrimination.

These are fine principles indeed, but they remain principles which fail to guide the activities of many national governments, and have an uncertain status in national (as opposed to international) law (Freeman, 1983).

The six subsequent principles on inter-country adoption remain standards adopted in moral rhetoric and exist as guiding principles only. They may serve however as the basis for specific agreements between individual "sending" and "receiving" countries. It is notoriously difficult to invoke standards or principles in United Nations charters as having legal or moral force if they have been merely adopted by the country in question, and not absorbed by statute in civil and criminal law. This point is illustrated be numerous case histories contained in the journal International Children's Rights Monitor, the Swiss-based organization Defence for Children International. For example, in 1986 the Monitor reported the case of a nine-year-old boy who was produced in court in the U.S.A. wearing leg shackles and handcuffs, to stand trial for an alleged murder. A U.N. convention on the treatment of prisoners, signed by the United States government in 1955 specifically forbids the use of chains to restrain juvenile offenders, whether alleged or convicted. When this was pointed out, the authorities replied: "This is the policy of Kissimmee detention center." Federal officials did not intervene. In another case (cited by Bagley and Thomlison, 1991) a 12-year-old girl was brought to adult court in California, with shackles on her wrists and legs. This girl had claimed that her father sexually assaulted her, but was unable to continue giving evidence at her father's trial. The distraught child was locked in an adult facility until she "discharged her contempt" of the court. By 1988 at least a dozen children under 16 were on death row in various states in the U.S.A. (Lewis et al, 1988) despite America being a signatory of the U.N. convention forbidding the execution of children.

The six U.N. articles pertaining to adoption, which have received widespread assent (albeit in lip-service) are:

Article 17: If a child cannot be placed in a foster or an adoptive family or cannot in any suitable manner be cared for in the country of origin, intercountry adoption may be considered as an alternative means of providing the child with a family.

Article 18: Governments should establish policy, legislation and effective supervision for the protection of children involved in intercountry adoption. Intercountry adoption should, wherever possible, only be undertaken when such measures have been established in the States concerned.

Article 19: In intercountry adoption, placements should as a rule be made through competent authorities or agencies with application of safeguards and standards equivalent to those existing in respect of national adoption. If no case should the placement result in improper financial gain for those involved.

Article 20: Special precautions should be taken to protect a child's legal and social interests when agents attempt to find children for adopters resident in another country.

Article 21: No intercountry adoption should be considered before it has been established that the child is legally free for adoption, and the informed consent of the competent authorities (including the child's biological parents) are available. It must be established through the relevant Embassy or High Commission that a child, once adopted in the sending country, would be free to enter the country of the adopting couple, and would be free to acquire the nationality of the receiving country.

Article 22: It must be established before arrangements are made for an intercountry adoption that the adoption order will be legally valid in both of the countries involved.

A number of European countries (notably, Germany, Sweden, Denmark and The Netherlands) have adopted these U.N. principles, and have incorporated their word or spirit into local legislation. Britain has not been one of those countries, and the number of intercountry adoptions each year (normally less than 300) is small in comparison with the number adopted in many other European countries (Tizard, 1991). However, in a twelve-month period in 1990 and 1991, over 400 children from Romania were brought to the UK for adoption.

At the time of writing (August, 1992) 53 nations are involved in a series of meetings of the Hague Conference on Private International Adoptions, trying to work out an agreed convention on intercountry adoptions which is widely accepted, and can be accepted into agreed principles of international law. The Secretary General of this conference was quoted in November, 1991 as saying: "The Conference ... is facilitating legitimate intercountry adoptions while offering protection for children against such abuses such as their kidnapping or outright sale." (Chavira and Constable, 1991). The finally agreed convention on international adoptions is expected to be ready some time in 1993, when a major diplomatic conference will be held (Department of Health, 1992).

Abuse and exploitation in intercountry adoption

Intercountry adoptions remain controversial for a number of reasons. The objections raised by critics include the following:

(a)   ICA is hazardous for the children involved, since they have to make adjustments to a culture which is profoundly different from the one they have left. In addition they may be subject to racial discrimination, marginalization and identity conflicts because of their ethnic difference from the majority of people in the culture where the adoptive parents live.

However, the evidence available to the present time (including that in later chapters in this book) suggest that the large majority of ICAs do not have negative outcomes. There are exceptions, such as the Amerindian children from Canada adopted by white Canadians and Americans - in the case of these children, as we argue in Chapter 13, stigmatization based on ethnicity does have profoundly harmful effects. For children from Southern and South-East Asia however, ethnic difference does not appear to be a factor in adjustment (Altstein and Simon, 1991).

(b)   ICA takes from the country potentially productive adults who could assist in that country's development.

There may be some grounds in this claim for some of the smaller Central American republics; but for countries like India and China population control is a major problem. Abandoned children in these countries are likely to grow up in large institutions. This experience, on the face of things, seems unlikely to help these individuals to become productive citizens. Rather, as in China they may be over-represented in the multi-million population which is kept in "administrative detention" - the State's solution to the problem of marginal or unwanted adults (AFP, 1992). Other countries such as Hong Kong, Costa Rica and Korea now only allow ICA for handicapped or special needs children for whom it is difficult or impossible to find adoptive homes locally.

(c)   The money spent on ICA would be better spent in providing services in developing countries which would prevent families being decimated and children abandoned because of extreme poverty.

The problem with this argument is that there is no guarantee that money which prospective adopters spend (on having social work assessments done, on medical checks for the child they wish to be adopted, on airfares in travelling to the country where the child resides, and in fees to lawyers who arrange the adoption) would be used instead for supporting local child welfare services. If all ICA were stopped, the money which the prospective adopters spend in acquiring an internationally-adopted child, would likely be spent in the couple's own country. Moreover, there is evidence from a number of case studies that once a couple have acquired an internationally-adopted child, they are then likely to support welfare services (through arrangements such as Foster Parent's Plan) in the country from which their child came.

(d)   Some countries who allow large numbers of children to be adopted overseas will as a result sponsor such adoptions as a solution to the problem of "unwanted" children, rather than providing in-country programs of family support.

Such a charge has been levelled against Korea, which has been the main supplier of babies for inter-country adoptions (Chun, 1989; Lewin, 1990). A related charge is that women will actually produce babies, knowing that lawyers will provide them with a fee
when they release the child for adoption.

(e)   It is alleged that some babies are actually stolen or kidnapped by criminal syndicates who market the baby for adoption. Other allegations are that unwilling mothers are coerced into giving up their child for adoption. It is clear that such abuses do occur, since there are a number of detailed and verified case histories, especially from Latin American countries (Fieweger, 1991). Some childless couples from North America, clearly desperate to adopt an infant from anywhere, and at almost any price offer a substantial temptation to criminal elements in developing countries, who meet the demands for infants in unscrupulous ways. Defence for Children International has documented a number of such abuses, including cases in which an impoverished woman is paid to say that the kidnapped child is hers, so that she can sign papers giving informed consent. Fieweger (1991) argues that many of these abuses go unchecked because the United States in particular has so far declined to sign any agreement in which sending and receiving countries would agree to adhere to the U.N. guidelines and principles on intercountry adoption. The only alternative, as occurred in Ecuador in 1989, is for the authorities to ban completely all intercountry adoptions (O'Shaughnessy, 1989).

There have also been allegations of Mafia involvement in the sale of babies for adoption in Naples (Boyes, 1988). Cases of the kidnapping of babies from peasant and transient women have also been made in Indonesia (UPI, 1980) and Bolivia (ICWR, 1984). In addition, agents in several parts of the developing world offer women in the poverty sector of large cities, substantial (in local terms) amounts of money to part with their babies for adoption (UNICEF, 1986). Countries from which children have been stolen and bought (according to apparently reliable reports) include Thailand, Guatemala, the Philippines, El Salvador, Sri Lanka, Romania, Taiwan, Turkey, and Peru (Chaponniere, 1983; Serrill, 1991). As Ngabonziza (1988) emphasized, until there is widespread incorporation of the U.N. principles into the laws of states participating in intercountry adoptions (including the funding of agencies which can oversee the conduct of such adoptions, making sure that no abuses take place) abuses of the intercountry adoption process are likely to continue. The United States is the major importer of babies for adoption, and through its lack of control over legal and social procedures through which intercountry adoptions are financed and arranged, this country is a major cause of the corrupt system which surrounds some intercountry adoptions.

Case study 1: United Kingdom

Britain's policy on inter-country adoption has developed in a slow and uncertain fashion. It is clear that professional social work organizations have been suspicious of and resistant to adoptions from overseas, for a variety of reasons. A survey by Bennett and Mostyn (1991) of 213 British couples who had adopted a child from overseas indicated that many of the respondents were dissatisfied with the hostile or indifferent attitudes of British social workers whom they had to consult. The authors of this survey report that: "There is clearly a crisis of confidence between prospective adopters and their Local Authority which has become worse over the years, since those adopting seven or more years ago were very likely to have had their Home Study conducted by the Local Authority ... Those who adopted within the last three years were significantly more likely to avoid the Local Authority. These social workers specializing in intercountry adoptions are, however not recognized by the British authorities, although their qualifications and reports are accepted abroad." (p. 9)

It appears that there is now an active policy amongst many local authorities in Britain to discourage adoptions from overseas "before Britain is deluged with foreign babies." According to the interviews with adopters reported by Bennett and Mostyn (1991) social workers often gave irrational or ethnocentric reasons for trying to discourage a couple from adopting overseas. Apparently many local authority social workers did not accept as adequate the motivation of the potential adopters' to be a "multi-racial/cultural family". There now appears to be a kind of reverse racism at work in many sectors of the human service profession in Britain - the idea that black children are reserved for black families, and white children for white families. Crossing these racial boundaries in any but token contact is seen as an undesirable manifestation of "white liberalism".

Ironically, the motivation to adopt overseas appears to have been stimulated in some cases by the difficult time the adopters had when they initially approached their local authority about an in-country adoption (Bennett and Mostyn, 1991, p. 41). One family who had adopted a black, British infant some years earlier were refused when they applied to the same local authority for another, similar child on the grounds that it was now policy to place black children only with black adopters.

Once the decision was made to adopt overseas (including an acceptance of the costs likely to be involved in travel, lawyers' and consultants fees, and so forth) most of the adoptions (85 percent) tended to be completed within nine months. In line with current trends towards open adoption, 96 of the 166 adoptive parents had actually met the birth mother, and many preserved mementos from the mother to pass on to the child as he or she grew older. Almost universally the adopting parents said that meeting the birth mother was a moving or useful experience.

The large majority of the adopters in this British survey were higher level professionals, a factor which may have accounted for their alienation from the professional social workers with whom they had to deal. Children from Sri Lanka accounted for 17 percent of the adoptees, followed by Brazil (16 percent), El Salvador (14 percent) and Thailand (9 percent). The average age of the 213 children adopted was nine months. Those from Thailand had the oldest average age of any group - 21 months at adoption. Those from Sri Lanka were, on average only 3 months old when adopted.

This study, carried under the auspices of the International Bar Association recommended a number of changes including the establishment of a central agency overseeing and co-ordinating the processes of intercountry adoption. This central agency would also act as an information clearing house on ICA. It was recommended also that British High Commissions and embassies overseas should receive clear directives from the Home Office and Foreign Office of Britain in how to deal with ICA, including the issuing of entry documents for the child once appropriate legal steps had been finalized for the approval of adoption in the child's own country. The report also recommended that the negative attitudes to ICA of many local authorities in Britain should be addressed through the appointment or designation of specialists in this field, and special workshops for training such individuals.

The British Agencies for Adoption and Fostering (BAAF) reacted to those criticisms in public debate, and the government in turn published a report on the reform of policies and regulations covering international adoption (Laurance, 1992). It appears that the government has largely accepted the recommendations of the International Bar Association, and has approved International Social Service as the body who will oversee intercountry adoptions in Britain. This choice clearly indicated that the government preferred ISS in this role, rather BAAF, which continued to voice negative views of intercountry adoption. It now appears that the U.N. principles on ICA may be adopted in British law and social work practice, with movement in Britain towards a more centralized role (as in the Netherlands) of a body having some power in monitoring and guiding responsible ICA practice, which can serve a child's best interests.

Barbara Tizard (1991), a noted British authority on child development, observed in a recent review of ICA:

As to the policy implications, it seems reasonable to conclude that, whilst children's needs are in most respects well met by intercountry adoption, a permanent and satisfactory home in their country of origin would save them from having to cope with problems of 'difference'. If such homes cannot be found, then in almost all respects their development is likely to be more satisfactory if adopted abroad than if abandoned in their country of origin. The earlier the adoption can be arranged, the smaller the chance that the child will have educational and behavioural problems. Political and ideological considerations are, of course, another matter, and are more likely to influence government policy considerations than is research evidence. (p. 756)

Case study 2: Korea

Korea has been a traditional sending country in ICA, but the role of this country is now changing, in ways which illustrate the problems and changing priorities in child care policy. Adoptions from Korea began after the civil war, in the 1950s, (Buck, 1964). At first these adoptions involved Eurasian children (with American fathers) but soon the practice of placing Korean babies overseas became institutionalized, with the aid of four large adoption agencies in the United States. In the decade 1979 to 1989 an average of 4,400 Korean babies were placed each year in the United States, by far the largest number from any country - followed by India, with an average of some 500 each year over the same period (Lewin, 1990). The majority of intercountry adopted children in Europe are also of Korean origin (Altstein and Simon, 1991).

The reasons why Koreans themselves did not adopt these children are similar to those in many other Asian countries - adoption was only considered as a means of perpetuating family lines in those without a male heir (Chun, 1989). The majority of children in residential care in Korea (as in China) are female. A very high birth rate in Korea up to the 1970s meant that there were many "surplus" children. Chun (1989) reports that the Korean government oversaw the international adoption of 20,963 children between 1955 and 1987, the majority going the United States, Germany and Denmark. In addition, at least another 30,000 infants were placed for overseas adoption by private agencies. The Netherlands and France have tended to adopt children from former colonies (eg Indonesia), or from overseas departments (as in the case of France).

Critics of ICA have pointed to Korea as an example of a country in which the possibility of placing "unwanted" children overseas had inhibited the development of local child welfare services. When Korea became a world showcase at the time of the 1988 Olympic Games a number of commentators wryly observed that Korea's chief export was still babies. The nation was clearly embarrassed by such commentary, and since that time the number of children released for overseas adoption has slowed. Much greater efforts are made to place a child locally, and now only children who fall into some "special needs" category are available for overseas adoption.

Despite the criticisms of Korean policy, the system had many benefits. The government of Korea had a keen interest in the process of adoption by both public and private agencies, which ensured that the Leysin guidelines were adhered to. There have been abuses in intercountry adoption (inducing parents to release children for financial reward; begetting of children for financial reward; and the actual stealing of children) - but such abuses have not, by all accounts, occurred in Korea.

Follow-up studies of children from Korea (reviewed elsewhere in this book; by Tizard, 1991; and by Altstein and Simon, 1991) have been remarkable for their agreement in showing the excellent outcomes for Korean children who grow up in white European or American families. Chun (1989) comments however that: "Studies of transcultural adoptions have so far shown remarkably positive results, but it is regrettable that the children investigated have been under 20 years of age. Adoption evaluation can be more precise if the adoptee is full-grown, with a fixed identity. I hope more studies on grown-up adoptees can be performed so that a better evaluation of our overseas adoption services can be achieved." (p. 260)

Case study 3: The Philippines

The Philippines has a long history of American influence, and many Filipinos have migrated to North America. Many overseas adoptions involving a Filipino child are in fact adoptions by relatives. However, the Philippines is assuming an increasing profile as a sending country in intercountry adoptions, since children without special needs are no longer available in Korea.

It was not until 1988 that the Philippines government, aware of a growing number of abuses of ICA including large sums offered to mothers to give up their child, enacted a law which placed all intercountry adoptions in the hands of government agencies in both the

Philippines and the receiving countries. At the time of writing the Philippine government had entered into bilateral agreements with Australia, Canada, Denmark, the Netherlands, Norway, German and Sweden. Negotiations are pending on an agreement with the United States, although there have been informal agreements with social service agencies serving U.S. military personnel in the Philippines on the overseas adoption of mixed-race children - these children usually have an American father and a Filipino mother.

Balanon (1989) indicates that at any point in time there are at least 8,000 children in residential care in the Philippines, without any parental contact. Many of these children would benefit from adoptive homes. However only about 2,000 within-country adoptions are finalized each year, and about 500 intercountry adoptions (a third by relatives) in the same period. The limited number of Filipino adopters can afford to be selective: "More Filipino families prefer a healthy female infant, fair-skinned with high-bridged nose and a fairly good family background." (Balanon, 1989 p.243). Children with some form of handicap, however mild are virtually impossible to place for adoption within the Philippines, as are children with a presumed "negative heredity" including mothers who were known to have been prostitutes, or to have criminal backgrounds.

Balanon (1989) points to new and worthwhile developments in the Philippines, including a link to agencies in Europe and America which "foster" children who remain with their families; and the early identification of children in residential institutions who have lost all parental contact, and are legally available for adoption.

Extreme poverty as a cause of child abandonment in the Philippines seem to be increasing. We agree with Davis (1987) that the policy of "children first" must include a more adequate policy of family support which can prevent parental death, and the forced abandonment of children. (1)

Case study 4: India

India is another country where economic conditions and the stability of family life have shown little improvement since the writer first began research on child welfare in that country (Bagley, 1979).

Both foster and adoptive care have developed slowly in India, and can by no measure provide the answer to the problems of the 25 million children in India today who live in institutions of one kind or another (Khan, 1991). The following figures were gathered by the Indian Council for the Promotion of Adoption, giving numbers in institutions of various kinds. Forty percent of the institutions have a sectarian basis; the majority of the sectarian institutions are run by Muslims, with Hindus and Christians providing a smaller number of homes. The reason so many Muslim children are in institutions relates to Muslim policy on adoption.

Table 1   Children in India in institutions, needing family care

Known cause of Institutional Care	1971	1976	1981	1991
Children aged 0-4 where:				
Father dead or absent	2,105,000	2,208,000	2,333,648	2,547,380
Mother dead or absent	1,315,000	1,465,000	1,526,530	1,342,114
Both parents dead, or child abandoned	34,000	32,000	31,000	29,618
All institutionalized children aged 0-4	24,124000	25,449,000	26,823,246	32,788,931

Note: These are the figures for children in institutions licensed by the various Indian States. Not included are a large number of children, probably over a million, placed directly in homes as domestic servants and who are aged less than 14.

Over the period 1976 to 1987 I regularly visited a number of institutions for children in the Bombay area, run by various religious groups. The standard of care is adequate from the point of view of health and nutrition and is certainly better than the lot of many children in the slums of the city; but the poor ratio of staff to children, and the strict regimes observed are quite different from those familiar in Western settings. The best arrangement I observed was that of a Hindu Women's Aid Society which provided a home for elderly women, who at the same time looked after children aged 3 to 10. The children are taught simple skills of craft and housework, and are found employment and marriage partners (through the Hindu system of arranged marriages) later on. I was less happy about the Catholic and Muslim institutions, particulary when the Catholic agencies had to engage in "rescue" work of young girls who had been brought up in institutions and who were now drifting into prostitution. Research by the Tata Institute of Social Sciences in Bombay has indicated that many of the adolescent prostitutes (for which Bombay is notorious) are recruited from girls with no stable family background.

In Bombay two-thirds of children are in institutions because their parent or parents are destitute, and cannot provide even a minimum of adequate care (Bagley, 1979). The remainder were either given up by the mothers because they were born out of wedlock, or were simply abandoned as infants. An abandoned infant is made a ward of the State, and placed in an institution, where about half will die within a few months. This is not usually because of the poor standards of care in the institutions (though epidemics of infection do take their toll) but because of the nutritional and endemic disease status of the child before he or she was abandoned, most of abandoned children are female, and about two-thirds of children in institutions are girls. This reflects the value placed on male children in traditional Indian society; in times of distress or extreme economic shortage, a girl will be given up rather than a boy.

The traditional practice of Hindu adoption as codified in the Hindu Adoption and Maintenance Act is a pale reflection of the complexities of traditional Hindu law, of which there are different schools, and different rules by caste and by sex. Traditionally, caste Hindus may adopt a male child if they have no male child as an heir. The child should be adopted from a family, usually related, of similar caste status. For the three highest castes the adoption involves an elaborate religious ceremony, but this is not required for the lowest of the four caste groups. The sub-castes, or untouchables are not allowed to adopt. Much work has been done in India towards the removal of caste barriers, but as a social force they remain strong and still carry certain legal statuses, as in the practice of adoption. No law exists by which Parsees, Christians and Muslims may adopt. Under Hindu law it is not possible for an abandoned child to be adopted, since its antecedents are not known. The majority of Hindu children in institutions are presumed to be from lowly backgrounds, and being children of low caste or untouchable parents they are unadoptable in terms of the Hindu Act. The Hindu Adoption Act of 1965 allows the adoption of a son, then of a daughter, then of a son, and then of a daughter, and so on, provided that the couple have no biological sons or daughters. However, the majority of children adopted under the Hindu Act are boys. The exact number is not known, since there is no obligation to legally register such adoptions (2).

The alternative procedure for non-Hindus, or Hindus who want to adopt a child whose caste antecedents are not known is to take out Guardianship proceedings, under the Guardians and Wards Act of 1890.

This Act is used too for inter-country adoptions, an agency or an individual being appointed a child's guardian for a temporary period until satisfactory arrangements for adoption can be made in the country from which the potential adopters come.

There is widespread agreement amongst the social workers in Hindu, Christian and secular agencies in Bombay and New Delhi that the present state of the law is unsatisfactory, and that a new Adoption Act is required. The Indian Council of Social Welfare, and the Indian Council for the Promotion of Adoption have been active in promoting a national adoption Bill, albeit unsuccessfully. The first Adoption Bill was presented to the national legislative body in 1955, but was withdrawn because of pressure from certain Ministers. A new Bill was drafted by the Indian Council of Social Welfare in 1965 and introduced after some local debate to the legislative assembly in 1967; it was finally introduced in Parliament by a Minister in 1972, and referred to a committee, which deliberated slowly, before abandoning the Bill. By 1990 no further progress in passing this Bill had been made. The Indian Association for the Promotion of Adoption was formed in 1970 to press for the passage of the Bill, and the greater acceptance of adoption and foster care in Indian. Most support for the Bill came from Bombay and the State of Maharashtra; the major difficulty was the steadfast opposition of the Muslim community to the Bill.

Traditional adoption practice and law had been based on the needs of communities for a stable system of inheritance, and not on any concept of the needs or welfare of the child. The changing view of the child in India was put forcefully by the Indian Council for Child Welfare in their journal in 1974: "..... The experience teaches us that it is really so: a child deprived of a family environment is always fatally injured in his possibilities of expression ; the balance of his development is destroyed; his general physical condition is affected; his psycho-emotional level is greatly inferior to the average level; he is injured in his speech. The child develops an attitude of sadness and indifference...."

However, Muslim opposition to a national Adoption Act has always been strong. The nature of Islamic opposition to the Adoption Bill can be judged from the Minute of Dissent given by Masquood Ali Khan, and two other Muslim colleagues in the report of the 45-member committee on the Adoption Bill, published in 1976. Mr. Khan proposed a subsidiary clause to the Bill, "This Act shall not apply to persons governed by the Muslim Law". This clause was unacceptable to the majority of the remainder of the committee. One reason for this may have been that Roman Catholic opposition to an earlier Bill on abortion had been ignored - but the plea then had been the same, that an Act offensive to the Catholic conscience should not legally apply to Catholics. Parliament could not accept a situation in which a national law should permit some, but not other members of the community differentiated on religious basis, to indulge in certain actions. The same logic applies to the Adoption Bill, reflecting the Indian constitutional guarantee that all, of whatever religion, must receive equal treatment in law.

It is clear from the lengthy evidence presented by Mr. Khan and his colleagues that the Bill caused a considerable stir in the Muslim intellectual community. The committee received thousands of letters from Muslims opposing the Bill, and hundreds of scholars and religious leaders gave verbal evidence to the committee opposing it. Fundamentally, the opposition is based on a verse in the Quran (Chapter 33:4), in which the absolute and binding word of God is addressed to His Prophet Mohammed: "... nor hath he made your adopted sons your real sons. This is only your saying by your mouths, whereas Allah sayeth the truth and guideth the way".

Mohammed adopted Hazrath Zaid as his son. This adopted son ultimately divorced the wife Mohammed had found for him. Because this adopted son did not by this action show due filial respect, the adoption was unpopular, and apparently led ultimately to divine injunction. Masquood Ali Khan and his colleagues argued that modern psychological evidence shows that adoptions frequently have a poor outcome, and that this is another manifestation of the divine wisdom. They continue in their evidence: "It is against the spirit of secularism that a particular religious belief is imposed upon others who do not subscribe to it. To say that the Bill is enabling in its character does not put it on a different footing from other civil laws. The divine character of the Muslim Jurisprudence can only be understood by those who either have faith in Islam or have made a deep study of the subject and hold a sympathetic view about the credulity of the Godly revelations to the Holy Prophet" (RSC, 1976).

The Muslim opposition to the Adoption Bill seems therefore to be severely uncompromising. The evidence given by the Muslim witnesses points to the well-known Islamic practice of fosterage - "in this country a number of orphanages testify to this fact". A family too may take on a related child, provided it is clear that he cannot inherit from this new family. While acknowledging that "hundreds of thousands of Muslim children in India are abandoned every year" the Islamic community in India have set their faces firmly against giving children without parents a normal family life. One detects a feeling of ambiguity on this issue throughout the Muslim world - Ismail (1977) writing on the future of the child in the Muslim world noted that children are protected by the severe sanctions against illegitimacy in Islam! Unfortunately, illegitimate

183

children that are produced have to be stigmatised in order to maintain the penalties against such behaviour. A conference on the future of children in the Islamic world declared, that Islam gives the child the right to life, social acceptance, nourishment, inheritance, affectionate treatment, protection against injustice, and the right to spiritual freedom. Illegitimate and abandoned children, presumably, are often excluded from such rights. Nowhere in the proceedings of this conference on the rights of the child is family life mentioned. It is notable however that in Libya, Tunisia, Malaysia, Indonesia and Algeria the Islamic community has accepted the secular practice of adoption.

The Islamic community in India, according to the evidence of Khan and his colleagues, has dismissed this apparent acceptance by Muslims of adoption in some countries, suggesting that these Acts "have been imposed by dictators without regard to the religious passions and sentiments of the people". What seems more likely is that the fierce opposition to adoption by Muslims in India relates to their position as a minority community, with feelings of insecurity accentuated by recent history of bloody clashes between Hindu and Muslim communities, and between India and Pakistan. The Islamic community is too, economically disadvantaged in India and in previous centuries attracted many converts from the untouchable class. In such a climate the more rigid tenets of Islam are accentuated.

According to our research and calculations, at least a quarter of a million children aged under five, in non-Muslim institutions, could be adopted tomorrow (there being no parental ties) if adoptive homes, either in India or overseas, were available. Research on conditions in institutions, and the long-term outcome for children brought up there is not encouraging.. While there are some excellent institutions which provide a showplace for the visitor, a more comprehensive survey provides a rather different picture.

Vigorous attempts have been made by various agencies, especially in Bombay, Delhi, Calcutta and Madras, to stimulate Indians to foster children or to take out Guardianship orders (Billimoria, 1984). Sometimes middle class families will take children for long periods, while working class families will take children needing temporary care. Indian welfare workers frankly admit that foster-care is not well-developed in India, for both cultural and economic reasons, and institutions will provide the main basis for substitute care for many year to come.

All of the workers we spoke to accepted that intercountry adoption provided a small but welcome relief to the problems of some children who would otherwise grow up in institutions, and intercountry adoption would need to continue on as large a scale as possible for a considerable period. If and when an Indian Adoption Bill is passed the way will be open for Indian couples to adopt within India, and the passage of the Bill may provide a social stimulus for such adoptions. Workers at the Indian Council of Social Welfare in Bombay, and the Indian Council for Child Welfare in New Delhi were sure too, that an adoption order made on a child before he or she left India would ensure more adequate safeguards, and allow pre- and post- adoption enquiries to be carried out on a more adequate basis.

One of the advantage of inter-country adoption from India is that adopters from overseas rarely make stipulations about the child's colour or social background. Class, caste and colour coincide in many cases, and the institutionalized children are usually from dark-skinned, lower class or caste backgrounds, while the potential adoptive or foster parents within India are medium or light-skinned, and from a higher social status. Skin colour remains a salient basis for social preference in India, as does caste.

The number of overseas adoptions from India has grown steadily since the late 1960s. Exact numbers are difficult to specify, but in the State of Maharashtra about 1,500 Guardianship orders are made a year involving children to be adopted overseas. According to the statistics for Maharashtra, the largest single number go to Sweden, followed by Belgium. The number going to the United Kingdom (about 50 a year) is tiny compared with the number going to these countries. These could indeed by mainly cases of Indian immigrants to Britain adopting related children. As one worker put it, the post-colonial connection has meant that people from Britain have little interest in India, in spheres of welfare, aid and adoption.

There is no evidence that from the surveys I made in India to indicate that the continued practice of inter-country adoption of Indian children was in any way harmful to the development of welfare services, or hindered the growth of indigenous fostering and adoption. Even if the amount of inter-country adoption from India were to double or triple, it would still make only a small dent in the estimated quarter of a million children who need adopting each year in India. The massive and continuing problems of poverty and associated problems in providing for a growing population in which a high proportion of people are aged 14 or less will plague India for many years, even with massive aid inputs from other countries. Only when these problems have been overcome can the policy of inter-country adoption be realistically reviewed. Meanwhile, the practice assures that a comparatively small number of children each year have an adequate home life which, in institutional care, they would have been denied.

In 1984 the Indian Supreme Court used a suit alleging baby selling as a vehicle for ruling that all intercountry adoptions had to supervized by government-approved agencies. This has led to a decline in the number of overseas adoptions, from 1,677 in 1988 to 1,272 in 1989. Efforts to provide permanent guardianship for children with Indian families have been relatively successful, the number so placed rising from 398 in 1988 to 1,075 in 1989. Nevertheless, the total number of children "adopted" both overseas and by local guardianship orders remains a tiny fraction of the numbers of children available for adoption, and in desperate need of family care. These official figures do not include traditional adoptions within the religious traditions of Hinduism. (2) No studies which have identified Indian adoptees as a specific group in follow-up work in ICA appear to be available. However, a number of European studies are available of intercountry adopted children which include those from India, without identifying specific outcomes for the Indian sub-group (Tizard, 1991). Norwegian researchers (Dalen and Saetersdal, 1987; Saetersdal and Dalen, 1991) studied outcomes for 182 children, the majority of whom came from India. Many of these children were in poor health on arrival, and also had problems of regression to early stages of development when they arrived. However, such physical dependency and (in many cases) loss of verbal skills would be likely to facilitate bonding with the new parents. Several years after arrival about 15 percent of these children had significant problems of behaviour and adaptation. Given the findings of other research (Kuehl, 1985; Altstein and Simon, 1991) we would expect these problems to diminish with time. Hoksbergen (1991) reports that a long-term study is in progress in the Netherlands comparing Indian children adopted in that country with Indian children in their mother country who were not adopted.

Case study 5: Romania

Various organizations working in the field of ICA - International Social Service, Terres des Hommes and the International Union for Child Welfare - are in agreement that intercountry adoptions should not be practised in the wake of war, famine or civil disruption. The case of Biafra in Nigeria is an oft-cited example in which large numbers of orphaned or displaced children were placed locally, when order and prosperity were restored. In 1988 authorities in what was then the Soviet Union took hundreds of orphaned children out of earthquake-stricken Armenia, for adoption in other Republics of the USSR, a practice condemned by Armenian exiles as representing a form of cultural genocide.

Despite the well-enunciated U.N. principles, the case of Romania provides yet another example of how not to conduct international adoptions. The traditional government of Romania was toppled in December, 1989 and a horrified world saw on their TV screens some of the 14,000 "abandoned" or apparently unwanted children in institutions of the worst kind. There was an immediate interest from many childless couples in the European and North America in adopting at least the minority of those children who were healthy, white infants.

However, it soon became clear that the adoptions initiated by these anxious couples often violated the U.N. principles on ICA. In conditions of turmoil and chaos the original parents were difficult to locate, and it appears that many of the children were placed for adoption before it was clear whether or not their biological parents had agreed to this. It was apparent too that many parents had given their children up both because of great poverty, and pressure from the state. The Romanian government, clearly preoccupied with many other issues of reform veered between banning all foreign adoptions for a period, then allowing them unchecked, finally reaching bilateral agreements with a number of countries, including Canada, for careful controls of the conduct and procedures associated with such adoptions (Globe, 1992).

A year earlier a reporter from the London Observer (Clark, 1991) was able to photograph apparently destitute women offering to "sell" their child to a potential adopter for a hundred pounds sterling. Another women was observed giving her two infant children to a Canadian woman for $500 (a year's wages for a workman). The bewildered young woman asked, through a translator "Is Canada in Romania?" The Romanian lawyer arranging this transaction charged a fee of $5,000. By the time Romania gained control of the situation, several thousand children had left the country with their adoptive parents.

Case study 6: China and Hong Kong

The People's Republic of China faces many problems of economic growth, population control, social organization, and social change. The usual response to problems is to formulate solutions at a national level, based on ideological reasons rather than on pragmatic grounds or human logic. The solution to the problem of overpopulation is both awesome and extraordinary. By state decree no couple is allowed to have more than one child, and various forms of coercion and control are directed towards this end.

Abortion and child welfare are closely linked in many countries, and lack of good child welfare and family support services are often cited as good grounds for abortion (Bagley, 1991c). In China too compulsory abortions are required for welfare reasons, since too many children will drain national resources in many areas.

John Aird (1990) entitles his book on birth control policy in China, Slaughter of the Innocents, indicating his view that compulsory, third-trimester abortions carried out in abattoir-like circumstances, without regard for the needs, wishes, bodily integrity or sensibility to pain (physical and psychological) of the women involved, are a violation of all humane principles. Hopefully, not even the most vigorous "freedom of choice" persons in the abortion debate would advocate such pseudo-medical interventions (3). Aird cites evidence from observers of the practical working of China's one-child policy. It must be emphasized that the Chinese government denies that the alleged events have taken place, or that the enforcement of third-abortions leads to abuses. Aird's informants (who are of course dissidents of one kind or another, and are subject to criminal sanctions) reported the routine practice of post-birth abortion (usually by smashing the skull, by the injection of alcohol into the fontanel, or by the stuffing of gauze into the foetus's mouth following delivery). Usually the foetuses put down in this manner are female (Aird, 1990, pp 28-9, 91-2, 135-6).

Clearly, a complicating factor in the one-child policy is the preference of many Chinese people for sons rather than daughters. This preference (shared with many other Asian cultures, including India) is a reflection of economic need, as well as traditional values. A couple whose first child is female are faced with a quandary, since there is pressure for them to have no more children. The sanctions for having a second child include loss of state benefits, housing and employment. Yet the couple who earnestly desire a son must, when a son is born, put their daughter into alternative care, or else abandon any female child as soon as she is born. A couple may secretly have a second child if their first child was female. If the second child is also female, the couple's dilemma is acute.

Official statistics in the People's Republic of China indicate that for every 100 female children surviving beyond birth in the period 1980 to 1997, 120 male children survived. Some observers have concluded that this implies infanticide on a massive scale, since under natural conditions the ratio would be 106 males born fro every 100 females. Since males have higher rates of perinatal mortality, the survival ratio after a child's first birthday should be about one female for every male. However, Swedish and Chinese demographers have offered a more optimistic interpretation of the recorded imbalance in favour of male children (Johansson, Nygren and Xuan, 1991). These researchers located about half of the missing 2.5 female children as residents in institutions or in foster survive, but are hidden from official demographic surveys by parents and relatives. Probably less than half a million female children were put down in the first year of life, in the period 1980 to 1987. Almost all of the children formally adopted in China are male, the adopters being infertile couples who want a son (4).

The survival of female children in institutions is not a matter of complete rejoicing however. A detailed description of an orphanage in Fuzhou, People's Republic of China may give the reader an idea of the conditions in which abandoned or unwanted children try and survive. In the Fuzhou State Orphanage there are about 70 children at any point in time. The large majority are girls. Almost all of the boys have some handicap or blemish. In China however, a child can be labelled as handicapped simply for being ugly, or having unsightly birthmarks (Chan, 1991). The children lie or sit in rows, without attention for many hours. Those that attempt to wander are tied with rags by their arms to chairs or cribs. Most learn to become passive within a few weeks. Youngsters two or three years of age sit or lie motionless in tiny wooden beds. Many remain in these beds for 24 hours a day, without bedding or pillows, attended from time to time for toileting, change of clothes, and feeding. Given the staff-to-child ratio, they are attended infrequently. No one talks to these children, and their verbal skills are rudimentary. The workers in this and other institutions are poorly-paid, and without training. Supervision of their activities is minimal. The children have no toys, and no-one plays with them. There are no outings, and no visitors. By the age of seven the inmates will graduate to a larger institution, with a harsher regime. Feeding of the infants is by a bottle propped into their mouth. No-one holds them.

Faced with a lack of resources with which to run these institutions properly, the Chinese government has co-operated with external agencies in making orphanage children available for overseas adoption, and several hundred prospective parents a month pass through Hong Kong en route for China to begin the first stage of adopting an infant. It appears however that unscrupulous middle-men can exploit this process, in ways which mean that the U.N. principles on international adoption are frequently violated.

Chinese law allows the adoption only of a child that has been abandoned. However, a class of middle-men has emerged who both violate this law, and forge documents which show that the child is free for adoption. Male and female reporters from the South China Morning

Post (Woolrich, 1992) visited Guangzhou, posing as potential adopters. They were offered two female children, one an infant and the other a toddler, for US$5,000. At no stage were they asked for documentation, such as a social work report from their country of origin. The papers offered by the intermediary purported to show that the children had been abandoned; in fact they had been fostered by women trying to hide their existence from the authorities. The intermediary told the journalists: "You have to say that you went to the orphanage yourselves, you must not tell them about me. They have to think the baby is a genuine orphan or they won't let you take it. You could tell them that her parents are dead." The intermediary (a Hong Kong businessman) claimed to have influence with senior Communist Party officials in Gaungdong Province. The documentation indicating that the journalists had now "adopted" the children were good enough to ensure clearance with the American embassy in Hong Kong for the entry of the children into the United States. In this case history it is, once again, the laissez faire policy of the United States which makes abuse of the inter-country adoption process so easy for wealthy couples.

Cantwell (1992) in a paper given to a conference on adoption policy produced evidence collected by Defence for Children International indicating that corrupt middle-men were earning huge profits by persuading women to give up children for small sums, and then producing forged papers for the potential adoptions. These abuses occur in China, Colombia, Brazil, Sri Lanka and the Philippines, and possibly elsewhere.

The wide availability of healthy infants in Southern China has had an effect on adoption practice in Hong Kong. A Chinese couple wishing to adopt will go across the border to Guangdong Province, rather than adopting a child locally. The locally available children usually have some handicapping condition, or have a suspected negative heredity (i.e. they are children of prostitutes, addicts, and the like). However, resident Europeans in Hong Kong have no difficulty in adopting such children, once the appropriate home studies have been carried out.

In June, 1992 the Beijing-based China Daily reported that the government of the People's Republic of China had set up a special centre for the processing of intercountry adoptions of chinese infants. The PRC government is clearly committed to supporting and regularizing the intercountry adoption process, which is seen as aiding the one-child policy. According the China Daily report the new centre will facilitate and speed up ICA. In 1992 the majority of the children adopted (all of them girls) were adopted by couples from Canada, United States, Germany and the Netherlands.

Health problems of children adopted internationally

One interesting issue is the health status of internationally adopted children, and how problems reflecting their earlier deprived status are linked with physical health, growth and emotional adjustment. I have been intrigued by this issue since one of my own adopted sons made a massive growth spurt which paralleled his emotional adjustment, following a period of settling in and recovery from malnutrition. French (1986) suggests from a clinical case study that children working through previous losses can also "grow" following this successful resolution, both physically and psychologically.

A number of researchers have addressed this issue. The work of Winnick et al (1975) showing that adopted children overcome what seemed to be massive and permanently handicapping conditions of malnutrition early in life has already been mentioned. Thompson (1986) presents similar evidence (on a severely-deprived Colombian child) showing that adoption by an American couple when the child was three years led to very satisfactory physically, scholastic and behavioural outcomes by the time the boy was 14. Cases such as this have considerable theoretical significance for developmental psychologists, since they demonstrate that even the most profound psychological and physical deprivation early in life can be overcome by the process of adoptive re-parenting.

Children adopted from tropical climates have been found to frequently suffer from environmentally-acquired diseases of the liver, lungs and gastro-intestinal system. Hotetter et al. (1989) found in a 52 children adopted in the United States, many with serious health problems which had not been detected by a superficial medical examination in the country of origin. The Dutch expert Rene Hoksbergen (1991) is the only specialist to have described the interplay between emotional and physical development in international adoptees. He argues that comprehensive medical examination and care is essential when the child arrives. In his study of 350 international adoptees, 20 percent were suffering from the effects of long-term malnutrition; 15 percent from intestinal and parasitic disorders; and 15 percent from skin diseases. A new worry is that children from countries such as Haiti may have been infected with the latent immune-deficiency virus.

Some critics of ICA (e.g. Lampo et al., 1988) have argued that the presence of such health risks is yet another argument against ICA. The counter argument is that if ICA can help some children overcome these potentially handicapping conditions, then it will certainly have been worth while.

Conclusions

In drawing conclusions about intercountry adoption, we share Rene Hoksbergen's ambivalent conclusions: in an ideal world there would be no need for ICA, and every country would have the material and spiritual resources to care for its own children, ensuring them all of the richness of family life, with minimum disruptions of care and attachment (Hoksbergen, 1985 & 1991). Yet, when properly conducted and supervized according to the U.N. principles, intercountry adoption can meet the needs of children for love, nurturance, cultural support and stimulation - even for children who are ethnically different from their adoptive parents. As Hoksbergen (1991) concluded:

> ... the 20,000 inter-country adopted children who have arrived in Holland in the last 20 years are very welcome and have a good chance of leading fulfilling lives. But we also have to see them as a symptom of ailing societies, societies, that in the interests of these children, have let them move far away from their homelands and birth parents. (Hoksbergen 1991, pp 156-7).

An important rider to this conclusion is that the society into which the adopted children are absorbed must itself be largely non-racist in its attitudes and behaviour towards the ethnic minority groups. The Netherlands has been particularly accepting of peoples from Asia, and has a long history of tolerance in the sphere or race relations (Bagley, 1973). The same cannot be said of Britain (Bagley et al., 1979), or of Canada (Bagley et al., 1989), and in those countries those who adopt ethnic minority children have had to face not only the usual problems of adoption, but also the pressures of a society which still has many racist elements.

The evolution of ICA should ideally move from the adoption of children overseas to one of within-country adoption in the developing country. Countries which traditionally have accepted children for overseas adoption would then accept only "special needs" children, parallel to the task of sponsoring the development of child welfare services within that developing country. Such evolution is clearly evident in countries such as Costa Rica and Korea.

A major problem in ICA has been the role of unscrupulous middle-men in developing countries, who pander to the powerful motivations to adopt a child which motivate couples from Europe and North America to seek a baby, at seemingly any cost. These often corrupt middlemen may bribe or deceive an impoverished women into surrendering her child. Informed consent in such a case cannot be given. Such abuses are seemingly easy to control - for example the Ministry of Social Welfare in the Philippines has set up a desk close to the emigration counter at Manila International Airport. The purpose of the duty social workers at this desk is to check infants and children travelling with adults who are not their legal guardians, as a check on "adoptions" which have bypassed official agencies; and to curb attempts by paedophiles to depart with children they have befriended, or bought. The possibility that paedophiles might be abusing the ICA system in order to gain access to children must be seen as the ultimate outrage, and violation of the principles of adoption. Unfortunately there is at least one case documented (see Chapter 13) in which unsuspecting authorities placed a boy for adoption with a single male from another country, who subsequently abused the child.

End notes

(1)   The reality of this problem has confronted me profoundly in the past five years, during which time I have been administering Canadian funds in the Philippines, identifying with the aid of Priests and lay-workers, street adolescents at risk of entering prostitution. The Canadian funds provide scholarships to help these young women to complete their education, offering in addition social and material supports to the families of origin. In the Philippines as in India much child abandonment is forced by extreme poverty.

(2)   When I asked my Hindu friend and colleague, Gajendra K. Verma to be God Father to my youngest daughter, the request initially caused some consternation, since in Hinduism the Christian concept of being a God Father is unknown. However, in a splendid ceremony Abigail was both inducted into Hinduism, and was formally adopted by her Hindu God Father. Abigail now has two fathers, and two religions, Christianity and Hinduism. I can assure the reader that Krishna and Christ co-exist peaceably in our household.

(3)   I became interested in abortion policy when, as a conscientious objector to compulsory military service in Britain, I worked as a hospital orderly. One of my tasks was to dispose of unwanted products of surgical operations - amputated limbs, foetuses, etc. Some of the aborted foetuses were still breathing, kicking and crying when I collected them for disposal. There was nothing I could do to keep them alive, but this experience impressed on me the grave ethical dilemmas in second and third-trimester abortions. My position on abortion has gone through various stages (Bagley, 1976; 1988d; 1991d). My current position is that termination of pregnancy involves few ethical dilemmas whilst the pregnancy is in the embryo stage, in the first 10 weeks of gestation. However, once the foetus has a central nervous system indicating "brain life" (the opposite of "brain death" which is well-described in the literature on critically ill neonates), then the destruction of this human personality should only be considered when another, greater wrong is anticipated such as requiring a rape or incest victim to carry a

foetus to term. I have argued vigorously that abortion should not be a routine solution to problems of poverty and lack of adequate child and child welfare services, low wages, lack of affordable housing etc. Adoption of course is a creative solution to the problem of "unwanted" children. In absolute terms, no child is ever unwanted. My argument (as befits a Quaker position) is that the appeal to the inherent goodness in human beings should be enough to prevent a child in utero being put down. The law should not be involved in this area, except to regulate and require good medical practice in terminations. I am impressed by Hindu metaphysics which imply that if one is born as a robber, a prostitute or an abortionist, salvation (in terms of favourable rebirth) lies in being a good and efficient thief or executioner. The Christian position (which does not differ greatly from the Hindu metaphysic) is to love the sinner unreservedly and without condemnation: all human beings and all human situations can be redeemed through love.

(4)   According to the references and sources cited by Aird (1990) - including Communist Party documents, and local press reports in China - traditional practices of female infanticide ended in 1949 with the establishment of the People's Republic of China. These practices were resurrected as the result of Communist Party pressure some 30 years later, when the program of enforced population control was at its height. In 1981 Deng Xiaoping urged family planning officials: "Use whatever means you must [to enforce the one child policy] but do it!". (Aird, 1990, p.92).

According to Chinese media reports appearing between 1981 and 1987, in many rural area women voluntarily aided Communist Party cadres in reviving pre-revolutionary practices, in putting down or abandoning new-born female children: "According to medical reports, unwanted female infants were often drowned at birth in buckets of water placed purposefully beside the delivery bed, or they were thrown down wells or into ponds, buried alive, or abandoned under bridges, in fields, by riversides, in railway stations, hospitals, or public toilets." (Aird, 1990, p.136). In addition, gravely ill female (but not male) infants were often denied admission to hospital - another factor accounting for the disproportionate number of surviving male children.

Further evidence of the trend towards genocide of female infants following the initiation of a more vigorous one-child policy in 1980 comes from an editorial in the Journal of Chinese Youth, in 1983. This editorial published an appeal under the heading "Let us save our new-born baby girls!". The editorial suggested that drowning babies or abandoning them in the open country side were "harsh and inhuman acts" based on "feudal" concepts which regarded males as people worthy of veneration, and females as objects of scorn. The Journal, a popular monthly read by many Chinese youth was responding to numerous letters on this topic from it's readers. In certain communes the boy/girl ratio of survival was said to be three to two. Besides the abandonment and genocide of female infants, many urban Chinese women were obtaining abortions when amniocentesis indicated that the foetus was of female sex.

For further information on the effects of China's one child policy see White (1992).

194

11 Adopted girls from Hong Kong in Britain: A twenty year follow-up of adjustment and social identity

Introduction

In 1981 we reported a follow-up study of 67 Chinese girls, then in their mid-teens to their early twenties, who had been adopted by British parents in the period 1962 to 1964 (Bagley and Young, 1981). All of these girls came from an orphanage in Sha Tin, Hong Kong which had been run by an Anglican Foundation. When the director retired it was decided to close the orphanage, and some 100 of the residents, all girls, were placed for adoption in Britain through Dr. Barnardo's Children's Society, and the National Children's Home. The girls had all been abandoned or surrendered in infancy as unwanted. All were physically healthy, though some had minor disabilities. In this period no non-disabled, infant males were abandoned or surrendered for adoption in Hong Kong.

Nothing is known about the family background of these girls, and there was no parental contact. No local adoptive homes could be found for these girls, whose ages ranged from a few months to nine years old. It seemed both logical and humane to seek adoptive homes in Britain through the two available agencies. Both these agencies had a Christian foundation, and the adopters included some Anglo-Chinese couples, reflecting the fact that some parents had worked as missionaries in China or in Hong Kong. About a quarter of the adoptive fathers were ministers of religion. In our follow-up of the adoptees it was an extremely pleasant task to drive across England to various country vicarages, and meet these elegant young women and their parents in rather gracious, rural surroundings.

In our initial follow-up we made contact with 76 of the 90 sets of parent who had adopted the 100 girls (some parents adopted more than one child). The sample selection was governed by the fact that these families lived not more than a day's drive from London, a strategy dictated by our limited funding resources! Once located, parents were very co-operative, and 67 of the 76 returned our initial questionnaire enquiring about educational and social progress, and various problems encountered. For our initial report (Bagley and Young, 1981) 51 of these parents and their 53 adopted children were interviewed, personally, a few more than once. Our usually strategy was for the male researcher (CB) to interview parents, and the female researcher (CB's partner, Loretta Young) to interview the daughter. Some standardized testing of self-esteem, identity and adjustment was undertaken with the girls.

Our theoretical assumptions in undertaking this research are grounded in ego-identity theory (Erikson, 1963 and 1968). Based on Erikson's identity theory, we assume that a child goes through successive "identity dilemmas" in which at various stages of development he or she has to synthesize what has been experienced earlier with new roles and psychological tasks which are demanded at different ages. Erikson proposed that there are eight life stages (six involving childhood, adolescence and young adulthood).

These stages begin the first year of life, involving basic trust versus mistrust of the caring figures; in the second year, autonomy versus shame and doubt; in the third to fifth years, initiative versus guilt; in the sixth to eleventh years, industry versus inferiority; in puberty and adolescence, identity development versus role confusion; and in young adulthood, intimacy versus isolation. Closely related to the development of identity in adolescence and young adulthood are Maslow's "need levels" for safety, physical nurturance, love and belonginess, self-esteem and self-actualization (Maslow, 1954; Shostrom, 1964; Ben-Porat, 1977). We have synthesized these and other accounts of personal development in a theory of identity and global self-esteem in relation to ethnic identity issues (Young and Bagley, 1982).

In the accounts of personal development of Erikson and Maslow, the success which an individual has in coping with his or her personal and social needs at any point in time is intimately related to the degree to which particular needs during earlier stages were fulfilled, or frustrated. Thus an adolescent who has successfully resolved or passed earlier stages of development in relation to current role obligations, and whose needs for an adequate sense of personal worth are met, can successfully cope with considerable stress later in life (he or she will posses adequate reserves of "ego strength") compared with an individual who has been relatively unsuccessful in identity synthesis in adolescence. An adolescent with multiple previous failures in identity stage development, and an interpersonal environment which has failed to meet certain basic needs (for love, warmth, belonginess and esteem development) may develop a "fixated identity": which does not permit further identity development, the development of altruism, the elaboration of cognitive and social skills, or in Maslow's terminology allow "self-actualization.

Identity development in the adopted adolescent has the special feature that the child must incorporate into identity structure the knowledge that the present parents are not biological parents, and that the original parent gave the child up for adoption or alternative care. Some writers have argued that this task may make the adopted child particularly likely to develop anxiety and neurosis, with various kinds of identity crisis in early and late adolescence (Sorosky, Baron and Pannor, 1984).

David Kirk (1964 and 1981) has argued that the identity problems implicit in the roles of both parents and children in adopting families can best be solved by openness about the adoption, honesty and enthusiasm about the child's natural origins, and a frank and cheerful acceptance of the idea that being an adopted chid is both different and special. Kirk produces evidence to show that parents who show "acknowledgment of difference" between natural and adoptive parenting lay the foundations for personality stability, ego strength, and good mental health in their adopted children. In adopted children whose ethnic group or colour is different from that of their parents, it is presumably more difficult for parents to deny or minimize the child's nature origins.

In transracial adoption, the acceptance or accentuation of difference model would seem to be easiest for the adopting parent to follow. In the case of inter-country adoptions, this would take the form of giving the child a knowledge of, and positive emotional orientation to both personal ethnicity and culture of origin. In theory at least this approach should produce the best outcomes in terms of identity development.

At the same time, we should note that adequate identity formation and feelings of self-worth cannot be developed without family support which provides feelings of love and belonginess, combined with stable and authoritative parenting which provides a structure of rules, rewards and sanctions, a stability of socialization figures, and consistency in their behaviours.

Without parental love, and establishment of boundaries within which the child learns and internalizes rules which can successfully guide behaviour in various roles, the child cannot develop an adequate sense of self, or self-worth. There is ample research showing the importance of these two antecedents of self-esteem, love and stability of family structure in the work of Coopersmith (1981) and Bagley, Verma, Mallick and Young (1979).

This theoretical framework has an important implication for research on outcomes in adoption. We take the view the human development is a complex process; the individual has to draw together, incorporate and make sense of many diverse social and psychological strands in forming his or her identity. Identity formation is a long-term process, and uncertainty and unhappiness at one point in a child or adolescent's development may simply be a transient phenomenon as the individual copes with certain problems in the formation of personal identity. Studies of "adjustment" (e.g. of adopted children) which are based on interviews at the only one point in time could present a misleading picture. In addition, studies of adjustment before the crucial stage of adolescent identity formation may well give an unduly limited or optimistic picture of adopting. Ideally, follow-up research on adoption will be undertaken at more than one point in development, with a final assessment based on the personal views of the adopted personal when he or she is a young adult.

There is a parallel ethical problem in such research. Interviewing children and their parents on the subject of adoption may elicit fears, worries or anxieties which may in the short run be disturbing; but in the long run it may well be helpful to face and cope with such problems. Researchers have the ethnical obligation to offer help, support and referral where this is needed. But such help may significantly affect the outcome that is being researched. In this "action research" framework, the act of research and itself influence the outcome positively.

The initial results

It was striking the degree to which these Chinese girls aged between 12 and 18 had become Anglicized; they spoke with regional accents, and they shared the interests, pursuits and values of their adopted brothers and sisters, and their school friends. This was true even of children adopted by Anglo-Chinese couples, or by couples who encouraged a strong interest in Hong Kong, and Chinese culture generally. This cultural interest and awareness was an intellectual rather than an emotional orientation, and was not generally a core part of identity. The adoptive

Chinese mother of one girl, adopted at age four, told us that by the time she was eight her daughter rebelled against having to learn Chinese script, saying, "But Mummy, this is no use to me. I want to be an English girl." At the age 18 when we first interviewed her, this child had become a highly intelligent, articulate and poised young woman with a clear and unambiguous consciousness of her Chinese background and ethnicity. At the same time she regarded herself as English in outlook and values. At 28 she was a successful young solicitor, practising business law with a large insurance company; married (to an Englishman); and expecting her first child.

There were varying styles of relating to the adopted children by parents. Some put a strong emphasis on Chinese culture of which they had knowledge, and which they admired and respected. Others did not mention these cultural factors, either because they wanted their daughter to be no different from her adopted siblings, or because the child herself resisted any form of cultural education. Children in this latter group were likely to be the youngest children adopted into large families (brothers were frequently and affectionately mentioned by the adoptees, as admired and respected figures.

Scholastically the picture was an encouraging one. Without exception, the situation in these families was one of material advantage (even amongst the ministers of religion!), marital stability, and positive intellectual stimulation and support. Reflecting, perhaps, this largely middle class background all of the children we interviewed and tested in the first follow-up were in comparison with a large comparison group of similar age and sex, functioning at least at an average level scholastically. About a third of the girls aged 16 or more were undertaking study for advanced level (university admission) examinations.

Recalling their primary school days, the majority of girls reported some teasing about their ethnic origins which disappeared by the time they entered secondary school; few lived in areas where immigration from Caribbean or the Indian sub-continent had occurred, and where "immigration" was an issue. The main form of inter-ethnic contact was with Chinese students and student nurses whom the parents would invite for visits. One family provided accommodation for a female Chinese student from the nearby Polytechnic for two years. These various contacts meant that the adopted girls often established links with Hong Kong which they could take up later. A preference for service professions (nursing, social work, etc.) involving some professional training was often expressed, and a quarter of the girls showed interest in working in Hong Kong, at some stage.

A particular problem for many families was the reaction of

relatives, ranging from those who were patronising (seeing the adoption as an act of charity, to be suffered nobly) to frank rejection. The parents often chose to ignore such relatives, cutting off contact; but when a grandparent took such a rejecting attitude there were often role strains when parent made it clear that their adopted daughter was as their own. One parent told us that this was the reason why they did not emphasize their daughter's Chinese background or identity.

Our overall conclusion from this first phase of interviewing was that this group of Chinese girls adopted by white, English families (five had Chinese mothers, but all had white, English fathers) had few problems of identity. Homes were without exception, warm and supportive; the only negative features was some degree of anxiety and over-protection in about ten percent of parents. Scores on a standardized measure of self-esteem (Bagley and Evan-Wong, 1975; Bagley, Verma and Mallick, 1979; Bagley, 1989) completed by the adopted girls confirmed this picture of good adjustment. The mean score of the 50 girls tested was 9.83 (SD 7.9). The higher the score, the poorer the self-esteem: the 100 control subjects matched for age and sex but not for social class had a mean score of 16.12 (SD 9.3), a highly significant difference. In other words, these adopted girls had markedly and significantly better self-esteem than a group of girls of similar age drawn from the general population.

To what extent were the adopted girls expressing defensive or socially desirable responses? We had some check on this from the identity constructs elicited for twenty of the adoptees; no girls exhibited "defensive high self-esteem" in the terms established by Weinreich (1979 and 1986). Nor did we find any cases of "identity foreclosure" or weaknesses in "identity diffusion". The identity structures of these adopted girls appeared to be integrated and healthy, in contrast to those observed in some of Weinreich's British subjects form ethnic minority groups. Weinreich (1979) had described the linking of out-group identification with rejection of self in minority adolescents; but these adopted girls were highly accepting of self (including their ethnicity), but nevertheless had strong cross-ethnic identifications.

Using the global evaluation of identity development, and the self-esteem measure as dependent variables, we carried out a number of multi-variate analyses in test of various hypotheses. It was found that level of self-esteem, and level of identity development or ego-strength did not show any statistically significant variation according to the degree to which parents emphasised the difference between cultural origins of the child, and themselves. This might have been because Kirk's hypothesis is not appropriate for a group whose manifest ethnicity makes the concealment of adopted status implausible. Age at placement was not related to later adjustment; nor was a history of early illness, minor congenital difficulties (e.g. cleft palate, difficulties of hearing or sight), or early fears of tantrums. All of these difficulties seemed to smooth out with the passage of years.

Type of family structure (number, age and sex of siblings) was not related to later adjustment; nor was parental death (2 cases) or divorce (1 case). We formed the opinion that the successful resolution of identity problems and dilemmas earlier in life; the fulfilment in Maslow's terms of various basic needs; strong bonding, and relationships based on love, affection and concerned tolerance; and an authoritative form of parenting based on firm grounding in moral precepts (often informed by religious belief and practice) created firm ego-strengths in these girls and young women.

Five of fifty families interviewed were experiencing some difficulty in relation to adolescent problems; or the daughters in these families complained that their parents were too protective or to strict. But these problems seemed relatively mild in comparison with some of the acute identity crises which some adolescents experience (e.g. the cases of acute adolescent distress described in our work in counselling of high school students - Bagley, 1975 and 1991b). Our hypothesis for the second long-term follow up was that the positive progress of these adoptees - many of whom had spent several years in a large institution and had also suffered abandonment (sometimes because of minor blemishes of appearance, or minor physical faults or problems), and had also sometimes suffered early malnutrition and illness - would be maintained as they entered adulthood, and began to self-actualize. In a sense this exercise is a kind of 35 Up perspective, like the famous TV series of a group of children studied at age 7, and followed up every seven years. We can predict broad patterns of outcome, but we are fascinated by the individual directions people have taken with their lives, and the unfolding (and sometimes the checking) of talents that this involves.

The follow-up at ages 22 to 28

Some nine years after the original follow-up, we interviewed as many of the Chinese adoptees as we could locate. We were able to find 44 of the original 50 young women we had interviewed; three of these were interviewed in Hong Kong, where the researcher is now living. We asked these women to reflect on their lives, and on the process of adoption; checked out their current occupational, educational and family careers;

and requested them to complete a number of standardized measures of mental health, self-esteem, self-sentiment, and self-actualization or self-development. Control or comparison subjects of similar age and sex were drawn from two community mental health surveys, which randomly sampled 1135 women from the population of Calgary, Alberta (Bagley, 1991a). Unfortunately no control group was available to us in Britain. We do know however from a comparative study of British and Canadian adolescents (in London and Calgary) that the Canadian adolescents have significantly better self-esteem than those in Britain (Bagley, 1989a). Thus, the Canadian controls group for the Chinese adoptees should yield conservative comparisons, with a bias against statistical significance if there is a cultural bias in Canada to better feelings of self-worth.

Two random control subjects (88 in all) were selected for each adoptee. All of the controls were white, and of British, Irish or other European ethnic origin. In the following measures there was no statistically significant difference between the adoptees and the controls on the following measures: the Middlessex Hospital Questionnaire (Bagley, 1980) which measures psychoneurosis, anxiety and depression; the revised Coopersmith self-esteem scale for adults (Bagley, 1986b); Shostrom's (1964) measure of personal orientation and self-actualization; and Cattell's measure of self-sentiment (Gorsuch and Catell, 1977) which is a measure of ego-strength and self-actualization with question such as "I want to know more about science, art and literature". Whether the young Chinese women have a more positive attitude to themselves and to their future than women in the general population of Britain is difficult to say; but what we can conclude from the Canadian comparison is that there are no grounds for suggesting any psychological problems in these adoptees, and every reason to be optimistic.

Table 1 indicates the generally high level of educational and occupational achievement of these young women, a reflection of their middle class backgrounds, the quality of the family life they had experienced, their good educational achievements in school, their high achievement motivation, and their good emotional stability. Some thirty percent were married, or engaged to be married, and nine percent of the 44 adoptees had one or more child. Only two of the thirteen women who were married or engaged to be married had a partner of fiancee who was not a white Englishman. Four of the adoptees had worked in Hong Kong for periods of time, and one (a nurse) had married a Hong Kong physician and had returned with her husband to the United Kingdom.

When questioned about their ethnic identity these young women universally identified themselves as English, and about a half however maintained a strong emotional or intellectual interest in Chinese culture and institutions. Their expressed satisfaction with their adopted families were high, and there were few expressed problems of identity (Table 2).

Conclusion

On the face of things, almost all of these young women have made excellent adjustment. Only three of the 44 in the second follow-up had manifest problems of mental health or adjustment, or were not performing at their full potential. All of these three women had high levels of anxiety which seemed to impair their ability to operate effectively in social and occupational spheres. In broad terms however we can say these adoptions had been highly successful, and support the idea that inter-country adoptions can be successful. It seems inevitable that the very process of absorption into an accepting family and culture will diminish both interest in and need for a clear ethnic identity which is different from that of the adopted culture. Few of these young women reported that they had been discriminated against or snubbed, socially or occupationally. Almost all seemed at ease in a variety of social and professional situations, and their high levels of educational an occupational advancement seem to bear out the impression that in a society which still discriminates against many ethnic minority groups (Verma et al. 1989) these women are well-accepted, and are leading successfully, well-fulfilled lives.

Inter-country adoption continues to be a controversial issue, and evidence of successful long-term adjustment in young people adopted across national had racial lines while reassuring, will not ultimately resolve the policy issues and dilemmas involved. Inter-country adoption will continue to have its critics (arguing for example that such adoptions distort patterns of child welfare in sending countries; that parents may surrender children for adoption for financial reward, or because they do not truly understand the meaning of adoption; and that rich but perhaps unsuitable parents can overcome legal barriers because of their wealth). Equally vociferous are advocates of inter-country adoption, who argue that the quality of the potential adopters is high, their motives are genuine, and they can offer excellent care for children who would grow up (or might even perish) in poor quality institutions. Recent British policy developments in this field, and the many legal and organizational difficulties which inter-country adopters in Britain now face are well summarized by Bennett and Mostyn (1991).

Our own policy argument is that all alternatives to inter-country adoption should be considered in the country of the child's birth; but if all in-country options are exhausted, then inter-country adoption should be considered as an option which can have distinct advantages for some children. Evidence on good adjustment from our own and other studies (reviewed by Silverman and Feigelman, 1990) clearly strengthens the arguments in favour of inter-country adoption. By the same standard however, evidence on poor outcomes for any particular group adopted across national and cultural lines must cause practitioners to think very carefully about the wisdom of such adoptions. Thus, in a study in Alberta, Canada (Bagley, 1990), we found that both white, in-racial adoptees and inter-country adoptees (from Central and South America, and Asia) had rather good adjustment in their adolescent years. But Native Indian (aboriginal) adolescent adoptees had dramatically poorer outcomes than the other adoptees. The reasons for this seemed to be the widespread prejudice and discrimination against Native people in Canada, and communities, peers and relatives of the adopters who could not accept the adopted child as part of the white community. The adoptive parents, in turn, were unable to transmit to the Native child an adequate sense of identity or self-esteem.

Since most of these Native youth were forcibly removed from their families by a colonialist child welfare system operating on ethnocentric assumptions, we advocated that social work effort should be put into support of extended Native families, who with minimum support were quite capable of caring for their own children.

The evidence from studies in a number of countries (U.S.A.- Simon and Altstein, 1991; Norway - Saetersdal and Dalen, 1991; Denmark - Rorbech, 1991; West Germany Textor, 1991; Netherlands - Hoksbergen, 1991; and Israel - Jaffe, 1991) indicates that prospective adopters face many hurdles in trying to adopt children from other countries. But outcomes for the inter-country adopted children in these studies appear to be very similar to children adopted in-country, and in adoptive families where parent and child are ethnically similar. In these studies children who were older or handicapped at the time of their adoption fared somewhat worse; but the same is true of in-country adoptions, and outcomes for these children are likely to be much more favourable than for children who were not adopted (Altstein and Simon, 1991).

Table 1
Educational, work and family situation of 44 adoptees aged 22 to 28 years

Completed or completing degree or diploma at University, Polytechnic or Institute of Higher Education	40.9%
Completed or completing professional training (e.g.law, nursing, accountancy, social work, education)	34.1%
Completed or completing a postgraduate degree or diploma	11.4%
Currently in professional or managerial post (Registrar General's Class I or II)	31.8%
Semi- or -unskilled post (Registrar General's Class IV or V)	2.3%
Currently unemployed	4.5%
Full-time homemaker, with children	9.1%
Married, or engaged to be married	29.5%

Note: Many individuals fall into more than one of the categories above.

Table 2
Perceptions of adoptions in 44 Chinese adoptees age 23 to 28

	"Strongly agree"	"Agree"	"Unsure"	"Disagree"	"Strongly Disagree"
Adoption provided me with the kind of family life I needed	90.9%	9.1%	0%	0%	0%
I have enjoyed my life as an adopted child	95.4%	4.6%	0%	0%	0%
I wish I had not been adopted	0%	0%	0%	0%	100%
I feel confused being an oriental person in white family	0%	0%	0%	9.1%	89.9%
I have confusion about my ethnic identity	0%	0%	2.5%	11.4%	86.0%
I have experienced discrimination because I am an oriental child in a white family	0%	0%	0%	9.1%	89.9%

12 Adopted from Vietnam: A ten year follow-up of British adoptees

Introduction

From my study as I write this chapter I look out over the South China Sea, at the junks, fishing smacks and cargo boats entering Hong Kong harbour. Everyday in the months before the monsoon season two or three of these boats have contained refugees from Vietnam. In 1991 over 10,000 fled Vietnam, which remains one of the world's poorest most oppressive regimes (Hieber, 1992). The refugees sit in camps in Hong Kong and elsewhere, waiting for freedom (for they are kept prisoner in Hong Kong), waiting for refuge in various parts of the world. Plans for compulsory repatriation have stalled, since those forcibly returned often flee a second time. In the desperate conditions of the camps where they are concentrated in Hong Kong, violence and death seem to be daily occurrences, as despair stagnates, and feeds interpersonal strife. Twenty four of the concentration camp in mates were burnt to death in February of 1992, spurring calls for the compulsory return of the escapees to the larger prison camp that is Vietnam.

A nurse working for the Ockenden Venture (which placed the Vietnamese children in our follow-up study) stayed on after the fall of Vietnam in 1975, for a year. On this experience she wrote that "The rich become poor, and the poor died." The lot of the ethnic Chinese minority in what was South Vietnam has been particularly hard. Used to roles as entrepreneurs and small traders, they were forbidden to operate as small-scale capitalists, and become both political and economic refugees.

In the chaos of Vietnam both before and after the military defeat of the southern forces, many children were orphaned or permanently separated from their parents. In 1977 about nine per cent of all children (some 880,000) in Vietnam were still separated from their biological families, most of them permanently (ICWR, 1977). Those who had been resident in children's homes were placed in foster care; the exception was the mixed-race children (with Vietnamese mother, and American father) who remained in institutional care. In 1988 an agreement between the United States and Vietnam established a special centre in Ho Chi Min City for such children (now adolescents) pending their repatriation to America. By May, 1991 136,000 of these young people (who were apparently rejected by most Vietnamese because of their physical appearance) had been resettled in the United States. They were placed with foster or adoptive homes or (for the young adults) in supported-living arrangements of various kinds (Mydans, 1991). The repatriation from Vietnam of these mixed children was scheduled for completion by mid-1992, by which time a further 80,000 of these young adults will have left Vietnam for the United States.

The year 1975 saw desperate scenes of chaos and escape, and among the plane-loads of refugees fleeing South Vietnam were groups of children who had previously been resident in orphanages of various kinds. The agencies which ran these orphanages were in some dilemma about evacuating their charges. Few of the children had been formally "surrendered" or released for adoption or alternative care in a formal sense, and indeed in the circumstances of war conventional social work procedures are rarely possible.

In course of time a few of the children exported in the airlift were reunited with their Vietnamese families, but it appeared that the large majority had lost all contact with their family of origin (ICWR, 1977). Many of the agencies bringing the children out of Vietnam expressed some anguish about this policy, but in retrospect the fate of the children who remained in Vietnam had been so deprived and marginal (eg Mydans, 1991) that doubts about the policy of placing children in adoptive homes in the West have largely disappeared. Indeed, we now face the phenomenon of Vietnamese families putting children in refugee boats in the hope that they can be adopted by Western families.

My own chapter in this story began in 1978 when with Loretta Young, I began work on the adjustment and identity of a group of Vietnamese children adopted by English parents. The Ockenden Venture which had placed these children had worked in Vietnam, and continues to work in refugee camps in Cambodia. Of the many thousands of children this group worked with in Asia, a small number (about 200) were placed with English adoptive families. We have systematically followed up twenty two of these children, sixteen boys and six girls, all born in Vietnam. Five of these children were mixed race origin, presumably with white fathers and Vietnamese mothers, although we had no information which could verify this. What is known is that the children had lost all parental contact in Vietnam, and a number of them had been found abandoned. All came out of Vietnam in an airlift of 99 institutionalized children and infants organized by a British newspaper, The Daily Mail.

Some of the older children remained in group care, but many of the younger children were adopted. The Daily Mail featured a number of the adoptees in an article of April 11, 1977. Amongst the children featured is a boy named Ian by his adoptive parents.

The newspaper reported:

> "Ian is nearly seven years old, and a truthful child. He was hiding with his father when his mother ran out and was shot dead before his eyes. Later, a party of nuns took him to a Saigon orphanage, through gunfire and bombing. His father too had gone. What makes the story convincing is the hole in his hip identifiable as a shrapnel wound. Ian says so much about Vietnam then switches off. He has a British flag in his bedroom. His friends are English now....."

The early years

These adoptees from Vietnam were aged between three and eight years when we began to study them in 1978. We interviewed the parents and talked discursively about the settling in process and the early problems encountered, and we joined in the support groups which these parents had established for themselves. At this stage no attempt was made to undertake any formal testing of the children. But from the parents we gleaned some consistent accounts of problems and progress.

When they arrived in Britain many of the children had problems of malnourishment, infestation with parasites, evidence of physical trauma (Ian was not alone in having been injured in crossfire or bombing), and some minor physical handicaps which were probably congenital in origin. Medical workers with PVO (Project Vietnam Orphan, the umbrella organization which oversaw the placement and care of the airlifted children) advised us that the more severely disabled or sickly children would have died in the first two years of life, so the children who survived could be counted as the hardy ones. Nevertheless, it was estimated that about half of the children would have died if they had stayed in the Vietnam orphanages.

Children were placed with adoptive parents after relatively brief periods of hospitalization or foster care and some went straight to adoptive parents, particularly when these had some medical or nursing qualification relevant to caring for sickly children. In fact, the adoptive parents reported that having to care for a sickly, dependent child was an important part of the bonding process.

Children used to sleeping on a mat on the floor, and eating a diet comprised mainly of rice took a little while (but never more than a few weeks) to adjust to western norms of sleeping and eating. Speed of learning and adjustment was a feature of the attachment of these children to their new families. However, as quickly as they learned English they forgot Vietnamese. One family, concerned at this asked a Vietnamese colleague to talk to their child regularly in Vietnamese; but this proved to be a disaster, since the boy's English language skills regressed and he began to have nightmares.

As they bonded to their parents (and to their new siblings, which were present in all but three of the adoptive homes) these children began to lose their memory not only of Vietnamese language, but of Vietnam itself. Two years after their arrival, none of the 22 children in our study could remember anything about their early lives. Occasionally memories broke through, but these had traumatic effect. One family described how they took their six year old daughter to a county show, which featured a helicopter landing. When the child saw the helicopter coming she was transfixed with terror, then flung herself face down, arms covering her head. He parents assumed that she was reliving an old trauma which involved a helicopter gunship.

Not only did these children learn English quickly, but once in infant and primary school they made rapid progress and appeared to be amongst the brightest of their classmates. No particular emotional or developmental problems were reported by parents two years after placement, and all of the children seemed to be doing well.

Ten years later

By the time we completed the follow-up interviews, the twenty two Vietnamese adoptees were in their middle or late teenage years. We interviewed parents (on their perceptions of the adoption, and any problems they had experienced) and the adopted children (on their perceptions of adoption, as well as some formal testing or current self-concept and identity formation). We also interviewed available siblings of these adopted children who were still at home, and thus obtained a comparison group of twelve teenagers (8 boys and 4 girls) who were, on average three years older than the adoptees. This is perhaps not the most ideal of comparison groups, but it is likely to hold constant some family factors which may influence adjustment in both adoptive and biological children.

Most of the adoptive parents had kept in touch with one another, and formed informal support groups. This strategy was particularly helpful when problems arising from the child's behaviour or the reactions of the community needed to be addressed. One of the adoptees had a chronic health problem (asthma), and another had needed surgery for an optical problem. Otherwise they had maintained good health, despite early problems of nutrition, and a variety of physical and psychological trauma. One of the teenaged adoptees achieved prominence in youth international badminton; another achieved success in national chess competitions. All of the adoptees, like their adopted siblings, were achieving at school at least an average level, although one adoptee required special tuition for problems of dyslexia.

Not one of the adoptees whom we followed up had maintained anything but an intellectual interest in Vietnam, a country which because of international politics they are unable to visit. Like the Chinese adoptees in Britain, whom we describe in another chapter in this book the Vietnamese children seemed totally absorbed in their neighbourhoods, and all of those of an age to date had English boyfriends or girlfriends, and a range of peers who included a variety of individuals from the ethnic minorities which make up multicultural Britain today.

Two of the adoptees, and one of the comparison group had psychological problems of sufficient seriousness that a professional counsellor or psychiatrist had to be consulted. These three individuals suffered from phobic anxiety; anorexia; and running from home associated with drug use, respectively. However, the self-concept levels (on the Coopersmith measure) of the adoptees and their siblings was similar, and within the normal range. On Weinreich's measure of individual identity two individuals (one adoptee, and one sibling) had elements of identity which were disparate, self-derogatory, or unintegrated. However, the Vietnamese youth seemed to ignore their personal ethnicity in mapping their identity formation - perhaps because they were reminded of it so infrequently by parents and peers.

"Ian" described in the previous section was now a handsome

teenager with a steady girl friend. He was attending a Sixth Form College, taking advanced level study in Maths and Physics. He had been accepted by a university to study engineering, subject to adequate grades in his advanced level examinations.

Although some of these adoptees were "just ordinary" and a few were troubled over various personality problems or stresses in their lives, we couldn't identity the fact of being adopted as such, as having any causal significance in the relatively minor psychological problems experienced by some of these adoptees. Again, the "eighty per cent" rule seems to apply - the large majority of both the adoptees and their siblings had a normal outcome, in terms of intellectual, social and personal development. The fact of being ethnically different from parents and siblings did not seem to have had any negative impact on the lives of these teenagers.

Our conclusion then (as with the Chinese adoptees) is that inter-ethnic and inter-country adoption can work when the wider community does not by and large hold negative stereotypes about the ethnic group in question, and the adoptive parents have the intellectual and emotional resources (including the support of a peer group of adopters) which can cope with most of the problems which are likely to arise in the adoptive parent of a "minority" adolescent. This situation is in marked contrast to the outcomes for the American Indian adolescents adopted by white, Canadian parents whom we describe in another chapter. For those adolescents, stigmatized and excluded by peers and the wider community, adoptive parents were unable in many cases to provide the ego-enhancing buffers which adopted children often need.

The powerful tenacity and widespread success which Vietnamese emigrants (including adoptees, refugees and "boat people") have demonstrated in adapting to life in Europe and North America is demonstrated in the study by Caplan, Whitmore and Choy (1989). This American research involved the intensive study of 1,384 families including 6,775 individuals, who were studied in 1981 and 1984. Children in these families had been malnourished, and were often traumatized by the hazards of war, flight and separation. The large majority spoke no English on arrival in the U.S.A.. Yet, within 40 months of their arrival, these children not only spoke English well, but as a group surpassed the achievement test norms of the average American student. Eighty percent of the children had, within five years of arrival at least a B average in English and Mathematics; 48 percent averaged A in mathematics, and many completed nationally in spelling competitions. On the California Achievement Test, 60 percent scored above the average for mainstream American students. While very few of these children were actually adopted, they do indicate a major spirit or trait of hardiness and achievement orientation in Vietnamese children. What will be interesting in years to come is to see whether adopted Vietnamese children in white families achieve as highly as their non-adopted, Vietnamese peers in the U.S.A.

13 Transracial adoption of Aboriginal children in Canada: A disturbing case study

Introduction

The first inhabitants of North American have in the past 150 years been subjected to extraordinary ravages of their traditional way of life, assaults which have threatened their very existence as independent nations. A system of oppression amounting to cultural genocide has resulted in the undermining of the family in many groups of Native people, with a consequent crisis in the care of children (Morse, 1984).

Native or aboriginal people in North America are (like the peoples of Europe) a collection of very diverse cultures, ranging from the Inuit in the North to the Pueblo in the South. The devastation by the European settlers of the ecological basis of the culture of many of these aboriginal people has led in turn to epidemics of disease, starvation, unemployment, hopelessness, and exploitation (Morrison & Wilson, 1986). In the mid-west of "Canada" and the "United States" the destruction of the buffalo by white settlers effectively destroyed a way of life and with it a nomadic, self-sufficient culture. Native leaders, defeated and demoralized, facing death from starvation and the guns of the conquering army, signed treaties whose implications were not understood (MacDonald, 1978). Effectively, however, Native people were relegated to tracts of isolated, barren land which had no apparent economic value. Only when oil, coal and natural gas were discovered on those "reserves" did white administrations move to dispossess aboriginal populations once again

214

(Morrison & Wilson, 1986).

The mineral and agricultural resources of the lands ceded by the aboriginal people have provided the basis for acquisition of capital and the facilitating of industrial development, which in turn allowed the new settlers in North America to attain average income levels which are higher than those of any country in the world. Two groups have not, however, been able to share in that prosperity - descendants of slaves imported from Africa to provide earlier capital development in agriculture, industry and trade; and the aboriginal people themselves. The early European settlers tried to enslave the conquered Amerindian peoples. However, in slavery aboriginal people tended to retreat into a depressed state, and in captivity and servitude died within a short while (Buchignani & Engel, 1983). It would indeed have been convenient for the settlers if all of the Amerindian people died out - as happened through systematic policies of genocide on the island that later became the Canadian Province of Newfoundland. This administratively convenient solution did not occur, and "the Indian problem" remains.

The Canadian situation

The international border between Canada and the United States was an arbitrary division along the 49th parallel, and paid no attention to the traditional lands of Native peoples. For many groups the US-Canadian division is an arbitrary and often humiliating barrier across their national territory. The Blackfoot Nation of Alberta, for instance, who once hunted buffalo over a wide area, are now confined to a small number of reserves, the largest in Northern Montana (USA) and the several others in Southern Alberta (Canada). The Blood reserve of the Blackfoot nation, near Lethbridge, Alberta, is the largest reserve in Canada. People from the various reserves are linked by kindred and marriage ties, and travel across the US border is common. Having to submit sacred and ritual objects to customs inspection is, for example, a humiliating experience.

The exact number of people of aboriginal descent in Canada is unknown, and census attempts to assess their numbers are seriously flawed (Bagley, 1988a). However, about four percent of the Canadian population have direct and major descent from the pre-colonized aboriginal people. First (about half of all aboriginal people) are those who have status under the Indian Act, their forbears having signed treaties with the Canadian government (MacDonald, 1978). Secondly are "non-status" aboriginal people (mainly in the Provinces of British

Columbia and Alberta) who were remote and "undiscovered" by the colonization process, did not engage in warfare with the early settlers, and did not sign treaties. These groups still struggle for retention of traditional territory, and claim sovereignty over a large part of British Columbia, a land mass the size of Europe. Thirdly are the Metis, originally formed from unions of Native people and early French settlers. Following the final defeat of the French, these people fled into northern areas of what are now Manitoba, Saskatchewan and Alberta (Buchignani & Engel, 1983). Their lot has always been ambiguous and more wretched than that of full-blood Indians, and after a revolt by Metis people in the 1880s (following which Metis leaders were hanged), they have been a doubly marginalized group. Because of endogamy over the past century, they are physically indistinguishable from most other aboriginal people. The Inuit (Eskimo) people of the far north number about 25,000 today (Johnston, 1983).

Current social and health conditions of aboriginal children

Although Canada is one of the world's richest countries, the material and health conditions of aboriginal people in Canada have been at a level which is similar to or below that of many Third World countries (CJPH, 1982). Native people (including children) are at least five times as likely to suffer serious injury or death through accidents (Diand, 1979; Bagley, et al., 1990). Death rates from various causes at younger ages are between 40 and 90 percent higher than in whites. Many Native people in rural areas for many years had no piped water, indoor plumbing or sewage disposal (Siggner & Locatelli, 1980). Houses are still of poor quality and often overcrowded. These housing conditions are a major cause of the very high rates of tuberculosis suffered by Native people (Talbot, 1983).

Housing conditions also underlie the very high rate of middle ear diseases and associated hearing loss in Native children but, the high rate of cerebral palsy in Native children is probably a reflection of the poor health of Native mothers prior to childbirth, rather than of housing conditions as such (Tervo, 1983). A Manitoba study has shown that Native children are often undernourished (Ellestad-Sayed et al., 1981). Unemployment rates in Native males range on most reserves from 80 percent in winter to 50 percent in summer (when seasonal, agricultural work at minimum wage can be obtained). Applying for financial assistance from welfare authorities means that a man must not only swallow his pride, but also have linguistic and social skills to negotiate what is often a confusing welfare system. The problem is compounded by the fact that it is rare for a welfare official to speak a Native language; but particularly in northern areas, many Native people speak little or no English. Often the task of applying for a welfare cheque is left to the woman in a family, and the money obtained is shared with male members of the family.

Our own work in Southern Alberta indicates that when welfare cheques are denied, or shared with members of the extended family, adults and children suffer days and even weeks of what can only be described as semi-starvation. Family and kin in Native communities share values, resources, skills, rituals and food. When food runs out, all suffer, including children.

As a consequence of haphazard or chronic undernutrition, poor perinatal conditions and poor housing conditions, Native children become ill, and die at a far greater rate than non-Native children (Valberg et al., 1979; Evers et al.; Nuttal, 1982; Spady, 1982). These differential rates of illness and death have lead some authors to suggest that the health of Native people is no better than that of inhabitants of many Third World countries, and that Canada's overseas relief agencies might do better to concentrate on conditions within Canada itself (Young, 1983).

The *Canadian Journal of Public Health* commented in an editorial in 1982 that:

> The infant mortality rates in our native people are worse than those of Indonesia or Nigeria. Compared to a child born into a white family in Toronto, the child born into an Indian family in the North-West Territories has only about a third as good a chance of surviving the first year of life; an Inuit child's chances have recently improved to the same level. Diseases of poverty, ignorance, overcrowding and squalor, chronic and acute respiratory disease, and gastroenteritis take a heavy tool among infants, children and young adults. (p. 297)

White social workers in Canada have approached the problems of child neglect and family disorganization which often occur in a people overburdened by poverty and poor health with practice models based on individual pathology; the structural aspects of the problem are almost universally ignored. the standard approach to a family in desperate need of adequate housing, income and health-care support has been to remove children when, in the words of child welfare legislation the parents are "unable or unwilling to provide the necessities of life." In other words, a family's extreme poverty constitutes valid grounds for removal of a child from his or her family (Alberta, 1984).

Child welfare policies and interventions

Canadian policy in the twentieth century towards Native people has been largely paternalistic, with attempts to guide Native people into assimilating into Canadian culture. The principle medium of this policy was the residential schools, run by Anglican and Catholic missionaries. Children were forcibly removed from parents and placed in schools which required abandonment (on pain of physical beating) of traditional dress, hair styles, religion, and language. Although the majority of these schools were abandoned in the 1960s and 1970s, their effect in terms of cultural genocide, is still apparent (Morse, 1984). Native people graduated from these schools demoralized, bewildered and unprepared for any but the most marginal existence. Indeed, with traditional hunting and trapping lifestyles destroyed, chronic unemployment for 80 percent of adult males is the norm.

Under these conditions, it is not difficult to understand why so many Native families contain members who are alcoholic or mentally ill. The majority of Native families exist in the most desperate poverty.

Native families are subject to the control of provincial Child Welfare Acts. These acts allow for the "protection" or removal of children when physical and other abuse or neglect is suspected. Since these are civil law statutes, the alleged abuse or neglect does not have to be proven at the stringent level of criminal law proceedings, and judges in family courts who award a provincial government permanent or temporary guardianship over a child usually act as little more than rubber stamps for social work decisions (Bagley, 1988b).

The effects of provincial child welfare interventions upon Native communities have been documented in the monographs of Johnston (1983) and Hepworth (1980). Although Native children constitute about five percent of the population of the prairie provinces (Manitoba, Saskatchewan and Alberta), in the early 1980s they constituted on average nearly 40 percent of children in residential care. The large majority of these children had become permanent wards of the Crown not through abuse, but because of alleged "neglect."

What this effectively meant was that white social workers perceived the conditions of family life to be too far below, or too different from those which pertained in the average white family. Social work practice in Canada in this respect resembled that of an earlier decade in the United States, which contributed to "the destruction of the American Indian family" (Ungers, 1977). According to the estimates of

Hepworth, Johnston and others, at least a quarter of all Native children are current or past clients of the child welfare system, compared with less than five percent of white children.

The child care settings to which the Native children were removed was of varying, but often inferior quality. The evidence from the province of Alberta (Thomlison, 1985) indicates that untrained white foster parents were the main resource used. These well-meaning people were often unequal to the task of caring for the bewildered and often disturbed Native children who had been removed from their biological parents, usually for trivial reasons. What followed was often a classic case of "drift," with children being moved between a series of foster homes. With each move the child would become increasingly disturbed, making a successful placement increasingly unlikely. By adolescence the child would usually be too disturbed to live in a family and would, after a series of behavioural or psychiatric crises in adolescence, be permanently institutionalized (Bagley, 1986).

Studies of adult prison populations have indicated that at least a third of those incarcerated in jails in the Prairie Provinces are of Native origin (Morse, 1984). A significant proportion of Native prisoners are debtors, who cannot afford to pay fines imposed for minor crimes.

Case studies of "Child Protection"

In the past five years we have collected detailed information on a number of cases of Native children removed from their parents by child protection workers. Case data were obtained through consultation with a number of Native bands who were attempting to regain children from the legal custody of the Province of Alberta; and through assessments of cases as an expert witness (Bagley, 1984).

A single, elaborated account of a case can expose weaknesses in a system of service delivery, and provokes the question: is this an isolated case, or do the identified weaknesses in the delivery and care system apply to many more cases than this one? In Alberta the case of a Metis child, Richard Cardinal (Bagley, 1986), exposed the weaknesses of an entire system. The boy in question, Richard Cardinal, had been removed with his three siblings from the care of relatives for reasons of poverty, parental alcoholism, and poor housing.

The children from this family went through a series of foster homes, and Richard was separated from his siblings at the age of seven. A further series of second-rate and sometimes abusive foster homes followed, and after various emotional crises and suicide attempts, Richard hanged himself at the age of 17. An official enquiry (Thomlison, 1985) indicated that the "care" Richard had received was typical of that received by many Native and Metis youth in the child welfare system. Research on 130 cases of youth suicide in Alberta indicated in fact that 11 percent were current or previous wards of the government, compared with an expected frequency in the general population of less than two percent - the case of Richard Cardinal was not an isolated one (Bagley, 1989a).

Two further cases illustrate the colonial nature of child welfare administration for Native children. These are cases known to the writer from consultancy with a consortium of Indian Bands in northern Alberta, seeking to gain control of child welfare service delivery systems:

> **Case A:** This girl was removed from her parents at the age of six weeks. She had a respiratory infection, and her parents (both aged 16) were living in an old car in March, in a harsh, northern climate. The child was removed by a social worker acting under the authority given by the Child Welfare Act of Alberta. The child was placed in a temporary foster home and in the following four years proceeded through six different foster homes, before being stabilized with a farm family in the southern part of the province, nearly 500 miles from her original home. By this time, her biological parents had married, and had two other children. Each month the parents and their two children made a two-day trip by bus to a social service office for a visit with their daughter; then they made the bus journey back to their northern reserve. By the age of 6 their daughter had bonded to her foster parents, and was completely acculturated. She fled from her biological parents when they came to visit, and fought with her younger siblings. Only her mother spoke any English, and the child could not speak her original, native language. The foster parents applied for and were granted an adoption order by the court. Shortly afterwards they moved to another province, and all contact with the child's culture of origin was lost.

> **Case B:** This 1-year-old boy was removed from his mother by social workers after the woman had moved to the city following her marriage breakdown. His mother lived in a miserable apartment, and had drinking problem. The alleged grounds for removal of the child were neglect, and the boy was briefly hospitalized for a respiratory infection. They boy's aunt moved to the city, and sought custody of the boy, but this was refused. The boy was placed with foster parents, and stabilized in his second

placement. The aunt, a woman in her 'fifties who had successfully raised a large family continued to press for custody of the boy. The foster parents in the meanwhile applied for an adoption order on the boy. They resisted all attempts by the boy's biological family to visit. A court finally ordered custody of the boy to the aunt, with visitation rights by the foster parents!

In both of these case (and in many others in Alberta with which I have been involved) social workers employed ethnocentric models of practice, ignoring both the economic factors which oppress Native people, and the cultural patterns of Native families in finding alternative ways to care for children. In particular, social workers have ignored the strengths of the extended family in which child care is shared between biological parents and aunts, grandparents and other relatives. The principle cultural value of the extended Native family is that of sharing: income, food and resources are shared; troubles are shared and solved within the extended family; and caring for children is shared too.

The adjustment of native children adopted by white parents

Large numbers of Native children in Canada were permanently removed from their biological parents in the 1970s and early 1980s. Extended families were rarely considered by social workers as a source of permanent care for these children. Many Native children became emotionally very disturbed through disruptions and varying quality of care, and by adolescence, had become unadoptable. Nevertheless, a large number of Native children were placed in white homes before adolescence, without regard to the child's original ethnicity and without regard to the child's need for cultural support in a society in a society which still holds many negative stereotypes of Native people (Morse, 1984). Table 1 shows that when Native children were adopted, the adopters in more than two-thirds of cases have been white. In character these are like some international adoptions: children from very poor families in developing nations are removed by colonial administrations and given to childless couples in a developed country.

Table 1

Adoption of status Indian children by Indian and non-Indian families in Canada

Year	By Indian Families	By White Families	Total	% Adopted by Whites
1971	45	235	280	83.9
1972	48	269	317	84.9
1973	100	328	428	76.6
1974	104	261	365	71.5
1975	99	247	346	71.4
1976	114	381	495	77.0
1977	127	385	512	75.1
1978	111	354	465	76.1
1979	156	433	589	73.5
1980	131	435	566	76.5
1981	118	401	519	77.2

Source: Johnston (1983), page 57.

What is the long-term adjustment of Native children adopted by white parents in Canada? Surprisingly, there is no systematic Canadian research on this important issue (Sachdev, 1984). Indeed, although there is much North American research on trans-cultural and trans-racial adoptions (Feigelman & Silverman, 1983), there is very little research indeed on outcomes for adoptions of Native children by whites. A few recent case studies exist, however, including those in a judicial report (Kimmelman, 1984) on the export of Native children to the United States for purposes of adoption; and reports of Native children adopted from Canada to the United Stated by pedophiles (Campagna & Poffenberger, 1988).

Hepworth (1981) had argued that adoptions of Native children were less well supervised (probably reflecting pressures on child welfare authorities by fiscal administrators). Subsequent evidence uncovered in the Kimmelman report on adoptions in Manitoba (1984) has supported this view.

The classic and oft-cited study (for there is little else to cite) on Native adoptions is David Fanshel's book, *Far From the Reservation*

222

(1972). Fanshel interviewed 392 sets of parents who had adopted Native children aged 0 to 11 years. The average age of the child at follow-up was 4.5 years, and only data from parental interviews is reported. Overwhelmingly, parents were satisfied with the child's initial adjustment:

> Even if the adjustment of the children proves to be somewhat more problematic as they get older - particularly during their adolescence when the factor of racial differences may loom larger - the overall prospect for their futures can be termed "guardedly optimistic." When one contrasts the relative security of their lives with the horrendous growing up experiences endured by their mothers...one has to take the position that adoption has saved many of these children from lives of utter ruination (Fanshel, 1972, p.339).

One implication of this conclusion (saving the children from "utter ruination") is that adoption of Native children by whites should increase if such children are to be "saved." In this respect, the movement to remove and adopt aboriginal children was part of the movement contributing to what Byler (1977) calls "the destruction of the American Indian family." French (1980) terms the practices of forced sterilization of Native women, and the compulsory removal and eventual adoption of their children as "contemporary versions of physical and cultural genocide." While this may be an overstatement of the aims of official policy, it is difficult to escape the view that social work practices in North American have undermined rather than supported the aboriginal family.

Adoption might be in the best interests of an individual child, but the issue becomes more contentious when the child has biological parents and extended families who both object to the adoption, and can offer a home for the child - albeit an economically poor one by North American standards.

We have argued that inter-country adoption is an acceptable outcome for children who have been orphaned or abandoned, with no possibility of making contact with kin networks (Bagley & Young, 1979; 1981). Inter-country adoptions are, according to a number of follow-up studies, rather successful in terms of the long-term psychological outcomes for the children involved (Bagley & Young, 1981; Feigelman & Silverman, 1983).

In contrast with this rather optimistic picture for oriental and black children adopted by whites in North America, limited clinical evidence (reviewed by Bagley, Wood & Khumar 1990) as well as our own clinical experience suggests that disrupted relationships and significant mental health problems are a common occurrence for Native adolescents adopter by white parents.

A Canadian study

We have argued that outcomes for adopted children can best be assessed in terms of how adolescents and their parents cope with "identity crises" (Young & Bagley, 1982). The results reported below represent the first report of a longitudinal study of adjustment of adopted adolescents from contrasted ethnic groups and family situations. An interview in early adolescence, for example, might identify a temporary adolescent crisis. It is important to review the whole of adolescence, with a review of their growing years by the adoptees themselves, when they have reached young adulthood. What might be seen as a "troubled adoption" at age 13, might be seen as successful by the time the individual is 18 (Bagley & Young, 1981).

The adoptive subjects in the present study were obtained from two sources: supplementary questions in a survey of child development in a large, random sample in Calgary (Bagley, 1988c); and similar questions in two surveys of community mental health (Ramsay & Bagley, 1986; Bagley, 1989b). These surveys of 1,990 adults yielded 93 families in which an adopted child was in his/her adolescent years; 19 of these families had adopted a child of Native origin, and seven had adopted a child from overseas. Further adopted adolescents were obtained for study through random telephone sampling in Calgary, until a pool of 37 Native and 20 inter-country children aged 13 to 17 was obtained for study.

All subjects were resident in the city of Calgary. From the pool of white adopted children, fairly close matches for the adopted Native children were obtained, and age and sex matched non-adopted, white control groups were obtained from the main sample. The comparability of the samples can be seen in Table 2. "Native" included children with full or part ancestry in a child of Native appearance. The inter-country adopted group were either oriental (55%) or South American (45%). All were classified as non-white, as were all of the Native children.

It should be stressed that we were anxious to obtain a randomly selected group of subjects for study, since the use of volunteer subjects might have meant a bias - for example, parents having difficulty in adoption might be more likely to volunteer. The overall positive response to the random sampling technique was 84.5 percent. We know from initial questioning the type of child adopted by the couple, and whether the child was currently at home or elsewhere (usually reflecting a breakdown in adoption). The proportion of "adoption breakdowns" was similar across those who agreed to an interview, and those who did not. White adoptees (the first comparison group) were sampled for purposes of the present study from a larger pool (N = 169) by age and sex, in order to obtain a balanced comparison with the other groups. All of the inter-country adoptions identified are included in the comparison samples. The Native adolescents were all resident on Reserves in rural areas; all had at least one sibling who had been removed by social services for alleged neglect, but these children, unlike their siblings, had never been removed from a biological parent, and all families had received social service support from their bands to prevent further family problems. At least half were, however, cared for by a grandmother or aunt for periods ranging from three months to 14.6 years.

Measures of adjustment used were the Coopersmith self-esteem inventory, a sensitive and well-validated instrument for measuring adolescent and young adult adjustment (Coopersmith, 1987c; Bagley, 1989c); and a measure of suicidal ideas and behaviour (Ramsay & Bagley, 1986). Suicidal ideas and acts of deliberate harm are now sufficiently common in adolescence (Bagley, 1989a) to be seen as an indicator of profound distress or identity crisis. All subjects were interviewed in their own homes. Parents (always mother, and sometimes father as well) and children were interviewed separately.

Results and discussion

Results (Table 2) indicate that Native child adoptions are significantly more likely than any other parenting situation to involve problems and difficulties, and a fifth of the Native adoptees had, by the age of 15, separated from their adoptive parents. A follow-up of the adoptees two years later indicated that nearly a half of the Native adoptees, and none of the inter-country adopted group had separated from parents because of behavioural or emotional problems, or parent-child conflict. Follow-up work with remaining groups is continuing.

Overall, the Native adoptees had significantly poorer self-esteem, and were also more than three times as likely than any other group to have problems of serious suicidal ideas or acts of deliberate self-harm in the previous six months. In contrast, the non-adopted Native adolescents had adjustment profiles that were not significantly different from those of non-adopted whites. Examination of white and Native adoptees by parental description of adjustment (Table 2) indicates that even within the group parents describe as having "no or some problem," adopted

Native children had significantly poorer levels of self-esteem, and higher scores on the suicidal ideation scale than the combined comparison groups.

Multiple regression (Table 3) has explored the relationships among variables in predicting self-esteem scores. Multiple regression is a technique which, in a series of steps, calculates the amount of variance explained in the dependent variable. Being "Native and adopted" was forced to enter the regression equation last, and this variable retains its significance in predicting low self-esteem, even when the effects of age at adoption are accounted for.

A tabulation of parental descriptions of adolescent problems (Table 4) suggests that although issues surrounding ethnicity were often perceived as problematic the adoptive parents were unwilling or unable to come to grips with issues of ethnic identity, and respect for the ethnic group to which the child originally came from. For both the Native and inter-country adopted children, parents put little stress on identity and ethnic issues, preferring to treat the child "just like one of us." A measure of identity integration (Weinreich, 1979) indicated however that in the Native adolescents adoptees tested, failure to integrate or respect ethnic identity was present in a half of the subjects. This was in contrast with the inter-country group, in which only 10 percent (two individuals) had similar types of identity conflict. In the non-adopted Native group, three adolescents (13%) showed marked identity confusion[1].

We conclude from this analysis that Native children do have significantly poorer adjustment than white adoptees. The exact cause of this poorer adjustment is unknown, but conflicts over ethnicity might be a factor. These results, and other clinical data suggest that Native adoptees are usually brought up with a consciousness of themselves as white, but increasingly find themselves subject to the stereotyping and rejection experienced by the average Native adolescent in urban Canada. Inter-country adopted children, despite their differing ethnicity, do not seem to experience similar kinds of rejection or conflict. This is a tentative conclusion, which needs testing and exploration in future work.

It is not entirely clear from the data why outcomes for the Native adoptee should be so much worse than those for white children adopted by white parents, and the inter-country adoptee. But what is clear is that Native children adopted by white parents in this sample do have much poorer levels of adjustment, more problems of depression, low self-esteem, and suicidal ideas as well as much higher levels of acting out behavior. Failure to integrate concepts of ethnic, social, personal and sexual identity (as indicated by Weinreich's measure) is the most powerful predictor of level of adolescent problems: problems of identify integration account for the majority of the variance in the correlation of being adopted with marked behaviour problems, as well as the correlation of being Native in predicting serious behaviour problems in adolescence. These findings leave us with the inference (which will be explored in future research with these subjects) that identity problems and identity confusion are of major importance in the development of behaviour problems which are associated with adoption breakdown in more than a fifth of the Native adoptees.

There is an implication too that Native children adopted by white parents needed special support (which few of them got) to buffer them against what appear to have been acute role dilemmas - the conflicting roles of being a Native child in a white family; of being a Native child in a city where there are relatively few Native people; and of having to bear the brunt of ethnic stimigmatization without the support of parents of similar ethnicity.

In contrast, the non-adopted Native children grew up in rural areas on Reserves in which there were cultural and family factors supporting their ethnic identity. It is notable too that the inter-country adopted group appeared to have few current problems. These findings are similar to other work on the adjustment of inter-country adopted children in North America (Feigelman & Silverman, 1983). In Calgary, people of oriental and Central and South American origin are numerous and visible in term of their commercial and professional success, and it may that the inter-country adopted children experienced fewer role conflicts with school and peers with regard to status, ethnic identity, and attachment to culture of origin. Ongoing work with this sample indicates that all of the inter-country adopted children were comfortable and accepted in inter-ethnic dating; but dating a white boy or girl was rare for the adopted Native adolescents.

A potential solution: Native sovereignty and control of child welfare services

Child welfare programs in Canada have not served Native families well, and have often undermined rather than supported these families. Children have been removed by child protection workers, often on trivial grounds, their extended families ignored as source of care. Native

Table 2
Comparison of three groups of adopted adolescents and non-adopted controls

Variable	Natives Adoptees (N=37)	White Adoptees (N=42)	Inter-country Adoptees (N=20)	Non-adopted, White (N=40)	Non-adopted, Native (N=23)
Mean age adopted (years)	2.4	1.8	3.5	-	-
Educational rank Father, % high school+	37.0%	36.0%	60.0%	35.0%	0.0%
Mother, % high school+	32.0%	36.0%	51.0%	30.0%	4.3%
Child's age at Interview (Years)	14.5	14.2	16.3	14.5	15.2
Maternal age at interview	48.6	50.2	54.8	45.3	38.9
% female	38.0%	40.0%	50.0%	40.0%	52.2%

Table 2 (Cont'd)

Mother's assessment of child-parent relations:					
No problems	18.9%	50.0%	65.0%	70.0%	56.5%
Some problems	24.3%	26.2%	20.0%	20.0%	26.1%
Many problems	35.2%	11.9%	15.0%	10.0%	17.4%
Profound problems (breakdown of parent-child relations and/or residential care)	21.6%	11.9%	0.0%	0.0%	0.0%
Adoptee's Self-Esteem					
Below 1st quartile of normative group	64.9%	30.9%	25.0%	22.5%	26.1%
Above 3rd quartile of normative group	10.8%	26.2%	35.0%	27.5%	21.7%

Table 2 (Cont'd)

Suicidal ideas or deliberate self-harm in past 6 months	40.5%	9.5%	10.0%	12.5%	8.7%

Significance (ANOVA): Significant variation at the 5% level or beyond across all five categories for:

- Parental assessment of problems
- Adoptee's self-esteem
- Adoptee's suicidal ideas or actions

230

Table 3   Multiple regression of variable predicting poor self-esteem in 159 adolescents

Variable	Simple Correlation	After Multiple Regression	Multiple Correlation
Subject's age	-.16	-.16	.16
Sex: female	.13	.09	.17
Maternal education	-.15	-.14	.20
Age in months child was adopted (O = non-adopted)	.26	.20	.28
Ethnicity: Native or Non-European	.24	.12	.33
Maternal age	-.09	.03	.33
Child is Native <u>and</u> adopted	.39	.25	.44

Note: Variables entered into the regression analysis in steps, ordered as above, with "Adopted and Native" entered last. Partial correlations of 0.18 and above after regression are significant at the 5% level or beyond.

Table 4 Problems of child-rearing identified by parents of adopted and non-adopted children

Variable	Natives Adoptees (N=37)	White Adoptees (N=42)	Inter-Country White (N=20)	Non-adopted Native (N=40)	Non-adopted Adoptees (N=23)
Child suffered racial harass-ment or insults in elementary school	51.3%	0.0%	15.0%	0.0%	34.8
Lack of identity integration *	48.6%	14.3%	10.0%	7.5%	13.0%
Child had neuro-logical or learning problem needing specialist treatment	10.8%	2.4%	0.0%	5.0%	4.3%

Table 4 (Cont'd)

Up to age 12, marked signs of aggression/ overactivity/ conduct disorder **	43.2%	9.5%	5.0%	10.0%	21.7%
Marked behaviour problems present at interview: one or more of rebellion; running from school or home; drug or alcohol use; delinquency; sexual acting out	59.5%	11.9%	15.0%	15.0%	17.4%

*   Cut-off point indicated by Weinreich (1979)[1].

**   Clinical cut-off on Rutter's behaviour disorder scale (Rutter, 1980) completed by mother.

233

children have been placed in various types of alternative care, ranging from boarding schools which were in themselves abusive, to foster homes uninterested in Native children, to white adoptive parents who have often been unable to meet the identity needs of Native children[2]. Overall administration of almost every aspect of the life of Native people covered by the Indian Act is retained by central government. These powers include those of education and social service, which are usually delegated to the provinces. Only rarely are Native bands allowed to administer their own social service systems: and only then under the paternalistic guardianship of the federal government. Canada seems unlikely in the present political climate to pass a law like the *Indian Child Welfare Act* (which allows autonomy in social service delivery in tribes choosing to do so - Simon & Altstein, 1981). Yet to appears to us that only by allowing Native people in Canada such autonomy will the problems of Native child welfare be solved. In parallel, the land claims which many Canadian bands have for return of traditional territory much also be conceded. This land was either seized illegally or was taken through "treaties" signed under duress, or signed without legal guidance as to what the implications would be.

Native peoples in Canada and North America have traditionally formed nations, with individual languages, customs and territories. Native people, together with the Metis (mixed) people in Canada are seeking to reinforce their group identity through the negotiation of their rights as individual nations. Within this search for political recognition lies a potential solution, namely that of applying the rules for controlling and monitoring the practice of inter-country adoption to adoptions between Native nations, and Canada and the U.S.A.

There are a number of ways of approaching this. First of all, independent Native nations could enact law which governs the removal of any child from the band for purposes of adoption[3].

In addition, or alternatively, both Canada and the Native nations could adopt the United Nations principles on inter-country adoption, which emerged from a conference at Leysin, switzerland addressing the many problems surrounding such adoption (Delupis, 1976).

The Leysin principles (UN, 1960) have been revised and updated in subsequent international meetings (Luecker-Babel, 1986), and the revised principles presented to the United Nations (UN, 1985) are broadly as follows:

(a)   The first priority is for a child to be cared for by his or her own parents.

(b) Where adoption is considered to be a suitable solution to the problem of providing a permanent family environment for a child, the informed consent of the child's biological parents should be sought, before any legal proceedings regarding adoption can be undertaken.

(c) Inter-country adoption should only be considered when no permanent home within the child's own country can be found.

(d) Inter-country adoption should only be undertaken when governments of the respective countries have agreed on the professional and legal principles to be followed in monitoring and supervising such adoptions.

(e) All assessments of children and potential parents should be made by properly qualified professionals, according to standards laid down by the two countries involved. In no case should the placement result in improper financial gain for those involved. Professionals involved should receive normal fees; but no financial inducement must be offered to any biological parent, or to any official.

(f) Special legal precautions should be taken to control the activities of third parties who attempt to arrange international adoptions.

(g) The order for adoption should be made in the country in which the child is born, and the prospective adopters must travel to that country for purposes of such legal hearings. The laws and rules concerning adoption should be agreed on by both countries involved.

(h) The prospective adopters should be professionally assessed in their country of domicile - if they are unsuitable as in-country adopters, then most certainly they would be unsuitable as inter-country adopters.

(i) The receiving country should appoint professionals who will monitor the child's progress in the receiving country for at least six months.

(j) All actions taken with regard to international adoption shall be taken in the best interests of the child, and for no other reason.

The potential which the child has for healthy psychological growth in the country of the adopters, in terms of adaptation, and acceptance by the wider community should be carefully considered before making an adoption order.

The adoptions of Native children from Canada, many of whom were taken to the United States and elsewhere, have not followed these principles. Children were handed to prospective adopters by child welfare authorities, clearly pleased to be relieved of a financial burden[4]. Adoption orders were made by the country, province or state in which the adopter resided, and no social work or legal monitoring was undertaken once the child was placed.

The case of Carla W. who returned to Canada in November, 1989 at the age of 25 illustrates the problems which can arise in an unsupervised international adoption, in which the Leysin principles were ignored entirely (York, 1989). Carla, a Native child, was removed from her parents by social workers in Winnipeg when she was five. As usual, the possibility of placing Carl with members of her extended family was ignored. Social workers, in this case, like adoptive parents and many other Canadians, seemed to view aboriginal culture and social organization with distaste, not something to be taken seriously or respected.

Carla was placed with a Dutch couple in Manitoba when she was aged eight. The couple immediately left for the Netherlands, and there were no further checks or follow-ups on Carla's status. The application of the United Nations principles on international adoption might have prevented the disasters that followed; but Canada has never followed these principles[5]. Carla was among the thousands of Manitoba Indian children who were adopted by white parents in the 1960s and 1970s. Hundreds of them were sent to the United States; some went further, to Europe.

After six months in the Netherlands, Carla's adoption broke down, for unexplained reasons. She was initially placed in a children's home, where Carla recalled that nuns would beat her because she wouldn't obey instructions - apparently because she didn't understand Dutch. She was then placed in a series of foster homes, in which by her own account she was both acutely depressed and rebellious. In the final home she was sexually abused, and had two children by her foster father. Both children were placed in care, and the foster father denied responsibility. When Carla returned to the Anishinaaboin nation she was met by the traditional chief in full regalia, accompanied by fifty members of her extended family. The Anishinaaboin and other nations in Canada are now trying to locate the children taken, against the community's will, and placed for adoption.

Conclusions

Native people in North America are struggling to survive both culturally and physically, following the devastations imposed on their traditional way of life and family systems by white settlers and their administrative apparatus. The approach of white settlers can be described as one of institutional racism, just as the manner in which whites in North America control black people, and exclude them form many arenas of public and social life is one of institutionalized oppression. Just as the adoption of black children by white parents has been problematic, in comparison with within-race adoptions and inter-country adoptions (Feigelman & Silverman, 1983), so the adoptions of Native children by whites has appears to be fraught with difficulty.

However, while there is some evidence of positive trends in identity development in black children adopted by white parents (Bagley & Young, 1979; Simon & Altstein, 1981). The same cannot be said for transracial adoptions of Native children. As Simon and Altstein (1981) have argued: "The case of Native Americans is a special one. Native Americans have been subjected to a singularly tragic fate, and their children have been particularly vulnerable." (p.69). Our own research supports such a conclusion.

The majority of adoptions of Native children by white parents in our survey (based on random sampling) had experienced difficulties, often profound. It should be added that attempts by some of these white parents to give the child a sense of identity as a Native person were not particularly successful - Native adolescents with profound identity problems were equally divided in our sample between parents who had ignored identity issues, and those who had tried to emphasize Native identity. We draw from these results the conclusion that the extreme marginalization of Native people in Canada means that there is little possibility for a Native child to adapt successfully in a white family. The few real "successes" in Native-white adoptions in our series occurred in children with mixed ancestry, who were able to pass themselves as white.

Our study is unique in having a control group of Native children who grew up with their parents on a rural reserve. These controls, who had relatively good psychological outcomes in adolescence were not randomly selected, but came from families identified by the band as needing help and support following the removal by provincial social services of an older child. The results from these non-adopted, Native adolescents are important, and this work deserves replication.

The answer to problems of Native communities lies, we have argued, in a combination of political, social and economic development. Those communities with the fewest problems (of crime, suicide, family breakdown, alcoholism, and removal of children by external authorities) in Alberta are the larger reserves in the south, with diversified economies providing income through ranching and leasing oil, coal and natural gas reserves (Bagley, Wood & Khumar, 1990). It is these nations too (particularly the Blackfoot nation, with whom we have worked extensively - Bagley, 1985) who are the closest to organizing indigenous systems of child welfare and adoption. Not only must the white power structure concede land claims by Native peoples, they must also foster development of Native nations as they foster the development of third world peoples. If Native nations and communities choose to allow children to be adopted by white families, then internationally agreed rules for inter-country adoption must be observed.

End notes

1.   Weinreich's method of identifying acute identity problems in adolescence is based on the theoretical merging of Kelly's personal construct theory, Eriksonian notions of identity formation, and Hauser's work on identity problems in black adolescents. Each adolescent tested produces a unique collection of elements (individuals or groups) which are construed in ways given by the subject. Each personal construct is then interpreted in the light of Hauser's work on identity formation. Because there is a subjective element in this interpretation, each set of personal constructs was interpreted by the writer and/or the two research assistants (Michael Wood and Helda Khumar) who undertook the interviewing; each profile was rated "blindly" by two individuals who had not interviewed the subject. When there was complete agreement between the two raters on profound failure of identity integration, a subject was assumed to have acute identity problems.

For example, John, aged 14 identified 11 elements relating to himself, his ethnic group, his school peers, his past self, his ideal self, his white parents, his Native parents, and Native people in general. As "a person with white parents" he evaluated himself positively in the past, but negatively now. Native people were evaluated positively in the past, but negatively now. His white brother had very positive ratings, while he had very negative, current ratings on the strong-weak dimension. White peers were seen as unfriendly, successful and strong. We used Weinreich's formulation for assessing the ratio of current identification with contra identifications (past, present and future) to obtain measures of failure of identity integration, or of identity fixation. For further details on the methods of analyzing personal constructs, see Fransella and Bannister (1977) and Weinreich (1986).

238

The identity problems of the Native adoptees in this study appear to much more profound than those of the adolescent black subjects adopted by white parents, analyzed in the study by McRoy and Zurcher (1983).

2.   It is ironic that only in 1988 in Canada did details being in emerge of the sexual abuse (among many other types of abuse) in the boarding schools for Native children, run by Catholic and Anglican missionaries. In September 1989, the Canadian Broadcasting Company ran an hour-long documentary in which many adult Native people spoke about these abuses. The last of these schools (in Manitoba), was closed in October, 1989 after parents complained about the severe and regular beating their children received. The missionaries defended such beating on biblical grounds.

3.   What are needed for both sending and receiving countries involved in inter-country adoption are model acts of the kind outlined by Simon and Altstein (1981) in their chapter on inter-country adoptions.

4.   The readiness of child welfare authorities to unburden themselves of seemingly unadoptable children is illustrated by the State of California, which in the late 1970s gave into the care of a religious organization 150 permanent wards, all of them black. The cult, the "People's Temple" took 39 of these children to Guyana with the tacit approval of the State of California, but in contravention to Californian law which forbad the removal of permanent wards. Once in Guyana, the children were beaten, terrorized, raped, and sexually tortured. They had to regularly rehearse taking poison. Wooden (1981) devotes a good part of his book on the Jonestown massacre to describing how easily children can be given away or disposed of once the state has assumed the role of legal parent. As Wooden points out, some 300 of those who died by poisoning in Guyana did not commit suicide; they were children and minors who had no option but to obey the adults who had terrorized them. In other words, these children were murdered.

5.   There is an "Adoption Desk" at the Federal government headquarters in Ottawa, with the role of advising parties in international adoptions. The writer asked the director of this agency in 1984 whether the Leysin principles were followed in Canada. The director replied by letter, saying he had never heard of these principles! For a statement of Federal policy on adoptions of Native children see *Adoption and the Indian Child,* available from the Adoption Desk, National Health and Welfare, Brooke Claxton Building, Tunney's Pasture, Ottawa, K1A 1B5, Canada.

14 Transracial adoption in Britain: A follow-up with policy implications

Transracial adoption we define as the adoption by parents (usually of white, European origin) of a an ethnically different child (usually of black, Afro-Caribbean origin). We are concerned in this chapter with adoptions of minority-group children born in the country in which they are adopted. Inter-country adoptions are often also inter-ethnic adoptions, with the added complication of adaptations of language and culture, especially for older adopted children. In research studies we have treated inter-country adoptions as a special case, to be considered separately from other inter-ethnic adoptions (Bagley and Young, 1981; Bagley, 1990). Another interesting type of parenting whose literature is relevant for, but should be considered separately from inter-ethnic adoption is the identity and psychological development of children of ethnically-mixed marriages (Bagley and Young, 1984; Bagley, 1991a).

Earlier writers on transracial adoption have pointed to mixed, but generally favourable outcomes in pre-adolescent follow-ups of transracial or inter-ethnic adoptions In Britain Tizard (1977) has written enthusiastically about the benefits of adoption for children who would otherwise grow up in institutional or unstable care, but also points to the potentially negative impact upon a black child's adjustment of white parents who ignore (or even denigrate) black culture, and have no contact with black people and their institutions. Gill and Jackson (1983) in another British study have shown that 60 per cent of white adopters with black, adolescent children had no black friends, and their children likewise had few contacts with black adolescents. Nevertheless, the majority of the adopted children had good levels of self-esteem, and few signs of behavioural maladjustment.

In the United States Ladner (1977) who studied 136 transracial adoptions, argued that "love is not enough" - while it's essential that parents love and care for their children, they should also esteem and interact with black culture, if they are to fully meet their black child's identity needs. As in the British research, a minority (but a crucially important minority) of white adopters had failed in the task of integrating themselves and their black child, with black social institutions and culture.

Since these earlier studies were undertaken the practice of placing black children with white parents has slowed in many regions, or has ceased altogether. In part this has been because social workers have been using more culturally appropriate models, supporting minority-group families under stress rather than removing children on grounds of alleged neglect or abuse (Bagley, 1990); in part because social agencies have become more active and adept in finding black homes for black children (Sandven and Resnick, 1987); and in part for political reasons, since vocal members of the minority community have attacked the idea of black children being brought up in white homes (Simon and Altstein, 1987; Stubbs, 1987). Nevertheless, black and other minority-group children are still being place transracially in Canada and the United States when their "special needs" (such as physical and mental disability) make them unacceptable to the still limited pool of black or minority group adopters.

Another policy dilemma concerns the status of mixed-race children, who have one white and one black biological parent. Advocates of mixed-race families, such as the British Harmony group (described by White, 1985) argue that mixed-race children are neither black nor white, but both, and form a special ethnic or cultural group (Bagley and Young, 1984). Why should a child with one white, biological parent not be placed with a white family, or with a family of a mixed marriage?

Further research from the United States has indicated the rather successful outcomes for transracial adoptions. Thus McRoy and Zurcher (1983) compared 30 black children placed with white parents, and 30 black children adopted inracially. A standardized measure of self-concept (the Tennessee scale) indicated no differences between the two adopted groups, and no statistically significant differences in comparison with normative groups for the test. Feigelman and Silverman (1984) studied

241

372 adoptive families with children from a variety of ethnic groups, and found that "the adolescent and school-aged transracial adoptees were no more poorly adjusted than their inracially adopted counterparts."

Confirmatory evidence comes from the study by Simon and Altstein (1987) of 98 transracial adoptions. Success rates (about 80 percent) in the adolescent years were very similar to success rates encountered by research on outcomes of both inracial adoption, and ordinary parenting. Put another way, about 10 percent of children from ordinary, non-adoptive families will have marked psychological problems; about 10 percent will have an intermediate level of problems; and 80 percent will be well-adjusted. These figures are the bench mark for evaluating outcomes of adoption, and a large number of studies (reviewed by Brodzinsky and Schecter, 1990) suggest that outcomes for those without handicap or disability and placed for adoption in infancy (including black children placed with white parents) have outcomes which are close to the 80 percent benchmark figure of good adjustment. Indeed, if adoptive families can achieve a 70 or 80 percent level of good adjustment with children who were adopted past infancy, and experienced many earlier traumas including neglect, abuse, and early neurological and physical problems (Cadoret, 1990), then adoptive parenting will have been particularly successful.

One of the paradoxes of transracial adoption in terms of the assumed problems of black children in white families in achieving satisfactory levels of ethnic self-esteem is that many black children brought up in black families appear to have problems in this regard. In various projective tests (e.g. using photographs of black and white people, and black and white colours and figures) black children in both the United States and Britain have tended to devalue blackness and black people, and have preferred white figures, even to the extent of denying and sometimes even denigrating their own blackness (Milner, 1975; Weinreich, 1979; Davey, 1982; Williams and Morland, 1976). The situation is changing in the direction of a more positive evaluation of self-characteristics by black children (Milner, 1983; Bagley and Young, 1988). Nevertheless, a fifth of the black, Jamaican children studied in Toronto in 1987 identified with white children, implicitly rejecting their own black identity compared with the 40 percent of the black Jamaican children in Britain we studied 12 years earlier, and 53 per cent of the black American children studied by Williams and Morland (1976), using the same projective test in the early 1970s.

The irony in the research evidence on transracial adoption is that despite negative assertions of some black political leaders about the effects of transracial adoption (cited in Simon and Altstein, 1977), black and mixed race children adopted by white parents actually have similar or better levels of ethnic identity, and more positive evaluations of black people than do black children growing up in black families. This is brought out in the studies of self-esteem in black adoptees (reviewed by Silverman and Feigelman, 1990), and most clearly by Johnson, Shireman and Watson (1987) who used the Clark Doll Test in their study of 42 black children adopted by white parents, and 45 black children adopted by black parents. Eighty percent of the within- race, adopted black children identified themselves as black, compared with 73 percent of the transracial adoptees (who contained more children who were mixed-race or fair-skinned). As Feigelman and Silverman (1983) point out, agencies have tended to place light-skinned black children and mixed-race children more frequently with white families; this has complicated comparisons of ethnic identity between transracial and inracial adopted children, since fair-skinned children might be more likely to identify themselves as white.

However, Simon and Altstein (1977) who also used the Clark Doll Test, and the Williams and Morland (1976) projective tests, reported:

> It appears that black children reared in the special setting of a multiracial family do not acquire the ambivalence toward their own race reported in all other studies involving young black children. Our results also show that white children do not consistently prefer white to other groups, and that there are no significant differences in the racial attitudes of any category of children. Our findings do not offer any evidence that black children reared by white parents acquire a preference for white over black. They show only that black children perceive themselves as black as accurately as white children perceive themselves as white. (Simon and Altstein, 1977, p. 158)

Transracial adoptions: Results of the earlier British study

In 1979 we reported on the current adjustment of 114 adopted and non-adopted children in Southern England, thirty of whom were of black or mixed-race origin, and had been adopted by white parents (Bagley and Young, 1979). These thirty children were compared with a similar number of white children adopted by white parents, a group of black and mixed-race children in foster or group care who had not been adopted, and a non-separated comparison group, obtained from school sources. We concluded from this work that the black and mixed-race, adopted children then aged between six and eight years old had generally good psychological outcomes in terms of a number of standardized measures of adjustment, despite the fact that some white parents had few black friends, and were unable or unwilling to transmit to their children any consciousness or pride in the heritage of being of black origin.

We examined various measures of adjustment against a number of background characteristics: racial awareness in parents was associated with higher social status, parental age, and existing children in the family. What this in effect meant was that parents who already had children of their own, and who made a conscious decision to adopt a mixed-race child were more racially aware than parents who adopted a child because of infertility. Twelve of the thirty parents had adopted because they couldn't have children "of their own"; only three of these had, from the outset, specifically intended to adopt a mixed-race child. The remaining nine had originally wanted to adopt a white baby but eventually approached agencies with a mixed-race child in mind when it became clear that no white children were available.

These couples whatever their original motivation were mature, kind, mentally healthy people, and appeared to make excellent parents. This was reflected in the good adjustment of the children they had adopted. But these adopted children, according to the racial identification measures we used, often tended to identify themselves as white (as frequently as black children in black families did). Our optimistic surmise in this original research was that since the foundations of good mental health and feelings of self-worth were laid during a crucial period of development, the transracially adopted children would possess the basic ego-strength to incorporate within their identify framework, at some later stage, positive concepts of their ethnic identity. In Hauser's (1971) phrase, we supposed that there would not be any "premature foreclosure" of identity in these children.

In the original study the mixed-race adopted children were considered as a group by themselves and in combination with the white adopted children to see if any background factors could predict current adjustment. Sex was not related to adjustment, so that Raynor's (1970) finding of better adjustment in mixed-race boys was not confirmed. Early health history, including birth weight and minor congenital malformations was not systematically related to later adjustment. Age of child at placement with adoptive parents (average age 23 months, range one month to four years); age at separation from natural mother; and factors related to previous foster care (including a history of abuse or neglect in five cases) bore no relationship to the children's current adjustment when they were, on average 7.3 years old. A possible reason for this finding was that, as in Seglow et al's (1972) study, the excellent care provided by the adoptive parents had counteracted the negative effects of early environmental and physical handicaps.

The follow-up of transracial adoptees

Twelve years after the original study we were able to locate 27 of the 30 black and mixed-race children adopted by white parents, and 25 of the 30 white children adopted by white parents. These young people completed a number of measures of mental health and adjustment including the Middlesex Hospital Questionnaire (Bagley, 1980); the Coopersmith self-esteem scale revised for use with adults and older adolescents (Bagley, 1989a); Weinreich's measure of identity (Weinreich, 1979 and 1986); two measures used by Stein and Hoopes (1985) in their follow-up study of adoptees - the Tan et al. (1979) ego identity scale, and the Offer et al. (1988) Self-Image Questionnaire. We also devised a questionnaire which asked the adoptees to reflect on the process of their adoption, and the degree of satisfaction that it had yielded them. Specific questions about ethnic identity were addressed to the black adoptees.

These instruments were chosen in order to address the measurement of identity and self-esteem, issues which previous writers on adoption have shown to be important (Stein and Hoopes, 1985; Hoopes, 1990; Brodzinsky, 1990). Our hypothesis, based on the previous findings of McRoy and Zurcher (1983) and Simon and Altstein (1987) is that there would be no differences in self- esteem, identity and adjustment between the two types of adoptees, black and white, both adopted by white parents.

The mean age of the 27 black and mixed-race adoptees at follow-up was 19.0 years; 14 were male. The white adoptees were on average 19.2 years old, with an age range (similar to the black adoptees) of 17 to 20 years. Twelve of these white adoptees were male. Eighty one percent of the transracially adopted children came from families where one or both parents were "middle class" (in occupations classified in the Registrar General's classes I and II), compared with 72 percent of the families of the white adoptees.

Results

Using a variety of dependent measures (psychoneurosis, self- esteem, and identity development in the adoptees) we tried to predict from the earlier data collected on the parents of the transracial adoptees and on the adoptees themselves, the outcomes for these young people when they were in their late 'teens. None of the potential predictors examined (social status and educational level of parents; presence of biological and adopted siblings; age at which child was placed; parents' motives for adopting; attitudes of parents to black culture, and contact with black friends; child's self-esteem and ethnic identity in the earlier period) predicted later outcome. When problems did emerge in the adolescent years, there was no apparent cause for this in the previously collected data on the adoptive families.

In Table 1 the two adopted groups (black and mixed race children adopted by white parents; and white children adopted by white parents) are compared. The two groups are similar in terms of parental age and social class profiles, and number of adopted and biological siblings in the adoptive families. The clinical profiles of the two groups of adoptees are very similar too. Profiles of psychoneurosis, depression and anxiety derived from the Middlesex Hospital Questionnaire have been expressed in terms of the quartiles for the combined groups. While there is a tendency for white adoptees to be more anxious, this difference did not reach the five percent level of significance.

Normative data from a large Canadian sample of young adults (Bagley, 1991a) has allowed cut-off points on the Middlesex Hospital Questionnaire to be calculated which indicate scores typical of those with a formal psychiatric diagnosis. Some 11.5 percent of the adoptees fall into this clinical range, a very similar proportion to that observed in the non-adopted, normative sample. Of the other measures, self-esteem and identity orientation are very similar between the two groups of adoptees, with no significant deviation from the available Canadian, U.S. and European norms for these measures (Bagley, 1989a; Offer et al., 1988). In other words, the clinical profiles of the two adopted groups are very similar, and do not appear to differ from these which would be expected of an unselected population of similar age.

The educational achievements of the two adopted groups (Table 2) are rather high, and reflect the advantaged, middle class status of most of the adoptive families. What is clear however from Table 3 is that the black and mixed-race adoptees move in a predominantly white milieu: the majority of their close friends, both female and male, are white (but 41 percent of the black adoptees have a "best girl-friend/boy-friend" who is black, mixed-race, Chinese or Indian, compared with 24 percent of the white adoptees). There is no reason however for lament in the fact that these black and mixed-race teenagers do have dating relationships with white boys and girls. What is clear from our data is that neither group of adoptees has any trouble in finding friends of either sex.

Both groups are largely positive about their adoption experiences (Table 4). Combining the information from the clinical tests and the interview data, we can say that three of the 25 white adoptees, and two of the 25 black and mixed race adoptees have ongoing psychological and adjustment problems, marked self-doubt, and some identity problems. But in none of these cases could we adduce factors in the adoption, or in the fact of being a black child in a white family, as having any causal significance in this maladjustment. As Tizard and Phoenix (1987) have argued, although transracial adoption may be qualitatively different from inracial adoption in terms of identity outcomes, such adoption is by no means inferior in terms of identity and adjustment. It is appropriate, in our view, to draw a parallel between "mixed adoptions" and "mixed marriages" - both appear to have generally successful outcomes in terms of the adjustment and identity development of the children involved. It would be reactionary to criticize the mixing of races which mixed marriages involve; likewise, it is reactionary to criticize mixed adoptions simply on the grounds that somehow the identity of the partners in this relationship will be changed.

Conclusions

The findings of the present study underscore those from previous American research on transracial adoption (Silverman and Feigelman, 1990). Such adoption, despite the lack of black consciousness on the part of many of the white parents involved, does appear to meet the psychosocial and development needs of the large majority of the children involved, and can be just as successful as inracial adoption.

Despite this optimistic finding, the practice of transracial adoption in meeting the needs of black children has greatly diminished in both Britain and the United States. There are both positive and negative reasons for this. It is likely that in Britain (as in Canada) families of Caribbean origin are stabilizing and becoming upwardly mobile, achieving the original goals of their migration (Thomas-Hope, 1982; Bagley and Young, 1988). Achieving economic stability is paralleled by family stability, leading to far fewer black children coming into care for whatever reason. Thus other things being equal (for example, the absence of racist practice by social workers) the actual need for adoptive homes for black children will decline.

Unfortunately, there seems to be a marked contrast between the stable, upwardly mobile patterns of family life which is feature of most migrants from the Caribbean to the United States, Canada and Europe, and the increase in instability in the family life in indigenous black Americans. As Silverman and Feigelman have observed, despite the demonstrable success of transracial adoption, it is only atypically considered as an option for the increasing number of black children entering institutional care in America:

> Perhaps the most disturbing part of our review of the transracial adoption literature is the extent to which it is ignored in formulating adoption policy. We are not recommending transracial placements as a panacea for the problems of family disintegration among nonwhite minorities in the United States. But their success suggests that they may at least be a useful resource. The effort to expand intraracial placement for minority children, however, does not require the cessation of transracial placements. At a time when few black leaders are sanguine about the deplorably low income and employment levels found among minority underclasses, as the rates of adolescent out-of-wedlock pregnancies continue to mount, transracial placement is a resource that cannot easily be ignore. (Silverman and Feigelman, 1990, p. 200)

In Britain, fortunately, the situation seems to be different, with a trend towards the embourgoisiment of the black family. Not only are black families releasing fewer children; stable, prosperous black families are more able to accept roles as foster and adoptive parents. Nevertheless, it appears that a significant number of black children in Britain remain in residential care because of the "blanket prohibition" of many local authorities to consider a transracial placement for a black child, or placement of a mixed-race child with a white couple (Jarvis, 1990; Bennett and Mostyn, 1991). The pressure group Children First argues that if the child's individual needs are to be met, transracial adoption should be considered as a serious possibility for many black and mixed race children in long-term, local authority care (Tubbs, 1986).

The failure of many local authorities in Britain to consider this option is puzzling, and is clearly not based on any good psychological or research evidence on the outcomes of transracial adoption (Tizard and Phoenix, 1987). Indeed, some local authority practice may be based on a naive anti-racist policy, which assumes that keeping black children separated from white families will somehow serve their interests, or protect them from racism. Such a view is both naive and absurd. It is clear that despite the existence of both institutional and personal racism in Britain, about twenty per cent of the white, British population do hold markedly non-prejudiced and accepting views of black people and their culture (Bagley et al, 1979). It is this sector of the white population which is particularly likely to be partner in the growing number of racially mixed marriages in Britain and in Canada (Bagley, 1991a). It is this sector of the population to which should be considered, after appropriate home studies by social workers, as transracial adoptive parents. Not only is this sector of the British population educated and enlightened, with many black friends and colleagues, and intercultural interests and contacts; they also express an interest in transracial adoption, an interest often frustrated by current local authority policy in Britain (Bennett and Mostyn, 1991). The movement towards interculturalism (defined and discussed in the British context by Verma and Bagley, 1984) is one of the most positive signs in ethnic relations today. In Canada, this concept is known as multiculturalism, the sharing and inter-relationship of cultures whose importance and integrity is generously supported by federal and provincial governments. This policy has for example, led to the rapid absorption and upward social mobility of immigrants from Jamaica (Bagley, 1989b; Bagley, Friesen and Coward, 1989). Multicultural adoption adoption is part of this optimistic blending and sharing of ethnic group cultures and heritages. Transracial adoption, like transracial marriage could be part of that growth. About a fifth of all marriages in Britain of a black person are between black and white partners. Could we hope for a similar ratio in transracial adoptions?[1]

End note

1.   In an ideal society, not divided on grounds of race or skin colour, physical features should be no more relevant in adoption placement than, say hair or eye colour. What is crucial is that the adopted children should be "chosen children" (Feigelman and Silverman, 1983) and that there should be an essential match between the psychological needs and commitments of parent and child. This is entirely compatible with the adoption of white children by members of other ethnic groups, and such practice does occur for example, in the North Western Territories and Yukon provinces of Canada, where white children are adopted by Native and Inuit families, in regions where whites are a small minority of the total population.

Table 1 Proportions of contrasted adopted adolescents in mental health and identity groupings

	Lowest (25%) (Excellent mental health)	Mid (50%)	Highest (25%) (Poorer mental health)	Significance
Total scale score - psychoneurosis				
Black adoptees (27)	22.2%	55.5%	22.2%	NS
White adoptees (25)	28.0%	44.0%	28.0%	
Both groups (52)	25.0%	50.0%	25.0%	
Depression				
Black adoptees (27)	25.9%	48.1%	25.9%	NS
White adoptees (25)	24.0%	52.0%	24.0%	
Both groups (52)	25.0%	50.0%	25.0%	

Table 1 (Cont'd)

Free-Floating Anxiety

Black adoptees	(27)	22.2%	63.0%	14.8%	NS
White adoptees	(25)	28.0%	36.0%	36.0%	
Both groups	(52)	25.0%	50.0%	25.0%	

<u>Problems in range of normative clinical group</u>

Black adoptees   (27)   11.1%   (3 individuals)
White adoptees   (25)   12.0%   (3 individuals)

<u>Self-Esteem Scale (Coopersmith - Revised)</u>

Black adoptees   (27)   Mean 32.88   SD 9.78   NS
White adoptees   (25)   Mean 30.49   SD 10.50

<u>Identity Measure: Percent with Fixated or Fragmented Identity</u>

Black adoptees   (27)   7.4% (2 individuals)   NS
White adoptees   (25)   8.0% (2 individuals)

Table 2 (Cont'd)

Tan Ego Identity Scale

Black adoptees (27)	Mean: 72.36	SD: 8.05
White adoptees (25)	Mean: 74.81	SD: 8.73

NS

Offer Self-Image Questionnaire

Black adoptees (27)	Mean: 49.85	SD: 11.69
White adoptees (25)	Mean: 53.79	SD: 13.04

NS

Table 2 Educational achievements of the two adopted groups

	Black (N=27)	White (N=25)
School Attainment		
Left school at 16 with some GCSE passes	40.0%	28.0%
Left school at 17 or 18 with some GCSE and/or A level passes	60.0%	72.0%
College Progress		
Attending technical or further education college full-time	33.3%	28.0%
Attending college part-time whilst employed	11.1%	8.0%
Working full-time, no college attendance	14.8%	12.0%
Not working, not attending college full or part-time	3.7%	8.0%
Attending/accepted by Polytechnic, University or Institute of Higher Education for full-time study	37.0%	40.0%

Note   No comparison of the above variables between black and white adoptees indicates any statistically significant differences.

Table 3 Ethnic status of best friends of black and white adoptees

	Black (N=27)	White (N=25)
Current best friend of <u>same</u> sex:		
Mixed race	4	1
Black	5	2
White	17	21
Oriental	0	1
South Asian	1	0
Current best friend of <u>opposite</u> sex:		
Mixed race	5	1
Black	5	3
White	16	19
Oriental	0	1
South Asian	1	1

Note   No comparison of differences between black and white adoptees indicates any statistically significant differences on the above variables.

Table 4 Perceptions of adoption in black and white adoptees

Item		"Strongly agree/agree"	"Unsure"	"Disagree/ strongly disagree"
Adoption provided me with the kind of family life I needed	Black (N=27)	96.3%	3.7%	0%
	White (N=25)	92.0%	4.0%	4.0%
I have enjoyed my life as an adopted child	Black (N=27)	96.0%	4.0%	0%
	White (N=25)	84.0%	12.0%	0%

Table 4 (Cont'd)

I wish I had not been adopted	Black (N=27)	0%	11.1%	88.9%
	White (N=25)	4.0%	4.0%	92.0%
I feel confused being a black or mixed race child in a white family	Black (N=27)	0%	7.4%	92.6%
I feel confused about my ethnic identity	Black (N=27)	0%	3.7%	96.3%
I have experienced discrimination because I am a black child in a white family	Black (N=27)	0%	7.4 %	92.6%

Note   No comparison between the two groups is statistically significant at the five per cent level or beyond.

15 Attitudes to transracial adoption in samples of Afro-Caribbeans in London, 1979 and 1989

Professionals and intellectuals from both the white and Afro-Caribbean communities in Britain often express strong opinions (usually in the absence of good empirical evidence) about the effects and desirability (or otherwise) of transracial adoptions. However these spokesmen and women are often self-appointed, or have uncertain constituencies. Information on how black people actually feel about transracial adoption is sketchy. They are rarely consulted as a caucus about how they feel about black and mixed-race children being adopted by white families; or about the resources actually available (or needed) within the black community for expanding the scope of adoptions of black children by black families.

Some radical black organisations in Britain have spoken out against transracial adoption as their counterparts in America have done, claiming that "the black community" disfavours transracial adoption. But it is not clear whether such organisations clearly speak for the black community; nor is it clear what the ordinary members of the black community in Britain think about transracial adoption.

Two surveys in America questioned the view that ordinary black people were generally opposed to transracial adoption; these surveys showed too the untapped potential for adopting black children which lies within the black community. Alicia Howard and her colleagues (1977) reported that 57 percent of a sample of 150 black residents of Dayton, Ohio had an open or accepting attitude to adoption of black children by white families. She concluded that, "...... the data suggest that the majority of blacks do not oppose the idea of transracial adoptions and a large majority could be described as favourable to this alternative under certain conditions. The majority of respondents felt that it is more important that a black child receive love from white parents than be placed in foster care or in an institution. While the respondents were concerned about the child's possible loss of identification with the black community, the need of the individual child were seen to be of prime importance."

The second American survey of black attitudes toward transracial adoption is by Rita Simon (1978) of 324 black adults randomly sampled in middle class/urban areas of the northern United States. Overall, 45 percent of those surveyed approved in principle, of the practice of white parents adoption black children. The main reason for this approval was the need of the children for a loving home; but a second reason was that the practice of transracial adoption would help to integrate the races. The main grounds in those objecting to transracial adoption were that black children would lose their identity, and that whites did not understand black culture. Nearly 20 percent of the sample said that they would be willing to and were interested in adopting a child if the government offered even minimal financial incentives ($50 a month).

A British survey of black attitudes to transracial adoption in 1979

The questionnaire used by Alicia Howard and her colleagues is ideal for use in a replication study, so we included this questionnaire in the study of a random sample of black families living in the London Borough of Merton. This survey, of 100 families was part of an enquiry into the adequacy of provision for the under-fives, and for older children. Black interviewers administered the questionnaires to families living in the western part of the Borough, adjacent to the Borough of Wandsworth.

The sample characteristics indicated a population, largely West Indian in origin but containing some Africans, that had been long settled in Britain and who had moved to Merton as part of a general trend of upward mobility. Over two thirds of respondents were in the age range 30 to 49; 64 percent were women; and 80 percent had one or more children. Sixty five percent owned or were buying their own house, and crowding or lack of amenities in the household was infrequent. Over two thirds of the mothers worked full time outside of the home, and the modal pattern of social class was of a skilled manual husband with a wife working in nursing or office work.

Table 1 gives the results of the survey of attitudes to adoption, the questions with slight alteration being those used in Howard's American survey. The index of acceptance of transracial adoption, based on combining two questions (responses to "I dislike the idea of black children being adopted by whites" and "I do not strongly object to whites adopting black children") indicated that in 1979 71 percent of the Merton sample were completely accepting of the idea of transracial adoption, compared with 57 percent of the American sample. It was clear that contrary to the views of some radical voices in the black community, the majority of ordinary black people in the sample did not oppose transracial adoption. Nevertheless, as in the American samples, they did express some fears about the possible erosion of identity, and alienation from the black community in black children growing up in white homes. Thus 42 percent of respondents thought that "Black children have special problems that whites cannot begin to understand and/or cope with"; but 85 percent nevertheless preferred a black child to grow up in a white adoptive home than in an institution or foster home.

At the outset, respondents were told that, "Adoption is the process by which a child is placed permanently with substitute parents, and all contact with the natural parents is broken. At the present time, many black and mixed race children are being placed for adoption with white parents. I would like to ask you opinion about some aspects of this policy, and I wonder if you would consider the following statements...." Following the questions taken from the American survey, we asked respondents whether they had considered adoption, and whether they would like to know more about adoption now. Nearly 70 percent said that they would consider adopting a specific child, and 61 percent wanted more information about adoption. Clearly there was much potential within the black community for adoption black children, which had not been reached by existing efforts.

An analysis of the characteristics of those favouring transracial adoption, and those interested in adoption themselves showed them to be largely the same people, and clearly their opinions on both of these issues were motivated by a concern for the needs of black children. Those supporting adoption, both transracially and potentially for themselves tended to be older respondents with growing or grown up families, owning their own houses. No sex differences in responses were observed.

It was salient that the women in the group expressing interest in adoption often had to work full time to maintain the family living standards, and if they did adopt it would have meant a marked drop in household income.   Over half of the respondents did agree that, "Generally speaking, blacks are financially less able to adopt than whites are". This response was similar to Rita Simon's argument for American blacks, that financial support for adoption was needed.   Those respondents most likely to express doubts about transracial adoption were younger, more often single without children themselves, and were likely to live in rented accommodation.

A British survey of black attitudes to transracial adoption in 1989

In 1989, using methods of sampling and interviewing which were precisely similar to those in the 1979 survey, we obtained a fresh random sample of black adults, living in the same area of South London.   Our initial approach was to the same houses which contained the respondents in the survey undertaken for the Merton Community Relations Council in 1979. Although age, sex and ethnicity (Caribbean ancestry/African ancestry/mixed ancestry) were matched in the 1989 survey with the profiles obtained in 1979, we did not interview the same individuals at both points in time.   However, eleven of the 1989 respondents were children of individuals interviewed in 1979.

Assuming that the two samples are reasonably representative of black community opinion (at least in the area of South London where the study was undertaken) there has clearly been a shift in views about the desirability of transracial adoptions. Indeed, by 1989 such adoptions had all but ceased in London. Our respondents' attitudes and opinions in 1989 resembled those of the younger people in the 1979 survey. In fact, that younger generation was now the older generation in the second survey. By 1989 about a third of the black respondents were strongly opposed to the idea of transracial adoptions. However, even in 1989 about half of the respondents were rather accepting of the idea of transracial adoptions. The proportions who would consider adopting a black child had risen from 39 percent in 1979 to 48 percent ten years later. Two thirds of the respondents in the 1989 survey said that they would like to know more about adopting a black or mixed race child. As in the earlier survey, in 1989 those who would approve of transracial adoption for meeting a child's needs for family life, were largely similar to the group who themselves are interested in adopting a black child. Those who expressed such an interest tended to be older individuals in stable family circumstances, had secure employment, and owned their house. The younger, more radical group were much less likely to be in a settled domestic situation, and were significantly less likely to be themselves interested in adoption or fostering of a black child.

At this time, Merton was not a borough noted for its employment of ethnic minority social workers, or for its policies in recruiting black and Asian foster and adoptive parents. Weise (1989) has indicated that policies for placing black children vary quite markedly between different English boroughs. She indicates for example that in 1986 the London borough of Hackney had 766 children in its care, three-quarters of them black, mixed-race or Asian. About a half of these children were placed in adoptive and foster homes, 90 percent of the black children who were placed going to black families.

Rickford (1990) draws unfavourable comparisons between five boroughs with a high proportion of ethnic minority families but with contrasting policies with regard to the recruitment of both black social workers, and the recruitment of minority group foster and adoptive parents. Lambeth for example had 210 black and Asian foster parents in 1989, while Birmingham West with a similar proportion of ethnic minority families, had only one set of foster parents from ethnic minorities. However, areas with a high proportion of minorities who are practising Moslems may recruit very few minority foster families because of the religious proscriptions on adoption and fostering which prevail in orthodox Islam.

It is clear from British work (including our own analysis of the National Child Development study data) that adoption has a much better outcome for the children concerned than does residential care (Triseliotis and Russell, 1984). There is good evidence to support the proposition that a transracial foster or adoptive placement, carefully supported by specialized social workers (using, for example, the groupwork model described by Mullender, 1988) is much preferable to long periods spent in residential care. In-racial, family placement is highly desirable; but nevertheless, many white families with careful selection, screening and support, can meet the needs for identity, love, care and stability which black children (like all children) need.

Table 1

Proportions of 100 black residents in a London Borough responding in various ways to questions about transracial adoption in 1979 and 1989

	Agree or Strongly Agree %		Disagree or Strongly Disagree %	
	1979	1989	1979	1989
"Being raised in white home might prove beneficial to a black child in need of adoption, if no black homes are available"	85	51	7	34
"Whites do not understand blacks enough to raise a black child"	39	64	55	29
"Black children adopted by whites do not understand blacks when they grow up"	55	74	38	21
"Blacks are responsible for adopting black children who are in need of adoption"	46	71	51	24
"Whites should be allowed to adopt only children of mixed backgrounds"	9	25	89	71
"I dislike the idea of black children being adopted by whites"	24	39	74	53
"Black children can never learn to adjust to living in a white adoptive home"	15	32	78	60
"Black children raised in institutions would be no worse off than those raised in white homes"	24	14	62	75
"Black children lose their sense of black identity when they are raised in white homes"	64	79	29	16
"Fewer problems arise from interracial adoptions than from foster homes and/or institutions"	49	54	17	25

Table 1 (cont'd)

	Agree or Strongly Agree %		Disagree or Strongly Disagree %	
"Generally speaking, blacks are financially less able to adopt than whites are"	56	45	35	40
"Black adoptions would increase in Britain if blacks were made aware of how to go about adopting a child"	68	81	15	12
"I do not strongly object to whites adopting black children"	91	58	6	24
"Liberal whites may be qualified to raise black children if they are willing sacrifice some of their white culture, in order to give the children a chance to obtain some black identity"	58	42	32	37
"Black children learn to be 'Prejudiced' against blacks when they are raised by white homes"	38	59	45	32
"Black identity is less important than giving a child love"	76	79	15	12
"Black children have special problems that whites cannot begin to understand and/or cope with"	42	75	43	31
"I would prefer a child being adopted by whites to having him/her lingering in a foster home or institution"	85	80	10	14

Table 1 (Cont'd)

	Yes %		No %	
	1979	1989	1979	1989
"Do you feel that blacks are less interested in adoption than whites are?"	69	55	19	35
"Have you ever considered adopting a black child?"	39	48	59	40
"If you knew of a black or mixed race child who really needed an adoptive home, would you consider adopting that child?"	69	70	19	23
"Would you like to to know more about the possibility of adopting a black or mixed race child?"	61	67	35	30

Combined index of acceptance of transracial adoption (Dislikes the idea of black children adopted by whites, plus Would not strongly object to whites adopting black children)	Completely accepting %	Ambiguous %	Somewhat Unfavourable %	Most Unfavourable %
London sample (100 people) 1979	71	10	10	9
London sample (100 people) 1989	56	8	24	12
Dayton, Ohio, U.S.A. (150 people) 1977	57	17	19	7

Note: Proportion responding "Don't know/unsure" omitted from the above table.

16 A survey of adopted children in two residential treatment centres: Methods of study and initial results

Introduction

In order to explore empirically some of the issues and problems raised in the preceding review of literature, and particularly those concerning disruption and maladjustment in adoption, a survey has been made of all children admitted to two residential treatment centres in an urban area in Western Canada over a ten-year period. The purpose of this work was to identify a sample of adopted children. The only general hypothesis tested is the null hypothesis, that any adopted children in the residential treatment centres will not differ in general characteristics from nonadopted children in these centres. In exploration and test of this hypothesis, a detailed comparison of adopted and a matched group of nonadopted children is presented in the following chapter. This chapter also presents the results of an epidemiological analysis of the characteristics of adopted children in two residential treatment centres.

These two centres serve rural and urban areas with a total population of about one million within the Province of Alberta. In addition, children are admitted from parts of British Columbia, and from the Northwest Territories. Children stay an average about six months, and both facilities have educational services on campus. Treatment involves the highest level of skill available, from psychologists, psychiatrists and social therapists.

The children (aged between 5 and 18) 'present' with the most serious disturbances imaginable; they have been acutely aggressive in home and community, have attacked and injured others, slashed, burnt, poisoned and hanged themselves, killed someone (in one case), burned down their homes and other property, attacked, beaten and poisoned their siblings and parents, run from home and wandered from an early age, abused alcohol and drugs, sexually assaulted others, prostituted themselves, and have engaged in many types of crime including armed robbery.

The largest of the two centres accepts children of all ages from five onwards. The other institution accepts older, (past the age of 11) slightly less disturbed adolescents. The average age of children in the two treatment centres was 13.5 years, the youngest being five and the oldest 18. Over 90 percent of the children were temporary or permanent wards of the province. A small number of children were treated in one centre on an 'out-patient' basis.

Methods of research

Permission was obtained from the directors of two institutions to access the files of children at the two centres, in order to identify any adopted children. This was possible for the period from early 1978 (when complete black files for both centres were available) until December, 1988. We did not seek to interview any the children or their families. Such a course was procedurally and ethically too difficult, but it must be recognized that personal interviews with adopted children and their families would throw further light on the possible causes of disruption in adoption.

After initially reviewing 20 files in each centre, a coding schedule was drawn up to record items which would be ascertained from a reading of the file. Details of current treatment and any therapeutic progress were recorded, and discharge status was also noted. It should be said that files, especially those prior to 1980, were not well organized and were characterized by haphazard organization, duplication, and puzzling gaps. Few follow-ups had been undertaken, and neither centre had a very clear idea of whether their therapeutic intervention had been successful to any degree.

What was most interesting was the lack of any focus in the therapeutic programs on the fact of a child having been adopted. Both centres stressed a behaviourial approach, and addressed the current problem behaviours rather than their early cause. Families were frequently involved in treatment, but as behaviourial reinforcers for treatment regimes designed to modify maladaptive behaviour. The fact of the child having been adopted was almost casually recorded in a number of cases, and its possible aetiological significance was rarely addressed in the case records. Family composition was more often addressed in terms of the possibility of parental support for current treatment, and the degree to which a child's return to the parental home could be achieved.

In a number of cases problems were longstanding, and the child had been in foster home or group care for some time (several years in the case of adolescents) prior to entry to the centre. In such cases early details of family history were sketchy, and it is possible that we have missed some cases of adoption when this fact was not recorded in the file.

Another problem in collecting data was the possibility that the interpretations by the writer of what constituted 'extreme' behaviour disturbance or family disruption were too subjective, and might be both biased and nonreplicable. We checked this possibility by asking a social work colleague to review twenty files, completing the check list we had devised after explaining to her the general criteria we had established for the coding system.

While there was complete agreement on such formal characteristics as sex and age of the child, there was less than complete agreement in other areas. Forty variables where subjective judgement might come into play (excluding sex and age) were compared between the two raters: the degree of agreement on the rating of the 800 pieces of information rated (20 cases, with 40 pieces of information in each) was as follows:

Complete agreement by both raters: 616 comparisons (77 percent)
Agreement in adjacent categories: 80 comparisons (10 percent)
Complete disagreement: 104 comparisons (13 percent)

While the level of agreement is far greater than a random possibility (the probability of such agreement occurring by chance is less than one in a thousand), it is clear that there is a significant margin of error in our judgement, and perhaps in that of our colleague. It could be that this level of measurement error is irreducible; error of this magnitude exists in most sociological and psychological research.

'Agreement in adjacent categories' refers in the main to ratings of behaviourial categories. Ratings in the 'apparently absent' and ' present to some degree' categories were judged to be adjacent; likewise ' present to some degree' and 'present to a marked degree' are in adjacent categories. One convention of coding was agreed on by the two raters: 'apparently absent' (scored zero) refers to either a clear report in the file that the specified behaviour or circumstance was not present or it was not mentioned. Usually the latter was the case. When methods of case recording are not standardized this frequently occurs, only symptoms or circumstance which are saliently present being noted.

In all, the four raters involved (C. Bagley, L. Young, M. Weir and M. Wood) read 519 case records to establish whether or not the child had been adopted - 61 of these 519 children (11.75%) were found to be adopted. Unfortunately many details of the early placement were not recorded, and virtually nothing is known of the birthparents of the adopted children, except in some cases of step-parent adoption. The paucity of information about the circumstances prior to and early in adoption is a reflection of the general lack of importance which most professional workers seem to attach to adoption as a variable which might be addressed in dealing with the child's current psychological condition.

Since in most files data were not organized in a systematic fashion, it was only after some time that we discovered whether or not the child was adopted. This had the advantage that the rating (which was undertaken for each case) often avoided the possibility of any halo effect - a bias in recording which might unconsciously occur once we learned that the child was adopted. It took approximately 45 minutes to read and record the relevant data on each of the 519 cases.

In a second phase of the study, age and sex matched controls for the 61 adopted children were drawn from the pool of 458 controls. Where more than one potential control existed, a random selection method was used. The case files of the 61 adopted children and the 61 controls were further reviewed, and data on the original coding sheet were checked. A special section on circumstances of the adoption, including age at adoption, was completed for the adopted children.

Methods of data analysis

Data were coded in numerical categories for analysis by the Statistical Program for the Social Sciences (Nie et al., 1975) through the Multics computer system of the University of Calgary. The statistics and measures of association reported in subsequent tables in this chapter were generated by the SPSS Crosstabs Program (Nie et al., Chapter 16). Following Labovitz (1967) we assumed too that interval-level assumptions could almost always be applied to ordinal level (ranked) variables. In the 2xN table, on which the following calculations are based, we present Cramer's V, which is derived from the value of Chi-Squared. Since degrees of freedom differ between the cross-tabulations reported in the following tables, only the significance of Chi-Squared is reported in the following tables. Cramer's V is independent of the number of cells in the table however, and has a range of 0 (no association) to 1 (complete association). Since V measures both linear and non-linear associations, it has no sign. The level of significance chosen was the conventional one of 0.05 (one in 20 chance probability of occurrence).

How many adoptions in Alberta?

In order to evaluate the significance of the proportion of adopted children in residential care for maladjusted children, it would be useful to have details of the numbers of children in general population of Canada who were see adopted. The best data we can find on this is taken from Eichler (1983) - see Table 1. This shows that the number of infant adoptions as a proportion of the total population under one year ranged from 2.7% in 1959 to a peak of 5.6% in 1971. The majority of the adopted children in the residential centres we surveyed were born in the period 1964 to 1970. One would expect, on a random selection basis that between 4 and 5 percent of any population born in the period would have been adopted in infancy. In fact, the data from the two centres indicate that 19 out of the 519 subjects identified - 3.7% - were adopted before age one. Given the problems of making comparisons between data for the whole Canada with data from a small, local sample it does appear that infant adoptions are not overrepresented in the population we have studied. There is no comparable data we can locate on the proportions of older children adopted. However, since virtually all ward adoptions in Alberta in the period 1964 to 1970 were adoptions of infants, and most non-ward adoptions were of children aged one or more, the available data on adoptions in Alberta suggest that in the relevant period about 50 percent of adoptions were of children aged 1 and over, and were non-ward adoptions (the majority being biological children of the mother who are adopted by a new spouse not biologically related to the child).

We could expect then, that some 2 to 3 percent of the children in any unselected population would have been adopted after age one. In fact 8.1 percent of the adopted children in the residential treatment centres were adopted after age one. Whether this is a statistically significant excess is really impossible to calculate, because of the many assumptions made in arriving at the two proportions. It is tentatively assumed however that the population of disturbed children studied does contain an excess of children adopted past their first year. Table 2 shows the actual ages at which the residential care children were adopted.

It seems a reasonable hypothesis that older children who are adopted past infancy, (because of possible disruptions and stresses of family life prior to adoption, and problems of adjusting after adoption) are particularly at risk for the development of severe behaviour problems, which would account for the overrepresentation of children adopted at a later age in populations of maladjusted children. It should be noted that the practice of placing for adoption older children who were permanent wards was not well developed in Alberta in the late 1960s and early 1970s, so it is unlikely that many of the late adoptions (apart from adoptions by foster parents, which account for 10 of the 61 adoptions in the population studied) were the result of the placement of 'special needs' children by social service agencies. Twenty-one of the 61 children were adopted by a step-parent; five were adopted by a relative; and 25 were adopted by an unrelated person.

Table 1 Adoption completions in Canada (excluding Northwest Territories and Yukon) as a percentage of the child population aged under one year, 1959-60 to 1976-77

	A No. of Completed Adoptions (thousands)	B All children Under 1 Year (thousands)	C A as a percentage of B
1959-60	12.8	479.2	2.7
1960-61	13.5	478.5	2.8
1961-62	13.7	475.7	2.9
1962-63	13.6	469.7	2.9
1963-64	14.3	465.8	3.1
1964-65	15.4	453.0	3.4
1965-66	16.4	418.6	3.9
1966-67	17.1	387.7	4.4
1967-68	17.9	370.8	4.8

Table 1 (Cont'd)

1968-69	19.1	364.3	5.2
1969-70	20.3	369.6	5.5
1970-71	20.5	372.0	5.5
1971-72	20.2	360.3	5.6
1972-73	18.9	357.9	5.3
1973-74	17.3	347.7	5.0
1974-75	16.7	341.0	4.9
1975-76	14.6	336.6	4.3
1976-77	16.2	347.7	4.7

Source: Adapted from Eichler (1983).

Table 2 Ages and types of adoption of 61 adopted children in two residential treatment centres

Age Adopted	Number	Percent of 61
0 to 11 months	19	31%
one year	10	16%
two years	5	8%
three years	7	11%
four years	4	7%
five years	4	7%

Table 2 (Cont'd)

six years	2	3%
seven years	2	3%
eight years	3	5%
nine years	4	7%
ten years	1	2%
Total	61	100%

Type of Adoption	Number	Percent of 61
Adopted by a non-relative	25	41%
Adoption by a relative	5	8%
Adoption by a step-parent	21	34%
Adoption by a foster-parent	10	16%
Total	61	100%

Descriptive results of comparison of adopted and non-adopted children

The adopted children are slightly older (mean age 13.8 years) than the remaining 458 children (mean age 13.4 years); and slightly more likely to be male (68 percent versus 64 percent). The home background of the two groups differed dramatically however - two-thirds of adopted children came from 'intact' families containing two parents compared with only one-third of the nonadopted children. A quarter of the nonadopted families were disrupted to some or a marked degree, disruption being defined by frequent quarrels, fights, violence, and parental drunkenness in child's presence, and a parent leaving for temporary periods before a final break. Only three percent of adoptive families experienced such disruption. However, a third of adopted children compared with 10 percent of nonadopted had a step-father, a statistically significant difference. The adopted parents were much more likely to be in high status occupations.

Adopted children are no more likely to occupy minority ethnic status than nonadopted; nor are there differences in rates of prior physical abuse. In some cases of older child adoptions, we were able to establish that physical abuse took place before adoption; but in some cases the stage in the child's life at which physical abuse took place was not clearly stated. Siblings of nonadopted children were significantly more likely to need agency treatment, and parents of nonadopted children were significantly more likely to have psychiatric or behavioural problems. In fact none of the adoptive parents was described as alcoholic, criminal or addicted; the problems they had related to psychiatric illness, usually anxiety neurosis or depression. In a few cases depression in mothers was said to be directly caused by the child's behaviour. Significantly fewer adopted children came from homes with a single mother.

When two categories of sexual abuse (in the family, and outside the home) are aggregated, significantly more of the nonadopted children were said to have suffered sexual abuse. Nonadopted children were also much more likely to have experienced inconsistent or unduly harsh discipline in the home.

In a comparison of symptoms, adopted children had significantly fewer problems of self-concept or in relating to peers. However, their problems had earlier onset than in the nonadopted, and they were likely to be described as hyperactive (a condition with earlier onset), and to be underachieving in school, despite average or above-average I.Q.. Nonadopted children were more likely to be aggressive to others; but adopted children showed a non-significant trend to be more aggressive to themselves, in terms of suicidal behaviour. Nonadopted children were significantly more likely to wander or run from home, and to engage in serious criminal behaviour. However, adopted children were somewhat more likely to have clinical neurological problems, and significantly more likely to have been prescribed medication for a neurological or behavioural problem. The most frequently prescribed medications were Ritalin (for overactivity), and various types of anticonvulsant. Adopted children also had significantly more problems of speech. Adopted children were significantly more likely also to have been enuretic or encopretic, and to have set fires. Finally, the adopted children were somewhat more likely to have been discharged to their parents or to a foster home - a reflection presumably of their somewhat lesser psychological pathology, and rather fewer aggressive or criminal activities.

Firesetting behaviour in the adopted children seemed to have remitted prior to admission, but it is interesting to note that in the psychoanalytical theory of child development the combination of enuresis or encopresis and firesetting is said to be, "closely related to hostility and aggressiveness of the child towards the mother; in fact it seems to indicate a bitterness of feeling and an irreconcilable attitude which makes the case a difficult therapeutic problem". (Mayer-Gross et al. 1971).

Conclusion

The first finding of note is than 11.75 percent of 519 children in two residential centres for severely maladjusted children in the area studied had been previously adopted. This proportion is similar to that reported by Edgar (1981) for Vancouver, and is probably in excess of the known proportion of adopted children in the community in the relevant period (Hepworth, 1980; Eichler, 1983).

The adopted children in this study came from more stable and higher status families, with a lower rate of disturbance in siblings and parents than in nonadopting families. The adopted child's problems had an earlier onset, and were more often marked by hyperactivity, and medical treatment for a neurologically-related condition. The adopted children were somewhat more suicidal, but less aggressive. They also had a more prominent history as firesetters, and had been more enuretic or encopretic in the past. While such symptoms may imply an underlying aggression to the adopted child's family, such children are not, overtly, more aggressive to their mothers.

Are the adopted children in residential care a unitary group, or do they include sub-groups with different symptom patterns and antecedent circumstances to the behaviour disorder? These issues will be explored in the next chapters, in which a more exactly matched group controlling for effects of sex and age, is compared.

17 Comparison of 61 adopted children and 61 control children in two centres for seriously disturbed children

Introduction

In the previous chapter the 61 previously adopted children in two residential care centres were compared with the remaining 458 children admitted during a 5-year-period. In the present chapter comparison of the adopted children with a more exactly matched set of controls is reported, and various forms of multivariate analysis with regard to the two groups will be presented.

Methods

A more exactly drawn control group, similar in sex and age (to the nearest six months), was drawn for each of the 61 adopted children from the 458 non-adopted children. Where more than one potential control subject existed, selection was made by a random procedure. The files of the 61 control subjects were reread, and any discrepancies in coding from the original study were checked. Some additional variables (including measures of early bonding) were collected. Controlling in this way introduces a more conservative test of difference between the two groups: some of the differences reported in the previous chapter could have been due to differences in age and sex profiles between the two groups. In addition, comparing 61 cases with 458 cases meant that, because of the large number of total cases, quite small differences (which have little clinical significance) could be statistically significant.

Results

Table 1 shows the results of this comparison. The trends of comparison are in many ways similar to those reported in the previous chapter. The adopted children were much more likely to have come from an intact family with normal psychological functioning, prior to admission. Siblings of the adopted children were less likely to be disturbed. The disturbance of the siblings of the control children appeared in most cases to reflect turmoil and conflict in the home, turmoil which was much less likely in the adoptive homes. Control children were more likely to have been sexually or physically abused prior to admission.

Adoptive parents were much more likely to be older and of higher status. The problems of the adopted children were likely to have begun earlier, and more often involved hyperactivity, aggression to a parent, fire-setting at home, neurological problems, and problems of depression and suicidal behaviour. The controls, by contrast, were more likely to show externalizing symptoms, such as aggression outside the home and delinquency. Adoptive parents were much more likely to report early bonding problems, and persistent health problems.

Differences in symptom level between adopted children and controls

Some indication of levels of symptom difference between adopted children and controls is given in Table 1, in which the results of cross-tabular analysis were presented. In Table 2 we present a comparison of symptom levels, following the calculation of mean scores, standard deviations and t-tests for testing significant differences, employing the standard SPSS program for this purpose (Nie et al., 1975). Symptom presence has been estimated on a 4-point scale ranging from 0 (not present) to 3 (marked sign).

These results confirm those of the cross-tabular analysis. Adopted children have significantly higher scores on indices of neurological problems. When externalized symptoms (aggression outside the family setting) are combined into an index, control children are seen to be significantly more disturbed in this area. By contrast, adopted children have higher scores (but not significantly so) on an index of internalized symptoms.

A striking difference between the two groups is on the variable of firesetting usually within the home but sometimes outside the home - adopted children are much more likely to do this. This clinical significance of this behaviour is intriguing, and it could be one reason why the adopted children while overall less aggressive, are likely to be institutionalized. Juvenile arson is looked at as one of society's most serious crimes, and might represent very deep-seated but unconscious hostility to the adopted parents (Karchmer, 1984).

Table 1

Comparison of adopted (N = 61) with age, and sex-matched, non-adopted controls (N = 61) in residential treatment centres for behaviourally disturbed children

Variable	Significance of Chi-Squared	Cramer's v	Trend
Intact family with two parents (adoptive or biological)	.000	.41	Ad: 67% Con: 31%
Gross, recent marital tension prior to admission	.004	.59	Ad: 8% Con: 53%
Behaviour problem in sibling(s) where present, needing agency treatment	.001	.36	Ad: 13% Con: 35%
Mother a single parent since child was five or younger	.002	.30	Ad: 8% Con: 33%
Stepfather before admission	.034	.32	Ad: 34% Con: 21%

Table 1 (Cont'd)

Mother has mental health or behavioural problem needing treatment	.415	.16	Ad: 15% Con: 21%
Father (where present) has mental health problem needing treatment	.076	.10	Ad: 5% Con: 18%
Clear evidence of turmoil and conflict in home, not caused by child's behaviour	.005	.32	Ad: 3% Con: 30%
Evidence of physical abuse prior to admission	.168	.15	Ad: 13% Con: 29%
Evidence of sexual abuse outside home prior to admission	.633	.06	Ad: 3% Con: 8%
Social status of supporting parent: professional or managerial	.000	.38	Ad: 54% Con: 20%
Evidence of inconsistent discipline in home prior to admission	.000	.44	Ad: 21% Con: 54%
Evidence of harsh discipline in home prior to admission	.478	.06	Ad: 21% Con: 28%
Father died prior to child's admission	1.00	.00	Ad: 3% Con: 3%
Mother died prior to child's admission	1.00	.00	Ad: 3% Con: 3%

Table 1 (Cont'd)

Child's emotional or behavioural problems began before fifth year	.041	.26	Ad: 25% Con: 3%
Child has marked problems of self-concept	.180	.11	Ad: 20% Con: 33%
Child has specific learning disorder (IQ 80+ but marked learning problem)	.507	.07	Ad: 5% Con: 4%
Child has general learning disorder (IQ less than 80 and generally poor achievement)	.690	.08	Ad: 5% Con: 4%
Child has presented with marked hyperactivity or restlessness	.097	.23	Ad: 30% Con: 13%
Child has displayed marked aggressiveness in home, school or community	.008	.32	Ad: 54% Con: 74%
Child has displayed marked aggression to mother	.075	.24	Ad: 13% Con: 2%
Child has displayed marked aggression to father (where present)	.173	.21	Ad: 10% Con: 5%
Child had displayed suicidal depression	.072	.24	Ad: 25% Con: 8%
Child had displayed suicidal gestures or attempts	.133	.20	Ad: 15% Con: 7%

Table 1 (Con't)

Child has wandered or run from home more than once, for more than a day	.122	.08	Ad: 30% Con: 31%
Child has committed a serious criminal offence (at least theft over $200)	.046	.16	Ad: 13% Con: 31%
Child has acted out sexually (promiscuity, prostitution et. al.)	.461	.04	Ad: 11% Con: 10%
Child had abnormal signs on neurological exam; or diagnosed neurological condition	.191	.20	Ad: 15% Con: 5%
Child has used illegal drugs alcohol or solvents	.226	.09	Ad: 5% Con: 10%
Child receiving medication for CNS or behavioural problem, now or in the past	.011	.17	Ad: 18% Con: 3%
Child has marked problems of speech	.111	.13	Ad: 6% Con: 0%
Child has marked problems of sight or hearing	.764	.11	Ad: 6% Con: 1%
Child has displayed encopresis or enuresis	.583	.10	Ad: 15% Con: 9%
Child has set fires	.042	.16	Ad: 19% Con: 7%

Table 1 (Cont'd)

Child has displayed marked aggression in community	.002	.33	Ad: 10% Con: 36%
Parent(s) mentally retarded	.468	.05	Ad: 0%
Parents judged to be over-ambitious for child	.097	.14	Ad: 15% Con: 2%
Discharge status (where discharged): return to original home	.114	.13	Ad: 29% Con: 20%
Parent recalls behavioural problems in child's infancy, up to 5th birthday	.061	.18	Ad: 25% Con: 15%
Parent recalls significant health problems, up to 5th birthday	.009	.20	Ad: 26% Con: 10%
Parent recalls problem of bonding to child, up to 5th birthday	.005	.28	Ad: 25% Con: 8%
Persistent problem of physical health after 5th birthday	.054	.20	Ad: 20% Con: 10%

Note: Ad = adopted group. Con = non-adopted controls.
Because of missing data, numbers for each comparison range from a minimum of 110 (55 in each group) to 122 (61 in each group). Cramer's v is a measure of association calculated by SPSS, and is derived from the value of Chi-squared. The level of probability accepted for purposes of statistical significance is .05.

Table 2   Comparison of symptom levels in 61 adopted subjects and controls

Variable	Adopted Children		Controls		t Value	P
	Mean	S.D.	Mean	S.D.		
Self-concept/identity problems	1.14	1.5	1.98	0.75	-4.51	.000
Isolation/withdrawal from peers	1.78	1.20	2.33	1.02	-2.53	.013
Hyperactivity	0.91	1.27	1.75	1.01	-3.82	.000
Aggression to peers/siblings	1.57	1.33	1.94	1.26	-1.49	.140
Aggression to mother	0.77	1.16	0.88	1.08	-0.54	.589
Aggression to father	0.66	1.07	0.36	0.84	1.60	.112
Depressed, anxious, withdrawn	1.18	1.32	1.40	1.14	-0.95	.345
Suicidal behaviour	0.53	1.20	0.29	0.93	1.20	.235
Running/wandering	1.34	1.27	2.23	0.81	-4.39	.000
Delinquency	1.54	1.06	2.10	0.95	-2.89	.005
Sexual acting out	0.55	1.09	0.56	1.11	-0.02	.985
Neurological problems	0.27	0.73	0.08	0.39	1.72	.089
Medication for behavioural or neurological problem	0.43	0.87	0.13	0.56	2.10	.038
Drug, alcohol or solvent use	0.36	0.86	0.69	1.13	-1.72	.088
Speech problems	0.16	0.68	0.08	0.28	1.24	.220

281

Table 2 (Cont'd)

Variable	Adopted Children Mean	S.D.	Controls Mean	S.D.	t Value	P
Hearing/sight problems	0.09	0.43	0.04	0.28	0.68	.497
Encopresis/enuresis	0.27	0.73	0.25	0.79	0.12	.903
Firesetting	0.46	0.91	0.02	0.19	3.50	.000
Robbery, serious assault	0.26	0.65	0.29	0.70	-0.16	.874
Specific learning disorder	0.70	1.01	0.92	1.18	-1.07	.289
General learning disorder	0.12	0.54	0.17	0.62	-0.43	.669
Index of externalized symptoms	10.48	4.80	13.38	3.68	-3.54	.001
Index of internalized symptoms	3.49	2.56	4.02	2.01	-1.85	.067

Note: Symptoms scored 0 = not present/no information and presumed not present; 1 = unsure/vague sign; 2 = some sign; 3 = marked sign.

Index of Externalized Symptoms Combines: Aggression to peers; aggression to father; aggression to mother; running from home; delinquency; sexual acting out; drug and alcohol abuse; fire-setting; marked aggression in the community (e.g., armed robbery).

Index of Internalized Symptoms Combines: Depression; withdrawal from peers; and suicidal behaviour.
S.D. indicates Standard Deviation, an estimation of the degree to which the observations are distributed around, or 'deviate' from the mean.

Table 3

Variables significantly discriminating 58 adopted from 58 non-adopted children in residential care centres, and degree to which canonical function predicts adopted versus non-adopted

Variable	Discriminant Function	Mean Values: Adopted	Controls
Degree of marital tension in home (less to more)	.47	1.48	2.18
Child's self-esteem impairment (less to more)	.358	1.16	2.00
Child runs or wanders from home/school	.349	1.25	2.20
One-parent family (0 = not; 1 = yes)	.346	0.09	0.31
Child is hyperactive (less to more)	-.306	1.70	0.94
Discipline of child is inconsistent	.292	0.27	0.60
Age at which marked behaviour disorder began (early to late)	.256	8.58	10.83
Child is delinquent (less to more)	.232	1.50	2.14
Child is aggressive/isolated in peer relationship (less to more)	.203	1.03	1.23
Child has step-parent (o = not; 1 = yes)	-.187	0.32	0.09

Table 3 (Cont'd)

Social class (low to high)	-.160	2.36	1.88
Child has medication for behavioural or neurological problem	-.136	0.45	0.17

<u>Discriminators of Adopted Children</u>

Actual Group	N	Predicted Group 1	Predicted Group 2
1. Adopted	58	50 (86%)	8 (14%)
2. Non-adopted	58	7 (12%)	51 (88%)

Percent of successful allocation of cases to predicted groups: 87%

Note: Only cases for which complete data were available were included in the analysis

---

Components of behaviour in adopted and non-adopted children

Principal components analysis is an extremely useful technique for classifying variables into distinct groups, components or "factors" (Nie et al., 1975). We used this technique to see if symptoms of disturbed behaviour have the same grouping between adopted and non-adopted children. It is theoretically possible that although adopted and nonadopted children constitute different groups, the co-variance of symptoms within each group occurs at approximately the same level. This would mean that basic patterns of symptom formation would be rather similar.

The number of components rotated were those which explained 50 percent of the variance amongst the correlations of the eighteen behavioural variables (plus sex, as a "marker" variable) included in the analysis. Four factors or components within each group (adopted and non-adopted) explained about 50 percent of the overall variance in each correlation matrix.

The significant loadings (greater than 0.3 according to the criteria of Nunnally, 1967) of the behavioural items, and the loading of sex, significant or otherwise, on the four factors in the adopted and non-adopted groups are presented in Tables 4 and 5. There are interesting differences. The most general factor (explaining 17 percent of variance) in the adopted children combines hyperactivity, medication for a C.N.S. problem, aggression to peers and siblings, speech problems, neurological signs, and fire-setting.

The parallel factor in the non-adopted controls is the second component or factor. This is not an exactly equivalent factor however, and hyperactivity and fire-setting actual load significantly on the first, more general "delinquency" factor in the control subjects. Component III in the adopted group and component IV in the controls appear to have equivalence: both represent the grouping of depression, suicidal behaviour, and sexual acting out. It is possible that these components of behaviour as well as component IV in the controls, are actually sequels of earlier sexual abuse in females, a possibility discussed in the next chapter.

The third component of behaviour in the adopted children involves delinquency, running from home, and drug use. This has some resemblance to component I in the control subjects.

Overall, we would conclude that the factors structure of behavioural symptoms in the two groups has more similarities than difference. Despite difference in prevalence of symptoms between the two groups, the grouping of symptoms between the adopted and non-adopted children is to a large extent, similar. Three components are with some variation, common to both adopted and non-adopted subjects. An additional component (no. II) in the adopted children involves aggression to parents, hyperactivity and running from home. This could be a behavioural syndrome specific to problems of the adopted child's identity. In the other hand, component IV in the non-adopted controls also identifies aggression to father and running from home. However, the loading of female sex on this component indicates the possibility that these symptoms could be reactions to earlier sexual abuse.

Table 4   **Principal components of behaviour disorder in 58 adopted children**

Component I	17% of Variance *
<u>Variable</u>	<u>Loading</u>
Medication for C.N.S. condition	.83
Neurological signs	.78
Hyperactive	.67
Aggressive to peers/siblings	.51
Fire-setting	.44
Speech problems	.33
Sex: male	.30

Component II	12% of Variance *
<u>Variable</u>	<u>Loading</u>
Aggression to mother	.82
Aggression to father	.80
Running from home	.35
Hyperactivity	.35
Sex: male	.02

Component III	11% of Variance *
<u>Variable</u>	<u>Loading</u>
Delinquency	.76
Running from home	.53
Drug use	.49
Aggression to peers/siblings	.32
Sex: male	.14

Table 4 (Cont'd)

Component IV	10% of Variance *
Variable	Loading
Suicidal Behaviour	.76
Depression	.73
Sexual acting out	.52
Drug use	.42
Problems of hearing or sight	.33
Sex: male	-.29

Table 5   **Components of behaviour disorder in 58 controls for adopted children**

Component I	18% of Variance *
Variable	Loading
Delinquency	.89
Sexual acting out	.42
Use of drugs	.42
Fire-setting	.38
Hyperactivity	.38
Sex: male	.06

Component II	13% of Variance *
Variable	Loading
Medication for C.N.S. condition	.78
Neurological signs	.70
Encopresis or enuresis	.74
Running from home	-.35
Sex: male	.32

Table 5 (Cont'd)

Component III	10% of Variance *
Variable	Loading
Depression	.83
Suicidal behaviour	.77
Sexual acting out	.54
Sex: male	-.30

Component IV	9% of Variance *
Variable	Loading
Running from home	.56
Aggression to father	.47
Fire-setting	.45
Encopresis or enuresis	.34
Sexual acting out	.36
Sex: male	-.27

---

* The variance explained is the total amount of variance in the correlation matrix or behavioural variables on which the principal components analysis is based.

Selected psychosocial factors which predict symptoms of maladjustment in 61 adopted children and 61 controls

Can psychosocial variable predict symptom occurrence in adopted children and in the non-adopted children at the same level? We had no particular hypothesis with regard to this, and undertook the analysis of predictive factors as an exploratory exercise, rather than as a hypothesis-testing one. Results could however have implications for the differential treatment and counselling of the two groups.

Age and sex are similar in adopted children and controls. These two variable predict symptom levels in somewhat different ways however, although there are trends toward similarity for the higher correlations (Table 7). Younger children in both groups are more likely to be aggressive to peers, hyperactive, and in need of medication; older children are more likely to be delinquent. Girls are more likely to display sexual acting out and drug use, in both groups.

Marital separation of the adopted child's parents (a relatively uncommon occurrence) is related to the child's manifestation of delinquency, and aggression to mother. Self-concept is to some extent diminished in the adopted children whose parents have separated, but this trend is more marked in the controls. Having a step-parent is associated with later onset of symptoms in both groups. Children who were adopted by a step-parent tended to be delinquent. Discharge to the step-parent was uncommon in both groups, presumably reflecting the fact that conflict with the step-parent was bound up with the child's maladjustment. Having a parent with behaviour or psychiatric problems was again negatively associated with discharge to parents, for obvious reasons. Mental health problems in mothers are associated with an index of "internalized" symptoms (including depression and suicide) in the adopted children, but with the index of "externalized" symptoms (including delinquency, and aggression outside the home) in the non-adopted children. Delinquency was particularly likely to be associated with parental problems, in the non-adopted controls.

Extreme family instability (rare in the adoptive parents) did not predict any aspect of behaviour; but was associated with some aggressive behaviour towards peers in the control subjects. Physical abuse (usually occurring before adoption, but sometimes after it) was a significant predictor of a range of behavioural symptoms in the adopted children. Abuse was linked to delinquency in children in the controls group, as well as in the adopted children.

Sexual abuse was linked to low IQ in the adopted children; and to aggression to father, suicidal behaviour, and delinquency in the controls. The link of sexual abuse and low IQ in the adopted children in puzzling, but may reflect a special type of vulnerability in some adopted children.

Table 7

Selected psychosocial factors correlating with symptoms of maladjustment in 61 adopted children and 61 controls

Age (Younger to Older) Correlations	Adopted	Controls
Aggression to or withdrawal from parents	-.47	-.35
Hyperactive	-.29	(-.21)*
Aggressive to peers/sibling	-.52	-.32
Child has required/requires medication for behavioural problems	-.35	-.29
Fire-setting behaviour	-.26	(.03)*
Child has IQ below 80 (GLD)	-.31	-.25
Child has speech problems	(-.18)*	-.27
Encopresis/enuresis	(-.05)*	.26

Sex (Female) Correlations		
Hyperactive	-.33	(-.18)*
Suicidal behaviour	.24	(.03)*
Sexual acting out	.41	.64
Neurological problems	-.23	(-.11)*
Medication for behaviour problems	-.22	(-.13)*
Drug abuse	.38	.35
Aggression to father	(-.14)*	-.24
Depression	(.06)*	-.28

One-Parent Family (Prior to Child's Fifth Birthday) Correlations		
Encopresis/enuresis	-.28	(.20)*
Aggression to or withdrawal from peers	(.02)*	-.38
Drug abuse	(.01)*	.28

290

Table 7 (Cont'd)

Marital Separation in 3 Years Before Admission	Adopted	Controls
Aggressive to mother	.27	(.09)*
Delinquent	.24	(.06)*
Child has self-concept problems	(.17)*	.25

Step-Parent

	Adopted	Controls
Discharge to original parent(s)	-.33	-.29
Age at which marked behavioural problems began (older)	-.30	-.32
Depressed	.27	(.07)*
Delinquency	(.15)*	.35

Mental Health or Behavioural Problems in Biological or Adoptive Mother in 3 years Before Admission

	Adopted	Controls
Discharge to original parent(s)	-.28	-.20
Suicidal behaviour	.24	(.03)*
Aggressive to siblings	(.08)*	.28
Delinquency	(.12)	.41
Runs or wanders from home/school	(.04)*	.24
Combined measure or externalizing symptoms	(.14)*	.23
Combined measure of internalizing symptoms	.27	(.15)*

Mental Health or Behavioural Problems in Biological or Adoptive Father in 3 Years Before Child's Admission

	Adopted	Controls
IQ less than 80 (general learning disorder)	-.44	(.19)*
Runs or wanders from home/school	.25	(.16)*

Table 7 (Cont'd)

Gross Family Instability in 3 Years Before Child's Admission	Adopted	Controls
Aggressive to/withdrawal from peers	(.03)*	.23
IQ less than 80 (GLD)	(.13)*	.24
Aggression to peers/sibling	(-.00)*	.30
Aggression to father	(.10)*	.23
Delinquency	(.09)*	.24

Child Has Suffered Physical Abuse (Including Before and After Adoption)		
IQ less than 80 (GLD)	-.36	(.16)*
Aggression to father	-.41	(.01)*
Depressed/anxiety	.34	(.12)*
Delinquency	.40	.30
Enuresis/encopresis	.24	(-.01)*
Child has problems of hearing or sight	(.10)*	.44

Child Has Suffered Sexual Abuse in Family (Including Before and After Adoption)		
IQ less than 80 (GLD)	.47	(-.04)*
Aggression to father	(.08)*	.44
Suicidal behaviour	(.06)*	.26
Delinquency	(.20)*	.29

Child Has Suffered Sexual Abuse Outside Home (Including Before and After Adoption)		
Sexual acting out	.34	.51
Neurological problems	(-.07)*	.32
Drug abuse	(-.08)*	.34

Table 7 (Cont'd)

Social Class of Parent (Low to High)	Adopted	Controls
Depression	.22	(.06)*
Aggression to father	(.03)*	.22
Runs/wander from home/school	(-.18)*	-.24
Drug abuse	(.01)*	.25
Delinquency	.22	-.24

Discipline Inconsistent (Sometimes Lax, Sometimes Authoritarian)

	Adopted	Controls
Child has self-concept problems	.28	(.07)*

Discipline Consistently Harsh and Authoritarian

	Adopted	Controls
Child has self-concept problems	(.15)*	.37
Aggression to peers/siblings	(-.11)*	.35
Combined index of externalizing symptoms	(.09)*	.30

Death of Father or Mother After Child's Fifth Year

	Adopted	Controls
Age at which behavioural problems began (older)	.22	(.10)*
Combined index of internalizing symptoms	.28	(.21)*
Suicidal behaviour	.25	(.04)*

Parent Have Unrealistically High Academic Expectations for Child

	Adopted	Controls
IQ less than 80 (GLD)	.54	(.06)*
Depression in child	.31	.22
Aggressive to father	(.00)*	.24
Sexual acting out	(-.06)*	.22

* Correlations of 0.22 and above are significant at the 5 percent level or beyond. Non-significant correlations are in brackets. All correlations are product moment correlations (Pearson's r).
GLD = general learning disorder

Social class factors are inversely related to delinquency in both groups (the higher the social status of parents, the less likely is the child to be delinquent). Depression is positively related to higher social status only in the adopted children. Overall however, it cannot be concluded that the difference in symptomatology observed between the adopted and nonadopted children are a function of social class differences. Inconsistent discipline is linked to poor self-concept in the adopted children only; and harsh discipline is linked to poor self-concept only in the controls. Harsh discipline predicts no symptom patterns in the adopted children; but predicts a number or externalizing or aggressive symptoms in controls.

Overall, this comparison of antecedents of symptoms in adopted and nonadopted children has revealed more differences than similarities. Although there is some similarity in symptom patterns or behavioural components, the antecedents of these symptoms appear to be different. It seems possible that the special identity which some adopted children acquire means that they react differently to stresses or trauma than nonadopted children. For sub-groups of adopted children of course, both stress and reaction type may be similar to patterns of stress and symptom formation in controls. The question of sub-groups, or types of adjustment in adoption will be discussed in the next chapter.

Age at adoption

The literature reviewed in earlier chapters suggests that age at adoption may be a factor in the child's adjustment. Some, but by no means all studies have indicated that children adopted past their first year have greater problems of adjustment. In the previous chapter we saw that just over half of the adopted children in residential care were adopted past their first year, and a fifth were adopted past their fifth year.

Table 8 shows the significant correlations of age at adoption. Stability of the home is associated with early adoption, while mental health or behavioural problems in a parent, and family disruption are associated with later adoption.

Physical and sexual abuse are associated with later adoption, as is harsh discipline, aggressive symptoms and delinquency. While early adoption is associated with higher social status in parents, such early adoptions are also associated with learning problems, self-concept problems, hyperactivity, CNS problems, encopresis or enuresis, firesetting, early onset of behaviour problems, early onset of physical health problems, and early bonding problems. It seems a reasonable inference from these correlations that a sub-group of disturbed adopted children exists whose problems are neurological in origin, and which do not reflect adoption past infancy.

Bonding problems in adoption

Bonding is a crucial psychological process in successful parenting (Goldberg, 1979). Bonding involves a commitment of adult to the child which includes a deep and abiding emotional bond, an "irrational" love which transcends individual circumstances, or the child's transgressions at any point in time. Young children too will, under normal circumstance, rapidly bond not only to their birth mother but also to a range of adult caretakers. Children also have the capacity to "forgive" or go on loving adults who are imperfect or even abusive caretakers.

In adoption, mutual bonding of the child and the new parents is crucially important if the adoption is to be successful. The evidence indicates that such bonding does take place in the large majority of adoptions. Bonding in adoption may be difficult however when the child has a medical condition which impairs that child's ability to respond normally or adequately to parental affection; when the child is older; when the child has been emotionally traumatized by early life experiences prior to adoption; and perhaps when the parent has ambiguities about being an adopter (Humphrey, 1967).

Measurement of bonding is not an easy task, especially in a retrospective study using secondary sources. In reading case records on the adopted children we looked for statements such as, "Child cried excessively.... would not cuddled .... did not respond easily to affection.... aggressive to parent(s) from an early age .... Parent had difficulty relating to the child." These are invalidated measures, and the inferences they involve may be questionable.

The measure was developed using the following indictors: 0 = no indication of bonding problems before fifth birthday (62 percent of cases); 1 = unsure or vague signs (13 percent); 2 = some problems in bonding, or difficulties in parent-child relationships in first two years after adoption (15 percent); 3 = clear signs of bonding or relationship problems (10 percent). The difficulty with this indicator is that it measures, to some extent, the incipient behaviour problem which finally led to the child's admission to residential care. This should be borne in mind in interpreting the correlations in Table 9. Note too that we have only attempted to measure bonding problems in the preschool period.

Table 8   **Significant associations of age at adoption (younger to older) in 61 subjects**

Variable	Significance of Chi-Squared	Direction of Relationship	Cramer's v*
Home contains two original adoptive parents	.048	Negative	.24
Mother has mental health or behavioural problems	.010	Positive	.30
Father has mental health or behavioural problems	.004	Positive	.27
Family disrupted prior to marital break	.016	Positive	.36
Physical abuse of child	.007	Positive	.41
Sexual abuse of child	.000	Positive	.25
Social status (lower to higher)	.014	Negative	.35
Discipline harsh	.000	Positive	.33
Age at which marked problems emerged	.000	Positive	.46
Problems of self-concept	.000	Negative	.28
Specific learning disability	.042	Negative	.31
Hyperactivity	.002	Negative	.45
Aggression	.012	Positive	.40

Table 8 (Cont'd)

Delinquency	.001	Positive	.24
Child has medication for CNS/ behavioural condition	.009	Negative	.25
Encopresis/enuresis	.000	Negative	.28
Firesetting	.019	Negative	.22
Parents have overly high expectations for child	.000	Positive	.37
Adoption by step-mother	.000	Positive	.52
Adoption by step-mother	.000	Positive	.41
Number of biological siblings in family also adopted	.000	Positive	.59
Parent reports behaviour problems in first five years	.020	Negative	.21
Parent reports health problems in first five years	.000	Negative	.30
Parent reports bonding problems in first five years	.000	Negative	.61
Physical health problems after five years	.000	Negative	.27

* Note: Cramer's v, which measure non-linear relationships, cannot have a sign. "Negative" indicates that the trait is associated with **earlier** adoption; "positive" indicates that the trait is associated with **later** adoption.

Table 9   **Significant associations of bonding difficulty in 61 adopted children**

Variable	Significance of Chi-Squared	Cramer's v
Degree of marital tension prior to child's admission	.008	.45
Mother's poor mental health or behaviour problem	.041	.28
Physical abuse of child (before adoption)	.014	.28
Social status of family (low to high)	.017	.44
Number of siblings (fewer to more)	.030	.34
Child's self-concept problems	.018	.43
Child's problems with peers	.033	.46
Hyperactivity	.041	.34
Aggressiveness	.069	.47
Neurological problems detected	.011	.33
Medication for CNS or behaviour	.000	.52
Discharge status (fewer returning to adoptive parents)	.048	.40
Age at adoption (older)	.000	.57
Behavioural problems began in infancy (before fifth birthday)	.001	.53
Mother's age (older)	.043	.45

The significant correlations presented in Table 9 do not consider problems of cause and effect. For example, bonding difficulties have a significant link with recent marital tension, and with mother's poor mental health. Were parents who were experiencing psychological difficulty and marital problems unable to bond properly? Or did behavioural or medical problems of the child which interfered with bonding cause, or exacerbate, parental problems? We have no way of knowing from these data. Hyperactivity and neurological problems were associated with bonding problems: this could mean that children's early behaviour, impaired by a neurological syndrome, makes parent-child relationships particularly difficult.

Interestingly, higher status parents, and older mothers appeared to have difficulty in the bonding relationship. This could mean that older, high status and previously childless women have particular difficulty in relating to infants and young children, especially those with a difficult temperament. Examination of sub-correlations supports this view to some extent: there does appear to be a sub-group of high status, older, childless mother who reported bonding difficulties, and whose child was later diagnosed as having a neurological syndrome underlying disturbed behaviour. Such mothers also tended to display poor mental health in the long-run, becoming increasingly anxious or depressed at their self-perceived failure as a parent.

We conclude from the analysis of bonding problems in the sample of adopted children that such problems are integrally related to the early onset of behavioural problems, particularly those involving hyperactivity and aggression.

Conclusion

In this chapter a detailed comparison of the 61 adopted children in the two residential care centres and the 61 children from the same two centres has been reported. The controls subjects were matched for age and sex.

Despite the matched similarities of the two groups of children, the adopted children were different from the non-adopted control subjects in a number of important ways. Although one-third of the control children had a single parent since before the child's fifth birthday, 30 percent of remaining control children had experienced turmoil and conflict between parents after the child's fifth birthday. Control children tended to react to stresses within the home by deviant reactions outside the home, reactions which usually took the form of delinquency, and aggression to others.   By contrast, adopted children tended to react either by internalized symptoms (depression and deliberate self-harm), or by aggression within the family setting. The most extreme form of this was firesetting in their own homes. In symbolic terms, burning one's home is both an act of aggression against oneself, and an aggressive action against one's family. Although our data give no direct evidence, it could be that being adopted gives children a special kind of "overprotected" identity, which does not allow children under stress to externalize aggression, either in psychological terms (as aggression against others rather than against the self,) or outside of the family itself. Social class factors may be influential here too, since the majority of adopted children came from middle class backgrounds, in contrast to the controls. However, social class factors can by no means explain all of the psychological differences between the two groups.

What is clear however, is that demographic and behavioural factors distinguish between the two groups at a highly significant level, so that adopted and non-adopted children can clearly be categorized as separate groups, despite the fact that a range of background factors were initially controlled for, and the fact that all the children adopted and non-adopted, were admitted to the same institutions, presumably on similar criteria.

The components of behaviour within the two groups are rather similar, except for the greater salience of a neurological component of behaviour in the adopted children. The presence of a neurological syndrome, associated with early onset of behaviour problems, hyperactivity, aggression to peers and siblings, and firesetting, particulary in boys, is an important feature of the adopted group. These problems occur in children placed in infancy with seemingly normal parents. However, the stresses of parenting a child with a difficult temperament seem to have exacerbated problems which some adoptive parents, especially mothers, may have had concerning the parenting role.

It could be that these parents were committed to an 'exclusive' parenting model for the apparently normal, white infant they adopted. But attempting to 'exclude' aspects of the child's behaviour which were genetic or organic in origin appears to have been an unwise strategy. This exclusion process may well have served to impair parental adaptability in coping with the adopted child's needs. Long childless, they eagerly expected a perfect, white infant. But what evolved was a "lack of fit" as Thomas and Chess (1977) call it, between the child's temperament and parental rearing style.

While these are speculations for which we have no direct supportive evidence, it is clear from evidence produced by Thomas and

Chess (1977) from the New York longitudinal study that a mismatch between child's temperament and parental rearing styles can actually cause the child's disturbed behaviour. In other words, the 'difficult', unresponsive child is by no mean destined to become a behaviour problem later on, even if this difficult temperament has a basis either in genetics, in acquired C.N.S. trauma, or in both.

There is no evidence in the present study of social service support for parenting a newly adopted infant, and parents themselves may have colluded in this exclusion process. However, it may be too that adopted children are more at risk in terms of the inheritance of certain behavioural characteristics, as the literature reviewed in an earlier chapter indicates. This implies that the environment in which the at-risk child grows up is of crucial importance. But social service and adoption agencies have been naive in attending to and supporting adoptive parents in this crucially important role. Adoptive parenting is, nevertheless, crucially different from normal parenting and requires different strengths, attitudes and skills.

This is true at whatever age the child is place for adoption. Again, there is little evidence that adoption agencies have supported parents who have adopted older children, many of whom experienced early trauma in their lives. Step-parents who adopt seem to be extremely unsupported in their difficult parenting role, and there is an important need for parent support services in this area.

18 Types or clusters of adjustment: Classification of adopted children by case study and statistical methods

Introduction

The following 'intuitive' division of the 61 cases of adopted children in the two centres for seriously disturbed children was undertaken before the statistical work of the previous two chapters, and before the statistical clustering reported later in this chapter. It is felt that the case material will enable the reader to appreciate more clearly the nature of the problems of these adoptive families. While causal patterns cannot be directly inferred from these case histories, placing seemingly similar cases in groups carries an implicit hypothesis of cause. In many cases, however, the original record does not discuss interactions in the family with specific reference to adoption.

It was extremely rare to find any acknowledgment or discussion in the main case records of the possibility that current behavioral problems might be due to particular relationships within the family which are typical of, or peculiar to, the institution of adoption. While it would be difficult to infer that the type of relationships which emerge in adoptive families are the sole cause of the very serious behavioural problems encountered in the adopted children, such relationships might interact with other factors which in combination could cause the behavioural problems. It is salutary that treatment programs for behaviourally disturbed children rarely look at early causes. Their aim is to manage or contain the difficult behaviour, using instead an educational or behavioural model which aims to teach the child new ways of coping with potentially stressful situations, and modifying his or her behaviour with the aid of environmental and family support.

I have excluded some very interesting and spectacular cases because of unique factors (such as medical history, crimes committed, or aspects of the family) which might have served to identify individuals. In the cases that follow, the letter of the alphabet which represents the child's name has been chosen at random.

The 27 cases presented below are meant to be illustrative of the various categories intuitively identified, rather than an exhaustive presentation. It may well be that there are additional categories or groups which my intuitive categorization has missed.

(a)   *Early adoption: Possible cause of maladjustment lies within the family?*

1.   M, now 15 years old, is the youngest of five adopted children in the family. Mother reports that M formed little attachment to her or any other members of the family ever since his arrival soon after birth. There have been severe temper tantrums, tremendous sibling rivalry, inappropriate behaviour, particularly in front of company, and general aggression. M has very few friends, showing no remorse or any feeling for anyone in the family. Parents have come to the point of divorce mainly, it is said, because of the impact of M's behaviour on family members. They present as concerned parents who in the past have been somewhat overprotective of the child but who are now confused and frustrated by his behaviour. M was totally out of control at home and at school on entry to the Centre. Records do not indicate details of adoption. Other adopted children in the family have, apparently, few problems. There is a sense in the records that the youngest child may have been scapegoated in order that the parents could concentrated on the older children's needs, albeit in a neurotic and overprotective fashion.

2.   P was adopted at age two and a half years. Parents reported numerous and severe temper tantrums since this time. Trouble with the law begin during his early adolescent years - stealing, etc. He was placed in an institution for one year and on return home destroyed property in the family home with a knife. He was later placed in Detention Centre but on discharge, ransacked the family home, stole his mother's car and threatened to kill her. At one time he "drugged her coffee" in an attempt to get rid of her.

Mother is said to be very critical of and blaming towards child. There have been severe marital problems much of which have been blamed on P. Mother is a "recent alcoholic". P presented as an isolated and alienated child. Relationships with others are "hostile and superficial". His frustration and outrage were thought to be the result of distorted family interactions. Records do not indicate the possible impact of adoption.

3. C was placed with a view of adoption at 3 months. She was finally adopted at 14 months of age. Mother reports that "it's been a fight ever since we adopted C.... She craves attention." Parents, and father in particular, find child deliberately annoying and irritating. Father has had open heart surgery and finds it difficult to tolerate stress. He generally copes by ignoring C. There is little communication between parents and child. There are two other children from father's previous marriage who are seemingly well functioning family members. There is a history of abuse of C by her adoptive parents and she presented at the Centre with severe behaviour problems in school, lying stealing, fighting, disrespectful, contempt of authority, poor peer relationships, distrustful, firesetting. Parents belong to a fundamentalist religious sect.

4. J, a male, was adopted in infancy into a family of two older natural girls. The family originates from one of the third world countries where having a male child is indeed very important. They have lived in several different countries over a short period of time and find living in Canada disappointing because of their low status jobs and problems with communication. Parents reported difficulties with J since they were in their home country, but they have managed to cope through other family members becoming closer and sharing "the burden" of J. There is extended family support and they also find their church affiliation quite helpful. They have been involved with several community agencies since their arrival in Canada. J was only recently told (at the age 12) of his adoption, the family having been helped to do this by a community agency. Apparently, he was not at all surprised to learn of his adoption as he had thought so for a long time. He has no resemblance to his other siblings or parents and indeed his behaviour sets him apart. J presented as an obese, bespectacled child, seemingly of mixed racial parentage. Parents were apparently not aware of his mixed heritage. He was

softspoken and conscious of his weight problem. He displayed acting out behaviour when stressed in his relationship with adults based on whether he could manipulate them. J was attention-seeking with few internal controls. There was 'outlandish dressing' and he has verbally expressed a desire to be female. Firesetting, stealing, masturbating in front of younger boys were some of the behaviours which J presented at the Centre. He was said to be performing poorly at school, and his behaviour was out of control. One worker's assessment of J was that he appeared to be a lost and unhappy child who is trying to find his identity and home in Canadian society. The child is moving towards acquiring a Canadian identity and his parents are being encouraged to support and understand this as much as possible. Parents were receptive to counselling but expected the help to be "on their terms". J was finally discharged home to his parents.

5. Q came to her present family at six days of age. She was adopted as an infant, is aware of her adoptive status and at age 13 has her parents' "permission" to seek her natural parents. Adoptive father is said to be an alcoholic and is involved with drug abuse. Parents are inconsistent with discipline and seemingly have told children repeatedly that she was conceived "while (her) mother was high on dope", and hence her negative behaviour pattern. Marital relationship was said to be poor. Q was enuretic to age nine years and involved herself with genital play and masturbation. In admission to the Centre, she presented with the following - out of control of parents, inappropriate attention-seeking behaviour, a history of sexual involvement with older males, reacting to stress in a hysterical manner, and drug abuse and glue sniffing. There is suspicion, but no direct evidence, that Q had been sexually abused by her father.

6. I was placed with her adoptive family at age 4 weeks, and adopted soon afterwards. She was said to have suffered colic as a baby. Parents had opposing viewpoints on childrearing methods, and nurturing was largely inconsistent and erratic. Child presented with behaviour problems at an early age but parents were unable to resolve their conflicts. They were finally divorced when I was 10 years old and I, along with her older adopted brother went to live with mother. Mother is reported to have scapegoated the children, and on occasions locked them out of the house when she could not cope with their behaviour. Father was not encouraged

to visit as mother felt he was a negative influence on the children's behaviour. Mother sought professional help, but she remained largely unable to cope. I had several foster home placements after this. Disruptions resulted largely from manipulative behaviour and lying. Problems on admission to the Centre at age 12 included - stealing from home, school and community; lying; poor relationships; "attempts to organize group wars"; inappropriate or promiscuous behaviour with boys and with an older peer group; extreme attention-seeking behaviour; and poor hygiene.

7.   W was placed with his adoptive family apparently as the result of a "private" adoption, at age six weeks, parents having been married for only 18 months at this stage. Both parents suffered somewhat deprived upbringing themselves. Maternal grandparents were said to have been very critical of their daughter in all spheres of her performance and this resulted in very poor self-concept. Documentation of behaviour problems during W's early years was not available, but these problems appeared to have escalated with adolescence. At the age 13, W presented - theft, armed robbery, truancy, manipulative behaviour, passive resistance to authority, firesetting, destructive behaviour, physical aggression towards his adopted sister, and abuse of his diet (he is diabetic). Parents were concerned individuals who attended several parenting and family life courses, but showed "an amazing lack of insight" into this child's problems. They displayed a considerable amount of guilt about the adoption disruption and felt that their early marital difficulties may well have contributed to the present situation. Family Therapy was deemed successful enough for W to be discharged to the care of his parents.

(b)   *Early adoption: Possible neurological problems causing disturbed behaviour?*

1.   S was placed with his present family with a view to adoption at 4 weeks and finally adopted before his first birthday. His birthweight was nine lbs; there were no noteworthy neonatal problems and his early development seems fairly normal. However, S suffered from encopresis until age four and at the time had a mental health referral. S's parents, a middle-class couple in their 50s who maintained a seemingly normal family life, had four biological children ranging in age from 28 to 21. They

were said to be caring parents who were concerned about the following behaviour in their son - extreme hyperactivity, hoarding and eating of garbage under his bed, eating garbage, aggression to other children. Very early on S was prescribed Ritalin for his hyperactivity but he had a toxic reaction to this drug and become confused and even more overactive. It was suggested that he had brain stem dysfunction. However, a complete neurological examination indicated no grossly pathological signs. S has had consultation with a speech pathologist and a neuropsychologist but it would seem that professionals have not been able to get a firm grip on his seemingly intractables problems. Prior to admission to this Centre, S went to live with foster parents but they too found him completely unable to respond to any of the normal types of parenting approaches they had to offer. Family therapy produced little improvement in S's behaviour. There is no documentation of the possible impact of S's adoptive status.

2. L is one of three adopted children who came to the family as babies. Her parents, in their early 50s, described her as having behaviour problems since her arrival - poor sleeping habits, and irritability. Later problems included enuresis, poor peer relations, firesetting, cruelty to animals, stealing, temper outbursts, destructiveness and aggression. Behaviour problems at school (noncompliance, lying stealing, poor relations) led to L's expulsion for school at age 14 and subsequent placement in a Special Class. On admission, her mother was concerned by the following behaviours displayed by L - stealing money and cigarettes, threatening to jump in front of a car, hitting mother and sister, lying, showing no remorse or fears. Workers found L to be argumentative, egocentric and with extreme temper outbursts. However, she seemed to respond well to structure and indeed responded better to her father than to her mother as he tended to capitalize on her strengths -reading, watching T.V., horse riding and listening to classical music. Mother was said to be frustrated and worn out by her daughter's behaviour.

3. T, now 17 years, was adopted at 17 months of age. There are three older children in the family. He was said by his parents to have been an active baby, "extremely hyperkinetic". Difficult at school begin very soon after admission because of his hyperactivity. He was prescribed Ritalin at age 6 years. As T

grew older, he became more uncontrollable and destructive at home. He was aggressive to family members and neighbourhood children and kept 'running' in spite of the employment of full time care workers. He has spent much of his childhood in group homes, foster homes and institutions. He has been involved with the law because of breaking and entering, entering the same house on different occasions and threatening the owner with a butcher's knife. On admission to the Centre, T presented with the following - delinquent behaviours, hyperactivity, running, physically and verbally aggressive, destructive, academically behind, emotionally labile, impulsive, immature. Temporal lobe epilepsy was suspected.

4.   R was placed soon after birth in a middle-class family of 4 biological children. There is also one younger sibling. He was adopted in infancy and mother reports that he has been difficult to handle since age two years - wandering off and always determined to do as he pleased. At age 7 R began coming home late from school. Later he stayed away all night and latterly for up to 4 days at a time. At age 9 he had an electroencephalogram, as there was a history of epilepsy in his biological parents. Nothing was found but he was placed on Ritalin. Prior to admission to the Centre, the family sought the help of various community agencies but their attempts were unsuccessful as R was uncooperative. He presented with the following - poor impulse control, manipulative, negative leader, aggressive to siblings, negative attention-seeking behaviour, inability to discuss feelings or show remorse.

(c)   *Adopted child's behavioural problems possibly genetic in origin with exacerbating factors in early life?*

1.   H was placed with his adoptive parents at age 4 weeks. As a child he was said to be restless, irritable and slept little, necessitating drug therapy. A generally unhappy, secluded child, he was very dependent on his mother in his early years, lacking self-confidence and having no external friends. His mother described him as a frustrating child, difficult to please. Medically, his status is unclear, but H has a form of mild cerebral palsy. Parents are very concerned, caring individuals who have sought several consultations on his intractable medical problem. Contact with

biological parents was denied by the Social Services Department when there was an indication that H's medical problem might be of genetic origin. On admission to institutional care in his early teens, H was said to have been setting fire to his school, made several suicide attempts (overdose of drugs, slashing his throat, jumping from his bedroom window) and generally displaying self-destructive attitudes. Parents are said to be dedicated to the care of this child, have good family relationships and are interested in child's future development.

2.   O spent the first four years of life with his biological parents and suffered physical abuse and was emotionally, socially and nutritionally deprived. He was adopted at age seven years into a middle-class family, the parents having high hopes for their children's achievement academically. As a child, O achieved his developmental milestones much later than his age peers, had many phobias and fears, engaged in rocking and headbanging, was shy and withdrawn. Adoptive mother's report of original parents suggests that father has a history of alcoholism and diabetes. Biological mother had a serious kidney problem of unknown nature and a history of mental retardation is said to be present in the biological family. At age 12, child presents with mild retardation; psychotic behaviour such as talking to fingers; history of soiling, eating inanimate objects such as chalk, soap, sponges; aggressive and inappropriate behaviour. O's behaviour swings from cooperative with an ability to comprehend, to inappropriately aggressive and unable to trust others. Marital relationship appears poor as the parents struggle to offer consistency and support to this troubled child.

3.   Y was born to married parents and suffered severe emotional and physical abuse and neglect throughout much of his early life. He was removed from his mother's care at age 18 months as he was found chained to his crib and covered with excrement. Y was placed in several foster homes and was finally adopted at age $4^1/_2$ years. Parents reported that they have always experienced difficulty with him. He was extremely difficult to manage, had problems with sleeping, eating huge quantities of food at night during his 'wanderings', stealing and lying. He has no close friends and his closest relationship is with his adoptive brother. Parents' greatest worry has been his violent thoughts, especially threats of killing family members. Y's biological mother had repeated

admissions to institutional care much of her life. She is described as being psychotic for much of the time, with paranoid delusions. She is also epileptic. His father has a history of mental deficiency and behaviour disorder. He has been charged with sexual offences in the past. Y presented at the Centre with following - poor peer relationships, low self-esteem, insecurity, threats to kill family members, out of control. He was said to have been severely physically abused (in early life) and emotionally deprived. Adoptive parents have a strong religious background. They were prepared to have child back in their home but made little changes themselves regarding relationship with the child.

4.   N was adopted at age 2½ following placement in 24 different foster homes since birth. She suffered with respiratory complaints during much of her early life and at one stage was diagnosed as being mentally retarded. Little has been documented of her behaviour during her early years but it was noted that her biological mother was a heroin addict and her father a drifter. N has been previously institutionalized because of self-destructive behaviour, running, violent outbursts, swearing, shoplifting, challenging authority, promiscuity, drugs and alcohol abuse. She has also had several group home and foster home placements but had to be discharged because of behaviour problems. At age 12, N presented with limited feelings of self-worth, feelings of loneliness, confusion, resentment and hostility. She is said to be self-centred, insecure and 'paranoid'. Relationship with peers is poor but she craves love, attention and warmth. Parents are a middle-class couple. N has been rejected by them totally but remains in contact (by telephone) with her adoptive sister.

(d)   *Adoption by stepparents or grandparents: Family problems possibly contributing to maladjustment?*

1.   U was adopted by his grandmother in infancy as his natural mother was unmarried at the time and wished to give him up for adoption. He was born in 1968 and found out about his adoption at the age of 12. He had apparently known about this for only a few months and on admission, presented as a child confused about life in general. He finds his adoptive mother hostile, irrational and difficult to get along with. He also finds his father vague and uninvolved except during periods of marital turmoil. U has been

involved in several delinquent acts since the age of 10 and has ben given a number of Probation Orders. He does not enjoy attending school, is defiant of authority and generally his parents find his behaviour beyond their control.

2. K, now 15 years old, was adopted by his stepfather after his parents' very tumultuous marriage ended in a divorce (date unknown). K also had a younger sister and soon after marriage, mother and stepfather had another child. Marital problems led to a second family breakdown and divorce. K's behaviour problems began after the second divorce. There was running and theft resulting in placement in an institution. He was returned to the care of his stepfather but this relationship soon broke down, after which he was placed in a foster home. Behaviour problems persisted and he at one time threatened to kill his foster mother. K was transferred to a parent counsellor home but this arrangement broke down because of his destructive behaviour.

3. V, aged 16, was adopted at age 6 by his stepfather following his mother's remarriage. Severe marital problems ensued in this marriage particularly regarding V's behaviour. Mother reported that V was difficult from birth -difficult delivery, irritability, fell from a table and hit his head at 2 months, rocked and headbanged from 1 year, diagnosed hyperactive at age 6. On admission, it was evident that father felt little commitment to B's welfare and indeed refused to pay the family's portion of maintenance while he resided at the Centre. He also refused to appear in court following one of V's antisocial acts. Parents did not agree on disciplinary measures. V's 'problem' on admission included the following - hyperactivity, theft, breaking and entering, behaviour problems in the classroom, academic difficulties, dysfunctional relationships with other family members, firesetting, out of control of parents.

4. X was the 15 year old illegitimate son of his current mother and was adopted by his stepfather at age four years. Stepfather was previously married and brought two children into this family. Soon after the marriage, X began displaying antisocial behaviours - defiant, destructive aggressive - and was seen by a psychiatrist for four years. Parents had two other sons and X's behaviour problems increased with each subsequent birth. He became increasingly aggressive to them. At school, X was aggressive to

younger children and damaged school property. There were several incidents of theft and acting out behaviour against people and property in the neighbourhood. X presented with the following on admission - behaviour problems at school, non-compliance, threats to harm teacher, truancy, vandalism, shoplifting, firesetting, impulsivity, poor peer relationships, power struggles with father, aggression to siblings. Parents are seemingly inconsistent with discipline and indeed do not agree on disciplinary measures. Father is as a strict disciplinarian while mother appears to be the 'excuse maker' for family members. Father tends to scapegoat child for family difficulties.

5.   A was adopted at age nine by her mother's second husband, 1 year after marriage. During the child's early teens, mother approached the Social Services Department as she felt unable to cope with A's truancy, running, cruelty to younger sibling (born to this marriage), moodiness and drug use. There have been several incidence of theft with consequent placement on probation. Reports suggest that mother is a very controlling, rather rigid individual with unrealistic expectations of child. Father seemed much more positively involved with his biological child than with A. Mother appeared very angry with child and this was evident in the bitter, depersonalising way she spoke of her. A was critical of the kind of parenting both she and her brother received. Psychological tests revealed a child with "a pathological hypomanic picture ... displaying periods of hyperactivity followed by depression... an exacerbation of her difficulties will produce a resultant break in reality contact." A appeared to use repression as a defense mechanism to control her impulsiveness. Family therapy was in the end apparently unsuccessful. Parents tried to protect their son from "all of this" and so refused to have him present in counselling sessions.

6.   D is the first of three children of mother's first marriage. She was adopted at age eight by mother's third husband, who assumed responsibility for five children in total, mother having taken on the care of two of her second husband's four children. Severe behaviour problems began soon after mother's third marriage though mother reports that D was a difficult child from birth - cried a great deal, had a variety of physical problems, demanding and obstinate. At age 12, D saw the start of several residential and foster home placements, indeed 29 such placements within 4

years. There was constant running lying, stealing, demonstration of low frustration level and explosive acting out behaviour within the home situation and at school. D lacked motivation to be involved in any treatment. Play and Family Therapy, Special Class placement have all been unsuccessful in alleviating some of D's difficulties - delinquencies, theft, breaking and entering, drug use, running, manipulative behaviour, extremely rapid mood swings, no remorse, aggressive to peers and siblings, immature, destructive to property, severe lack of trust with peers and adults, behaviour problems at school. There is total rejection by mother, and father appears uninvolved with the rest of the family. Mother notes, however, that there certainly have been problems since he joined the family when child was seven years old. Mother has remained hostile towards child and claims that the other children are "flirting" with delinquent behaviour. She feels that "it is time to concentrate on them."

(e) *Adoption by foster parents: Early experiences possibly contributions to maladjustment?*

1. B was one of 3 adopted children in the family, and the 2 older daughters are now married and living away from home. Parents were initially his foster parents, the placement having taken place at age 3 weeks because of malnutrition and neglect by biological mother. B was adopted at age 3 years. Father spent periods away from the family home and because of his ill health and chronic nightmares, B spent a lot of the time in the marital bed as his adoptive mother "nursed" him. B's school attendance was poor mainly due to his health problems but it is noteworthy that as soon as his health improved, his behaviour problems began (age 12). A poor relationship with his father developed so that communication was non-existent by the time of his admission to this Centre. Parents are particularly concerned about his sexual acting out behaviour - attempted to sexually assault a widow in her 60s. One occasion when father was absent from the home, he forcibly attempted sexual intercourse with his mother. B was said to be full of remorse following this incident and threatened to take his own life. B is now very much scapegoated in his neighbourhood and parents are reluctant to be involved in any placement decision.

(f)   *Adoption of older child: Prior experiences or health problems possibly contributing to maladjustment?*

1.   E was removed from his drug addicted mother as an infant and had several changes of foster home placements until his adoption at age five years. However this adoption was disrupted three years later, and his parents separated one year following this. E lived with his adoptive mother and common law husband for some time, but after this he ran away from and was placed in a foster home which he later smashed. He was sexually acting out with his foster siblings and was generally very aggressive to both adults and children. E's behaviour included breaking furniture in his home, running, extreme aggression to adults and children, theft, sexual assault of other children.

2.   This boy, W, was adopted at age five, suffering very poor health prior to his adoption from overseas. His behaviour rapidly settled into disruptive episodes with frequent temper tantrums. An electroencephalogram suggested parietal lobe dysfunction and he has been treated with a number of antidepressants. This child suffers from night terrors and frequent nightmares. He has threatened to set fire to the family home in order to kill his parents, though he has not actually done so. He has in the past built an elaborate series of weapons and booby-traps to attack his older siblings (also adopted), his teacher and his father. Parents are concerned individuals who are understandably disappointed with the outcome following a great deal of personal investment.

3.   Adopted at age four years, G is said to have experienced behavioural and social difficulties since adoption - stealing from family member within one year of adoption , lying, masturbation (excessive), self stimulation during classroom hours. G was told of her adoption at age 10 years and since this time has thought much about her natural parents, contrasting them unfavourably with her adoptive parents. She feels parents are not attentive to her unless she displayed negative behaviour e.g. running. There are constant arguments with her parents with G expressing a desire to return to a previous foster home. Problems reported by parents on admission included - theft, poor sense of reality, negative attention-seeking behaviour, identity problems relating to her adoption, self abuse, poor self-esteem, lying, poor peer relationships, immaturity, impulsivity, volatility. G displayed

constant twitching of extremities, slurred speech and hysteric tendencies suggestive of earlier sexual abuse. Parents are deemed to have a good, stable marital relationship.

4.   F was adopted at age seven years following several foster and adoptive home breakdowns. After two years in his present adoptive home, he began setting fires to the home and farm. Parents reported the following on child's admission to the Centre - does not form meaningful interpersonal relationships (though has good relationship with his two siblings), and has difficulty expressing feelings and emotions. F appears to have repressed much of the psychological pain and rejection experienced so far. He is a very anxious child with a poor self-image. At age 12, he is encopretic. Individual psychotherapy has been of little help and F has continued to set fires. He has been totally rejected by his parents.

5.   Z is one of a pair of twins both adopted at the age of nine years by a distant maternal relative and her husband. The couple are said to be of average intelligence, very caring but possessing little parenting skills. Little is known of the child's previous, disrupted family life. Both parents have difficulty in being consistent in their approach to discipline and indicated that the child was very much like her mother and male twin - "rascals." On admission, the female twin was withdrawn and also had feelings of inferiority, poor sense of identity, sexual identity problems, chronic running, promiscuity, breaking and entering and truancy. Family therapy led to some improvement in Z's difficulties and she was discharged home to the care of her adoptive parents.

Conclusions from the study of case material

Setting our material in the form of case histories can be both revealing and frustrating. The frustration arises from the fact that, despite a fascination of detail, problems of linking later maladjustment to earlier events in the child's life become more, rather than less difficult. For this reason these groupings (accounting, overall, for two-thirds of the adoptees) must be considered as very tentative. For example, though genetic effects have been inferred in some cases, this can by no means be proved from the data available. Moreover, mental illness in a biological parent is often linked to disruption and poor care in the child's early years. Further, the child's problems resulting from genetic history and early environment may interact negatively, in some cases, with latent problems in the adoptive family.

Not a single case record examined focused specifically on the problems of adoptive parenting mentioned in the literature reviewed in previous chapters. For this reason it is not possible to explore the rather subtle aspects of family interaction in the present sample. It is salutory however that with only a couple of exceptions, the disturbed adolescents themselves were not recorded as making comments on their adoptive status as a problem. It may be that the workers failed to ask questions which would reveal this; or perhaps the children were so overwhelmed by the reactions of adults to their maladjustments that they were unable to conceptualize the more subtle aspects of adoptive family relationships. Children, having little experience outside their own families would in any case have no comparative base for describing their own families as unusual or abnormal.

What these data do not tell us, and what systematic follow-up studies of adoption must establish, is the degree to which different kinds of adoptive families are at risk for disruption to a lesser or greater degree. We cannot answer such an epidemiological question from this essentially clinical data. What is implied however, is that more systematic support and follow-up adoptions by placement agencies might prevent some of the extreme disruptions described here. Adoptions by step-parents are also, in some cases, problematic and deserve greater attention by preventive social services.

Classification of adopted children by methods of numerical taxonomy

It seems possible to subject the data on the adopted children to complex statistical analysis. Methods exist for classifying subjects into groups, so we applied the cluster analysis program available in the Biological and Medical Data Program Package (BMDP - Engelman, 1983).

This technique calculates the similarity of each case to each other case, based on the absolute mean differences on all indicators (variables) entered into the analysis. This technique in BMDP is called 'centroid linkage'. In a series of steps, the two most dissimilar cases are selected, and similar and dissimilar cases are selected until a basic set of clusters emerges. The nearest cluster for each other cluster is then estimated.

The variables put into the cluster analysis were the nine factor scores for each case from an SPSS principal components analysis of the data. In order to reduce the number of variables in this principal components analysis to 34 (since the higher the ratio of subjects to variables, the more stable the factor structure), symptoms were grouped into four clusters according to a prior principal components analysis reported in the previous chapter.

The factor score output for the nine components from the second principal components analysis, accounting for 53 percent of the variance or intercorrelation amongst the 34 variables was subjected to the clustering program. Twelve clusters of individuals emerged, and we have selected for analysis and comparison the eight clusters to which a set of behavioural symptoms was linked.

In summary, the procedures followed were:

(1)   Principal components analysis of behavioural symptoms for 61 adopted children identified four basic groupings.
(2)   These groupings were used to form four basic sub-scales of behaviour.
(3)   These four scales, plus thirty psychosocial variables were subjected to a further principal components analysis, extracting nine factors accounting for 53 percent of the variance. Three cases for which some data was missing were excluded from this analysis.
(4)   The factor scores for each individual on the nine principal components were subjected to cluster analysis using the centroid linkage method.
(5)   The clusters of individual were linked in some cases, and collapsed into four basic clusters.

One problem in extracting clusters is that of deciding what variables characterize these clusters. For this purpose an easy-to-use, descriptive technique was employed: the trait was assigned to the group if more than half of the cases possessed the trait. In the case of the variables of age and social status, distribution around the median for all cases (more than 66 percent above or below) was used as the inclusion category. In the case of symptom clusters, at least two of the variables had to be scored in an extreme direction for more than half of the cases, for that symptom cluster to be assigned to the group of individuals.

The groups or clusters of individuals which emerged are listed in Table 1. Only those clusters for which a behavioural cluster has been assigned, according to the above criteria, are represented. The sub-clustering of these groups is represented in Table 2. Group A contains the single, large cluster (with 11 cases), which represents children adopted early in life, with neurological symptoms, hyperactivity and fire-setting, physical, motor and sensory health problems of early onset and often still persisting, difficult temperament in infancy, and early onset of behavioural problems. The depression of the adopted mother (in 7 of the 11 cases) appeared from the case material to be a reaction to, rather than a cause of, her child's deviant behaviour. Overall, a picture emerges of well-meaning but distressed parents who have been unable to cope with the overactive and often antisocial behaviour of their adopted child, whose problems seem related to CNS damage acquired during or before birth, or which might even be genetic in origin.

Group B (13 cases) contains the two higher order clusters III and V. Both clusters are similar in representing children whose depression and suicidal behaviour probably reflect the abuse they suffered before adoption. Nevertheless, there are indications that these adoptive parents were often unable to cope, even at the outset, with the needs of these often difficult children and instead focused unrealistically on the child's academic potential. This Group includes three cases (3/4 in Cluster V) who were adopted by foster parents. Although the case histories provide no direct evidence, there is an implication that the social service departments who placed these children in foster care and adoption had failed to prepare and support the parents in caring for these at-risk and potentially difficult children. For example, sexual abuse in childhood is now known to have in many cases long-term, adverse sequels for the child (Bagley and King, 1990); but this seems not to have been acknowledge or recognized by the social workers placing the children.

Group C (9 cases) includes Cluster IV and VII in which disruption in the adoptive home appears to be causally related to deviant behaviour in the child. In one cluster, lower class parents seem to have been overly strict with the child (but whether this was a vain attempt to control the child's acting-out behaviour, or actually caused it is not clear). It is possible that these families failed to acknowledge difference, or meet the child's identity needs, although again we have no direct evidence of this. In the linked Cluster VII, the adopted child lived in a climate of emotional and marital tension, had in three cases probably been sexually abused by the father, and later displayed marked aggression to both father and mother, as well as depression, suicide attempts, and sexual acting out. Finkelhor (1984) argues that the incest taboo is weakened in the case of adopted children; this could be the case with the girls in this group for whom there is clear evidence of failure by adoptive parents to meet the child's developmental needs.

Group D (16 cases) includes 14 step-parent adoptions (all by a step-father) in the adopted children. The common symptom cluster in these children was delinquency, running from home, drug use, and aggression to other children. Cluster II within this Group represents step-

318

fathers who have alternatively used extreme discipline and extreme indulgence to win over or control the errant step-child, without success. Cluster VI represents those step-fathers who may have sexually abused their stepchild, while Cluster VIII represents three children all of whose fathers had died. A common feature of these children is the later onset of acting out symptoms. Adoption for Cluster II and VI will have legally closed access to, or by the biological father, with what effects on the child's identity development the case records do not say.

Table 1   **Cluster analysis of 58 adopted children residential care for maladjusted children**

Cluster I   11 cases

> Age: younger
> Age of onset of behavioural problems (younger)
> Symptom cluster: hyperactivity, neurological problems; lower IQ, Aggressive to peers/sibling
> Health problems early in life, and still persisting
> Child difficult in infancy (restless, crying, slow in milestones)
> Adoptive mother's poor mental health (depression)
> Child's age at adoption (younger)
> Sex: male

Cluster II   9 cases

> Gross marital tension in home 3 years before child's admission
> Stepfather
> Mental health/behavioural problems in father
> Inconsistent discipline, veering from lax to harsh without rational cause
> Age of onset of behavioural problems (older)
> Child has been unable to relate or bond to stepfather
> Symptom cluster: Delinquency; running; drug use.

Table 1 (Cont'd)

Cluster III   9 cases

Child has experience of marked physical abuse and neglect prior to adoption
Child had problems in bonding to adoptive parents
Age adopted: older
Mental health/behavioural problems in father (in 4 out of 5 cases in biological father)
Mental health/behavioural problems in mother (in 3 out of 5 cases in biological mother)
Parents have unrealistically high academic expectations for child
Child has experienced sexual abuse prior to adoption
Symptom cluster: Anxiety/depression; suicidal behaviour; sexual acting-out
Child sexually abused in the community after adoption

Cluster IV   5 cases

Sex: Male
Number of other adopted children in family: more
Age of onset of behavioural problems: younger
Behavioural problems in sibling(s)
Discipline consistently harsh and authoritarian
Social status of family: lower
Symptom cluster: Delinquent; runs; drug use

Cluster V   4 cases

Social status of family: higher
Age of onset of behaviour problems: older
Adoption of a foster child
Number of other adopted children in family: more
Symptom cluster: Anxiety/depression; suicidal behaviour

Table 1 (Cont'd)

Cluster VI   4 cases

    Suspicion of sexual abuse in family
    Discipline harsh and authoritarian
    Age at adoption: older
    Number of biological children of adoption parent(s): more
    Symptom cluster: Delinquent; runs; drug use

Cluster VII   4 cases

    Gross marital tension in home in 3 years before admission
    Sex: female
    Age of onset of behaviour problems: older
    Symptom cluster: Aggression to mother; aggression to father
    Symptom cluster: Anxiety/depression; suicidal behaviour; sexual
    acting out
    Suspicion of sexual abuse in existing family

Cluster VIII   3 cases

    Mother single parent when child 5 or younger
    Death of father
    Step-father at present time
    Symptom cluster: Delinquent; runs; drug use
    Age: older
    Behavioural problems in a sibling
    Age behavioural problems began: older

Note: Characteristics assigned to cluster if <u>more than</u> half of the cases possessed the characteristic. For symptom or behavioural groupings, at least two of the symptom had to be present in a marked degree for the behavioural cluster to be assigned to the group. Rank of listing within each group reflects prevalence of item in the cluster.

Table 2   Groupings of cluster of 58 adopted children

Cluster I	Cluster III plus Cluster V	Cluster IV plus Cluster VII plus Cluster VIII	Cluster II plus Cluster VI
becomes	becomes	becomes	becomes
GROUP A (11 cases)	GROUP B (13 cases)	GROUP C (9 cases)	GROUP D (16 cases)
"Neurological problems in children adopted in infancy; hyperactivity"	"Children adopted past infancy; previous trauma; depressd and suicidal"	"Abuse in adoptive home"	"Adoption by step-parent; delinquency in child"

Unclassified: 9 cases undifferentiated by any behavioural profile.

Comparison of clustering of adopted children by numerical and case study techniques

Two methods of clustering cases have been presented: one is based on a detailed consideration of individual case material; the other on a formal and complex statistical method. Do these methods give comparable results? To answer this question the statistical classification of the 58 adoptees (for whom complete data was available) has been compared with the case study method presented earlier in this chapter. In the six types in the case study analysis, the neurological problems group were joined with the "possible genetic problems" group; and the "foster parent adoption" group were linked with the children adopted past infancy, with whom they had a number of similarities.

Table 3 presents the results of the comparison of the two methods of classification. The two methods clearly have much in common, classifying cases which are conceptually similar in the majority of cases.

The two "neurological" groups have the highest degree of concordance, and the "unclassified" groups the lowest concordance. Although not perfect, this degree of concordance does give some confidence in the validity of the two methods of clustering cases.

General conclusions

Two methods of clustering the cases of severely maladjusted, adopted children have, despite differences in lower-order grouping been largely in agreement in identifying four main types of maladjustment. The typology has immediate implications for understanding, prevention and treatment of disruption adoption.

The first type involves children whose chronic neurological problems (often involving hyperactivity and aggression to peers and siblings) are probably related either to genetic factors or to organic trauma in the perinatal period. Although parents have supported these difficult children as best they can, mothers especially are often exhausted and depressed. This group contains significantly more boys than girls. It is possible that adopters of these apparently "normal" white infants operated on the "denial of difference" model of adoption identified by Kirk (1981). This might well have made the parenting of a behaviourally difficult child more difficult. Although we have no direct evidence, it is hypothetically probable that being more detached from the child, and treating him in a more objective fashion (with the aid of continued professional guidance and support) would have prevented negative feedback loops which often characterize parenting in families with a neurologically impaired child (Bell, 1979).

What is clear however, is the need for support for more skilled and effective parenting which these families needed, but did not receive, in the early years. If, as previous evidence (reviewed above) suggests, adopted children are more at risk for behavioural conditions which are genetic or traumatic in origin, then the placing agencies should have offered much closer monitoring and support in the early years following placement. But there is no evidence that the agencies did this: rather they seem to have connived in a process of adoption in which the new parents took the child "as if" it were their own, not as a child with special needs which might require special parenting and support.

The disruption of later adoptions (the second group) seems directly attributable to the unresolved and long-term effects of trauma which occurred before the adoption took place. Again, social work agencies should have offered much fuller support for the parents of these obviously at-risk children: but there is no evidence from the case records that any such support was offered.

The problem of abuse and disruption in adoptive families, including behavioural abnormality in a parent, and gross marital problems which the child's deviance seems to reflect, is a more difficult one to address. The best kind of prevention here might well involve better screening of marital and mental health problems in potential adopters before any placement is approved.

The final group, step-parent adoptions, is the most problematic in terms of both prevention and intervention strategies. The number of 'blended' families is increasing as the amount of divorce and remarriage increases in Canada (Eichler, 1983). One administrative solution would be to make it impossible for a man or woman to adopt the children of their new spouse, substituting instead the possibility of guardianship, following the precedent set by the 1975 Children Act in Britain. This would at least allow access by a non-custodial, biological parent and might also allow better supervision and support of the new child care arrangements by social service agencies. Step-parent adoptions are not true adoptions in a sociological or legal sense; disruption of these parenting arrangements should not be counted as adoption failures, as has been the case in the past.

Table 3 Comparison of case study and statistical methods of classfiying adoption children in residential centres for maladjusted children

Statistical Method Grouping	A: Neurological Problems	B: Later Adoption	C: Abuse in Adoption	D: Step-Parent Adoption	Unclassified	Total
Case Study Grouping:						
a. Maladjustment in adopted' family	0	1(10%)	6(60%)	3(30%)	0	10
b. Neurological problem	8(89%)	0	0	1(11%)	0	9
plus						
c. Possible genetic problems						
d. Step-parent adoptions	0	1(7%)	1(6%)	11(73%)	2(13%)	15
e. Foster parent adoption	1(8%)	9(69%)	1(8%)	1(8%)	1(8%)	13
plus						
f. Adoption of older children						
Unclassified	2(18%)	2(18%)	1(9%)	0	6(54%)	11
Total	11	13	9	16	9	58

Note: Percentages calculated horizontally
Significance: Chi-squared (16 d.f.), 29.86, p = 0.1

19 Adjustment in adoption: Conclusions

Adoption is a powerful, permanent and yet changing institution. Finding new parents for children whose previous parental care can no longer be sustained is a powerful way of meeting the psychological and social needs of some children. The changes which adoption practice is undergoing should serve to strengthen this special type of child care practice. The research of the two previous decades, reviewed in some detail in earlier chapters points to ways in which adoption practice has changed. A number of important research studies and pioneering practice models have shown too how social work in adoption can be improved.

The traditional form of adoption within kinship and clan networks will continue in many parts of the world, and can with profit be used as a resource in economically developed countries too. As we stressed in Chapter 13, social workers have neglected extended families as a resource in the temporary or permanent care of children whose own parents cannot care for them. This failure, resulting from culturally biased methods of practice, has led to large numbers of children from disadvantaged ethnic minorities being permanently removed from their family and culture of origin, with placement in families of the dominant class or ethnic group. In the case of aboriginal children in North America (including Canada) this practice has often had disastrous consequences.

In other minority communities (for example, black people in Britain) more vigorous efforts to find relatives or community members who could care for a child in need should be attempted. In our survey of the attitudes of black people in the London Borough of Merton towards transracial adoption, as well as their personal interest in adoption, we found many people who were interested in such practice. Ironically, we also know of black children from this same area who were placed with white foster parents a considerable distance away.

Prevention is always better than cure, and in many cases a family can be kept together with various kinds of support including a child care worker visiting the family each day, as well as material subsidies and rehousing where necessary. Administrators and politicians would do well to remember that such strategies are likely to be cost effective in the long run, forestalling the need for expensive institutional and therapeutic care for neglected or abused children.

Consider the following case vignette from Calgary, Alberta:

A single mother with four children aged 3 to 9 had a drinking problem. After treatment (during which time her children were in care for three weeks) she was given a subsidized housing unit, and a child care worker came to the house each day to provide a model for parenting skills. The child care worker gave the mother advice and encouragement, and she began a course in professional cookery at an adult vocational centre. Without warning, the government of Alberta (in October, 1988) decided to cut back drastically on all ancillary social work services, because of an apparent budget crisis. Within three days the child care worker was pulled from Mrs. M's home, and she was left to fend for herself. She gave up the vocational training course to stay home in order to look after her children. But her drinking began again, and the children became neglected. A social worker apprehended the children, and they were placed in residential care, and then in a foster home. The oldest boy in the family began to exhibit serious behavioural problems and was moved to another foster home within a year. The cost of keeping these children in various kinds of substitute care for a year was about $40,000. The child care worker's daily visits to he home would have cost less than half of this. After a year there was no prospect of the children's return home. The mother had to give up her family dwelling unit since she no longer had children with her; she moved to a single women's hostel. Adoption was being considered for the two youngest children in this family. The two older children, likely to stay in care, could cost the Province more than a million dollars in social service support and therapy by the time they are 18.

In this case professional social work practice which could have supported the family in staying together was undermined by Treasury officials whose only goal was to save money in the short run. Supportive social work for families under stress can both prevent the need for children being taken into care and can in the long run save many millions of dollars.

While various forms of support can often prevent parent-child separation, there are situations of extreme abuse or neglect in which healing of parents is not possible. For example, Oliver (1985) in a study of multi-problem families in an English county has shown that successive generations of children in such families are likely to suffer extreme physical, sexual and emotional abuse before they themselves grow into adults with high rates of crime, mental illness and abuse of others, including their own children. Oliver argues that the only way to break into this cycle of abuse is to remove a child early in life and place that child for adoption, as part of a decisive and clearly-defined plan of permanency for the child's welfare.

The research which we have reviewed, and much of the data presented in the chapters above have shown that adoptive parenting can be a powerful factor in shaping the lives of young children as they become successful adults. Despite some negative genetic loading and the possibility of physical and emotional trauma of the child in the perinatal period, children in positive environments are likely to develop into normal adults. At least two thirds of children who are removed from dysfunctional families in which outcomes for them would have been very poor, have highly successful outcomes in adoptive families. This is clearly shown in the longitudinal data from the National Child Development study analysis in Chapter 6.

Adoptive parenting can be as successful as regular parenting in every respect. But herein lies an important dilemma. Once parent and adoptive child have bonded to one another there is a tendency, a temptation for the adoptive parent to treat the new child exactly if that child were his own. Indeed, as David Kirk pointed out, reactions from relatives and community members to the effect that the parent loves the child "almost as if it were your own" are very hurtful. Kirk's solution to this dilemma is well known: treat the child in a loving a way, but not as you would a biological child. Respect and love the child's origins, and help him in turn to respect and love the culture from which he came:

328

this is a specially important in transracial and intercountry adoption.

Like Hoksbergen we are ambiguous about intercountry adoption. Surely, these adoptions can be very successful. But in course of time all countries should develop to the extent that they can provide family care for all children. For some countries like India and China, that day may be very far off.

Adoptive parents are usually selected because they have good mental health and marital stability, and are successful in their various careers. This enables them to be, in most cases, excellent parents. Yet there is often an element of anxiety in adoptive parenting which reflects the role dilemmas of adoption, as well as the anxieties associated with infertility. This anxiety often leads to over-protective parenting which in turn can lead to sub-clinical levels of anxiety in adoptive parenting.

The study of previously adopted children who enter residential treatment centres indicates that this is sometimes a reflection of overanxious parents seeking services for prophylactic reasons - trying to prevent a problem from developing. This can have positive outcomes provided that the child is not unfairly labelled as deviant. Our study of adopted children in residential treatment centres in Calgary, Alberta has shown both that parents of adopted children can be highly anxious, and refer their children for specialist help sooner than other parents; and also that sometimes an adopted child can be negatively labelled or even abused by his adopters.

These findings underline the fact that if adoption (and not just special needs adoption) is to work well, parents need to be carefully prepared for the arrival of the child, knowing as much about his or her background as possible. Once placement has been made, the temptation for social workers to retreat and leave the family alone "as if" the adopted child were like a biological child, should be avoided. Adoption will be strengthened by the continued support of social workers, and the parents should feel free, without guilt or stigma, to call on the agency for help and advice whenever this seems necessary.

Our clinical study of disrupted adoptions in Alberta indicates that adopted children in residential care can be divided into four main groups. The first group includes children adopted in infancy, who developed behavioural problems at an early age. The nature of these problems suggests either that they stem from CNS impairments during the perinatal period, or genetic causes, or both. Many of these children had problems of learning, overactivity and attention deficit disorder. Adoptive parents reacted in various ways to these problems, ranging from the helpful involvement to resigned acceptance through to scapegoating and rejection.

A second group of adoptees who experienced disruption had few ascertainable problems which were neuropsychological or genetic in origin, and appeared to be reacting to stress, neglect and even abuse in their adoptive families. Fortunately this "dark side of adoption" as Ounsted (1970) put it appears to involve a very small proportion of adoptive families. However, a larger group of adoptions which were experiencing difficulty were those in which a child was not separated from his or her biological mother, but was formally adopted by the mother's new partner. Step-parenting involves many difficulties (Wallerstein and Kelly, 1980), and usually social work counselling is sought in such adoptions only at a late stage, when family therapy interventions have a much poorer chance of success.

The fourth group of disrupted adoptions involved children who were past infancy when adopted, and had often experienced abuse, neglect and broken bonding, often over a period of several years. In these children a period of residential treatment can be seen as part of an ongoing programme of care. Clinically, several factors are relevant: the adopted children in all of the four groups have fewer severe behaviour disorders than non-adopted children in residential treatment; these clinical problems are more likely to involve aggression against the self or the child's home and family, rather than externalized aggression in the community; families themselves were much more likely to be intact and non-pathological in the case of adoptees; and the adoptees were more likely than others to return to their families of origin. We have described other kinds of gross pathology from our work at these residential treatment centres (Bagley and Sewchuk-Dann, 1991). Adopted children were only atypically involved in the behaviours (sexual assaults against others) described in that study.

Adopted children have special tasks in identity formation, as well as stressors in their lives (possible negative genetic history, early CNS impairment or damage, minor or major congenital handicaps, separation from biological mother, as well as possible abuse and neglect). Given these various negative pressures, the very positive outcomes for 70 or 80 percent of children must be considered rather remarkable. The adoptive family is a powerful therapeutic agency for many children. Although therapeutic foster care can sometimes achieve these ends, adoption has the distinct advantage of providing a permanent commitment between parent and child, based on mutual bonding which lasts long after the adopted child has become an adult. This finding has emerged from a number of important follow-up studies of special needs adoption in America and Britain (Barth and Berry, 1988; Derdeyn, 1990; Hill and Triseliotis, 1991). A number of writers have outlined models of adjustment in adoption, sometimes reflecting different theoretical backgrounds (McRoy at al., 1988). The gloomy views of psychoanalytical writers (e.g. Brinich, 1990) are not borne out either by the Scandinavian follow-up studies (Bohman and Sigvardsson, 1990), nor the British National Child Development survey (Chapter 6 in the present volume; and Maughan and Pickles, 1990). Large scale epidemiological studies using an appropriately matched control group have shown that in many respects adopted children's outcomes as young adults are in the large majority of cases similar to those in any other intact, caring family. Nevertheless, there are some conditions which are either specific to some adoptees (a mild neurosis which takes the form of an anxious over-dependency on the adoptive parents), or which have a higher incidence in adoptees (such as overactivity, sometimes associated with learning problems). What we can say with some assurance is that if these children had grown up in institutions, outcomes for them would likely be much worse. Nevertheless (with the exception of certain multi-problem families) it is likely that outcomes might have been just as good if social service, income and housing support had enabled the birth parent or parents to keep their children, instead of the ultimate adoption by unrelated individuals following a period in residential child care.

We are largely in agreement with Brodzinsky's (1990) stress and coping model of adjustment in adoption, but would add to this social learning model elements of a symbolic interactionist framework, which seems to explain some of the negative findings we report in Chapter 13 with regard to the adjustment of Amerindian adoptees in Canada.

Finally, some personal messages to adopters: there is an element of luck in adoption - if your child has a sweet temperament and adapts quickly and well, rejoice; but remember, if your child seems to have a difficult temperament (Bagley, 1991c) try and adapt yourself to the child's needs by finding a "goodness of fit" between your temperament and his (Chess and Thomas, 1986). If you expect the best of your child, and structure your interactions accordingly, the best should emerge. But remember too "love is not enough" - you must acknowledge, respect and interact with the symbols of your child's ethnicity and ethnic culture as well.

For adopted children the message is this: searching for your roots can be great fun. I've accompanied my father on this journey, as well as my two adopted sons. You may be surprised, astonished, dismayed or delighted: but the journey is part of your growth in discovering the past, and moulding your future.

References

ABAFA (1981). *Access to Birth Records: The Impact of Section 26 of the Children Act 1975.* London: Association of British Fostering and Adoption Agencies.

Aird, J. (1990). *Slaughter of the Innocents: Coercive Birth Control in China.* Washington, D.C.: AEI Press.

Altstein, H. and Simon, R. (1991). Summary and concluding remarks. In H. Altstein and R. Simon (Eds). *Intercountry Adoption: A Multinational Perspective* (pp 192-193). New York: Praeger.

American Humane Society, Child Abuse in America. Paper given to International Congress on Child Abuse, Montreal, September 1984.

Andersen, R. (1989). The nature of adoptee search: adventure, cure or growth? *Child Welfare,* 68, 623-635.

Andreson, I. (1992). Behavioural and school adjustment of 12 and 13-year old internally adopted children in Norway. *Journal of Child Psychology and Psychiatry,* 33; 427-439.

Andrews, R. (1978). Adoption: legal resolution or legal fraud? *Family Process,* 17, 313-328.

Anthony, E. (1987). Risk, vulnerability and resilience: an overview. In E. Anthony and B. Cohler (Eds). *The Invulnerable Child.* (pp 3 to 48). New York: Guilford Press.

APP (1991). *16 Million in Labour Camps*, Paris: Agence France Press Report, February 10, 1991.

Bachrach, C. (1983). Children in families: Characteristics of biological, step- and adopted children. *Journal of Marriage and the Family*, 45, 171-179.

Bachrach, C. (1986). Adoption plans, adopted children, and adoptive mothers. *Journal of Marriage and the Family*, 48, 243-253.

Bagley, C. (1973). *The Dutch Plural Society: A Comparative Study in Race Relations*. London: Oxford University Press.

Bagley, C. (1975). Suicidal behaviour and suicidal ideation in adolescents: a problem for counsellors in education. *British Journal of Guidance and Counselling*, 3, 190-208.

Bagley, C. (1976). On the sociology and social ethics of abortion. *Ethics, Science and Medicine*, 3, 21-32.

Bagley, C. (1977). Adoption and the powerful effects of environment. *Adoption and Fostering*, 88, 45-47.

Bagley, C. (1977). The welfare of the child. In S. Curtis (Ed.) *Child Adoption* (pp 40-63) London: Association of British Adoption and Fostering Agencies.

Bagley, C. (1979) Inter-ethnic marriage in Britain and America: *Sage Race Relations Abstract*, 3, 1-21.

Bagley, C. (1979). Social policy and development: the case of child welfare, health and nutritional services in India. *Plural Societies*, 10, 3-26.

Bagley, C. (1980a). The factorial reliability of the Middlesex Hospital Questionnaire in normal subjects. *British Journal of Medical Psychology*, 53, 53-58.

Bagley, C. (1980b). Policy formation and evaluation of inter-country adoptions. University of Surrey, Department of Sociology, mimeo.

Bagley, C. (1983). Dutch social structure and the alienation of black youth. In C. Bagley and G. Verma (Eds.). *Multicultural Childhood: Education, Ethnicity and Cognitive Styles* (pp 180-196). Aldershot, U.K.: Gower.

Bagley, C. (1984). Child protection and the Native child. *Perception*, 28, 17-20.

Bagley, C. (1985). Field dependence and verbal reasoning in Blackfoot, Japanese and Anglo-Celtic children in Southern Alberta. In R. Diaz-Gurrero (Ed.), *Cross-Cultural and National Studies in Social Psychology* (pp 191-208). Amsterdam: Elsevier.

Bagley, C. (1986a). Child abuse by the child welfare system. *Journal of Child Care*, 2, 64-69.

Bagley, C. (1986b). Social and scholastic adjustment in children with epilepsy and infantile fits: a 16-year follow-up of a national sample. In B. Hermann and S. Whitman (Eds.) *The Social Dimensions of Epilepsy.* (pp 85-104). New York: Oxford University Press.

Bagley, C. (1988a). Lies, dammed lies, and Indian ethnicity in the Canadian census. *Ethnic and Racial Studies,* 11, 230-233.

Bagley, C. (1988b). Child abuse and the legal system: The question of bias. In S. Martin (Ed.), *Judges and Equality Issues* (pp 140-149),Toronto: Carswell Legal Publication.

Bagley, C. (1988c). Day care and child development. *Early Childhood Care, Health and Development,* 39, 134-146.

Bagley, C. (1988d). Helping women and protecting the fetus. *Policy Options,* May, 31-32.

Bagley, C. (1989a). Self-concept and achievement in British and Anglo-Canadian high school students. *Canadian and International Education,* 18, 77-78.

Bagley, C. (1989d). Helping women and protecting the fetus. *Policy Options,* May 31-32.

Bagley, C. (1989b). Development of a short self-esteem measure for use with adults in community mental health surveys. *Psychological Reports,* 65, 13-14.

Bagley, C. (1989c). Profiles of youthful suicide: Disrupted development and current stressors. *Psychological Reports,* 65, 234.

Bagley, C. (1989d). Development of a short self-esteem measure for use with adults in community mental health surveys. *Psychological Reports,* 65, 13-14.

Bagley, C. (1990). Adoption of Native Children in Canada: a policy analysis and a research report. In H. Altstein and R. Simon (Eds.). *Intercountry Adoption: a Multinational Perspective* (pp 55-79). New York: Praeger.

Bagley, C. (1991a). The prevalence and long-term sequels of child sexual abuse in community sample of young, adult women. *Canadian Journal of Community Mental Health,* 10, 103-116.

Bagley, C. (1991b). *Family Poverty and Children's Behavioural and Learning Problems.* Waterloo, Ont.: Monograph of the Centre for Social Welfare Studies, Wilfrid Laurier University.

Bagley, C. (1991c). Factor structure of temperament in the third year of life. *Journal of General Psychology,* 118, 291-297.

Bagley, C. (1991d). Social services and abortion policy. In I. Gentles (Ed.). *A Time to Choose Life: Women, Abortion and Human Life.* (pp 95-106 and 227-230). Toronto: Stoddart.

Bagley, C. (1992a). Development of an adolescent stress scale for use by school counsellors: construct validity in terms of depression, self-esteem and suicidal ideation. *Psychology in the Schools International*, 13, 31-49.

Bagley, C. (1992b). Psychological and social adjustment in racially-mixed marriages. *International Journal of Marriage and the Family*, 1, 41-54.

Bagley, C. (1992c). Child sexual abuse and its long-term outcomes: a review of some British and Canadian studies of victims and their families. *Annals of Sex Research*, 4, 23-48.

Bagley, C. and Evan-Wong, L. (1975). Neuroticism and extraversion in responses to coopersmith's self-esteem inventory. *Psychological Reports*, 36, 253-254.

Bagley, C., Friesen, J. and Coward, H. (1989). *The Evolution of Multiculturalism in Canada*. Calgary: Institute of Humanities.

Bagley, C. and King, K. (1990). *Child Sexual Abuse: The Search for Healing*. London: Tavistock-Routledge.

Bagley, C. and Sewchuk-Dann, D. (1991). Characteristics of 60 children and adolescents who have a history of sexual assault against others: evidence from a controlled study. *Journal of Youth and Child Care*, Fall Special Issue, 43-52.

Bagley, C. and Thomlison, R. (1991). "Understanding and preventing the sexual abuse of children." In C. Bagley and R. Thomlison (Eds) *Children Sexual Abuse: Critical Perspectives on Prevention, Intervention, and Treatment*. (pp 1-8). Toronto: Wall and Emerson.

Bagley, C., Verma, G. and Mallick, L. (1979). Pupil self-esteem: a study of black and white teenagers in British schools. In G. Verma and C. Bagley (Eds), *Race, Education and Identity*. (pp 176-191). London: MacMillan.

Bagley, C., Verma G. and Mallick, K. (1979). *Racial Prejudice, the Individual and Society*. Aldershot: Gower.

Bagley, C., Verma, L., Mallick, M. and Young, L. (1979). *Personality, Self-esteem and Prejudice*. Aldershot: Gower.

Bagley, C., Wood, M. & Khumar, H. (1990). Suicide and careless death in Native populations: A Canadian case study. *Canadian Journal of Community Mental Health*, 29, 127-1142.

Bagley, C. and Young, L. (1979). The identity, adjustment and achievement of transracially adopted children: a review and empirical report. In G. Verma and C. Bagley (Eds.). *Race, Education and Identity* (pp 192-219). London: MacMillan.

Bagley, C. and Young, L. (1980). Views of black adults on mixed adoption. *Community Care*, 304, 16-18.

Bagley, C. and Young, L. (1981). The long-term adjustment of a sample of inter-country adopted children. *International Social Work*, 23, 16-22.

Bagley, C. and Young, L. (1982). Policy dilemmas and the adoption of black children. In J. Cheetham (Ed.). *Social Work and Ethnicity* (pp120-139). London: Allen and Unwin.

Bagley, C. and Young, L. (1983). Class, socialization and cultural change: antecedents of cognitive style in children in Jamaica and England. In C. Bagley and G. Verma (Eds.) *Multicultural Childhood: Education, Ethnicity and Cognitive Styles*. (pp 16-26). Aldershot, U.K.: Gower Press.

Bagley, C. and Young, L. (1984). The welfare, adjustment and identity of children of mixed marriage. In G. Verma and C. Bagley (Eds). *Race Relations and Cultural Differences*. (pp 247-258). London: Croom Helm.

Bagley, C. and Young, L. (1988). Evaluation of color and ethnicity in young children in Jamaica, Ghana, England and Canada. *International Journal of Intercultural Relations*, 12, 45-60.

Bagley C. and Young, L. (1990). Depression, self-esteem and suicidal behaviour as sequels of sexual abuse in childhood: research and therapy. In G. Cameron (Ed.) *Child Maltreatment: Expanded Concepts of Helping*. (pp 183-209) New York: Lawrence Erlbaum.

Baker, L. (1986). Estimating genetic correlations among discontinuous phenotypes: an analysis of criminal convictions and psychiatric-hospital diagnoses in Danish adoptees. *Behavior Genetics*, 16, 127-137.

Balanon, L. (1989). Foreign adoption in the Philippines: issues and opportunities. *Child Welfare*, 68, 241-254.

Barth, R., Berry, M., Carson, M., Goodfield, R. and Feinberg, B. (1986). Contributors to disruption and dissolution of older-child adoptions. *Child Welfare*, 65, 395-371.

Barth, R. and Berry, M. (1988). *Adoption and Disruption: Rates, Risks and Responses*. New York: Aldine de Gruyter.

Bass, C. (1975). Matchmaker - matchmaker: older-child adoption failures. *Child Welfare*, 54, 505, 512.

Beck, A. Weissman, A., Lester, D. & Trexler, L. (1974). The measurement of pessimison: The hopelessness scale. *Journal of Consulting and Psychology*, 42, 861-865.

Beisky, J. (1985). Daycare: development effects and the problem of quality care. *Canadian Children*, 9,53-74.

Bell, R. (1979). Parent and child and reciprocal influences. *American Psychologist*, 34, 821-826.

Ben-Porat, A. (1977). Guttman scale test for Maslow need hierarchy. *Journal of Psychology,* 97, 85-92.

Benet, M. (1976). *The Politics of Adoption.* New York: Free Press.

Bennett, M. and Mostyn, B. (1991). *The Intercountry Adoption Process from the U.K. Adoptive Parents Perspective.* London: International Bar Association, Section on General Practice.

Berbaum, M. and Moreland, R. (1985). Intellectual development within transracial adoptive families: retesting the confluence model. *Child Development,* 56, 207-216.

Berlin I. (1978). Anglo adoption of Native Americans: Repercussions in adolescence. *Journal for the American Academy of Child Psychiatry,* 17, 387-388.

Berry, M. (1991). The effects of open adoption on biological and adoptive parents and the children: the arguments and the evidence. *Child Welfare,* 68, 637-645.

Berry, M. and Barth, R. (1990). A study of disrupted adoptive placements of adolescents. *Child Welfare,* 69, 209-225.

Billimoria, H. (1984). *Adoption: An Indian Experience.* Bombay: Himalayan Publications.

Bisett-Johnson, A. (1984). Adoption within the family. In P. Sachdev (Ed.), *Adoption: Current Issues and Trends.* Toronto: Butterworth.

Black, R. (1983). Genetics and adoption: A challenge for social work. In M. Dinerman (Ed.), *Social Work in a Turbulent World.* Maryland: National Association of Social Workers.

Blitz, J. and Glenwick, D. (1989), Peer relations and behaviors of adoptive children in residential treatment. *Psychological Reports,* 64, 157,-158.

Blotcky, M., Looney, J. and Grace K. (1982). Treatment of the adopted adolescent: involvement of biologic mother. *Journal of the American Academy of Child Psychiatry,* 21, 28-285.

Bohman, M. (1970). *Adopted Children and Their Families: A Follow up Study of Adopted Children, Their Background, Environment and Adjustment.* Stockholm: Proprius.

Bohman, M. (1973). Unwanted children - a prognostic study. *Child Adoption,* 72, 13-25.

Bohman, M. (1981). The interaction of heredity and childhood environment: Some adoption studies. *Journal of Child Psychology and Psychiatry,* 2, 195-200.

Bohman, M., Cloninger, R., Sigvardsson, S. and Von Knorring, A. (1982). Predisposition to petty criminality in Swedish adoptees. *Archives of General Psychiatry,* 39, 24-38.

Bohman, M. and Sigvardsson, S. (1980). Negative social heritage.

Adoption and Fostering, 101, 25-31.

Bohman, M. and Sigvardsson, S. (1990). Outcome in adoption: lessons from longitudinal studies. In D. Brodzinsky & M. Schechter (Eds). *The Psychology of Adoption* (pp 93-106). New York: Oxford University Press.

Borgman, R. (1982). The consequences of open and closed adoption for older children. *Child Welfare,* 61, 217-226.

Boswell, J. (1989). *The Kindness of Strangers.* London: Allen Lane.

Bowlby, J. (1973). *Attachment and Loss Vol. II: Separation.* New York: Basic Books.

Bowlby, J. (1979). *Attachment and Loss Vol. III:, Loss, Sadness, and Depression.* London: Hogarth Press.

Bowlby, J. (1980). *The Making and Breaking of Affectional Bonds.* London: Tavistock.

Bowman, E., Blix, S. and Coons, P. (1985). Multiple personality in adolescence: relationship to incestual experiences. *Journal of American Academy of Child Psychiatry,* 24, 109-114.

Boyes, R. (1988). What am I bid for a boy? *The Times,* July 13, 1988.

Braden, J. (1981). Adopting the abused child: love is not enough. *Social casework,* 62, 362-367.

Brinich, M. (1990). Adoption from the inside out: a psychoanalytic perspective. In D. Brodzinsky and M. Schechter (Eds). *The Psychology of Adoption.* (pp 42-61).

Brinich, P. and Brinich, E. (1982). Adoption and adaptation. *Journal of Nervous Mental Diseases,* 170, 489-493.

Brodzinsky, D. (1984). New perspectives on adoption revelation. *Adoption and Fostering,* 8, 27-32

Brodzinsky, D. (1987). Adjustment to adoption: a psychosocial perspective. *Clinical Psychology Review,* 7, 25-47.

Brodzinsky, D. and Brodzinsky, A. (1992). The impact of family structure on the adjustent of adopted children. *Child Welfare,* 71, 69-75.

Brodzinsky, D., Radice, C., Huffman, L. and Merkler, K. (1987). Prevalence of clinically significant symptomatology in a non clinical sample adopted and nonadopted children. *Journal of Clinical Child Psychology,* 16, 350-356.

Brodzinsky, D. (1990). A stress and coping model of adoption adjustment. In D. Brodzinsky and M. Schechter (Eds). *The Psychology of Adoption* (pp 3-24). New York: Oxford University of Press.

Brodzinsky, D. and Schechter, M. (Eds). (1990). *The Psychology of Adoption.* New York: Oxford University Press.

338

Brodzinsky, D., Schechter, D., Braff, M. and Singer, L. (1984). Psychological and academic adjustment in adopted children. *Journal of Consulting and Clinical Psychology*, 133, 1316-1318.

Buchard, T. Lykken, D., McGve, M., Segal, N. and Tellegen, A. (1990). *Science*, 250, 223-250.

Buchignani, N. & Engel, J. (1983). *Cultures in Canada: Strength in Diversity*. Edmonton: Weigl Publishers.

Buck, P. (1964). *Children for Adoption*. New York: Random House.

Butler, V. (1986). Private adoption in British Columbia. *The Social Worker*, 54, 155-159.

Byler, W. (1977). Removing children: the destruction of American Indian families. *Civil Rights Digest*, Summer, 19-27.

Byma, S. (1969). Overseas adoptions threaten development of local services. *Child Welfare*, 50, 7-11.

Cadoret, R. (1990). Biologic perspectives of adoptee adjustment. In D. Brodzinsky and M. Schechter (Eds). *The Psychology of Adoption, (pp 25-41)*. New York: Oxford University Press.

Cadoret, R. and Cain, C. (1980). Sex differences in predictors of antisocial behaviour in Cadoret, R. and Gath, A. (1978). Inheritance of alcoholism in adoptees. *British Journal of Psychiatry*, 132, 252-258.

Cadoret, R., Cunningham, L., Loffus, R. and Edwards, J. (1976). Studies of adoptees from psychiatrically disturbed biological parents: medical symptoms and illnesses in childhood adolescence. *American Journal of Psychiatry*, 133, 1316-1318.

Campagna, D. & Poffenberger, D. (1988). *The Sexual Trafficking in Children*. Dover, Mass.: Auburn House Publishing.

Campbell, L. (1979). The birthparent's right to know. *Public Welfare*, 137, 22-27.

Cantwell, N. (1992). Abuse of the intercountry adoption process. Paper given to International Conference on Adoption, Manila, April 5, 1992.

Caplan, N., Whitmore, J. and Choy, M. (1989). *The Boat People and Achievement in America: A Study of Family Life, Hard Work, and Cultural Values*. Ann Arbor: University of Michigan Press.

Cardon, L., DiLalla, L., Plomin, R., DeFries, J., and Fulker, D. (1990). Genetic correlations between reading performance and IQ in the Colorado Adoption Project. *Intelligence*, 14, 245-257.

Carey, W., Lipton, W. and Myers, R. (1974). Temperament in adopted and foster babies *Child Welfare*, 53, 352-258.

Cederblad, M. (1982). *Children Adopted from Abroad and Coming to Sweden After Age Tree*. Stockholm: Swedish National Board for

Intercountry Adoption.

Chan, W. (1991). Parenting stress and support for mothers of mentally handicapped children in GuangZhou. M.Soc.Sc. dissertation, University of Hong Kong.

Chaponniere, C. (1983). A question of interests: inter-country adoption. *International Children's Rights Monitor*, 1, 2-5.

Chess, S. and Thomas, A. (1986). *Temperament in Clinical Practice.* New York: Guilford Press.

Chestang, L. (1972). The dilemma of biracial adoption. *Social Work,* 17, 100-115.

Child Welfare League of America (1978). *Standards For Adoption Service.* New York: Child Welfare League of America.

Children's Home Society of California (1977). *The Changing Face of Adoption.* Los Angeles: The Society.

Chun, B. (1989). Adoption and Korea. *Child Welfare*, 68, 255-260.

Churchill, S. (1979). *No Child Is Unadoptable.* London: Sage Publications.

CJPH (1982). Editorial: Health of Native Canadians - its relevance to world health. *Canadian Journal of Public Health,* 73, 297-298.

Clark, K. and Clark, M. (1930). Emotional factors in racial identification and preferences in Negro education. *Journal of Negro Education,* 11, 341-350.

Clark, V. (1991). How can you sell your kids for $500? *The Observer* (London), January 27, 1991.

Clarke, A. and Clarke, A. (1976). *Early Deprivation: Myth and Evidence.* London: Open Books.

Cloninger, C., Sigvardsson, S., Bohman, M., Von Knorring, A. (1982). Predisposition to petty criminality in Swedish adoptees. *Archives of General Psychiatry,* 39, 1242-47.

Cohen, J. (1981). *Adoption Breakdown With Older Children.* University of Toronto: Monograph Series of the Faculty of Social Work.

Coleman, J. (1974). *Relationships in Adolescence.* London: Routledge and Kegan Paul.

Coopersmith, S. (1981). *The Antecedents of Self-Esteem.* Palo Alto, CA: Consulting Psychologists Press.

Cordell, A., Nathan, C. and Krymow, V. (1985). Group counselling for children adopted at older ages. *Child Welfare,* 64, 113-124.

Costin, L. and Wattenberg, S. (1979). Identity in transracial adoption: a study of parental dilemmas and experiences, in G. Verma (Ed.), *Race, Education and Identity.* London: MacMillan.

Coyne, A. and Brown, M. (1985). Developmentally disabled children can be adopted. *Child Welfare,* 64, 607-615.

Coyne, A. and Brown, M. (1986). Agency practices in successful adoption of developmentally disabled children. *Child Welfare,* 65, 45-51.

Crellin, E., Kellmer Pringle, M. and West, P. (1971). *Born Illegitimate.* Windsor: National Educational Research Foundation.

Cull, J. and Giill, W. (1982). *Manual for the Suicide Probability Scale.* Los Angeles: Western Psychological Services.

Culley, J. (1970). A study of the self-concept, self-acceptance, and ideal self of adopted and nonadopted adolescent children. *Dissertation Abstracts.* Series A, 5658-5059 (Unv. of South Dakota, 1970).

Cullom-Long, M. (1984). Address to Yesterday's Children, Association of Adult Adoptees. Seattle, May 1984.

Cunningham, L., Cadoret, R., Loftus, R. and Edwards, J. (1975). Studies of adoptees from psychiatrically disturbed biological parents: Psychiatric conditions in childhood and adolescence. *British Journal of Psychiatry,* 126, 533-549.

Curtis, P. (1986). The dialectics of open versus closed adoption of infants. *Child Welfare,* 65, 437-445.

Dalen, M. and Saetersdal, B. (1987). Transracial adoption in Norway. *Adoption and Fostering,* 11, 41-46.

Daniel, D., Plomin, R. and Greenhalgh, J. (1984). Correlates of difficult temperament in infancy. *Child Development,* 55, 1184-1194.

Davey, A. (1982). Ethnic identification, preference and sociometric choice. In G. Verma & C. Bagley (Eds). *Self-Concept, Achievement and Multicultural Education.* London: MacMillan.

Davie, R., Butler, N. and Goldstein, H. (1972). *From Birth to Seven.* London: Longman.

Davis, L. (1987). *The Philippines: People, Poverty and Politics.* London: MacMillan

Day, C. (1979). Access to birth records: General register office study. *Adoption and Fostering,* 98, 17-28.

Day, D. (1979). *The Adoption of Black Children: Counteracting Institutional Discrimination.* Lexington: Lexington Books.

DCI (1986). Statement on International Adoption by Defence for Children International. *International Children's Rights Monitor,* Vol 3, Part 2.

De Fries, J., Plomin, R., Vandenberg, S. and Kuse, A. (1981). Parent-off spring resemblance for cognitive abilities in the Colorado adoption project: Biological, adoptive, and control parents and one-year-old children. *Intelligence,* 5, 245-277.

De Hartog, J. (1969). *The Children.* London: Atheneum Press.

De Leon, J. (1980). *The Challenge of Adopting Older Children.* New Jersey: Spaulding For Children.

Delupis, I. (1976). *International Adoptions and the Conflicts of Laws.* Stockholm: Almquist and Wiksell.

Department of Health (1992). *Inter-Departmental Review of Adoption Law.* London: Department of Health.

Depp, C. (1982). After reunion: perceptions of adult adoptees, adoptive parents, and birth parents. *Child Welfare,* 1982, 61, 115-119.

Derdeyn, A. (1990). Foster parent adoption: the legal framework. In D. Brodzinsky and M. Schechter (Eds.) *The Psychology of Adoption.* (pp 332-348). New York: Oxford University Press.

DoH, (1990). *Discussion Paper No.1: The Nature and Effect of Adoption and Two Background Papers on International Perspectives and Research Relating to Adoption.* London: Department of Health.

Drotar, D. and Stege, E. (1988). Psychological testimony in foster parent adoption. *Journal of Clinical Child Psychology,* 17, 164-168.

Dukette, R. (1984). Value issues in present-day adoption. *Child Welfare,* 63, 233-243.

Edgar, M. (1981). Presentation to the First National Child Care Conference, University of Victoria, May 1981.

Eichler, M. (1983). *Families in Canada Today.* Toronto: Gage Publishing Limited.

Eldred, C., Rosenthal, D., Wonder, P., Kety, S., Schulsinger, F., Welner, J. and Jacobsen, B. (1976). Some aspects of adoption in selected samples of adult adoptees. *American Journal of Orthopsychiatry,* 46, 279-290.

Ellestad-Sayed, J., Haworth, J., Coodin, F. & Diling, L. (1981). Growth and nutrition of preschool Indian children in Manitoba. *Canadian Journal of Public Health,* 72, 127-133.

Engleman, L. (Ed). (1983). *BMDP Statistical Software.* Berkeley: University of California Press.

Ensminger, R. (1984). Adoption reunions - an emotional triangle. *The Social Worker,* 52, 69-73.

Erikson, E. (1968). *Identity, Youth and Crisis.* New York: Norton.

Essen, J. and Wedge, P. (1982). *Continuities in Childhood Disadvantage.* London: Heinemann.

Evers, D. & Rana, C. (1983). Morbidity in Canadian Indian and non-Indian children in the second year, *Canadian Journal of Public Health,* 74, 191-194.

Fanshel, D. (1972). *Far From the Reservation: The Transracial Adoption of American Indian Children.* Metuchen, New Jersey: Scarecrow Press.

Feigelman, W. and Silverman, A. (1983). *Chosen Children: New Patterns of Adoptive Relationships.* New York: Praeger.

342

Feigelman, W. and Silverman, A. (1984). The long-term effects of transracial adoption. *Social Service Review,* December, 588-602.

Feigelman, W. and Silverman, A. (1986). Adoptive parents, adoptees, and the sealed records controversy. *Social Casework,* April, 219-226.

Ferri, E. (1976). *Growing Up in a One-Parent Family.* Windsor, U.K.: National Foundation for Educational Research.

Festinger, T. (1986). *Necessary Risk: A Study of Disrupted Adoptive Placement.* Washington, D.C.: Child Welfare League of America.

Fieweger, M. (1991). Stolen children and international adoptions. *Child Welfare,* 70, 285-191.

Finkelhor, D. (1984). *Child Sexual Abuse.* New York: Collier MacMillan.

Fisher, F. (1973). *The Search for Anna Fisher.* New York: Arthur Field Books Inc.

Fitzgerald, J. (1979). After disruption. *Adoption and Fostering,* 98, 11-16.

Frances, A. (1982). Child with new parents is amenable at home but has problems at school. *Hospital and Community Psychiatry,* 33, 263-264.

Fransella, F. & Bannister, D. (1977). *A Manual for Repertory Grid Technique.* New York: Academic Press.

Freedman, M. (1970). *Family and Kinship in Chinese Society.* Stanford University Press.

Freeman, M. (1983). *The Rights and Wrongs of Children.* London: Frances Printer.

French, L. (1980). An analysis of government sterilization and adoption practices involving Native Americans. *International Child Welfare Review,* 45, 37-40.

Geissinger, S. (1984). Adoptive parents' attitudes toward open birth records. *Family Relations,* 33, 579-585.

Gibb, F. (1990). Adoption law overhaul may lead to less secrecy. *Times* (London), September 22.

Gill, O. and Jackson, B. (1982). Transracial adoption in Britain. *Adoption and Fostering,* 6, 30-35.

Gill, O. and Jackson, B. (1983). *Adoption and Race.* New York: St Martin's Press.

Globe, (1992). Deal limits adoptions of Romanian children: Canadians must send applications through government authorities. *Globe and Mail* (Toronto), February 8, 1992.

Goldberg, S. (1979). Premature birth: consequences for the parent-infant relationship. *Science,* 67, 214-220.

Goodwin, J., Cauthorne, C. and Rada, R. (1980). Cinderella syndrome:

children who simulate neglect, *American Journal of Psychiatry,* 137, 1223-1225.

Goodwin, D., Schulsinger, F., Knop, J., Mednick, S. and Guze, S. (1977). Alcoholism and depression in adopted-out daughters of alcoholics. *Archives of General Psychiatry,*

Goody, J. (1969). Adoption in cross-cultural perspective. *Comparative Studies in Society and History,* 11, 55-78.

Gorsuch, R. and Cattell, R. (1977). Personality and socio-ethical values: the structure of self and superego. In R. Cattell and R. Dreger (Eds). *Handbook of Modern Personality Theory,* (pp 675-708). New York: Wiley.

Gottesman, I. and Shields, J. (1982). *Schizophrenia: The Epigenetic Puzzle.* London, Cambridge University Press.

Grantham-McGregor, S. and Buchanan, E. (1982). The development of an adopted child recovering from severe malnutrition. *Human Nutrition: Clinical Nutrition.* 36c, 251-256.

Green, H. (1983). Risks and attitudes associated with extra-cultural placement of American Indian children: a critical review. *Journal of the Academy of Child Psychiatry,* 2, 63-67.

Gritter, J. (1989). *Adoption Without Fear.* New York: Bantam Books.

Groth, M., Bonnardel, D., Devis, D., Martin, J. and Vousden, H. (1987). An agency moves toward open adoption of infants. *Child Welfare,* 66, 247-257.

Grow, L. and Shapiro, D. (1974). *Black Children, White Parents.* New York: Child Welfare League of America.

Groze, V. (1991). Adoption and single parents: a review. *Child Welfare,* 70, 321-332.

Haimes, E. and Timms, N. (1984). Counselling and the Children Act 1975. *Adoption and Fostering,* 8, 42-46.

Haimes, E. and Timms, N. (1985). *Adoption, Identity and Social Policy: The Search for Distant Relatives.* Aldershot: Gower.

Hardy, D. (1984). Adoption of children with special needs: a national perspective. *American Psychologist,* 39, 901-904.

Hardy, D. (1984). Adoption of children with special needs. *American Psychologist,* 39, 8, 901-904.

Hartman, A. (1984). *Working With Adoptive Families Beyond Placement.* New York: Child Welfare League of America.

Hauser, S. (1971). *Black and White Identity Formation.* London: Wiley.

Hazel, N. (1986). *Ten Years on: A Pioneer Teenage Fostering Scheme.* Canterbury: Kent Family Placement Service.

Henry, F. and Ginzberg, E. (1975). *Who Gets The Work: A Test of Racial Discrimination in Employment.* Toronto: The Social

Planning Council of Metropolitan Toronto.

Hepworth, P. (1980). *Foster Care and Adoption in Canada.* Ottawa: Canadian Council on Social Development.

Hepworth, H. (1981). *Trends and Comparisons in Canadian Child Welfare Services.* Ottawa: Health and Welfare Policy Development Branch, Government of Canada.

Herbert, M. (1984). Causes and treatment of behaviour problems in adoptive children. In P. Bean (Ed.). *Adoption: Essays in Social Policy, Law and Sociology.* London: Tavistock.

Hiebert, M. (1992). Dynamics of despair: poverty condemns minorities to margins of society - lack of education, poor health plagues minorities. *Far Eastern Economic Review,* April 23, 26-30.

Hill, M. and Triseliotis, J. (1991). Subsidized adoption across the Atlantic. *Child Welfare,* 70, 383-395.

Hockey, A. (1980). Evaluation of adoption of the intellectually handicapped: a retrospective analysis of 137 cases. *Journal of Mental Deficiency Research,* 24, 187-202.

Hodges, J. and Tizard, B. (1989). IQ and behavioural adjustment of ex-institutional children. *Journal of Child Psychology and Psychiatry,* 30, 53 98.

Hoksbergen, R. (1985). Adopting a foreign child: Principles governing the handling of this complex phenomenon in the Netherlands. *International Child Welfare Review,* 64, 34-44.

Hoksbergen, R. (1986). *Adoption: A World Survey.* Berwyn, U.S.: Swets North American.

Hoksbergen, R. (1991). Intercountry adoption coming of age in The Netherlands. In H. Altstein and R. Simon (Eds). *Intercountry Adoption: A Multinational Perspective,* (pp 141-160). New York: Praeger.

Hoksbergen, R., Joffer, F. and Waardenburg, B. (1977). *Adopted Children at Home and at School.* Lisse: Swets and Zertlinger.

Holman, R. (1973). *Trading in Children.* London: Routledge and Kegan Paul.

Holman, R. (1975). Unmarried mothers, social deprivation and child separation. *Policy and Politics,* 3, 25-41.

Holmes, D. (1979). Adopting older children. *Children Today,* 8, 6-9.

Hoopes, J. (1990). Adoption and identity formation. In D. Brodzinsky and M. Schechter (Eds). *The Psychology of Adoption* (pp 144-166). New York: Oxford University Press.

Hoopes, J. and Sherman, E. (1969). Adjustment profiles of adopted and non-adopted children. Paper given to Annual Meeting of the American Psychiatric Association, Boston (Abstracted in

International Medical Tribune, March 13, 1969, p.4).

Horn, J. (1983). The Texas adoption project: adopted children and their intellectual resemblance to biological and adoptive parents. *Child Development,* 54, 268-275.

Hornby, H. (1986). Why adoptions disrupt and what agencies can do to prevent it. *Children Today,* 15, 7-11.

Hostelter, M., Iverson, S., Dole, K. and Johnson, D. (1989). Unsuspected infectious diseases and other medical diagnoses in the evaluation of internationally adopted children. *Pediatrics,* 83, 559-565.

Howard, A., Royse, D. and Sherl, J. (1977). Transracial adoption: the black community perspective. *Social Work,* 2, 177-189.

Howe, D. (1987). Adopted children in care. *British Journal of Social Work,* 17, 493-505.

Humphrey, M. (1967). *Hostage Seekers: A Study of Childless and Adopting Couples.* London: Longman.

Humphrey, M. and Ounsted, C. (1964). Adoptive families referred for psychiatric advice. *British Journal of Psychiatry,* 110, 549-555.

Humphrey, H. and Humphrey, M. (1989). Damaged identity and the search for kinship in adult adoptees. *British Journal of Medical Psychology,* 62, 301-309.

ICWR (1977). Vietnam orphans. *International Child Welfare Review,* 32, 13.

ICWR (1984). Bolivia: trading in children. *International Child Welfare Review,* 61, 3.

Ingham, J., Kreitman, N., Miller, P., Sashidharan, S. and Surtees, P. (1986). Self-esteem, vulnerability and psychiatric disorder in the community. *British Journal of Psychiatry,* 148, 375-385.

Ismael, S. (1977). The future of the child in the Muslim world. *International Child Welfare Review,* 34, 25-33.

Jackson, B. (1979). Inter-racial adoption, in S. Wolkind, (Ed.). *Medical Aspects of Adoption and Foster Care.* Heinemann.

Jackson, L. (1968). Unsuccessful adoptions: a study of 40 cases who attended a child guidance clinic. *British Journal of Medical Psychology,* 41, 389-398.

Jaffe, E. (1991). Foreign adoptions in Israel: private paths to parenthood. In H. Altstein and R. Simon (Eds). *Intercountry Adoption: A Multinational Perspective* (pp 161-182). New York: Praeger.

Jaffee, B. and Fanshel, D. (1970). *How they Fared in Adoption.* New York: Columbia University Press.

Jervis, M. (1990). Trans-racial adoption. *Social work Today,* February 8, 16-17.

Johansen, M. (1992). Innu want help to find their adopted children. *Evening Telegram* (St. John's Newfoundland). March 29, 3.

Johansson, S., Nygren, O. and Xuan, Z. (1991). *On Intriguing Sex Ratios Among Live Births in China in the 1980s.* Stockholm: Central Bureau of Statistics.

Johnson, B. (1981). The Indian Child Welfare Act of 1978: implications for practice. *Child Welfare,* 60.

Johnson, P., Shireman, J. and Watson, K. (1987). Transracial adoption and the development of black identity at age eight. *Child Welfare,* 66, 45-55.

Johnston, P. (1983). *Native Children and the Child Welfare System.* Toronto: James Lorimer and Company.

Jones, B. (1974). Adoption in Kenya. *New Society,* November 21, 483-484.

Kadushin, A. (1984). Principle values and assumptions underlying adoption practice, in P. Sachev (Ed.) *Adoption: Current Issues and Trends.* Toronto: Butterworths.

Kadushin, A. (1970). *Adopting Older Children.* New York: Columbia University Press.

Kagan, R. and Reid, W. Critical factors in the adoption of emotionally disturbed youths, *Child Welfare,* 65, 63-73.

Karchmer, C. (1984). Young arsonists. *Social Science and Public Policy,* 22, 78-85.

Katz, L. (1980). Adoption counselling as a preventive mental health speciality. *Child Welfare,* 6, 22-36.

Katz, L. (1986). Parental stress and factors for success in older-child adoption. *Child Welfare,* 65, 569-578.

Kelly, G. (1955). *The Psychology of Personal Constructs.* New York: Morton.

Kendler, K., Gruenberg, A. and Strauss, J. (1982). An independent analysis of the Copenhagen sample of the Danish adoption study of schizophrenia. *Archives of General Psychiatry,* 39, 639-642.

Khan, M. (1991). The foster care system in India. *Child Welfare,* 70, 243-259.

Kim, D. (1977). How they fare in American homes: a follow-up study of adopted Korean children. *Children Today.* 6,22-36.

Kim, D. (1978). Issues in transracial and transcultural adoption. *Social Casework,* October, 477-486.

Kim, S., Hong, S. and Kim, B. (1979). Adoption of Korean children by New York area couples: a preliminary study. *Child Welfare,* 58, 419-427.

Kimbell, K. (1990). Adopting a more honest approach to adoption.

Globe and Mail (Toronto), July, 4, A18.

Kimmelman, J. (1983). *Interim Report of Review Committee on Indian and Metis Adoptions and Placements.* Winnipeg: Government of Manitoba.

Kimmelman, J. (1984). *Report on the Adoption of Native children.* Winnipeg: Government of Manitoba.

Kirk, D. (1964). *Shared Fate: A Theory of Adoption and Mental Health.* London: Collier-MacMillan.

Kirk, D. (1981). *Adoptive Kinship: A Modern Institution in Need of Reform.* Toronto: Butterworths.

Kirk, D. and McDaniel, S. (1984). Adoption policy in Great Britain and North America. *Journal of Social Policy,* 13, 1, 75-84.

Kirmain, L. (1983). Adoption: a public health perspective. *American Journal of Public Health,* 73, 1158-1160.

Kraus, J. (1978). Family structure as a factor in the adjustment of adopted children. *British Journal of Social Work,* 8, 327-337.

Kuehl, W. (1985). *When Adopted Children of Foreign Origin Grow Up.* Osnabrueck: Terre des Hommes.

Kufeldt, K. (1981). *Temporary Foster Care.* Ph.D. Thesis, University of Calgary.

Labovitz, S. (1967). Some observations on measurement and statistics. *Social Forces,* 46, 151-60.

LaBuda, M., DeFries, J., Plomin, R. and Fulker, D. (1986). Longitudinal stability of cognitive ability from infancy to early childhood: genetic and environmental etiologies. *Child Development,* 57, 1142-1150.

Ladner, J. (1977). *Mixed Families: Adopting Across Racial Boundaries.* London: Doubleday.

Lambert, L. and Streather, J. (1980). *Children in Changing Families.* London: MacMillan.

Lampo, A., Proost, G. and Marneffe, C. (1988). Foreign adopted children - children at risk? Paper given to *8th International Congress of Child Abuse and Neglect,* Rio de Janero, September, 1988.

Larned, R. (1960). *International Social Service: A History, 1921-1955.* Geneva: International Social Service.

Laurance, J. (1922). Law to be tightened on foreign adoption. *The Times,* January 8, 1992, p.3.

Lee, R. and Hull, R. (1986). Legal, casework, and ethical issues in "risk adoption". *Child Welfare,* 62, 450-454.

Leitch, D. (1986). *Family Secrets.* London: Heinemann.

LePere, D., Davis, L., Couve, J. and Mcdonald, M. (1986). *Large Sibling Groups: Adoption Experiences.* Washington, DC: Child Welfare

League of America.

Lewin. T. (1990). South Korea slows export of babies for adoption. *New York Times,* February 19, 1990.

Lewis, D. Lovely, R., Yeager, C., Ferguson, G., Friedman, H., Sloane, G., Friedman, H., and Pincus, J. (1988). Intrinsic and environmental characteristics of juvenile murderers. *Journal of the American Academy of Child and Adolescent Psychiatry,* 27, 582-587.

Lifton, B. (1986). *Lost and Found: The Adoption Experience.* New York: Dial Press.

Lindholm, B. and Tavliatos, J. (1980). Psychological adjustment of adopted and non adopted children. *Psychological Reports,* 46, 307-310.

Lindsay, J. (1987). *Open Adoption: A Caring Option.* Bvena Park, CA: Morning Glory Press.

Lipman, M. (1984). Adoption in Canada: two decades in review, in P. Sachdev (Ed.). *Adoption: Current Issues and Trends.* P. Sachdev (Ed.), Toronto: Butterworth.

Locurto, C. (1990). The malleability of IQ as judged from adoption studies. *Intelligence,* 14, 275-292.

Lowing, P., Mirsky, A. and Pereira, R. (1983). The inheritance of schizophrenia spectrum disorder: a reanalysis of the Danish adopted study data. *American Journal of Psychiatry,* 140, 1167-1171.

Luecker-Babel, M. (1986). International adoption - agreement at last? *International Children's Rights Monitor,* 3, 7-13.

MacDonald, R. (1978). *Canada III: The Uncharted Nations: A Reference History of the Canadian Tribes.* Vancouver: The Evergreen Press.

Maluccio, A. and Fein, E. (1983). Permanency planning: a redefinition. *Child Welfare,* 53, 195-201.

Mandell, B. (1973). *Where Are The Children?* Toronto: Lexington Books.

Marcus, C. (1979). *Adopted: A Canadian Guide for Adopted Adults in Search of Their Origins.* Toronto: International Self-Counsel Press.

Marcus, C. (1981). *Who is My Mother?* Toronto: MacMillan.

Martin, H. and Beezley, P. (1977). Behavioural observations of abused children. *Developmental Medicine and Child Neurology,* 19, 372-387.

Maslow, A. (1954). *Motivation and Personality.* New York: Harper and Row.

Maughan, B. and Pickles, A. (1990). Adopted and illegitimale children growing up. In L. Robins and M. Rutter (Eds.) *Straight and*

Devious Pathways From Childhood to Adulthood, (pp 36-61) Cambridge: Cambridge University Press.

Maurer, R., Cadoret, R. and Cain, C. (1980). Cluster analysis of childhood temperament data on adoptees. *American Journal of Orthopsychiatry,* 50, 522-534.

Mayer-Gross, A., Slater, E. and Roth, M. (1971). *Clinical Psychiatry.* London: Cassell.

McDowell, B. (1985). The matching process. Address to Calgary Chapter of the Alberta Adoptive Parents Association, Calgary, January 30, 1985.

McEwan, M. (1973). Readoption with a minimum of pain. *Social Casework,* 54, 350-353.

McRoy, R., Grotevant, H. and Zurcher, L. (1988). *Emotional Disturbance in Adopted Adolescents.* New York: Praeger.

McRoy, R. and Zurcher, L. (1983). *Transracial and Inracial Adoptees: The Adolescent Years.* Springfield: Charles C. Thomas.

McWhinnie, A. (1967). *Adopted Children - How They Grow Up.* London: Routledge.

Mednick, S., Gabrielli, W. and Hutchings, B. (1984). Inheritance of crime in adoptees. *Science,* 224, 4561.

Melone, T. (1976). Adoption and crisis in the Third World: thoughts on the future. *International Child Welfare Review,* 28, 21-25.

Melville, J. (1983). Looking for mother. *New Society,* December 8, 391-393.

Menlove, F. (1965). Aggressive symptoms in emotionally disturbed adopted children. *Child Development,* 36, 519-532.

Mica, M. and Vosler, N. (1990). Foster-adoptive programs in public social service agencies: toward flexible family resources. *Child Welfare,* 69, 433-470.

Milner, D. (1973), Racial identification and preference in black British children. *European Journal of Social Psychology,* 3, 281-195.

Milner, D. (1983). *Children and Race: Ten Years on.* London: Penguin Books

Mitchell, A. (1991). Adoption slipping through the cracks. *Globe and Mail* (Toronto), March 8, 1991.

Montagu, A. (1977). On the non-perception of 'race' differences. *Current Anthropology,* 18, 743-744.

Moreno, J. (1953). *Who Shall Survive? Foundation of Sociometry, Group Psychotherapy and Sociodrama.* New York: Beacon House.

Morin, R. (1977). Black child, white parents: a beginning biography. *Child Welfare,* 56, 576-583.

Morrison, R. & Wilson, C. (1986). *Native Peoples: The Canadian Experience*. Toronto: McClelland and Stewart.

Morrow, W. (1984). Custom adoption law. In P. Sachdev (Ed.). *Adoption: Current Issues and Trends*. Toronto: Butterworth.

Morse, B. (1984). Native Indian and Metis children in Canada: victims of the child welfare system. In G. Verma & C. Bagley (Eds), *Race Relations and Cultural Differences*. London: Croon-Helm.

Mullender, A. (1988). Groupwork as the method of choice with black childern in white foster homes. *Groupwork*, 2, 158-172.

Munsinger, H. (1975). The adopted child's I.Q.: a critical review. *Psychological Bulletin*, 85, 623-659.

Mydans, S. (1991).Children rejected in Vietnam find a sad sanctuary in U.S.A. *New York Times*, May 28, 1991 A1 and A9.

Nelson, K. (1985). *On the Frontier of Adoption: A Study of Special-Needs Adoptive Families*. Washington, DC: Child Welfare League of America.

Ngabonziza, D. (1988). Inter-country Adoption: in whose best interest? *Adoption and Fostering*, 12, 35-40.

Nie, N., Hull, C., Jenkins, J., Steinbrenner, K. and Bent, D. (1975). *Statistical Package for the Social Sciences*. London: McGraw Hill.

NORCAP (1987). Access to birth records in Scotland. *Adoption and Fostering*, 11, 55.

Norvell, M. and Guy, R. (1977). A comparison of self-concept in adopted and nonadopted adolescents. *Adolescence*, 12, 443-448.

Nunnally, J. (1967). *Psychometric Theory*. New York: McGraw Hill.

Nuttall, R. (1982). The development of Indian Boards of Health in Alberta. *Canadian Journal of Public Health*, 73, 300-303.

NYT (1990). Romania is prohibiting adoption by foreigners. *New York Times*, February 9, 1990.

Offer, D., Ostrov, E., Howard, K. (1981). *The Adolescent: A Psychological Self-Portrait*. New York: Basic Books.

Offer, D., Ostrov, E., Howard, K. and Atkinson, R. (1988). *The Teenage World: Adolescents' Self-Image in Ten Countries*. New York: Plenum.

Oliver, J. (1985). Successive generations of child maltreatment: social and medical disorders in parents. *British Journal of Psychiatry*, 147, 484-490.

O'Shaughnessy, H. (1981). Bid to halt trade in snatched babies. *The Observer*, August 2, 1981.

Ounsted, C. (1970). The dark side of adoption. *Child Adoption*, 63, 23-36.

Palmer, A., Harper, G. and Rivinus, T. (1983). The 'adoption process' in the inpatient treatment of children and adolescents. *Journal of the American Academy of Child Psychiatry,* 22, 286-293.

Pannor, R. and Baran, A. (1984). Open adoption as standard practice. *Child Welfare,* 63, 245-250.

Pannor, R. and Nerlove, E. (1977). Fostering understanding between adolescents and adoptive parents through group experiences. *Child Welfare,* 56, 537-545.

Parker, G. (1982). Parental representations and affective symptoms: examination for an hereditary link. *British Journal of Medical Psychology,* 55, 57-61.

Pavoa, J. (1982). Identity and adoption. Department of Counselling, University of Harvard, unpublished paper.

Pilger, J. (1978). Do you remember Vietnam? Independent Television, London, documentary transmitted October 3, 1978.

Pilotti, F. (1985). Intercountry adoption: a review from Latin American. *Child Welfare,* 64, 25-34.

Powers, D. (Ed.) (1983). *Adoption for Troubled Children: Prevention and Repair of Adoptive Failures Through Residential Treatment.* New York: The Haworth Press.

Powers, D. (1984). The hurried adoption of older children: lessons from the American experience. *Association For Child Psychology and Psychiatry Newsletter,* 6, 11-18.

Pruzan, (1977). *Foreign Children Adopted in Denmark.* Copenhagen: Socialforsknings Instituttet, Monograph No. 77.

Ramsay, R. & Bagley, C. (1986). The prevalence of suicidal behaviors, attitudes and associated social experiences in an urban population. *Suicide and Life-Threatening Behavior,* 15, 151-160.

Ray, A. (1990). Possible biologic determinants of suicide. In D. Lester (Ed.) *Current Concepts of Suicide.* Philadelphia: The Charles Press.

Raynor, L. (1977). Twenty-one plus and adopted. *Adoption and Fostering,* 87, 38-46.

Redmond, W. and Sleightohlm, S. (1982). *Once Removed: Voices From Inside the Adoption Triangle.* Toronto: McGraw-Hill Ryerson.

Reid, W., Kagan, R., Kaminsky, A. and Helmer, K. (1987). Adoption of older institutionalized youth. *Social Casework,* 68, 140-149.

Rex, J. (1972). *Race Relations and Sociological Theory.* London: Heinemann.

Rice, T., Fulker, D. and DeFries, J. (1986). Multivariate path analysis of specific cognitive abilities in the Colorado Adoption Project. *Behavior Genetics,* 16, 107-114.

Rickford, F. (1990). Out of the background. *Social Work Today,* February 22, 8-9.

Robertson, D. (1974). Parental socialization patterns in interracial adoption, Ph.D. Thesis, University of California, Los Angles.

Rogeness, G. (1988). Psychopathology in hospitalized, adopted children. *Journal of the American Academy of Child Psychiatry.*

Rorbech, M. (1990). *Denmark, My Country: Conditions of 18-25 Year Old Foreign Born Adoptees in Denmark.* Copenhagen: Danish National Institute of Social Research, Monograph No. 30.

Rorbech, M. (1991). The conditions of 18 to 25-year-old foreign-born adoptees in Denmark. In H. Altstein and R. Simon (Eds). *Interrcountry Adoption: A Multinational Perspective.* (pp127-139). New York: Praeger.

Rosenberg, E. and Horner, T. (1991). Birthparent romances and identity formation in adopted children. *American Journal of Orthopsychiatry,* 61, 70-77.

Rosenberg, E. and Kaplan, H. (1982). *Social Psychology of the Self-Concept.* Arlington Heights: Harlan Davidson.

Rosenthal, J., Groze, V. and Aguilar, G. (1991). Adoption outcomes for children with handicaps. *Child Welfare,* 70, 623-630.

Rosenthal, P. (1982). Triple jeopardy: family stress and subsequent divorce following the adoption of racially and ethnically mixed children. *Journal of Divorce,* 4, 43-55.

Rowe, J. (1971). Reality in adoption, *In* Social Work in Adoption. London: Longman.

RSC (1976). *Report of the Joint Committee on the Adoption of Children Bill.* New Delhi: Rajya Sabha Secretariat.

Rush, F. (1980). *The Best Kept Secret: Sexual Abuse of Children.* New York: McGraw Hill.

Russell, D. (1984). *Sexual Exploitation.* Beverley Hill: Sage Publications.

Rutter, M. (1980). *Changing Youth in a Changing Society.* Cambridge: Harvard University Press.

Sachdev, P. (1984). *Adoption: Current Issues and Trends.* Toronto: Butterworths.

Sachdev, P. (1984). Unlocking the Adoption Files: A social and legal dilemma, in *Adoption: Current Issues and Trends.* P. Sachdev (Ed.), Toronto: Butterworths.

Sachdev, P. (1990). *Unlocking the Adoption Files,* Toronto: Lexington Books.

Sachdev, P. (1991). Achieving openness in adoption: some critical issues in policy formulation. *American Journal of Orthopsychiatry,* 61, 241-249.

Sack, W. and Dale, D. (1982). Abuse and deprivation in failing adoptions. *Child Abuse and Neglect,* 6, 443-451.

Saetersdal, B. and Dalen, M. (1991). Norway: inter-country adoption in a homogenous country. In H. Alstein and R. Simon (Eds). *Intercountry Adoptions: A Multinational Perspective* (pp 83-108). New York: Praeger.

Sager, C., Brown, H., Crohn, H., Engel, T., Rodstein, E. and Walker, L. (1983). *Treating the Remarried Family.* New York: Brunner/Mazel.

Sandmaier, M. (1986). *When Love is Not Enough: How Mental Health Professionals Can Help Special-Needs Adoptive Families.* Washington, D.C.: Child Welfare League of America.

Sandven, K. and Resnick, M. (1990). Informal adoption among black adolescent mothers. *American Journal of Orthopsychiatry,* 60, 210-215.

Sanford, M. (1974). A socialization in ambiguity: child lending in a British West Indian society. *Ethnology,* 13, 393-400.

Sants, H. (1978). Genealogical bewilderment in children with substitute parents, in *Child Adoption.* London: Association of British Adoption and Fostering Agencies.

Scarr, S. and Weinberg, R. (1976). I.Q. test performance of black children adopted and biological children. *Intelligence,* 1, 170-191.

Schaffer, J. and Lindstrom, C. (1989). *How to Raise an Adopted Child.* New York: Crown Publishers.

Schechter, M. and Bertocci, D. (1990). The meaning of search. In D. Brodzinsky & M. Schechter (Eds). *The Psychology of Adoption* (pp 62-90). New York: Oxford University Press.

Schechter, M., Carlson, P., Simmons, J. and Work, H. (1964). Emotional problems in the adoptee. *Archives of General Psychiatry,* 10, 109-118.

Schireman, J. and Johnson, P. (1986). A longitudinal study of black adoptions: single parent, transracial and traditional. *Social Work, 31, 172-176.*

Schneider, S. and Rimmer, L. (1984). Adoptive parents' hostility toward their adopted children. *Children and Youth Services Review,* 6, 345-352.

Scully, A. (1985). Personal Communication from the Permanent Ward Unit, Edmonton Social Service Region, Alberta

Seglow, J. and Pringle, J. (1972). *Growing Up Adopted.* London: National Foundation for Educational Research.

Serrill, M. (1991). Wrapping the earth in family ties. *Time,* November 4 1991, 38-45.

Shapiro, D. (1984). Fostering and adoption: converging roles for substitute parents. In P. Sachdev (Ed.), *Adoption: Current Issues and Trends.* Toronto:Butterworths.

Shepherd, M., Oppenheim, B. and Mitchell, S. (1973). *Childhood Behaviour and Mental Health.* London: University of London Press.

Shireman, J. and Johnson, P. (1985). Single-parent adoptions: a longitudinal study. *Children and Youth Services Review,* 7, 321-334.

Shostrom, E. (1964). A test for the measurement of self-actualization. *Educational and Psychology Measurement,* 24, 207-218.

Siggner, A. & Locatelli, C. (1980). *An Overview of Demographic, Social and Economic conditions among Manitoba's Registered Indian Population.* Winnipeg: Government of Manitoba, Corporate Policy Research Office.

Silverman, A. and Feigelman, W. (1981). The adjustment of black children adopted by white families. *Social Casework,* 62, 529-536.

Silverman, A. and Feigelman, W. (1990). Adjustment in interracial adoptees: an overview. In D. Brodzinsky and M. Schechter (Eds). *The Psychology of Adoption* (pp 187-200). New York: Oxford University Press.

Simon, R. (1975). An assessment of racial awareness, preference and self identity among white and adopted non-white children. *Social Problems,* 43-57.

Simon, R. and Altstein, H. (1977). *Transracial Adoption.* New York: Wiley.

Simon, R. and Altstein, H. (1981). *Transracial Adoption: A Follow-up.* Lexington: Heath.

Simon, R. and Altstein, H. (1987). *Transracial Adoptees and Their Families: A Study of Identity and Commitment.* New York: Praeger.

Singer, L., Brodzinsky, D. and Ramsay, D. (1985). Mother-infant attachment in adoptive families. *Child Development,* 56, 1453-1551.

Sink, D. (1983). Making the Indian Child Welfare Act work: missing social and governmental linkages. *Phylon,* 51, 360-366.

Skeels, H. (1966). Adult status of children with contrasting early life experiences. *Monographs of the Society for Research in Child Development,* 31, 105.

Skodak, M. and Skeels, H. (1949). A final follow-up study of 100 adopted children. *Journal of Genetic Psychology,* 75, 85-125.

Small, J. (1979). Discrimination against the adoptee. *Public Welfare,* 37, 38-43.

Smith, D. and Sherwen, L. (1988). *Mothers and Their Adopted Children:*

The Bonding Process. New York: Tiresias Press.

Sobol, M. and Cardiff, J. (1983). A sociopsychological investigation of adult adoptees' search for birth parents. *Family Relations,* 32, 477-483.

Sontage, L. (1960). The possible relationship of prenatal environmental to schizophrenia. In D. Jackson (Ed.), *The Etiology of Schizophrenia.* New York: Basic Books.

Sorich, C. and Siebert, R. (1982). Toward hunanizing adoption. *Child Welfare,* 61, 207-216.

Sorosky, A., Baran, A. and Pannor, R. (1975). Identity conflicts in adoptees. *American Journal of Orthopsychiatry,* 45, 18-27.

Sorosky, A., Baran, a. and Pannor, R. (1976). The effects of the sealed record in adoptees. *American Journal of Psychiatry,* 133, 900-903.

Sorosky, A., Baran, A. and Pannor, R. (1984). *The Adoption Triangle.* New York: Doubleday.

Spady, D. (1982). *Between Two Worlds.* Edmonton: The Boreal Institute, Occasional Publication, No.16.

Stein, L. and Hoopes, J. (1985). *Identity Formation in the Adopted Adolescent.* New York: Child Welfare League of America.

Stubbs, P. (1987). Professionalism and the adoption of black children. *British Journal of Social Work,* 17, 473-492.

Talbot, P. (1983). *Tuberculosis on Indian Reserves in Manitoba.* Winnipeg: Federal Health and Welfare, Regional Office, Manitoba.

Tan, A., Kendis, R., Fine, J. and Porac, J. A short measure of Eriksonian Ego Identity. *Journal of Personality Assessment,* 41, 279-284.

Teasdale, T. and Owen, D. (1984). Social class and mobility in male adoptees and non adoptees. *Journal of Biosocial Science,* 16, 521-530.

Teasdale, T. and Owen, D. (1986). The influence of paternal social class on intelligence and educational level in male adoptees and non-adoptees. *British Journal of Educational Psychology,* 36, 3-12.

Ternay, M., Wilborn, B. and Day, H. (1980). Perceived child-parent relationships and child adjustment in families with both adopted and natural children. *Journal of Genetic Psychology,* 146, 261-272.

Tervo, R. (1983). The Native child with cerebral palsy at a children's rehabilitation centre. *Canadian Journal of Public Health,* 74, 242-245.

Textor, M. (1991). International adoption in West Germany: a private affair. In H. Altstein and R. Simon (Eds). *Intercountry Adoption: A Multinational Perspective* (pp 109-126). New York: Praeger.

The Government of Alberta (1984). *The Child Welfare Act of Alberta.*

356

Edmonton: Government of Alberta.

Thomas - Hope, E. (1982). Identity and adaptation of migrants from the English-speaking Caribbean in Britain and North America. In G. Verma and C. Bagley (Eds). *Self-Concept Achievement and Multicultural Education.* London: MacMillan.

Thomas, D., Gecas, V., Weigert, A. and Rooney, E. (1974). *Family Socialization and the Adolescent Determinants of Self-Concept, Conformity and Counter-Culture Values.* Lexington: Lexington Press.

Thomas, S. and Chess, A. (1977). *Temperament and Development.* New York: Brunner-Mazel.

Thomlison, R. (1985). *Report on the Death of a Metis Foster Child.* Edmonton: Alberta Social Services, Government of Alberta.

Thompson, A. (1986). Adam - a severely-deprived Colombian orphan: a case report. *Journal of Child Psychology and Psychiatry*, 27, 689-695.

Tizard, B. (1977). *Adoption: A Second Chance.* London: Open Books.

Tizard, B. (1991). Intercountry adoption: a review of the evidence. *Journal of Child Psychology and Psychiatry,* 32, 743-756.

Tizard, B and Phoenix A. (1987). Black identity and transracial adoption. *New Community,* 15, 427-437.

Tod, R. (Ed.), (1971). *Social Work in Adoption.* London: Longman.

Toynbee, P. (1986). *Lost Children: The Story of Adopted Children Searching for their Mothers.* London: Hutchinson.

Triseliotis, J. (1973). *In Search of Origins: The Experience of Adopted People.* London: Routledge and Kegan Paul.

Triseliotis, J. (1974). Identity and adoption. *Child Adoption.* 78, 27-34.

Triseliotis, J. (1980). *New Developments in Foster Care and Adoption.* London: Routledge and Kegan Pual.

Triseliotis, J. (1985). Adoption with contact, *Adoption and Fostering,* 9, 19-24.

Triseliotis, J. and Russell, J. (1984). *Hard to Place: The Outcome of Adoption and Residential Care.* London: Heinemann.

Tubbs, M. (1986). Real children mean more than academic arguments. *Social Services Insight,* July 12, 2-3.

UN (1984). *Proceedings of the Sixth Committee of the General Assembly:* Geneva: United Nations Document A/C.6/39/SR.62.

Unger, S. (Ed.) (1977). *The Destruction of American Indian Families.* New York: Association on American Indian affairs.

UNICEF (1986). Adoption of babies in Sri Lanka. *Action for Children,* 1, 11.

United Nations. (1960). *Report of Leysin Seminar on Inter-Country*

Adoption. Geneva: United Nations Document UN/TAO/SEM/Rep. 2.

United Nations. (1985). *Draft declaration on social and legal principles relating to the protection and welfare of children, with special reference to foster placement and adoption, nationally and internationally.* New York: United Nations General Assembly Document A/40/998-6 Dec, 1985.

UPI (1990). Midwife held in babies for $40. Jakarta: United Press International New Report.

Valberg, L., Birkelt, N., Hoist, J., Zamenchik, J. & Pelletir, O. (1979). Evaluation of the body iron states of Native Canadians. *Canadian Medical Association Journal,* 120, 285-289.

Van Dusen, K., Mednick, S., Gabrielli, W. and Hutchings, B. (1983). Social class and criminality. *Journal of Criminal Law and Criminology,* 74, 249-252.

Verdier, P. (1988). 'Limited adoption' in France. *Adoption and Fostering,* 12, 41-45.

Verhulst, F., Althous, M. and Verlusi-Bierman, M. (1990). Problem behavior in international adoptees. *Journal of the American Academy of Child and Adolescent Psychiatry,* 29, 94-111.

Verma, G. and Bagley, C. (1984). Multicultural education: problems and issues. In G. Verma and C. Bagley, (Eds). *Race Relations and Cultural Differences* (pp 1-14). London: Croom Helm.

Verma, G., Mallick, K., Neasham, T., Ashworth, B. and Bagley, C. (1988). *Education and Ethnicity.* London: MacMillan.

Von Knorring, A., Bohman, M. and Sigvardsson, S. (1982). Early life experiences and psychiatric disorders: An adoptee study. *Acta Psychiatric Scandinavia,* 65, 283-291.

Von Overbeck, A. (1977). Should the Hague convention an inter-country adoption be ratified? *International Child Welfare Review,* 33, 25-32.

Wallerstein, J. and Kelly, J. (1980). *Surviving the Breakup: How Children and Parents Cope With Divorce.* New York: Basic Books.

Ward, M. (1984). Subsidized adoption: new hope for waiting children. In P. Sachdev (Ed.), *Adoption: Current Issues and Trends.* Toronto: Butterworth.

Ward, M. (1987). Choosing adoptive families for large sibling groups. *Child Welfare,* 66, 259-268.

Ward, M and Lewko, J. (1987). Support sources of adolescents in families adopting older children. *American Journal of Orthopsychiatry,* 57, 610-616.

Weider, H. (1977b). The family romance fantasies of adopted children.

Psychoanalytic Quarterly, 46, 185-200.

Weider, H. (1991). On being told of adoption. Psychoanalytic Quarterly, 46, 1-22.

Weil, R. (1984). International adoptions: the quiet migration. International Migration Review, 18, 276-293.

Weinberg, R. (1983). The Minnesota adoption studies: genetic differences and malleability. Child Development, 54, 260-267.

Weinreich, P. (1979). Cross-ethnic identification and self-rejection in a black adolescent. In G. Verma and C. Bagley, (Eds). Race, Education and Identity. London: MacMillan.

Weinreich, P. (1986). Manual for Identity Exploration Using Personal Constructs. Conventry, UK: ESCR Centre for Research in Ethnic Relations, University of Warwick.

Weise, J. (1988). Transracial Adoption: A Black Perspective. University of East Anglia, Norwich: Social Work Monograph No. 60.

Weiss, A. (1983). Symptomatology of adopted and non-adopted adolescents in a psychiatric hospital. Adolescence, 20, 764-774.

Weitzel, W. (1984). From residential treatment to adoption: a permanency planning service. Child Welfare, 53, 361-365.

Wells, K. and Reshotko, P. (1986). Co-operative adoption: an laternative to independent adoption. Child Welfare, 65, 177-188.

Wender, P., Rosenthal, D., Kety, S., Schulsinger, F., Welner, J. (1974). Crossfostering: A research strategy for clarifying the role of genetic and experiential factors in the etiology of schizophrenia. Archives of General Psychiatry, 30, 121-128.

White, H. (1985). Black Children, White Adopters. Norwich: University of East Anglia Social Work Monograph No. 31.

White, T. (1992). The population factor: China's family planning policy in the 1990s. In W. Joseph (Ed). China Briefing, 1991 (pp 97-118). Boulder, COL: Westview Press.

Williams, J. and Morland, K. (1976). Race, Color and the Young Child. Chapel Hill, NC: University of North Carolina Press.

Winnick, M., Meyer, K. and Harris, R. (1975). Malnutrition and environmental enrichment by early adoption. Science, 190, 1173-1175.

Wishard, L. and Wishard, W. (1979). Adoption: The Grafted Tree. San Franciso: Cragmont Press.

Wolkind, S. (1979). Psychological development of the adopted child. In Medical Aspects of Adoption and Foster Care. S. Wolkind (Ed.), London: Heineman.

Wong, J. (1991). Sino-Canadian baby boom gives infant girls a chance. Globe and Mail (Toronto), March 28, A1 and A8.

Wood, J. (1972). *A Study of the Long-Term Adjustment of Children of Korean Heritage Adopted By American Families.* Eugene, Ore: Holt.

Wooden, K. (1981). *The Children of Jonestown.* New York: McGraw-Hill.

Woolrich, P. (1992). China's unwanted children. *South China Morning Post,* May 17, 1992, A1 and B1.

Yogman, M., Herrera, C. and Bloom, K. (1980). Perinatal characteristics of newborns relinquished at birth. *American Journal of Public Health,* 73, 1194-1196.

York, G. (1989). Carla comes home. *Toronto Globe and Mail,* November, 11, 1.

Young, T. (1983). The Canadian North and the Third World: is the analogy appropriate? *Canadian Journal of Public Health,* 74, 239-241.

Young, L. & Bagley, C. (1982). Self-esteem, self-concept and the development of black identity: A theoretical overview. In G. Verma & C. Bagley (Eds.), *Self-Concept, Achievement and Multicultural Education* (pp 41-59). London: MacMillan.

Subject index

Aboriginal peoples of North
America 84, 86, 88,
123-134, 172, 204,
214-238, 326
Abortion policy 39-40, 172, 182,
188-194
Abuse, emotional 7, 57-60
Abuse, physical 7, 59-62,
125-134, 218, 242,
244,272, 275, 277, 294,
303-325, 328
Abuse, sexual 7, 59-62, 171,
222, 239, 272, 275, 277,
285, 289, 294, 303-315
Acceptance of difference 8-30,
35, 42-44, 55-60,
(Kirk model) 82, 84, 134,
197-198,
See also Role handicap
200-201, 323, 328-9
Addiction and alcohol problems

279, 286-287, 305-315
Adolescent adoptees 21-37, 52,
62, 76, 78-83, 198-201,
204, 220-238, 246-255,
303-325
Adoption as a social institution
1-14, 33, 37, 68-70, 96,
117, 326
Afro-Caribbeans 40-249, 256-262
Africa, adoptions from 151-152,
158, 161-163
Age at adoption 21-24, 28, 50-52,
59, 63-64, 77-82, 241-235,
268-269, 270, 288-289, 296,
303-325
Aggression to adoptive parents
273, 285, 291, 293 303-325
Aggressive behaviour disorders
18-35, 48-70, 233, 264-265,
272-3, 275-8, 281-3,
303-325

Anxiety, and adoption 14-15, 19-33, 36, 49,
See also Fertility problems 67-68, 77, 94, 114-120, 202, 331
Asia, adoptions from 135-194
Attitudes to adoption 83, 124-134, 192, 256-262, 327
Australia, adoptions in 152, 156

Biological factors in adjustment of adoptees 19-27, 38-47
Birth mother/birth parents 2-3, 18-23, 39, 44, 57,
See also Single parents 60-61, 90-93, 122, 179,
See also Step-parents 309, 319, 328
Black community 73-75, 256-262, 327
Black identity 27-29, 73-81, 242-4, 256-262
Bonding in adoption 7-8, 49-66, 113, 210, 274-275, 294-296, 303, 330
Boys, preference for 188-195

Canada, adoptions in 2, 84-86, 88, 115, 121, 152, 172-173, 189, 193, 214-238, 241-2, 247, 249, 264, 268, 304-5, 326-329
Central nervous system problems 23-26, 39-40, 47-48, 52, 87, 123-134, 242, 272, 275, 281, 284, 287, 290, 294, 297, 306-325, 329
China, adoptions from 84, 151, 173, 187-190,
See also Hong Kong 194, 329
Child psychiatric clinics 48-70
Children first, principle in adoption work 138-140, 169-180
See also Leysin Principles
Clinical studies of adoptees 38, 48-70, 303-325
Cluster analysis 316-325
Colombia, adoptions from 87
Control groups, in adoption research 15-37, 50-51, 90-113, 273-274
Criminal behaviour, 19, 33, 44-47, 272, 275,
in adoptees 287-291, 303-325
Custom adoptions 135-141, 214-238, 326

Dating and marriage in adoptees 68-69, 201-203, 234-238
Death of adoptive parent 20, 55, 103, 113, 277, 319
Delinquency, see Criminal Behaviour
Denmark, adoptions in 22-23, 42-45, 42-46, 88, 171, 178
Depression in adoptees 21-22, 34, 45-46, 114-120, 281, 287, 290, 318-325
Depression in adopters 49
Disruption of adoption 59-63, 94-95, 304-325

Ego-Strength 32, 55-56, 196-197, 201,

See also Erikson's model
244

Encopresis in adoptees 306-315

Enuresis in adoptees 306-315

Environmental effects in adoptees' adjustment 15-47, 90-113

Epilepsy in adoptees 106, 308

Erikson's identity model 32, 56-57, 196-197

Ethnic identity of adoptees 71-89, 195-206, 211-212, See also Black identity 237-239, 251-252

Exclusive versus inclusive model of adoption 1-10 (See also Role handicap)

Extended families, role of 58, 78, 89, 140-141, 201, 217, 220-223, 227, 230 236, 304-306

Family interaction and family problems 3-4, 49-54, 78, 302, 304, 316

Family romance fantasies of adoptees 56-58, 60-61

Family structure and adoption 271, 275-6

Fetal alcohol syndrome 121-134

Firesetting by adoptees 51, 273, 276, 279, 282, 286, 290, 294, 304-315

Follow-up studies of adoption 14-37, 39-46, 50, 76-78, 90-113, 316-325, 328, 330-331

Foster care and adoption 9-13, 18, 22,26, 47, 63-64, 92, 126-134, 219-221, 234, 244, 257, 266, 269, 273,

313-315

France, adoptions in 67, 177

Genetic factors in adjustment 19-20, 27, 38-47, 95, 114, 308-309, 329

Germany, adoptions in 88, 159-163, 171

Girls, abandonment of 10-14, 187-194
See also Boys, preference for

Goodness of fit model 43-44, 300, 331
See also Temperament

Greece, adoptions from 150

Guardianship and adoption 8-9, 171-186

Handicapped children and adoption 90-91, 121-134, 178, 209-210, 245

Height of adoptees 29, 39, 93

Health problems of adoptees 82-83, 97-102, 180-187, See also Medical problems 191-193, 220, 275, 287, 297, 303-325, 314-315

Home studies for adopters 113, 141-142

Hong Kong 135, 151-154, 165, 187-190, 195-206

Hyperactivity in adoptees 44, 52, 281-287, 296, 302-325

Identity of adoptees 28-32,53-58, 65-70, 135,
See also Black identity

211, 224-234, 294, 300

See also Self-concept

Illegitimacy and adoption 1-13, 24-25, 39, 91-113

See also Single parents

"In care" children 15, 90-113, 214-238, 247

See also Foster care 303-325, 327

See also Residential care

India, adoptions in and from 137, 158, 163-1644, 179-186, 193, 329

Intelligence level of adoptees 27, 41-43, 61, 83, 82-83, 126, 289, 291

See also School achievement

Infertility and adoption 3-5, 69, 244, 300

Intercountry adoption 71-89, 135-206, 234-240, 329

International Social Service 138-157, 176, 186,

International Union for Child Welfare 160-166, 186

Islam and adoption 168, 179-186

Israel, adoptions in Jamaica 88, 89, 242

Kinship and adoption 214-238

See also Custom adoption

See also Extended family

Korea, adoptions from 77-79, 82-85, 87, 148-154, 173, 177-178

Labelling effects in adoption

47, 48-53, 78, 303-305, 312, 313, 329

Latin America, adoptions from 77, 87, 134-154, 174

Legal aspects of adoption 5-12, 63, 122, 136-174, 218-9, 234, 324

Legal risk adoption 63

Leysin Principles of intercountry adoption 138-166, 167-174, 209-210, 234-239

Maladjustment in adoptees 14-37, 43-46, 48-70, 72-89, 90-113, 221-239, 303-325

Maternal separation 36-37, 90-113

Medical problems in adoptees 48, 121-134, 303-325

See also Health problems

Mental handicap 9-10, 61, 280

Mental health of adoptees 15-37, 15-37, 71-89, 114-120, 225-234, 244-255, 277-300,303-325

Mental health of adopters 36, 71-89, 114-120, 277, 296, 303-318

Mixed marriages 201-226, 240, 247, 249

Mixed race children, identity and adoption of 71-89, 241, 243, 249, 71-89, 241, 243, 249, 304

National Child Development Study 23-26, 38, 48,90-113, 328, 331

Native peoples of Canada 86, 122-134, 214-238

See also Aboriginal nations
Neglect of children 218, 225
Netherlands, adoptions in 11, 171, 191, 236
Norway 86-87, 15-16, 186
Nutrition of adoptees 82-83, 94

Older child adoptions 58-65, 314-315
Open adoption 6-8, 57-58, 61, 66-70
Overprotection of adoptees 28, 32, 303, 329
See also Anxiety in adopters

Parent-child relationships 8-9, 12, 14-16, 25, 46, 54-60, 81, 95, 198-201, 293-299
Perinatal stressors 24, 39-45, 90-113
Permanency planning 9, 61, 128-134
Personality disorders 43-46
Philippines, adoptions from 178-179, 193
Policy development in adoption 12-18, 57, 65-68, 81, 135-194, 203-204, 260-26
Preferential adoptions 3-4, 69
Private adoptions 121-134
Psychoanalytic view of adoption 21, 53, 60-61, 331
Prophylactic referrals 48-52, 90-96

Residential care and adoption 26, 10-13, 26-27, 50, 62, 64, 163, 179-187, 195, 218, 219, 234, 257, 260, 264-273, 279, 286, 302-325, 327-330
Revelation of adoption 17, 22-23, 34-35, 304
Role conflicts of adopters 1-6, 30, 55-56, 92, 189-199, 227, 229, 279, 286
Romania, adoptions from 140, 157, 163, 167, 186-187
Running from home 291

Schizophrenia and adoption 22-23, 44-47, 52
Scholastic achievements of adoptees 25-26, 36, 41-53, 90-113, 210-212, 246, 253
Search for biological parents 5-8, 40, 65-67
Self concept and self-esteem of adoptees 31-35, 53-56, 76-84, 114-120, 196-206, 211, 241, 245-255, 278, 281, 293, 296, 303-315
Sex differences in adjustment 4, 16, 18, 23, 34, 40-41, 274-286
Sexual acting out 303-315
See also Abuse, sexual
Siblings of adoptees 53, 63-65, 77, 275-276, 303-315, 363
Single parents 40, 272, 276
See also Illegitimacy
Social class and adoption 10-11, 16-37, 39, 52, 93, 115, 125, 202-205, 273, 277, 294, 299
Social work in adoption 10-31, 48-62, 113, 121-134,

141-142, 217-219, 223, 241, 247, 260, 301, 323-324, 326-328, 329

Special needs adoption 2-8, 32, 48-70, 121-134, 121-134, 178

Step-parent adoptions 8-9, 64-65, 272, 276, 297, 310-313, 330

Subsidies for adopters 63-64

Suicidal ideas and behaviour 114-120, 225, 230, 278 303-315

Support for adoptive parents 60, 63, 70, 77-78, 323-4

Sweden, adoptions in 18-23, 39-46, 148, 152, 171, 177, 185

Switzerland 135-166

Symbolic interactionism 53, 331
See also Labelling

Temperament of adoptees 43-44, 46-47, 146, 153, 300-303

Terre des Hommes 146, 158-160, 174, 186

Thailand, adoptions from 174

Transracial adoption 9, 30, 35, 40-43, 54-55, 62, 71-89, 121-134, 154, 172, 178, 195-206, 214-239, 240, 326-327

Unsealing adoption records 6-8, 66-67

United Kingdom, adoptions in 6-8, 23-25, 48-66, 76, 86, 90-113, 137, 147,

151-153, 175-177, 185, 328, 330

United Nations, agreements on adoption 135-194, 234-239

United States, adoptions in 5, 8-15, 21-23, 41-44, 50-51, 59-60, 71-89, 137, 147, 151-153, 170-179, 185, 170-177, 190, 208, 215, 234, 236, 241, 248

Vietnam, adoptions from 21-23, 207-213

Weight of adoptees 24, 39, 90-113
See also Nutrition